STAND OUT

Evidence-Based Learning for College and Career Readiness

1

THIRD EDITION

LESSON PLANNER

ROB JENKINS

STACI JOHNSON

Australia • Brazil • Mexico • Singapore • United Kingdom • United States

Stand Out 1: Evidence-Based Learning for College and Career Readiness, Third Edition
Rob Jenkins and Staci Johnson
Lesson Planner

Publisher: Sherrise Roehr

Executive Editor: Sarah Kenney

Senior Development Editor: Margarita Matte

Development Editor: Lewis Thompson

Director of Global Marketing: Ian Martin

Executive Marketing Manager: Ben Rivera

Product Marketing Manager: Dalia Bravo

Director of Content and Media Production: Michael Burggren

Production Manager: Daisy Sosa

Media Researcher: Leila Hishmeh

Senior Print Buyer: Mary Beth Hennebury

Cover and Interior Designer: Brenda Carmichael

Composition: Lumina

Cover Image: Portra Images/Getty Images

Bottom Images: (Left to Right) Jay B Sauceda/ Getty Images; Tripod/Getty Images; Portra Images/Getty Images; James Porter/ Getty Images; Mark Edward Atkinson/ Tracey Lee/Getty Images; Hero Images/ Getty Images; Jade/Getty Images; Seth Joel/ Getty Images; LWA/Larry Williams/ Getty Images; Dimitri Otis/Getty Images

For product information and technology assistance, contact us at
Cengage Learning Customer & Sales Support, 1-800-354-9706
For permission to use material from this text or product, submit all requests online at **cengage.com/permissions**
Further permissions questions can be emailed to
permissionrequest@cengage.com

Lesson Planner
ISBN 13: 978-1-305-65541-6

National Geographic Learning/Cengage Learning
20 Channel Center Street
Boston, MA 02210
USA

Cengage Learning is a leading provider of customized learning solutions with office locations around the globe, including Singapore, the United Kingdom, Australia, Mexico, Brazil, and Japan. Locate your local office at: **international.cengage.com/region**

Cengage Learning products are represented in Canada by Nelson Education, Ltd.

Visit National Geographic Learning online at **NGL.Cengage.com**
Visit our corporate website at **www.cengage.com**

Printed in the United States of America
Print Number: 02   Print Year: 2016

ACKNOWLEDGMENTS

Ellen Albano
Mcfatter Technical College, Davie, FL

Esther Anaya-Garcia
Glendale Community College, Glendale, AZ

Carol Bellamy
Prince George's Community College, Largo, MD

Gail Bier
Atlantic Technical College, Coconut Creek, FL

Kathryn Black
Myrtle Beach Family Learning Center, Myrtle Beach, SC

Claudia Brantley
College of Southern Nevada, Las Vegas, NV

Dr. Joan-Yvette Campbell
Lindsey Hopkins Technical College, Miami, FL

Maria Carmen Iglesias
Miami Senior Adult Educational Center, Miami, FL

Lee Chen
Palomar College, San Marcos, CA

Casey Cahill
Atlantic Technical College, Coconut Creek, FL

Maria Dillehay
Burien Job Training and Education Center, Goodwill, Seattle, WA

Irene Fjaerestad
Olympic College, Bremerton, WA

Eleanor Forfang-Brockman
Tarrant County College, Fort Worth, Texas

Jesse Galdamez
San Bernardino Adult School, San Bernardino, CA

Anna Garoz
Lindsey Hopkins Technical Education Center, Miami, FL

Maria Gutierrez
Miami Sunset Adult, Miami, FL

Noel Hernandez
Palm Beach County Public Schools, Palm Beach County, FL

Kathleen Hiscock
Portland Adult Education, Portland, ME

Frantz Jean-Louis
The English Center, Miami, FL

Annette Johnson
Sheridan Technical College, Hollywood, FL

Ginger Karaway
Gateway Technical College, Kenosha, WI

Judy Martin-Hall
Indian River State College, Fort Pierce, FL

Toni Molinaro
Dixie Hollins Adult Education Center, St Petersburg, FL

Tracey Person
Cape Cod Community College, Hyannis, MA

Celina Paula
Miami-Dade County Public Schools, Miami, FL

Veronica Pavon-Baker
Miami Beach Adult, Miami, FL

Ileana Perez
Robert Morgan Technical College, Miami, FL

Neeta Rancourt
Atlantic Technical College, Coconut Creek, FL

Brenda Roland
Joliet Junior College, Joliet, IL

Hidelisa Sampson
Las Vegas Urban League, Las Vegas, NV

Lisa Schick
James Madison University, Harrisonburg, VA

Rob Sheppard
Quincy Asian Resources, Quincy, MA

Sydney Silver
Burien Job Training and Education Center, Goodwill, Seattle, WA

Teresa Tamarit
Miami Senior Adult Educational Center, Miami, FL

Cristina Urena
Atlantic Technical College, Fort Lauderdale, FL

Pamela Jo Wilson
Palm Beach County Public Schools, Palm Beach County, FL

ABOUT THE AUTHORS

Staci Johnson

Ever since I can remember, I've been fascinated with other cultures and languages. I love to travel and every place I go, the first thing I want to do is meet the people, learn their language, and understand their culture. Becoming an ESL teacher was a perfect way to turn what I love to do into my profession. There's nothing more incredible than the exchange of teaching and learning from one another that goes on in an ESL classroom. And there's nothing more rewarding than helping a student succeed.

Rob Jenkins

I love teaching. I love to see the expressions on my students' faces when the light goes on and their eyes show such sincere joy of learning. I knew the first time I stepped into an ESL classroom that this is where I needed to be and I have never questioned that resolution. I have worked in business, sales, and publishing, and I've found challenge in all, but nothing can compare to the satisfaction of reaching people in such a personal way.

Along with the inclusion of National Geographic content, the third edition of **Stand Out** boasts several innovations. In response to initiatives regarding the development of more complexity with reading and encouraging students to interact more with reading texts, we are proud to introduce new rich reading sections that allow students to discuss topics relevant to a global society. We have also introduced new National Geographic videos that complement the life-skill videos **Stand Out** introduced in the second edition and which are now integrated into the student books. We don't stop there; **Stand Out** has even more activities that require critical and creative thinking that serve to maximize learning and prepare students for the future. The third edition also has online workbooks. **Stand Out** was the first mainstream ESL textbook for adults to introduce a lesson plan format, hundreds of customizable worksheets, and project-based instruction. The third edition expands on these features in its mission to provide rich learning opportunities that can be exploited in different ways. We believe that with the innovative approach that made **Stand Out** a leader from its inception, the many new features, and the new look, programs, teachers, and students will find great success!

Stand Out Mission Statement:

Our goal is to give students challenging opportunities to be successful in their language-learning experience so they develop confidence and become independent lifelong learners.

TO THE TEACHER

ABOUT THE SERIES

The **Stand Out** series is designed to facilitate *active* learning within life-skill settings that lead students to career and academic pathways. Each student book and its supplemental components in the six-level series expose students to competency areas most useful and essential for newcomers with careful treatment of level-appropriate but challenging materials. Students grow academically by developing essential literacy and critical-thinking skills that will help them find personal success in a changing and dynamic world.

THE STAND OUT PHILOSOPHY

Integrated Skills

In each of the five lessons of every unit, skills are introduced as they might be in real language use. They are in context and not separated into different sections of the unit. We believe that for real communication to occur, the classroom should mirror real life as much as possible.

Objective Driven Activities

Every lesson in **Stand Out** is driven by a performance objective. These objectives have been carefully selected to ensure they are measurable, accessible to students at their particular level, and relevant to students and their lives. Good objectives lead to effective learning. Effective objectives also lead to appropriate self, student, and program assessment which is increasingly required by state and federal mandates.

Lesson Plan Sequencing

Stand Out follows an established sequence of activities that provides students with the tools they need to have in order to practice and apply the skills required in the objective. A pioneer in Adult Education for introducing the Madeline Hunter WIPPEA lesson plan model into textbooks, **Stand Out** continues to provide a clear and easy-to-follow system for presenting and developing English language skills. The WIPPEA model follows six steps:

* **W**arm up and Review
* **I**ntroduction
* **P**resentation
* **P**ractice
* **E**valuation
* **A**pplication

Learning And Acquisition

In **Stand Out**, the recycling of skills is emphasized. Students must learn and practice the same skills multiple times in various contexts to actually acquire them. Practicing a skill one time is rarely sufficient for acquisition and rarely addresses diverse student needs and learning styles.

Critical Thinking

Critical thinking has been defined in various ways and sometimes so broadly that any activity could be classified to meet the criteria. To be clear and to draw attention to the strong critical thinking activities in **Stand Out,** we define these activities as *tasks that require learners to think deeper than the superficial vocabulary and meaning.* Activities such as ranking, making predictions, analyzing, or solving problems demand that students think beyond the surface. Critical thinking is highlighted throughout so the instructor can be confident that effective learning is going on.

Learner-Centered, Cooperative, and Communicative Activities

Stand Out provides ample opportunities for students to develop interpersonal skills and to practice new vocabulary through graphic organizers and charts like Venn diagrams, graphs, classifying charts, and mind maps. The lesson planners provide learner-centered approaches in every lesson. Students are asked to rank items, make decisions, and negotiate amongst other things.

Dialogues are used to prepare students for these activities in the low levels and fewer dialogues are used at the higher levels where students have already acquired the vocabulary and rudimentary conversation skills.

Activities should provide opportunities for students to speak in near authentic settings so they have confidence to perform outside the classroom. This does not mean that dialogues and other mechanical activities are not used to prepare students for cooperative activities, but these mechanical activities do not foster conversation. They merely provide the first tools students need to go beyond mimicry.

Assessment

Instructors and students should have a clear understanding of what is being taught and what is expected. In **Stand Out**, objectives are clearly stated so that target skills can be effectively assessed throughout.

Formative assessments are essential. Pre- and post-assessments can be given for units or sections of the book through ExamView®—a program that makes developing tests easy and effective. These tests can be created to appear like standardized tests, which are important for funding and to help students prepare.

Finally, *learner logs* allow students to self-assess, document progress, and identify areas that might require additional attention.

SUPPLEMENTAL COMPONENTS
The **Stand Out** series is a comprehensive tool for all student needs. There is no need to look any further than the resources offered.

Stand Out Lesson Planners
The lesson planners go beyond merely describing activities in the student book by providing teacher support, ideas, and guidance for the entire class period.

- **Standards correlations** for **CCRS, CASAS,** and **SCANS** are identified for each lesson.
- **Pacing Guides** help with planning by giving instructors suggested durations for each activity and a selection of activities for different class lengths.
- **Teacher Tips** provide point-of-use pedagogical comments and best practices.
- **At-A-Glance Lesson Openers** provide the instructor with everything that will be taught in a particular lesson. Elements include the agenda, the goal, grammar, pronunciation, academic strategies, critical thinking elements, correlations to standards, and resources.
- **Suggested Activities** go beyond what is shown in the text providing teachers with ideas that will stimulate them to come up with their own.
- **Listening Scripts** are integrated into the unit pages for easy access.

Stand Out Workbook
The workbook in the third edition takes the popular **Stand Out Grammar Challenge** and expands it to include vocabulary building, life-skill development, and grammar practice associated directly with each lesson in the student book.

Stand Out Online Workbook
One of the most important innovations in the third edition of **Stand Out** is the online workbook. This workbook provides unique activities that are closely related to the student book and gives students opportunities to have access to audio and video.

The online workbook provides opportunities for students to practice and improve digital literacy skills essential for 21st century learners. These skills are essential for standardized computer and online testing. Scores in these tests will improve when students can concentrate on the content and not so much on the technology.

Activity Bank
The activity bank is an online feature that provides several hundred multilevel worksheets per level to enhance the already rich materials available through **Stand Out**.

DVD Program
The **Stand Out Lifeskills Video Program** continues to be available with eight episodes per level; however, now the worksheets are part of the student books with additional help in the lesson planners.

New to the third edition of **Stand Out** are two National Geographic videos per level. Each video is accompanied by four pages of instruction and activities with support in the lesson planners.

ExamView®
ExamView® is a program that provides customizable test banks and allows instructors to make lesson, unit, and program tests quickly.

STANDARDS AND CORRELATIONS
Stand Out is the pioneer in establishing a foundation of standards within each unit and through every objective. The standards movement in the United States is as dominant today as it was when **Stand Out** was first published. Schools and programs must be aware of ongoing local and federal initiatives and make attempts to meet ever-changing requirements.

In the first edition of **Stand Out**, we identified direct correlations to SCANS, EFF, and CASAS standards. *The Secretary's Commission on Achieving Necessary Skills,* or SCANS, and *Equipped for the Future,* or EFF, standards are still important and are identified in every lesson of **Stand Out**. These skills include the basic skills, interpersonal skills, and problem-solving skills necessary to be successful in the workplace, in school, and in the community. **Stand Out** was also developed with a thorough understanding of objectives established by the *Comprehensive Adult Student Assessment Systems* or CASAS. Many programs have experienced great success with their CASAS scores using **Stand Out**, and these objectives continue to be reflected in the third edition.

Today, a new emphasis on critical thinking and complexity has swept the nation. Students are expected to think for themselves more now than ever before. They must also interact with reading texts at a higher level. These new standards and expectations are highly visible in the third edition and include *College and Career Readiness Standards.*

Stand Out offers a complete set of correlations online for all standards to demonstrate how closely we align with state and federal guidelines.

IMPORTANT INNOVATIONS IN THE THIRD EDITION

New Look
Although the third edition of **Stand Out** boasts the same lesson plan format and task-based activities that made it one of the most popular books in adult education, it now has an updated look with the addition of National Geographic content, which will capture the attention of the instructor and every student.

Critical Thinking
With the advent of new federal and state initiatives, teachers need to be confident that students will use critical thinking skills when learning. This has always been a goal in **Stand Out**, but now those opportunities are highlighted in each lesson.

College And Career Readiness Skills
These skills are also identified by critical thinking strategies and academic-related activities, which are found throughout **Stand Out**. New to the third edition is a special reading section in each unit that challenges students and encourages them to develop reading strategies within a rich National Geographic environment.

Stand Out Workbook
The print workbook is now more extensive and complete with vocabulary, life skills, and grammar activities to round out any program. Many instructors might find these pages ideal for homework, but they of course can be used for additional practice within the classroom.

Media And Online Support
Media and online support includes audio, video, online workbooks, presentation tools, multi-level worksheets, ExamView®, and standards correlations.

CONTENTS

Numeracy/ Academic Skills	CCRS	SCANS	CASAS
• Clarification strategies • Pronunciation • Focused listening	RI1, SL2, SL3, L2, RF2	• Listening • Speaking • Sociability	**1:** 0.1.1, 0.1.4, 0.2.1 **2:** 0.1.2, 0.1.4, 0.2.2 **3:** 0.1.5, 0.1.6, 2.2.1
• Focused listening • Predicting • Reviewing • Self-evaluation	RI1, R12, RI5, RI7, SL1, SL2, SL4, L1, L2, L5, RF2	**Most SCANS are incorporated into this unit, with an emphasis on:** • Acquiring information • Interpreting and evaluating information • Writing (Technology is optional.)	**1:** 0.1.2, 0.2.1 **2:** 0.1.2, 0.1.3, 1.1.4 **3:** 0.1.2 **4:** 0.2.4 **5:** 2.3.1 **R:** 0.1.2, 0.1.3, 0.2.1, 0.2.4, 1.1.4, 2.3.1, 4.8.1 **TP:** 0.1.2, 0.1.3, 0.2.1, 0.2.4, 1.1.4, 2.3.1
• Categorizing • Classifying • Focused listening • Graphs • Predicting • Reviewing • Self-evaluation	RI1, RI2, RI5, RI7, SL1, SL2, SL4, L1, L2, RF2, RF3	**Most SCANS are incorporated into this unit, with an emphasis on:** • Allocating money • Serving customers • Organizing and maintaining information • Decision-making (Technology is optional.)	**1:** 1.1.3, 1.3.7, 2.5.4 **2:** 1.3.3, 1.3.8, 1.3.9, 1.6.4 **3:** 1.2.1, 1.3.9 **4:** 1.3.9 **5:** 0.1.2, 1.1.9, 1.3.9 **R:** 0.1.2, 1.1.9, 1.2.1, 1.3.3, 1.3.8, 1.3.9, 1.6.4 **TP:** 0.1.2, 1.1.9, 1.2.1, 1.3.3, 1.3.8, 1.3.9, 1.6.4, 4.8.1

CONTENTS

Numeracy/ Academic Skills	CCRS	SCANS	CASAS
• Brainstorming • Classifying • Critical thinking • Focused listening • Making graphs • Predicting • Reviewing • Self-evaluation	RI1, RI2, RI5, RI7, SL1, SL2, SL4, L1, L2, L5, RF2, RF3	**Most SCANS are incorporated into this unit, with an emphasis on:** • Allocating money • Understanding systems • Creative thinking • Seeing things in the mind's eye (Technology is optional.)	**1:** 1.3.8, 7.2.3 **2:** 1.2.1, 1.2.4, 1.3.8 **3:** 0.1.2, 1.1.7, 1.3.8, 7.2.6 **4:** 1.1.3, 1.2.1, 1.2.2, 1.3.8 **5:** 1.3.8, 2.6.4, 7.2.3 **R:** 0.1.2, 1.1.3, 1.1.7, 1.2.1, 1.2.2, 1.2.4, 2.6.4 **TP:** 0.1.2, 1.1.3, 1.1.7, 1.2.1, 1.2.2, 1.2.4, 2.6.4, 4.8.1
• Classifying • Focused listening • Pie charts • Reviewing • Self-evaluation • Venn diagrams	RI1, RI2, RI5, RI7, W2, SL1, SL2, SL4, L1, L2, L4, L5, RF2, RF3	**Most SCANS are incorporated into this unit, with an emphasis on:** • Acquiring and evaluating information • Creative thinking • Seeing things in the mind's eye (Technology is optional.)	**1:** 1.1.3, 1.4.1 **2:** 1.1.3, 1.4.1, 4.8.1, 7.2.3 **3:** 1.4.2 **4:** 1.4.2 **5:** 1.4.1, 1.4.2, 2.2.1 **R:** 1.4.1, 1.4.2 **TP:** 1.4.1, 1.4.2, 4.8.1
• Brainstorming • Classifying • Focused listening • Reviewing • Scanning for information • Self-evaluation	RI1, RI2, RI5, RI7, W2, SL1, SL2, SL4, L1, L2, L4, L5, RF3	**Most SCANS are incorporated into this unit, with an emphasis on:** • Acquiring and evaluating information • Reading • Seeing things in the mind's eye • Sociability (Technology is optional.)	**1:** 1.1.3, 2.5.1, 2.5.3, 7.4.4 **2:** 1.1.3, 1.9.1, 1.9.4, 2.2.1, 2.2.2, 2.2.5 **3:** 1.3.7, 2.2.1, 2.5.4 **4:** 2.1.7, 2.1.8 **5:** 0.2.3 **R:** 0.2.3, 1.1.3, 2.1.7, 2.1.8, 1.9.1, 2.2.2 **TP:** 0.2.3, 1.1.3, 2.1.7, 2.1.8, 1.9.1, 2.2.2, 4.8.1

CONTENTS

Numeracy/ Academic Skills	CCRS	SCANS	CASAS
• Clarification strategies • Focused listening • Graphs • Predicting • Ranking • Reviewing • Self-evaluation • Venn diagrams	RI1, RI2, RI5, RI7, SL1, SL2, SL4, L1, L2, L4, L5, RF2, RF3	**Most SCANS are incorporated into this unit, with an emphasis on:** • Interpreting and communicating information • Understanding systems • Decision making (Technology is optional.)	**1:** 3.1.1 **2:** 3.1.1, 6.6.5 **3:** 0.1.3, 3.3.1, 3.3.2, 3.3.3 **4:** 0.1.2, 2.5.1 **5:** 1.1.3, 3.5.9, 7.1.1 **R:** 2.5.1, 3.1.1, 3.3.1, 3.3.2, 3.3.3, 3.5.9 **TP:** 2.5.1, 3.1.1, 3.3.1, 3.3.2, 3.3.3, 3.5.9, 4.8.1
• Clarification strategies • Classifying • Focused listening • Peer editing • Ranking • Reviewing • Scanning • Self-evaluation • Venn diagrams	RI1, RI2, RI5, RI7, RI9, W2, SL1, SL2, SL4, L1, L2, L5, RF2, RF3	**Most SCANS are incorporated into this unit, with an emphasis on:** • Organizing and maintaining information • Understanding systems • Creative thinking • Decision making (Technology is optional.)	**1:** 4.1.8 **2:** 4.1.3, 4.1.6, 4.1.8 **3:** 4.1.2, 4.1.8 **4:** 0.1.1, 0.1.6, 4.1.5, 4.6.1 **5:** 4.4.1, 4.4.4 **R:** 4.1.2, 4.1.3, 4.1.6, 4.1.8, 4.1.5, 4.4.1, 4.4.4, 4.6.1 **TP:** 4.1.2, 4.1.3, 4.1.6, 4.1.8, 4.1.5, 4.4.1, 4.4.4, 4.6.1, 4.8.1
• Focused listening • Note-taking • Organizational strategies • Predicting • Reviewing • Self-evaluation	RI1, RI2, RI5, RI7, SL1, SL2, L1, L2, L4, L5, RF3	**Most SCANS are incorporated into this unit, with an emphasis on:** • Understanding systems • Monitoring and correcting performance • Knowing how to learn • Self-management (Technology is optional.)	**1:** 7.4.1 **2:** 7.1.4, 7.4.1, 7.4.9 **3:** 2.5.5, 7.1.1 **4:** 7.1.1, 7.5.1 **5:** 7.1.1, 7.1.2 **R:** 7.1.1, 7.1.4, 7.4.1, 7.4.9, 7.5.1 **TP:** 4.8.1, 7.1.1, 7.1.4, 7.4.1, 7.4.9, 7.5.1

For other national and state specific standards, please visit: **www.NGL.Cengage.com/SO3**

INTRODUCING
STAND OUT, Third Edition!

Stand Out is a six-level, standards-based ESL series for adult education with a proven track record of successful results. The new edition of *Stand Out* continues to provide students with the foundations and tools needed to achieve success in life, college, and career.

Stand Out now integrates real-world content from National Geographic

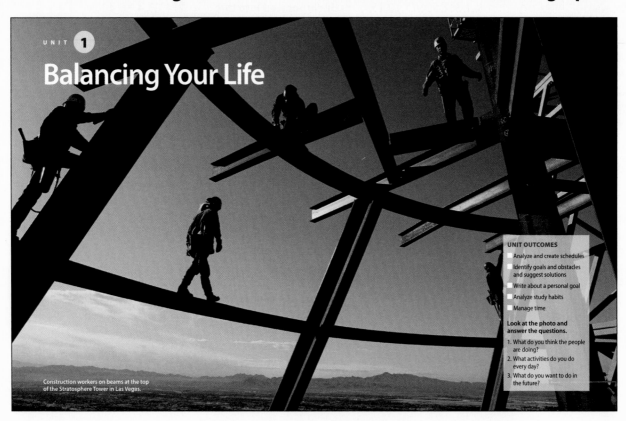

UNIT **1**

Balancing Your Life

UNIT OUTCOMES
- Analyze and create schedules
- Identify goals and obstacles and suggest solutions
- Write about a personal goal
- Analyze study habits
- Manage time

Look at the photo and answer the questions.
1. What do you think the people are doing?
2. What activities do you do every day?
3. What do you want to do in the future?

Construction workers on beams at the top of the Stratosphere Tower in Las Vegas.

- *Stand Out* now integrates high-interest, real-world content from National Geographic which enhances its proven approach to lesson planning and instruction. A stunning National Geographic image at the beginning of each unit introduces the theme and engages learners in meaningful conversations right from the start.

Stand Out supports college and career readiness

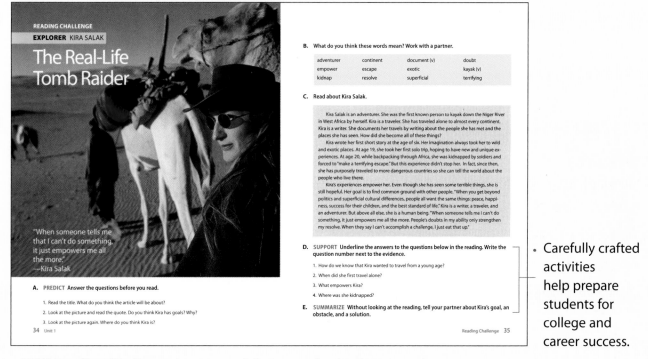

• **Carefully crafted activities help prepare students for college and career success.**

• **NEW Reading Challenge** in every unit features a fascinating story about a **National Geographic explorer** to immerse learners in authentic content.

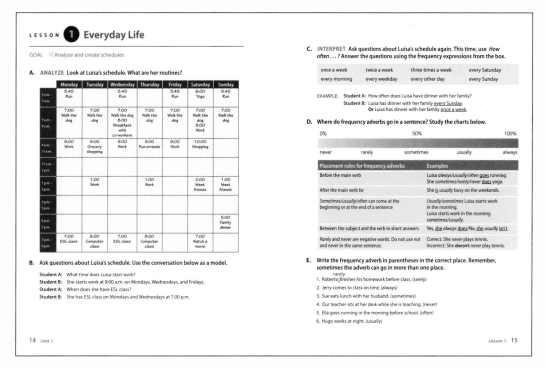

• **EXPANDED Critical Thinking Activities** challenge learners to evaluate, analyze, and synthesize information to prepare them for the workplace and academic life.

- **NEW Video Challenge** showcases **National Geographic footage and explorers**, providing learners with the opportunity to synthesize what they have learned in prior units through the use of authentic content.

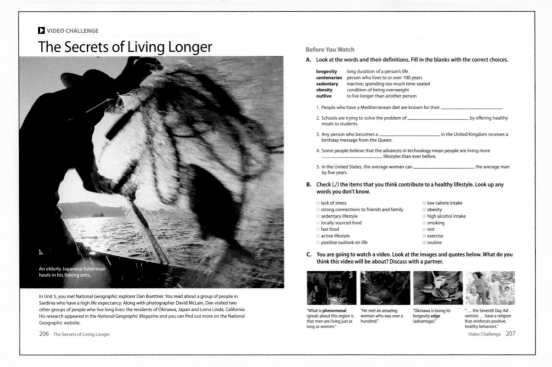

▶ VIDEO CHALLENGE

The Secrets of Living Longer

An elderly Japanese fisherman hauls in his fishing nets.

In Unit 5, you met National Geographic explorer Dan Buettner. You read about a group of people in Sardinia who have a high life expectancy. Along with photographer David McLain, Dan visited two other groups of people who live long lives: the residents of Okinawa, Japan and Loma Linda, California. His research appeared in the *National Geographic Magazine* and you can find out more on the National Geographic website.

206   The Secrets of Living Longer

Before You Watch

A. Look at the words and their definitions. Fill in the blanks with the correct choices.

longevity	long duration of a person's life
centenarian	person who lives to or over 100 years
sedentary	inactive; spending too much time seated
obesity	condition of being overweight
outlive	to live longer than another person

1. People who have a Mediterranean diet are known for their _____

2. Schools are trying to solve the problem of _____ by offering healthy meals to students.

3. Any person who becomes a _____ in the United Kingdom receives a birthday message from the Queen.

4. Some people believe that the advances in technology mean people are living more _____ lifestyles than ever before.

5. In the United States, the average woman can _____ the average man by five years.

B. Check (✓) the items that you think contribute to a healthy lifestyle. Look up any words you don't know.

- ☐ lack of stress
- ☐ strong connections to friends and family
- ☐ sedentary lifestyle
- ☐ locally sourced food
- ☐ fast food
- ☐ active lifestyle
- ☐ positive outlook on life
- ☐ low calorie intake
- ☐ obesity
- ☐ high alcohol intake
- ☐ smoking
- ☐ rest
- ☐ exercise
- ☐ routine

C. You are going to watch a video. Look at the images and quotes below. What do you think this video will be about? Discuss with a partner.

"What is **phenomenal** (great) about this region is that men are living just as long as women."

"He met an amazing woman who was over a hundred."

"Okinawa is losing its longevity **edge** (advantage)."

" … the Seventh Day Adventists … have a religion that reinforces positive, healthy behaviors."

Video Challenge   207

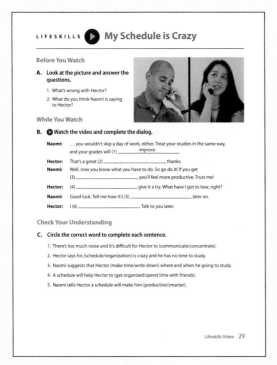

LIFESKILLS ▶ **My Schedule is Crazy**

Before You Watch

A. Look at the picture and answer the questions.
   1. What's wrong with Hector?
   2. What do you think Naomi is saying to Hector?

While You Watch

B. ▶ Watch the video and complete the dialog.

Naomi: … you wouldn't skip a day of work, either. Treat your studies in the same way, and your grades will (1) _improve_

Hector: That's a great (2) _____, thanks.

Naomi: Well, now you know what you have to do. So go do it! If you get (3) _____, you'll feel more productive. Trust me!

Hector: (4) _____ give it a try. What have I got to lose, right?

Naomi: Good luck. Tell me how it's (5) _____ later on.

Hector: I (6) _____ Talk to you later.

Check Your Understanding

C. Circle the correct word to complete each sentence.

1. There's too much noise and it's difficult for Hector to (communicate/concentrate).
2. Hector says his (schedule/organization) is crazy and he has no time to study.
3. Naomi suggests that Hector (make time/write down) where and when he going to study.
4. A schedule will help Hector to (get organized/spend time with friends).
5. Naomi tells Hector a schedule will make him (productive/smarter).

Lifeskills Video   29

- The **Lifeskills Video** is a dramatic video series integrated into each unit of the student book that helps students learn natural spoken English and apply it to their everyday activities.

Pages shown are from *Stand Out*, Third Edition Level 3

- **NEW Online Workbook** engages students and supports the classroom by providing a wide variety of auto-graded interactive activities, an audio program, video from National Geographic, and pronunciation activities.

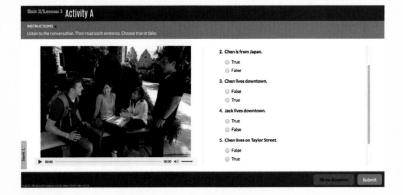

- **UPDATED Lesson Planner** includes correlations to **College and Career Readiness Standards (CCRS), CASAS, SCANS** and reference to **EL Civics** competencies to help instructors achieve the required standards.

- **Teacher support** *Stand Out* continues to provide a wide variety of user-friendly tools and interactive activities that help teachers prepare students for success while keeping them engaged and motivated.

Stand Out supports teachers and learners

LEARNER COMPONENTS

- Student Book
- Online workbook powered by My**ELT**
- Print workbook

TEACHER COMPONENTS

- Lesson Planner
- Classroom DVD
- Assessment CD-ROM
- Teacher's companion site with Multi-Level Worksheets

Welcome

Welcome

- Introduce the unit. Greet students by saying *Hello* and *Hi*.
- Ask students to look at the photos. Elicit the greetings people say to each other when they meet for the first time. Write any useful vocabulary on the board.
- Discuss the unit outcomes with students. Ask them if they know anyone's phone number or any classroom instructions. Write any useful vocabulary on the board next to the vocabulary for greetings you elicited earlier.

Life Skills Link

In this unit, students will learn how to greet people they meet for the first time. They will also learn how to ask for and give a specific piece of information.

The skills students learn in this unit can be applied to almost every area of EL Civics as they help students to function effectively within U.S. society.

PRE-UNIT

Welcome

UNIT OUTCOMES

☐ Greet people

☐ Say and write phone numbers

☐ Follow instructions

INSTRUCTOR'S NOTES

_____

_____

_____

_____

_____

UNIT OUTCOMES

- Greet people
- Say and write phone numbers
- Follow instructions

GRAMMAR

- Contractions: *I'm*
- Verb *Be*
- Imperatives

VOCABULARY

- Greetings
- Numbers
- Study words
- Classroom commands

EL CIVICS

The skills students learn in this unit can be applied to the following El Civics competency area:

- Personal Information

CASAS

Lesson 1: 0.1.1, 0.1.4, 0.2.1
Lesson 2: 0.1.2, 0.1.4, 0.2.2
Lesson 3: 0.1.5, 0.1.6, 2.2.1

SCANS

Many SCANs skills are incorporated in the unit with an emphasis on:

- Listening
- Speaking
- Sociability

CCRS

RI1, SL2, SL3, L2, RF2

LESSON **1** Hello!

GOAL ▪ Greet people

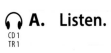 **A. Listen.**

CD 1
TR 1

Goal: Greet people
Grammar: *I'm*
Pronunciation: /m/
Academic Strategy: Focused listening
Vocabulary: Greetings

Agenda

- Greet each other.
- Practice greetings.
- Listen and write.
- Learn names.
- Talk to five classmates.

Resources

Multilevel Worksheet: Pre-Unit, Lesson 1, Worksheet 1
Workbook: Pre-Unit, Lesson 1
Audio: CD 1, Tracks 1–5
Heinle Picture Dictionary: Classroom, pages 18–19
Stand Out 1 Assessment CD-ROM with ExamView®

Pacing

- 1.5 hour classes   ■ 2.5 hour classes
- 3+ hour classes

STANDARDS CORRELATIONS

CCRS: SL2, SL3, L2, RF2
CASAS: 0.1.1, 0.1.4, 0.2.1
SCANS: **Basic Skills** Reading, writing, listening, speaking
EFF: **Communication** Read with understanding, speak so others can understand, listen actively

Preassessment *(optional)*   ■■■
Use the Stand Out 1 Assessment CD-ROM with ExamView® to create a pretest for the Pre-Unit.

Warm-up and Review   2–5 mins. ■■■
Shake hands and introduce yourself to students as they enter the classroom. Ask each student: *What is your name?* At this point, don't expect students to be able to produce this question.

BEST PRACTICE

Cultural differences

Students may have a different concept of what is an appropriate handshake. In the U.S., we shake hands by firmly curling our fingers around the other person's hand and maintaining eye contact. It is important to teach this style of handshake by modeling it and explaining it verbally.

After greeting about ten students, ask the class if they remember the students' names you have just met. Point to each student and state his or her name. Encourage the class to help.

Introduction   2 mins. ■■■
Point to the agenda on the board and state the goal: *Today, we will greet people.* Greet a student by saying *hi* and shaking his or her hand. Write *hi* and *hello* on the board and then point to the word *greetings* on the agenda.

Presentation 1   15 mins. ■■■
Ask students to open their books to page 3.

A. Listen.

Greet several students using the words and expressions on page 3. As you greet students, have the class point to the word or phrase in their books that you say. Then, as a class, listen to the recording.

LISTENING SCRIPT   CD 1 TR 1
The listening script matches Exercise A in the Student Book.

Write the greetings on the board in the form of a conversation. Practice by having students repeat the lines of the conversation after you. Then, work toward having them perform the conversation on their own. The conversation on the board might look like this:

Student A: Hello!
Student B: Hi. How are you?
Student A: Fine, how are you?
Student B: Fine.

Practice 1

5 mins. ■■■

Ask students to practice the conversation with several partners, using appropriate handshakes and eye contact. Encourage them to meet as many students as possible until you tell them to stop.

Evaluation 1

5 mins. ■■■

Observe students as they greet each other. You may also have students demonstrate in front of the class.

Presentation 2

15–20 mins. ■■■

Greet a few students again and say: *Welcome to our class.* Encourage students to say *thank you.* Write *thank you* on the board. Have students repeat the phrase until they understand and feel comfortable saying it.

Note: Many students will have trouble pronouncing the /th/ sound in *thank* properly. You might interrupt the lesson to demonstrate how to do it correctly. Explain that they should put the tongue between the teeth and push air past the tongue before moving on to the vowel sound.

B. Complete the conversations and practice them with a partner.

Do this activity as a class and practice the rhythm of the new conversations. Ask students to practice performing these conversations in pairs.

C. Read the greetings.

Go over the greetings in the box with students. Use them in conversations and have students point to them as they hear them in preparation for the focused listening in Exercise D.

Practice 2

5 mins. ■■

D. Listen and complete the conversation.

> LISTENING SCRIPT 🎧 CD 1 TR 2
>
> **Roberto:** *Hi. I'm Roberto. How are you?*
> **Gabriela:** *Hello. My name is Gabriela. I'm fine, thanks.*
> **Roberto:** *Welcome to our class.*
> **Gabriela:** *Thank you.*
> **Roberto:** *Our teacher is Miss Smith.*

Evaluation 2

7–10 mins. ■■

Ask students to check each other's work for spelling errors. At this level, students may have difficulty with peer-editing, but with repeated practice, they will become more accurate. Students may be uncomfortable at first with the task of finding mistakes in their peers' work. Stress the importance of spelling and methodically walk students through each word on the board.

B. Complete the conversations and practice them with a partner. Answers may vary.

Sample answers are given.

1. **Felipe:** _____Good morning_____. Welcome to our class.

   Student: Hello. Thank you.

2. **Gabriela:** Hi! _____How are you_____?

   Duong: Fine, thanks. _____How are you_____?

3. **Eva:** _____Hello_____. Welcome to our class.

   Student: Hi. Thank you.

C. Read the greetings.

hi	hello	welcome	How are you?
good morning	good afternoon	good evening	

TR 2
D. Listen and complete the conversation.

Roberto: Hi. I'm Roberto. _____How are you_____?

Gabriela: _____Hello_____. My name is Gabriela. I'm fine, thanks.

Roberto: _____Welcome_____ to our class.

Gabriela: Thank you.

Roberto: Our teacher is Miss Smith.

E.　Listen and repeat.

Hi! I'm Gabriela.
G-A-B-R-I-E-L-A.

Hello. I'm Duong.
D-U-O-N-G.

YES/NO QUESTIONS

Can you repeat that?
Can you speak slower?
Can you spell that again?

F.　Listen and repeat.

Aa　Bb　Cc　Dd　Ee　Ff
Gg　Hh　Ii　Jj　Kk　Ll
Mm　Nn　Oo　Pp　Qq　Rr
Ss　Tt　Uu　Vv　Ww　Xx
Yy　Zz

CONTRACTIONS

/m/　I'm

G.　Listen and write.

1. Hi! I'm _____ Susan _____.

2. Hello! My name is _____ Bill _____.

3. How are you? I'm _____ Ana _____.

4. Hi! My name is _____ Tony _____.

H.　Greet five people in your class. Ask them to spell their names. Write their names.

Answers will vary.

1. _____

2. _____

3. _____

4. _____

5. _____

Presentation 3

15–20 mins. ■■■

Wad up a piece of paper or bring a small soft ball into class and start a chain of questions. First, say: *My name's (your name)*. Then, throw the ball to a student and help him or her to say the sentence substituting his or her name. Write the phrase on the board to help students see what they are saying. Next, ask the first student to throw the ball to another student. Students should continue the activity until everyone has had a chance to say the sentence.

You may want to interrupt the activity for a short mini lesson on the */m/* sound if students are having trouble saying *my* and *name*.

PRONUNCIATION

/m/

Students may avoid touching their lips together when pronouncing the /m/ in *I'm*. Help students pronounce the /m/ first in isolation and then as part of the phrase they are practicing. Emphasizing the sound will help students distinguish it from other sounds. Don't single out students who are having problems with the target sound. After several students have made similar errors, go over the pronunciation of the sound again. You may want to have each student in turn say *I'm* just to be sure they understand that they must put their lips together. Again, be careful not to overcorrect.

E. Listen and repeat.

Write the two names on the board and ask students to join you as you spell the two names while pointing to each letter.

LISTENING SCRIPT

CD 1
TR 3

The listening script matches the conversation in Exercise E.

F. Listen and repeat.

Write the alphabet across the board. Have students listen to and repeat each letter. Write *Gabriela* under the *G* on the board. Write *Duong* under the *D*.

LISTENING SCRIPT

CD 1
TR 4

A B C D E F G H I J K L M
N O P Q R S T U V W X Y Z

Practice 3

5 mins. ■

G. Listen and write.

LISTENING SCRIPT

CD 1
TR 5

1. *Hi! I'm Susan.*
2. *Hello! My name is Bill.*
3. *How are you? I'm Ana.*
4. *Hi! My name is Tony.*

Evaluation 3

5 mins. ■

Ask volunteers to write the four names on the board from the practice activity under the corresponding letters in the alphabet.

Refer students to *Stand Out 1 Workbook*, Pre-Unit, Lesson 1 for more practice with the *be* verb.

Go to the *Activity Bank* online for suggestions on promoting digital literacy and using the Internet to enhance this lesson.

Application

5–7 mins. ■■■

H. Greet five people in your class. Ask them to spell their names. Write their names.

Ask students to write the names they learn in the spaces provided.

MULTILEVEL WORKSHEET

Pre-Unit, Lesson 1, Worksheet 1: Say *Hello*

INSTRUCTOR'S NOTES

Goal: Say and write numbers
Grammar: *Is, are*
Academic Strategy: Pronunciation
Vocabulary: Numbers, *hours, week, students, address, phone number*

Agenda

☐ Review names.
☐ Read a paragraph and complete a chart.
☐ Say and write numbers.
☐ Listen and write numbers.
☐ Learn how to say and write phone numbers, addresses, and zip codes.
☐ Ask for and write personal information.

Resources

Multilevel Worksheet: Pre-Unit, Lesson 2, Worksheet 1
Workbook: Pre-Unit, Lesson 2
Audio: CD 1, Tracks 6–8
Heinle Picture Dictionary: Numbers, pages 2–3; Calendar, pages 6–7; The Telephone, pages 16–17
Stand Out 1 Assessment CD-ROM with ExamView®

Pacing

■ 1.5 hour classes ■ 2.5 hour classes
■ 3+ hour classes

STANDARDS CORRELATIONS

CCRS: RI1, L2
CASAS: 0.1.2, 0.1.4, 0.2.2
SCANS: **Information** Acquire and evaluate information
Basic Skills Reading, writing, listening, speaking
Personal Qualities Sociability
EFF: **Communication** Read with understanding, convey ideas in writing, speak so others can understand, listen actively

Warm-up and Review   10–12 mins. ■■■

Write the alphabet across the board as you did in Lesson 1. Ask students to come to the board and write their names under the first letter of their first names. To help students understand the instructions, do a few students' names yourself. After students sit down, ask them to greet each other, practicing American-style handshakes and saying *hello*. You may refer to the previous lesson to help students remember the vocabulary.

Introduction   5 mins. ■■■

Count the number of students' names under each letter. Count out loud and encourage students to count along with you. Write the number of students under each letter whose name starts with the letter. State the goal: *Today, we will say and write numbers.*

Presentation 1   15 mins. ■■■

Write these words on the board: *students*, *hours*, and *week*. Help students understand the meaning of each word. Ask students to stand. Use gestures as well as verbal cues to request them to point at certain objects in the room. Have them point to one another, to a clock, and to a calendar. If there is no calendar in the room, quickly create one on the board. You might add a few other objects to round out the activity.

Ask students to sit down. Using the clock as a visual, say all the numbers from 1 to 12 and have students repeat them. Do the same while pointing at the calendar. Then, count the number of students in the class out loud, encouraging students to count with you.

A. Look at the picture. Describe what you see. Say how many students there are. Say where the teacher is.

Ask students to open their books and look at the picture. Briefly talk about the picture. Have students describe what they see. Ask them to say how many students there are and where the teacher is.

B. Read the paragraph. Circle the numbers.

This activity is still part of the presentation. At this stage, students are not expected to understand every word in the paragraph. The goal is to give students exposure to numbers within a text and to help them understand the general meaning of the paragraph.

First, read the paragraph out loud and then ask questions, such as: *What is the teacher's name? How many students are in the class?*

Practice 1   3 mins. ■■■

C. SURVEY Complete the chart about your class.

This should be an easy activity for students. Some students may have trouble completing or understanding a simple chart. In *Stand Out*, students will complete many charts, so it is important to help those who have difficulty.

Evaluation 1   3 mins. ■■■

Observe students as they work and check their charts.

LESSON ② What's your number?

GOAL ■ Say and write numbers

WORKPLACE CONNECTION
Exercise C: Collect and organize information.

A. Look at the picture. Describe what you see. Say how many students there are. Say where the teacher is.

B. Read the paragraph. Circle the numbers.

Welcome to Miss Smith's class. There are ⓬ students in the class. The students study for ⓢⓘⓧ hours every week. The school address is ⑲ Lincoln Street, Irvine, California ⑨②⑥⓪②.

C. SURVEY Complete the chart about your class. Answers will vary.

Teacher's name	
Number of students	
Number of hours	
Zip code	

D. Listen and practice saying the numbers 0 to 20.

0 zero/oh	1 one	2 two	3 three
4 four	5 five	6 six	7 seven
8 eight	9 nine	10 ten	11 eleven
12 twelve	13 thirteen	14 fourteen	15 fifteen
16 sixteen	17 seventeen	18 eighteen	19 nineteen
20 twenty			

E. Listen and write the numbers you hear. Then, spell them out.

1. _____5_____   _____five_____
2. _____8_____   _____eight_____
3. _____9_____   _____·nine_____
4. _____19_____   _____nineteen_____
5. _____2_____   _____two_____

F. Listen and write the missing numbers.

My name is Gabriela. My address is _____14_____ Main Street. The zip code is _____06119_____. My phone number is _____401-555-7248_____. There are _____nine_____ students in my class.
(Spell out)

Presentation 2

5–8 mins. ■■■

D. Listen and practice saying the numbers 0 to 20.

> **LISTENING SCRIPT**
> CD 1
> TR 6
>
> *0 1 2 3 4 5 6 7 8 9 10*
> *11 12 13 14 15 16 17 18 19 20*

After students have listened to the audio, call out different numbers and ask students to point to the numbers they hear in their books.

Prepare students for focused listening by talking about things in the classroom and asking students to point to the numbers in the book. For example, you might say: *There are 18 desks in the classroom.* Help students understand that they don't have to know what a desk is to do the activity; they only need to recognize the numbers they hear.

BEST PRACTICE

Natural speech

Natural speech is important in the classroom. Unnaturally slowing down or over-enunciating could make students frustrated when they listen to native speakers outside of the classroom and are unable to understand them. Help students learn the strategies they will use in such instances by speaking at an authentic pace and in a natural fashion.

Practice 2

12–15 mins. ■■

E. Listen and write the numbers you hear. Then, spell them out.

> **LISTENING SCRIPT**
> CD 1
> TR 7
>
> 1. *five*
> 2. *eight*
> 3. **Duong:** *Hello, Gabriela.*
>   **Gabriela:** *Hi, Duong.*
>   **Duong:** *How many students are in your class?*
>   **Gabriela:** *I think there are nine.*
> 4. **Duong:** *My class is bigger.*
>   **Gabriela:** *Really? How many?*
>   **Duong:** *We have 19 students.*
> 5. **Duong:** *Maybe my class is bigger because it is shorter.*
>   **Gabriela:** *How long is your class?*
>   **Duong:** *It is two hours a day.*

BEST PRACTICE

Focused listening

Focused listening is prevalent throughout the *Stand Out* series. The recordings are at an authentic speed and are filled with language students may not understand. The purpose of a focused-listening task is to help students develop the ability to pull meaning out of complex and natural conversations by identifying key words.

It's important to remind students to listen for overall meaning every time you do a focused-listening activity, so they don't become frustrated and stop listening all together.

F. Listen and write the missing numbers.

> **LISTENING SCRIPT**
> CD 1
> TR 8
>
> *My name is Gabriela. My address is 14 Main Street. The zip code is 06119. My phone number is 401-555-7248. There are nine students in my class.*

In the second part of the practice, students are asked to put multiple numbers together. If they have problems, play the recording as many times as necessary.

Evaluation 2

5 mins. ■■

Write the short paragraph from Exercise F on the board with space for the answers. Ask volunteers to write their answers on the board.

BEST PRACTICE

Encourage student participation

Whether classes are quiet or not, always look for opportunities to encourage student participation. This doesn't have to be elaborate in planning. Rather, a simple twist can turn an ordinary activity into a more engaging one. Consider the following:

1. Whenever you need to write something on the board, ask yourself if one or more volunteers can do it instead.
2. When it comes to problem solving, fill-in-the-blank, and open-ended questions, have students work in pairs or groups to come up with answers before trying individual responses.

Presentation 3

8–10 mins. ■■■

G. Read about Gabriela and Eva.

Do this activity as a class. Help students understand the new vocabulary, specifically *zip code*, *address*, and *phone number*. Ask questions about the information below the pictures. Ask the class and individuals for answers.

Prepare students for the practice by writing addresses, phone numbers, and zip codes on the board and asking them to help you label them as such.

You can make a game of this by forming three teams of students. Have the teams line up in three lines with the front of each line facing the board, 10–15 feet away from the board. In front of each team on the board, write the three target items: *zip code*, *phone number*, and *address*. Then, call out a phone number, address, or zip code. The first person in each line should slap the correct label. (Fly swatters work well here.) The first team to slap the correct word gets a point.

Practice 3

5–8 mins. ■

H. Look at the numbers. Write the information in the chart.

Evaluation 3

2–5 mins. ■

Ask students to compare answers and then go over them as a class.

Refer students to *Stand Out 1 Workbook,* Pre-Unit, Lesson 2 for more practice with *It is* and *It's*.

Go to the *Activity Bank* online for suggestions on promoting digital literacy and using the Internet to enhance this lesson.

Application

7–10 mins. ■■■

I. Write the numbers. Say the numbers to your partner. Listen and write your partner's numbers.

The goal here is to practice saying and writing numbers. Addresses will be the focus of another lesson; however, with the skills students learned in the first lesson, they should be able to give their addresses with the number and the name of the street. Students may not know how to spell their street names. Emphasize that the numbers are the most important part of the activity. After finishing this activity, students may also be encouraged to learn how to write and spell their complete addresses.

MULTILEVEL WORKSHEET

Pre-Unit, Lesson 2, Worksheet 1: Personal Information

INSTRUCTOR'S NOTES

_____

_____

_____

_____

_____

_____

_____

_____

_____

_____

_____

_____

_____

_____

G. Read about Gabriela and Eva.

Name: Gabriela Ramirez
Address: 14 Main Street
Zip code: 06119
Phone: 401-555-7248

Name: Eva Malinska
Address: 333 Western Circle
Zip code: 06119
Phone: 401-555-3534

H. Look at the numbers. Write the information in the chart.

2945 Broadway	916-555-2386	415-555-7869	72643
800-555-2675	9235 Sundry Way	98724	8 Palm Circle
213-555-5761	78231	9921 Johnson Street	23145

Address	Zip code	Phone
2945 Broadway	72643	916-555-2386
9235 Sundry Way	98724	415-555-7869
8 Palm Circle	78231	800-555-2675
9921 Johnson Street	23145	213-555-5761

I. Write the numbers. Say the numbers to your partner. Listen and write your partner's numbers. *Answers will vary.*

	You	Your partner
1. The number of people in your family	_____	_____
2. Your phone number	_____	_____
3. Your address	_____	_____
4. Your zip code	_____	_____

GOAL ▇ Follow instructions

A. **Write the words under the pictures.**

listen	read	speak	write

1.

_____write_____

2.

_____listen_____

3.

_____read_____

4.

_____speak_____

B. **Listen and point to the correct picture.**

CD 1
TR 9

C. **Complete the instructions. Use the words from the box in Exercise A.**

1. _____**Write**_____ your name on the paper.

2. _____Listen_____ to the audio and repeat.

3. _____Write_____ your answers on the board.

4. _____Read_____ the story and answer the questions.

5. _____Speak_____ with your partner about the picture.

Goal: Follow instructions
Grammar: Imperatives
Academic Strategies: Focused listening, clarifying
Vocabulary: Classroom commands

Agenda

- Review numbers.
- Complete instructions.
- Listen to new words.
- Listen and follow directions.
- Practice conversations with a partner.

Resources

Multilevel Worksheet: Pre-Unit, Lesson 3, Worksheet 1
Workbook: Pre-Unit, Lesson 3
Audio: CD 1, Tracks 9–10
Heinle Picture Dictionary: Listen, Read, Write, pages 20–21
Stand Out 1 Assessment CD-ROM with ExamView®

Pacing

- 1.5 hour classes
- 2.5 hour classes
- 3+ hour classes

STANDARDS CORRELATIONS

CCRS: SL2, SL3, L2
CASAS: 0.1.5, 0.1.6, 2.2.1
SCANS: **Information** Acquire and evaluate information
Basic Skills Listening, speaking
EFF: **Communication** Speak so others can understand, listen actively

Warm-up and Review   10 mins.

Ask students to go to page 8, Exercise I. Ask them to find a different partner and do the activity again.

Introduction   5 mins.

Ask students to stand up. Model the action so that they understand. Then, ask them to turn right and left as you model the actions. Then, ask them to turn around. Finally, ask them to sit down. Point to the agenda and give the goal: *Today, we will learn to follow instructions.*

Presentation 1   15–20 mins.

Students will learn the four vocabulary words—*write, listen, read,* and *speak*—through pantomiming. Before students open their books, pantomime the different vocabulary words several times. Some students may call out the words. Write them on the board. Then, repeat the activity with *stand up, sit down,* and *take out your books/pencil/paper.*

Ask students to open their books and look at the words and pictures. With student input, name the four people in the pictures. Create sentences about each person. Don't expect students to create sentences at this time. As you say each sentence, ask students to point to the picture it refers to.

A. Write the words under the pictures.

Write the four words from the box on the board as headings to four columns. Help students with additional new vocabulary to go with each word. For example, include *to the radio* under the heading *listen.* Next, say the words and ask students to pantomime. Finally, prepare students for the focused-listening practice. Remind them that they don't need to understand every word to do the activity.

Practice 1   7–10 mins.

B. Listen and point to the correct picture.

LISTENING SCRIPT   🎧 CD 1 TR 9

1. *I am a busy woman. I have to write everything down that I do and that I need to do. I write everything to stay organized.*
2. *I am a happy person. I speak to my friends every day. I also think it is important to speak English in the United States.*
3. *I like to listen to music. When I listen to music in English, I learn a lot.*
4. *I read every chance I get.*

C. Complete the instructions. Use the words from the box in Exercise A.

Evaluation 1   5 mins.

On the board, write the sentences as they appear in the student book in Exercise C. Have volunteers complete them.

Presentation 2

10–15 mins. ■■■

D. Match the sentences with the pictures. Write the letter.

Go over any new vocabulary in the pictures that students are unfamiliar with. Walk students through the matching activity. This may be the first matching activity students have done.

Say the sentences and ask students to repeat them. Pantomime different actions and ask students to say the sentences, first as a group, and then individually.

Next, say the words and ask students to pantomime as they did in the previous presentation.

Practice 2

7–10 mins. ■■

E. Listen and follow the instructions.

In this activity, play the recording several times. Ask students to follow the directions in the first listening section.

LISTENING SCRIPT

CD 1
TR 10

Please stand. Please sit down. Please read page one in your book. Please listen carefully. Please take out a sheet of paper. Please write your name on a sheet of paper.

Evaluation 2

7–10 mins. ■■

Observe students pantomiming the actions.

INSTRUCTOR'S NOTES

D. **Match the sentences with the pictures. Write the letter.**

a.

b.

c.

d.

e.

f.

g.

h.

___*d*___ 1. Please stand up.

___*h*___ 3. Please sit down.

___*a*___ 5. Please open your book.

___*e*___ 7. Please write.

___*c*___ 2. Please read.

___*b*___ 4. Please take out a sheet of paper.

___*f*___ 6. Please listen carefully.

___*g*___ 8. Please help Juana.

E. **Listen and follow the instructions.**

CD 1
TR 10

F. Read the conversation.

Teacher: Please open your books to page fifteen.

Student: What page?

Teacher: Page fifteen. That's one, five.

Student: Thank you.

G. Practice with a partner.

Student B's book is closed. Student A says:

1. Please open your book to page six.

2. Please open your book to page fourteen.

3. Please open your book to Unit 4, Lesson 2.

4. Please open your book to the vocabulary list on pages 213 and 214.

H. Practice with a partner.

Student A's book is closed. Student B says:

1. Please open your book to page three.

2. Please open your book to page twelve.

3. Please open your book to Unit 7, Lesson 3.

4. Please open your book to the charts on page 215.

I. Give instructions to a partner.

1. Please stand up.

2. Please take out your book and open to page fifteen.

3. Please sit down.

4. Please write my name on a sheet of paper.

5. Please read my name.

J. Guess the instruction. Act out an instruction and your partner guesses it.

Presentation 3

10–15 mins. ■■■

Open and close a book in front of the class several times. Open the book and show students what page you are on. Show them the page and say the page number.

F. Read the conversation.

Practice the conversation together. Help students use correct intonation, especially when they ask the clarification question.

Write the following clarification questions on the board: *Excuse me? Pardon me? What page? What did you say?* Say a sentence quickly so students can't understand it. Explain that they can ask for clarification by using one of these phrases.

Carefully explain how to do the two practice activities, Exercises G and H. Role-play the exercises with a volunteer in front of the class. Help them understand what is meant by *Student A* and *Student B*.

Practice 3

7–10 mins. ■

G. Practice with a partner.

H. Practice with a partner.

Evaluation 3

5 mins. ■

Ask volunteers to do the activity in front of the class.

Refer students to *Stand Out 1 Workbook*, Pre-Unit, Lesson 3 for more practice with imperatives and action verbs.

Go to the *Activity Bank* online for suggestions on promoting digital literacy and using the Internet to enhance this lesson.

Application

5–7 mins. ■■■

I. Give instructions to a partner.

Have students practice giving and following the instructions. Make sure they switch roles.

J. Guess the instruction. Act out an instruction and your partner guesses it.

MULTILEVEL WORKSHEET

Pre-Unit, Lesson 3, Worksheet 1: Classroom Instructions

Assessment

■■■

Use the Stand Out 1 Assessment CD-ROM with ExamView® to create a post-test for the Pre-Unit.

INSTRUCTOR'S NOTES

_____
_____
_____
_____
_____
_____
_____
_____
_____
_____
_____
_____
_____
_____
_____
_____
_____
_____
_____
_____
_____
_____
_____
_____
_____
_____

Talking with Others

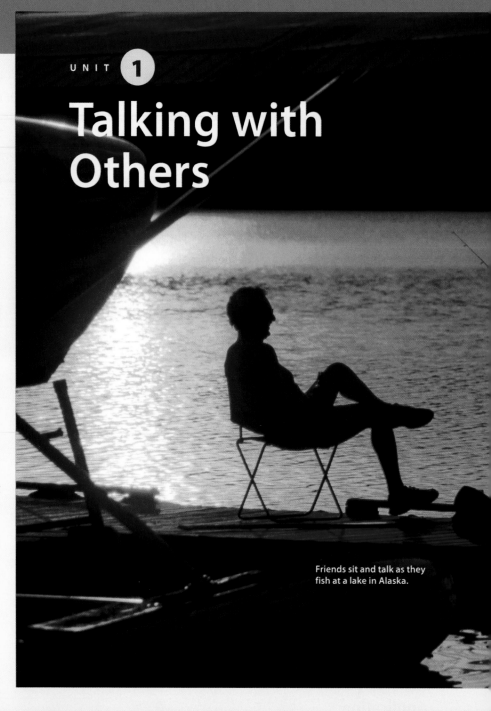

UNIT **1**

Talking with Others

Friends sit and talk as they fish at a lake in Alaska.

About the Photo

This photo shows two men at sunset fishing at a lake in the Kanai Peninsula, Alaska. The Kenai Fjords National Park in the Kenai Peninsula is popular among tourists who visit the region for hiking and wildlife spotting. One popular method of transport is by floatplane. The planes have the ability to take off from and land on water, making it easy for hikers to explore the region. Many cruises also pass through the park and allow visitors to see animals such as sea lions, puffins, porpoises, bears, and various whales.

- Introduce the unit. Ask students to talk with each other for a brief moment. Then, ask students what they talked about. Discuss as a class.
- Ask students to look at the photo and have a volunteer read the caption out loud.
- Read and ask each question. Then, ask students what they think the people are talking about. Discuss as a class.
- Ask volunteers to read the unit outcomes. Give students an example for each.

UNIT OUTCOMES	GRAMMAR	VOCABULARY	EL CIVICS
• Ask for and give personal information • Describe people • Describe family relationships • Express preferences • Plan a schedule	• Simple present: *Be* • his/her • Simple present: *Have* • Adjective order • Simple present: *Like* • *From … to*	• Personal information • Height, weight, hair colors and styles • Family • Entertainment • Clock times	The skills students learn in this unit can be applied to the following El Civics competency areas: • Personal Information

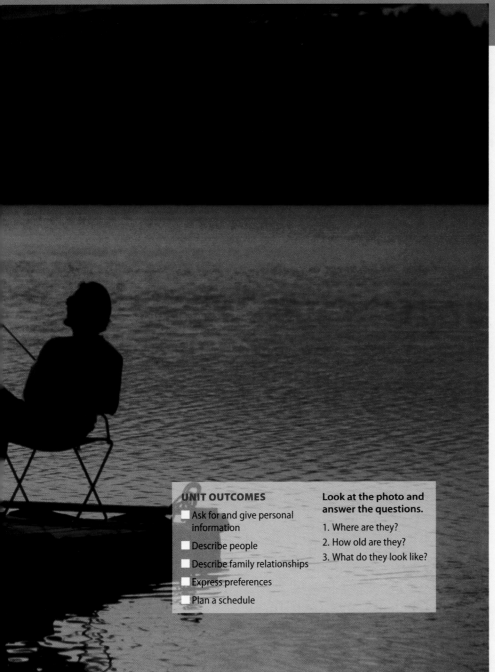

Life Skills Link

In this unit, students will learn how to introduce themselves and how to give out information to people they meet for the first time. They will also learn how to describe people around them and members of their families, as well as express their preferences.

Workplace Link

All lessons and units in *Stand Out* include basic communication skills and interpersonal skills important for the workplace. They are not individually identified. Other workplace skills are indicated. They include *collecting and organizing information, making decisions and solving problems,* and *combining ideas and information.*

UNIT OUTCOMES

- ☐ Ask for and give personal information
- ☐ Describe people
- ☐ Describe family relationships
- ☐ Express preferences
- ☐ Plan a schedule

Look at the photo and answer the questions.

1. Where are they?
2. How old are they?
3. What do they look like?

CASAS	SCANS	CCRS
Lesson 1: 0.1.2, 0.2.1 Lesson 2: 0.1.2, 0.1.3, 1.1.4 Lesson 3: 0.1.2 Lesson 4: 0.2.4 Lesson 5: 2.3.1 Review: 0.1.2, 0.1.3, 0.2.1, 0.2.4, 1.1.4, 2.3.1, 4.8.1 Team Project: 0.1.2, 0.1.3, 0.2.1, 0.2.4, 1.1.4, 2.3.1	Most SCANS are incorporated into this unit, with emphasis on: • Acquiring information • Interpreting and evaluating information • Writing (Technology is optional.)	RI1, RI2, RI5, RI7, SL1, SL2, SL4, L1, L2, L5, RF2

LESSON ① Where are you from?

A. Look at the picture. Where is Roberto from? Roberto is from Mexico City.

B. INTERPRET Read more about Roberto.

My name is <u>Roberto Garcia</u>. I'm a new student in this school. I'm from Mexico City, <u>Mexico</u>.
I'm <u>43</u> years old and I'm <u>married</u>. I'm very happy in my new class.

C. CLASSIFY Write the underlined words from Exercise B about Roberto in the chart below.

First name	Last name	Country	Age	Marital status
Roberto	Garcia	Mexico	43	married

D. Complete the sentences about Roberto.

(age)   1. Roberto Garcia is _____43_____ years old.

(country)   2. He is from _____Mexico_____.

(marital status) 3. He is _____married_____.

Goal: Ask for and give personal information
Grammar: Simple present: *Be*
Academic Strategy: Focused listening
Vocabulary: Personal information

Agenda

- Line up in alphabetical order.
- Give personal information.
- Talk about Roberto.
- Learn new vocabulary.
- Use the *be* verb.
- Ask for and give personal information.

Resources

Multilevel Worksheets: Unit 1, Lesson 1,
    Worksheets 1–2
Workbook: Unit 1, Lesson 1
Audio: CD 1, Tracks 11–13
Heinle Picture Dictionary: Nationalities,
    pages 44–45; Documents, pages 42–43
Stand Out 1 Assessment CD-ROM with ExamView®

Pacing

- 1.5 hour classes
- 2.5 hour classes
- 3+ hour classes

STANDARDS CORRELATIONS

CCRS: SL2, L1, L2, L5, RF2, RF3
CASAS: 0.1.1, 0.1.2, 0.1.4, 0.2.1
SCANS: **Basic Skills** Reading, writing, listening, speaking
EFF: **Communication** Read with understanding, convey ideas in writing, speak so others can understand, listen actively

Preassessment *(optional)*

Use the Stand Out 1 Assessment CD-ROM with ExamView® to create a pretest for Unit 1.

Warm-up and Review   10–15 mins.

Write the alphabet across the board as you did in the Pre-Unit. Begin to write students' first names on the board under the appropriate letters. Ask three students to stand up. Show them how to form a line in alphabetical order by first name. Ask the class to help you do the same with a few more students. Then, ask the class to complete the line by putting themselves in alphabetical order.

Introduction   5 mins.

Ask students to open their books and look at the picture of Roberto. Ask about Roberto. Students may not understand your questions at this point. Ask questions like: *Where is he from? Is he married? How old is he?* State the goal: *Today, we will learn how to give personal information.* Then, point to the agenda.

Presentation 1   10–15 mins.

On the board, write: *Where are you from?* Ask a few students where they are from. Expect one-word answers. Point to yourself and say: *I'm from (your country).* Ask more students the same question. Follow up by asking the class, *Where's (Selma) from?* Using the same procedure, ask: *Are you married?*

A. Look at the picture. Where is Roberto from?

B. INTERPRET Read more about Roberto.

Read the paragraph with the class. Then, read it again, but insert your own information. If you don't want to say your age, cover your mouth at that point and uncover it to finish.

Practice 1   3–5 mins.

BEST PRACTICE

Questioning strategies

The questions in the introduction are based on what students will learn in this lesson. Students are not expected to answer them at this point, but a few students may be able to guess their meaning.

Give students twenty seconds before you help them answer questions, and ask each question more than once. If students are unable to respond, answer the question by asking another. For example, *Where is he from? Is he from China?* This process will allow students to give a yes or no response. Don't ask about the correct country in your first question. After asking about a few different countries and eliciting negative responses, give students the answer by asking: *Is he from Mexico?*

C. CLASSIFY Write the underlined words from Exercise B about Roberto in the chart below.

Students may have trouble with the word *age*, but allow them to figure out what it means through process of elimination.

D. Complete the sentences about Roberto.

Evaluation 1
3–5 mins. ■■□

Go over the answers in the student book with the class. Ask the class or individual students the questions about Roberto: *What's his name? Where is he from? Is he married? How old is he?*

Presentation 2
8–10 mins. ■■□

The goal here is to help students understand the words associated with each idea. So, for example, if they are asked their marital status, they will be able to answer equally as well as if they are asked if they are married.

E. Look at the pictures.

Do this activity as a class. Make sure that students understand the words *single*, *married*, and *divorced*. Write *marital status* on the board. Then, have students look at the pictures in Exercise E. Ask them to predict the marital status of each student. Then, review the word *age* and ask students to guess the age of each student. Finally, ask students to predict the country (or you may write on the board *country of origin*) of each student.

F. Match the questions with the answers.

This exercise reinforces what students have learned. Walk around the classroom and check students' answers as they work.

Practice 2
5–7 mins. ■■□

G. Listen and complete the missing information.

Show students what to listen for in this focused-listening activity. Remind them that they don't need to understand every word.

<table>
<tr><td>BEST PRACTICE</td></tr>
</table>

Repeated listening

It may become necessary with focused listening to play the recording more than once. You may ask students to compare answers with each other before you play a recording again.

Note: Focused listening is at an authentic pace to help students learn the strategies they need to function outside of the classroom.

LISTENING SCRIPT

CD 1
TR 11–13

1. *Eva Malinska is happy to be in the United States. She wants to learn English. In Warsaw, Poland, she learned a bit of English. She wants to help other people in her family learn English. She is divorced and 60 years old.*
2. *Gabriela Ramirez is 26. She listens to the radio and reads the newspaper every day. She wants to learn English quickly. She is single and from Buenos Aires, Argentina.*
3. *Felipe is a student and also works hard. He is a salesman and goes to school at night. He is 33 years old. He is married with three kids. He talks to his family in Cuba once a week.*

Evaluation 2
7–10 mins. ■■□

Check students' understanding by describing different things about the students in Exercise G. For example, say: *divorced*. Students should respond: *Eva*. You can also ask students to respond nonverbally by showing the number of fingers that correspond to Picture 1, 2, or 3. After giving one-word descriptions, say complete sentences.

Finally, ask the four questions in Exercise F about each picture. Then, ask students to take on the role of the three students in Exercise G and ask the questions of each other using *you*.

<table>
<tr><td>BEST PRACTICE</td></tr>
</table>

Monitoring student responses

An easy way to monitor student responses is to have students respond verbally with a word. Say: *divorced*. Students recognize that Eva is divorced and respond: *Eva*.

With the above method, however, the stronger students sometimes overwhelm students who need more time to think when asked for a verbal response. You may choose other ways for students to respond where students are less likely to "go along with the crowd." One such method could be to use 3-by-5 index cards with an answer choice on each. For example, each card could have different names (Eva, Gabriela, or Felipe). Students then hold up the correct card after you give the cue. If you choose to do this method, have students create the cards themselves so they also get writing practice.

Another way is described in this lesson. Students will respond by showing the number of fingers that correspond to each picture. Start this method by first only saying the target word. Next, embed the word in a sentence and then embed all the words in a paragraph.

E. Look at the pictures.

single

divorced

married

F. Match the questions with the answers.

1. Where are you from?
2. What's your name?
3. Are you married?
4. How old are you?

a. Yes, I'm married.
b. I'm from Mexico.
c. I'm 43 years old.
d. Roberto.

G. Listen and complete the missing information.

CD 1
TR 11-13

1.

Name: _Eva Malinska_

Age: _60_

Marital status: _divorced_

Country: _Poland_

2.

Name: _Gabriela Ramirez_

Age: _26_

Marital status: _single_

Country: _Argentina_

3.

Name: _Felipe Rodriguez_

Age: _33_

Marital status: _married_

Country: _Cuba_

WORKPLACE CONNECTION
Exercise J: Interact appropriately with team members; Interpret and communicate
information; Collect and organize information.

H. **Study the chart with your classmates and teacher.**

Simple Present: *Be*			
Subject	*Be*	**Information**	**Example sentence**
I	am	43 years old	I **am** 43 years old.
He, She	is	single from Argentina	He **is** single. (Roberto **is** single.) She **is** from Argentina. (Gabriela **is** from Argentina.)
We, You, They	are	single married from Russia	We **are** single. You **are** married. They **are** from Russia.

I. **Write sentences about the people below.**

Trinh Hong

33 years old

Single

Cambodia

Duong Bui

33 years old

Married

Vietnam

Alan Hart

64 years old

Divorced

United States

1. (marital status) Duong ___is married___.

2. (marital status) Alan ___is divorced___.

3. (marital status) Trinh ___is single___ and Alan ___is divorced___.

4. (age) Trinh and Duong ___are (both) 33 years old___.

5. (age) Alan ___is 64 years old___.

6. (country) Alan ___is from the United States___.

J. **SURVEY** **In a group, interview three students. Complete the table.** Answers will vary.

What's your name?	Where are you from?	How old are you?	Are you married?

Presentation 3

H. Study the chart with your classmates and teacher.

Remember, at this stage, some students will have trouble understanding a chart like this one. Go over it carefully. Drill students by asking questions about the pictures below the chart and about themselves. Help students to use complete sentences. Write their responses on the board in complete sentences.

BEST PRACTICE

Drills

Drills can be a good way to help students become familiar with vocabulary, grammar structures, and proper pronunciation. They also help students to gain confidence, especially when performing together with their classmates. However, drills should not be the sole practice or method used to help students memorize something or acquire a grammar structure. There are several ways to drill (choral repetition, substitution, build up, backward build up, etc.). If particular drills are overused, there is a risk of losing meaning for structure.

Practice 3

I. Write sentences about the people below.

Ask students to complete the sentences in their books and then to copy them into a notebook.

Evaluation 3

Ask students to write their responses on the board and go over them as a class.

Refer students to *Stand Out 1 Workbook*, Unit 1, Lesson 1 for more practice with *be*.

Go to the *Activity Bank* online for suggestions on promoting digital literacy and using the Internet to enhance this lesson.

Application

J. SURVEY In a group, interview three students. Complete the table.

Ask students to form groups or form them in a way that you would like. Ask students in a Round Robin fashion to ask questions and record answers. The Round Robin would work like this: Student A asks Student B a question. Student B answers and all students record the answer. Then, Student B asks Student C, and so on. Demonstrate this several times before asking students to do it on their own.

MULTILEVEL WORKSHEETS

Unit 1, Lesson 1, Worksheet 1: Names and Countries

Unit 1, Lesson 1, Worksheet 2: The Verb *Be*

INSTRUCTOR'S NOTES

_____

_____

_____

_____

_____

_____

_____

_____

_____

_____

_____

_____

_____

_____

_____

Goal: Describe people

Grammar: *his/her;* simple present: *have;* adjective order

Pronunciation: /v/

Academic Strategy: Focused listening

Vocabulary: Colors, hairstyles, height, weight, age

Agenda

- Review personal information.
- Describe people.
- Learn about height, weight, age, hair and eye color.
- Listen and practice sentences.
- Describe hair.
- Complete a driver's license.

Resources

Multilevel Worksheets: Unit 1, Lesson 2, Worksheets 1–3

Workbook: Unit 1, Lesson 2

Audio: CD 1, Tracks 14–18

Heinle Picture Dictionary: Face and Hair, pages 32–33, Documents, pages 42–43

Stand Out 1 Assessment CD-ROM with ExamView®

Pacing

- 1.5 hour classes
- 2.5 hour classes
- 3+ hour classes

STANDARDS CORRELATIONS

CCRS: RI1, RI7, SL2, L1, L2, RF3

CASAS: 0.1.2, 0.1.3, 1.1.4

SCANS: **Information** Acquire and evaluate information

Interpersonal Participate as a member of a team

Thinking Skills Think creatively

EFF: **Communication** Speak so others can understand, listen actively, observe critically

Decision Making Solve problems and make decisions

Interpersonal Cooperate with others

Warm-up and Review   8–12 mins. ■■■

Ask a few students where they are from. Write their names and country of origin on the board. If you have a homogeneous group from one country, ask what city they are from. Take a class poll and create a graph. Put the number of students on the vertical axis and the countries, cities, or states on the horizontal axis. Make copies of the graph template on the **Multilevel Worksheets** CD-ROM to allow students to create their own graph.

Introduction   2 mins. ■■■

Write *tallest* on the board. Direct three students to the front of the room. Ask the class which student is tallest. Help students understand. Have students form a line from shortest to tallest. State the goal: *Today, we will learn how to describe people.*

Presentation 1   15–20 mins. ■■■

Show the class your driver's license or other identification. Tell students that the card has important information on it such as your birth date and your height. Remind them of the word *tall* and introduce them to the word *short*.

A. INTERPRET Look at Felipe's license. Complete the sentences.

Go over Felipe's license with the class. Check for understanding and prior knowledge. For example, ask what color Felipe's eyes are. Then, complete the sentences together. Since this is the presentation stage, students are still learning the new vocabulary.

Spend some time helping students understand the U.S. system of measurement and ways to write inches and feet. Many students will be familiar with the metric system. Show them how a foot equals 12 inches. Bring a tape measure, ruler, or yardstick in to emphasize the point. Take the time to measure several students against the board. Mark their heights with a line and label the measurements.

Go over colors for hair and eyes. Have a few students describe their eye and hair color.

Go over the grammar box. Use *his* and *her* in sentences describing students in the class. Stress the pronunciation for *her*. Students may concentrate on the /e/ sound, and the word ends up sounding like *air*. Help them to see that the vowel is swallowed up by the /r/.

Practice 1   7–10 mins. ■■■

B. Look at the licenses below. Complete the sentences about Duong and Eva.

Have students complete and practice the sentences in pairs. Student A says the part written in the book and Student B gives the information that they have filled in.

LESSON ② What does he look like?

GOAL ■ Describe people

WORKPLACE CONNECTION
Exercise A: Collect and organize information; Perform basic computations.
Exercises B: Collect and organize information.

A. INTERPRET Look at Felipe's license. Complete the sentences.

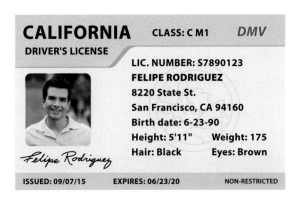

WRITE OUT

5'11" = five feet, eleven inches
= five-eleven

1. Felipe is ____five feet, eleven inches____ tall.

2. He is ____175____ pounds.

3. His hair is ____black____.

4. His eyes are ____brown____.

5. He is ____Answer will vary by year.____ years old.

6. His address is ____8220____ State Street.

HIS / HER

Duong

His hair is black.

His eyes are brown.

Eva

Her hair is white.

Her eyes are blue.

B. Look at the licenses below. Complete the sentences about Duong and Eva.

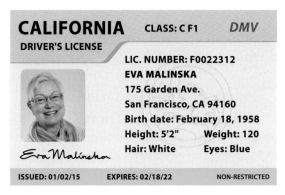

1. Duong is _five feet, six inches_ tall. (height)

2. He is ____165____ pounds. (weight)

3. His ____hair is black____. (hair)

4. His ____eyes are brown____. (eyes)

1. Eva is _five feet, two inches tall_ ____ tall. (height)

2. She is ____120____ pounds. (weight)

3. Her ____hair is white____. (hair)

4. Her ____eyes are blue____. (eyes)

C. Study the chart with your classmates and teacher.

Simple Present: *Have*		
Subject	**Verb**	**Example sentence**
I, You, We, They	have	I **have** black hair. You **have** white hair.
He, She, It	has	He **has** brown eyes. She **has** blue eyes.

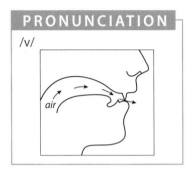

PRONUNCIATION

/v/

CD 1
TR 14-17

D. CLASSIFY Listen and complete the chart.

Name	Height	Hair	Eyes	Age
1. Roberto	5'11"	black	brown	43
2. Trinh	5'1"	black	brown	33
3. Gabriela	5'5"	black	brown	26
4. Alan	5'9"	red	green	64

CD 1
TR 18

E. Listen to and practice the conversation.

Student A: What does <u>Roberto</u> look like?

Student B: <u>He</u> has <u>black hair</u> and <u>brown eyes</u>.

Student A: How tall is <u>he</u>?

Student B: <u>He</u> is <u>five feet, eleven inches tall</u>.

Student A: Thank you.

F. Practice the conversation with information about Trinh, Gabriela, and Alan.

She has brown hair and brown eyes. She is tall.

Evaluation 1   7–10 mins. ■■■

Ask students to write their sentences on the board and then go over them as a class.

Presentation 2   15–20 mins. ■■■

Write *have* and *is* on the board as headings for two columns. These words can be problematic when describing people because students may confuse them in similar expressions.

Ask questions about height, hair, eyes, and age. Refer to the licenses on the previous page if students are uncomfortable giving their ages. Students at this level are not expected to use correct question form so it isn't necessary to have them ask the questions. Students will probably answer in short answers and not complete sentences. When they answer, write complete, correct sentences on the board using *have, has,* and *is.* After you have a good sample of sentences, circle all the verbs. Next, write *height, hair color, eye color,* and *age* as column headings on the board. Ask students to help put the words *is, have,* and *has* in the correct columns.

C. Study the chart with your classmates and teacher.

Go over the chart carefully. Ask students to create additional example sentences.

PRONUNCIATION

/v/

Review the pronunciation of *have* while going over the grammar. A good way to help students with the /v/ sound is to have them bite their lower lip. Make sure they don't hide their upper teeth with their upper lip. Ask them to smile and bring the corners of their mouths out and up, exposing their teeth.

Another way to teach this sound is to contrast it with /f/, which most students will be able to produce. Ask them to pronounce words that begin with /f/. Then, show them how to make the /f/ voiced by activating the voice box.

Practice 2   15–20 mins. ■■

The listening that follows is the first of a two-part practice. First, the vocabulary is checked in the listening. Then, students will use *has* to describe people in a conversation.

D. CLASSIFY Listen and complete the chart.

Play the recording several times so students have an opportunity to hear all the information. Allow students to compare their answers.

> ### LISTENING SCRIPT
> CD 1
> TR 14–17
>
> 1. **A:** *Excuse me. I am looking for Roberto Garcia.*
>   **B:** *I don't think I know him. What does he look like?*
>   **A:** *He has black hair and brown eyes, I think.*
>   **B:** *And his height . . . how tall is he?*
>   **A:** *He is five feet, eleven inches tall. He is probably 43 years old.*
>   **B:** *Oh, he's in Room 114.*
>   **A:** *Thanks!*
>
> 2. **A:** *Do you see Trinh over there?*
>   **B:** *I don't see her.*
>   **A:** *She is 5 feet, 1 inch tall and has black hair and brown eyes.*
>   **B:** *Oh, I see her now. Is she about 33 years old?*
>   **A:** *That sounds right.*
>
> 3. **A:** *Excuse me. I am looking for Gabriela Ramirez. She is tall, maybe 5 feet 5 inches. She has black hair and brown eyes. She is 26 years old.*
>   **B:** *No, I haven't seen her.*
>
> 4. **A:** *My name is Alan.*
>   **B:** *Please describe yourself.*
>   **A:** *I am 5 feet 9 inches tall. I have red hair and green eyes. I am 64 years old.*

E. Listen to and practice the conversation.

Go over the conversation, modeling correct intonation. Show students how to substitute information from the chart in Exercise D.

> ### LISTENING SCRIPT
> CD 1
> TR 18
> *The listening script matches the conversation in Exercise E.*

F. Practice the conversation with information about Trinh, Gabriela, and Alan.

Evaluation 2   5–7 mins. ■■

Ask students to perform their conversations in front of the class.

Presentation 3

10–15 mins. ■■■

G. Discuss the words with your classmates and teacher.

Integrate the grammar from the grammar box in your discussion. Flip through the book and ask students to find examples of different hairstyles and hair colors. Use *have*. Say *He has blond hair* instead of *He is blond* to avoid confusion.

Practice 3

10–15 mins. ■

H. DESIGN In a group, choose and draw the hair color and style for each face.

Let students discuss this activity the best they can in English. Then, ask students to describe what they have created in their groups. Have students take turns describing the people.

Evaluation 3

7–10 mins. ■

Ask students from each group to report one of their creations.

Refer students to *Stand Out 1 Workbook*, Unit 1, Lesson 2 for more practice with *have* and *be*.

Go to the *Activity Bank* online for suggestions on promoting digital literacy and using the Internet to enhance this lesson.

Application

5–7 mins. ■■■

I. APPLY Complete the driver's license with your information.

Have students describe themselves by completing the driver's license. If time permits, have students look at their partners' work and report the information to a third student. Have them describe the second student based on the information from the driver's license.

MULTILEVEL WORKSHEETS

Templates: Bar Graph

Unit 1, Lesson 2, Worksheet 1: Height and Weight

Unit 1, Lesson 2, Worksheet 2: Eyes and Hair

Unit 1, Lesson 2, Worksheet 3: The Verb *Have*

INSTRUCTOR'S NOTES

G. Discuss the words with your classmates and teacher.

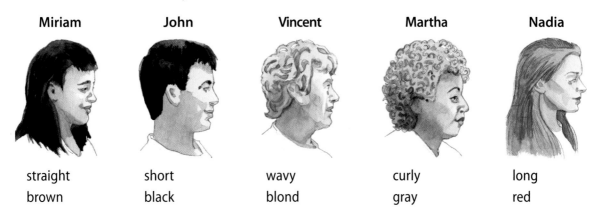

Miriam	John	Vincent	Martha	Nadia
straight	short	wavy	curly	long
brown	black	blond	gray	red

> **ADJECTIVES**
>
> Adjectives come before the noun. Always say colors just before the noun.
>
>   1   2
>
> Miriam has *straight brown* hair.

H. DESIGN In a group, choose and draw the best hair color and style for each face.

Jane	Gustavo	Andre	Maria

I. APPLY Complete the driver's license with your information. Answers will vary.

DRIVER'S LICENSE

Name:_____

Age:_____   Weight:_____

Height:_____   Eyes:_____

Address:_____

City:_____

State:_____   Zip Code:_____

Your Photo Here

LESSON ③ Roberto's family

GOAL ■ Describe family relationships

A. Look at the picture. Who is in the picture? What are they saying?

Antonio
Rebecca
Roberto
Duong
Lidia

B. Listen to the conversation.

CD 1
TR 19

Roberto:	Duong, this is my mother, my father, and my sister.
Antonio:	Nice to meet you, Duong. Where are you from?
Duong:	I'm from Vietnam.
Antonio:	Do your parents live here in the United States?
Duong:	No. Right now they live in Vietnam.

C. Look at the people from the picture above. Write the words from the box under the pictures.

friend	son	parents	sister	brother

brother   sister

son   parents

friend   friend

AT-A-GLANCE **PREP**

Goal: Describe family relationships
Grammar: *Be* verb
Pronunciation: Prominence
Academic Strategies: Predicting, focused listening
Vocabulary: Family

Agenda

- Read drivers' licenses.
- Describe family relationships.
- Learn family vocabulary.
- Listen for vocabulary in family trees.
- Ask questions about families.
- Make a family tree.

Resources

Multilevel Worksheets: Unit 1, Lesson 3, Worksheets 1–2
Workbook: Unit 1, Lesson 3
Audio: CD 1, Tracks 19–20
Heinle Picture Dictionary: Family, pages 26–27
Stand Out 1 Assessment CD-ROM with ExamView®

Pacing

- 1.5 hour classes
- 2.5 hour classes
- 3+ hour classes

STANDARDS CORRELATIONS

CCRS: RI1, RI7, SL1, SL2, L1, L2, L5
CASAS: 0.1.2
SCANS: **Information** Acquire and evaluate information, interpret and communicate information
Basic Skills Reading, writing, listening, speaking
EFF: **Communication** Read with understanding, convey ideas in writing, speak so others can understand, listen actively

Warm-up and Review   10–12 mins.

If you haven't already, do the application activity from the previous lesson. Ask students in groups of three to describe a student based on his or her driver's license information. Student A reads Student B's license and describes Student B to Student C. If they have done this activity, have them review it orally.

Introduction   5–7 mins.

Write *brother* and *sister* on the board. Ask individual students how many brothers and sisters they have. Count the total number of brothers and sisters in the

class including yours. State the goal: *Today, we will learn how to describe family relationships.*

Presentation 1   15–20 mins.

Draw a family tree on the board. Start with your parents. Draw a line from the parents to a child (you). Make sure you present *parents* as one of the vocabulary words. Add brothers and sisters. Describe your family. You may choose to add grandchildren. You are demonstrating what you hope students will be able to do by the end of class, so include vocabulary that you think will be most useful. Ask for help describing relationships to see what students already know and don't know.

Instruct the class to study the picture at the top of the page. Next, ask the questions in the box and ask students to close their books.

A. Look at the picture. Who is in the picture? What are they saying?

Instruct the class to study the picture at the top of the page. Next, ask the questions in the direction line.

B. Listen to the conversation.

Play the recording with books closed. Students just listen. Play the recording a second time and ask students to write down any family vocabulary they hear. Play the recording a third time. This time, students follow along in their books and underline the family vocabulary.

BEST PRACTICE

Eliciting information

Whenever possible, we suggest that you elicit as much information from students as they can give. By doing this, you will create a student-centered classroom. This method will also help you assess what students already know. Students are much more engaged when they are contributing to the lesson instead of passively listening to the teacher.

LISTENING SCRIPT   🎧 CD 1 TR 19
The listening script matches the conversation in Exercise B.

Note: Practice 1 (Exercise C) and Evaluation 1 appear on next page.

Practice 1

3–10 mins. ■■■

C. Look at the people from the picture above. Write the words from the box under the pictures.

Extend this activity by writing sentences on the board. Ask students to complete them in their notebooks. For example:

> Roberto is Lidia's brother.
> Lidia is _____.

Evaluation 1

5 mins. ■■■

Walk around and check students' work.

Presentation 2

10–15 mins. ■■■

D. Discuss the words with your classmates and teacher.

Reinforce what students have already learned by using the family tree you created on the board to go over the new vocabulary.

Go over the picture and the family tree with students. Discuss them using the target vocabulary. Without listening, students will not know the relationships for sure. Encourage them to guess and predict what the recording will say.

BEST PRACTICE

Predicting

An important part of listening is anticipating what will be heard. Predicting is an academic skill that students will begin to develop at this level. Predicting will help students to focus on what they are listening for and, consequently, be more prepared to pick out the target information.

Practice 2

5–7 mins. ■■

E. PREDICT Look at the picture and write the names on the family tree. Then, listen to check your answers.

Before students listen, have the class predict names to go on each line of the family tree by looking at the picture.

LISTENING SCRIPT

🎧 CD 1 TR 20

My name is Roberto Garcia. I am very happily married. My wife's name is Silvia. This is a picture of my family. The older man and the woman in the picture are my parents. My mother's name is Rebecca, and my father's name is Antonio. I have one sister, Lidia, and one brother, Julio. The girl and the boy are my children, Juan and Carla.

Evaluation 2

3 mins. ■■

Ask questions, such as: *Who is Silvia?* Students might answer: *She is Roberto's wife.*

INSTRUCTOR'S NOTES

_____
_____
_____
_____
_____
_____
_____
_____
_____
_____
_____
_____
_____
_____
_____
_____
_____
_____

D. Discuss the words with your classmates and teacher.

father	wife	children	grandson	uncle
mother	husband	grandfather	granddaughter	niece
brother	son	grandmother	aunt	nephew
sister	daughter			

E. CD 1 TR 20 **PREDICT Look at the picture and write the names on the family tree. Then, listen to check your answers.**

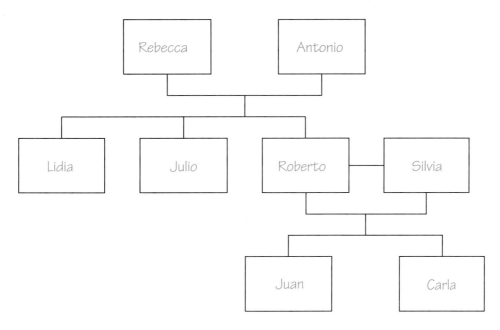

F. **Practice the conversation.**

Student A: Who is <u>Silvia</u>?

Student B: <u>Silvia is Roberto's wife</u>.

Student A: Who are <u>Antonio and Rebecca</u>?

Student B: They are <u>Roberto's parents</u>.

> **BE VERB**
>
> He **is** Roberto's brother.
> They **are** Roberto's children.

> **STRESS**
>
> **Emphasis**
> ➤ **WHO** is Silvia?
> ➤ **WHO** are Antonio and Rebecca?

G. **Work with a partner. Ask questions about Roberto's family on page 21.**

H. **CREATE** **Complete the family tree for your family.** Answers will vary.

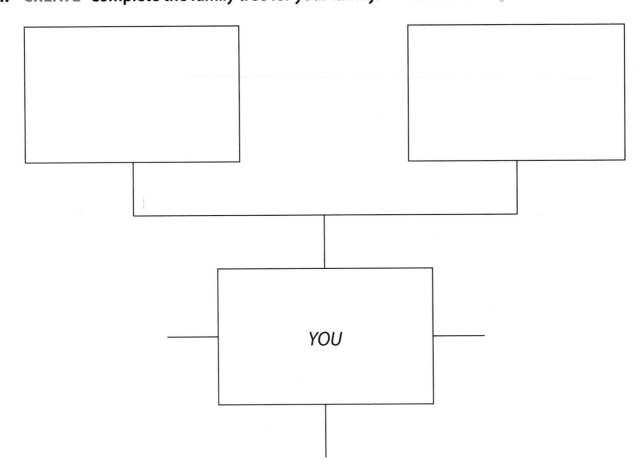

I. **Find or draw a picture of your family and share it with the class.**

Presentation 3   10–15 mins. ■■■

F. Practice the conversation.

On the board, write: *Who is . . . ?* Help students understand what kind of information is required in response to a question that begins with this phrase. Review the singular and plural forms of the *be* verb found in the small grammar box.

Go over the conversations. Make sure students use good intonation in their practice.

PRONUNCIATION

Prominence

Show students which words get emphasis. Usually, the question word will receive emphasis. Also, the names of people get more emphasis than the *be* verb, which gets no emphasis.

It is hard to teach which words are most important in questions and statements like these because it really depends on the context. For example, if the question is: *Is Silvia Roberto's sister?*, the answer might be: *Silvia is Roberto's WIFE*. *Wife* in this example becomes more important because a correction is taking place.

In the example here, it is more likely that *Roberto* will be emphasized over *wife*.

Practice 3   5–7 mins. ■

G. Work with a partner. Ask questions about Roberto's family on page 21.

Make sure that students understand they can use the conversations in Exercise F as models.

Evaluation 3   2 mins. ■

Observe students as they do the practice exercise.

Refer students to *Stand Out 1 Workbook*, Unit 1, Lesson 3 for more practice with *have* and *be*.

Go to the *Activity Bank* online for suggestions on promoting digital literacy and using the Internet to enhance this lesson.

Application   5–7 mins. ■■■

H. CREATE Complete the family tree for your family.

Ask students to describe their family to a partner or to a group after they complete their family trees.

I. Find or draw a picture of your family and share it with the class.

MULTILEVEL WORKSHEETS

Unit 1, Lesson 3, Worksheet 1: Family Tree

Unit 1, Lesson 3, Worksheet 2: Family Vocabulary

INSTRUCTOR'S NOTES

_____

_____

_____

_____

_____

_____

_____

_____

_____

_____

_____

_____

_____

_____

_____

_____

_____

_____

_____

_____

Goal: Express preferences
Grammar: Simple present: *Like*
Pronunciation: Prominence
Academic Strategies: Venn diagrams
Vocabulary: Entertainment

Agenda

▉ Write a paragraph.
▉ Listen to things Roberto and Silvia like.
▉ Use *like*.
▉ Read about Carla's and Juan's likes.
▉ Make a Venn diagram.

Resources

Multilevel Worksheets: Unit 1, Lesson 4, Worksheets 1–2
Workbook: Unit 1, Lesson 4
Audio: CD 1, Track 21
Heinle Picture Dictionary: Daily Activities, pages 34–35
Stand Out 1 Assessment CD-ROM with ExamView®

Pacing

■ 1.5 hour classes   ■ 2.5 hour classes
■ 3+ hour classes

CCRS: R3, SL1, SL2, SL4, L1, L2, L5
CASAS: 0.2.4
SCANS: **Basic Skills** Writing, listening, speaking
Thinking Skills See things in the mind's eye
EFF: **Communication** Convey ideas in writing, speak so others can understand, listen actively

Warm-up and Review   15–20 mins. ■■■

Write two paragraphs on the board about your family. Keep them simple and short. This will be a model for students. They might look something like this:

My Family
My name is Jim Smith. I am married. I have two children. I have one daughter and one son. I love my family.

My Family
My name is Jim Smith. My parents are John and Judy. I have three brothers. I love my family.

Ask students to copy one of the paragraphs or, if you feel they can do it, ask them to rewrite one of the paragraphs with their own personal information.

Introduction   2 mins. ■■■

Write the word *like* on the board. Mention something that you like. You might want to say that you like your students. Ask students what they like. Make a list on the board. State the goal: *Today, we will learn how to express preferences.*

Presentation 1   10–12 mins. ■■■

Ask students to open their books and go over the meaning of each new vocabulary item in Exercise A. Draw a Venn diagram on the board. Make a list of the items on the page you like. Ask a student for the items he or she likes. Record the information in the Venn diagram. Alternatively, you could make copies of the Venn diagram template on the **Multilevel Worksheets** Activity Bank and distribute them to students. Students can then do this activity along with you. Use this activity to prepare students for the focused listening.

Practice 1   10–20 mins. ■■■

A. Listen. Put an *R* by things Roberto likes and an *S* by things Silvia likes.

Play the listening several times.

LISTENING SCRIPT   CD 1 TR 21
Roberto and Silvia are happily married. Roberto likes movies, games, and books. Silvia likes parks, restaurants, and music. They both like sports, computers, and TV.

This activity can be expanded by asking students to complete a Venn diagram for Roberto and Silvia.

B. Complete the sentences.

Have students complete this activity individually.

Evaluation 1   7–10 mins. ■■■

Ask volunteers to write their completed sentences on the board. Have them check their answers to the previous listening activity based on their sentences.

LESSON ④ I like sports and music

WORKPLACE CONNECTION
Exercise B: Collect and organize information.

🎧 **A.** **Listen. Put an *R* by things Roberto likes and an *S* by things Silvia likes.**

CD 1
TR 21

movies ____R____   music ____S____   sports ____R, S____

games ____R____   computers ____R, S____   TV ____R, S____

books ____R____   restaurants ____S____   parks ____S____

B. **Complete the sentences.**

1. Roberto likes ____movies____.   2. Roberto likes ____games____.

3. Roberto likes ____books____.   4. Silvia likes ____music____.

5. Silvia likes ____restaurants____.   6. Silvia likes ____parks____.

7. They both like ____sports____.   8. They both like ____computers____.

9. They both like ____TV____.

C. Study the chart with your classmates and teacher.

Simple Present: *Like*			
Subject	**Verb**	**Noun**	**Example sentence**
I, You, We, They	like	movies, music, sports, games, computers, TV, books, restaurants, parks	I **like** computers. You **like** games. We **like** music. They **like** books.
He, She, It	likes		He **likes** parks. She **likes** restaurants.

D. Complete the sentences with the correct form of *like*.

1. Antonio _____ likes _____ computers.

2. Rebecca _____ likes _____ parks.

3. Antonio and Rebecca _____ like _____ movies.

4. We _____ like _____ games.

5. The students _____ like _____ books.

6. I _____ Answers will vary. _____ .

E. COMPARE AND CONTRAST Read the Venn diagram about Roberto's children.

Answers will vary.

Carla likes ...
- restaurants
- books

Carla and Juan like ...
- movies
- music

Juan likes ...
- sports
- computers

Presentation 2
10–15 mins. ■■■

C. Study the chart with your classmates and teacher.

As you go over the chart, show students that other verbs follow the same rule as *like(s)*. Students are only working with *like* in this lesson, but you can use it as an introduction to the simple present. Drill students on the verb tense.

BEST PRACTICE

Drills

Drills can be a good way to help students become familiar with vocabulary, grammar structures, and proper pronunciation. They also help students to gain confidence, especially when performing together with their classmates. However, drills should not be the sole practice or method used to help students memorize something or acquire a grammar structure. There are several ways to drill (choral repetition, substitution, build up, backward build up, etc.). If particular drills are overused, there is a risk of losing meaning for structure.

D. Complete the sentences with the correct form of *like*.

Have students choose an item that they like from the chart in Exercise C.

E. COMPARE AND CONTRAST Read the Venn diagram about Roberto's children.

Discuss the Venn diagram in Exercise E.

Practice 2

5–7 mins. ■■

F. Create sentences and repeat them to a partner.

Ask students to write sentences about the Venn diagram. Then, ask them to read their sentences to a partner.

Evaluation 2

7–10 mins. ■■

Ask for volunteers to write a (different) sentence about the Venn diagram on the board.

Presentation 3

15–20 mins. ■■□

Review the chart on the previous page again and drill once more.

Practice 3

15–20 mins. ■

G. CLASSIFY Write Silvia's and Roberto's information from Exercise A into the Venn diagram.

Evaluation 3

5 mins. ■

Walk around the classroom and check students' work.

Refer students to *Stand Out 1 Workbook*, Unit 1, Lesson 4 for more practice with *like* and the simple present tense.

Go to the *Activity Bank* online for suggestions on promoting digital literacy and using the Internet to enhance this lesson.

Application

5–7 mins. ■■■

Review the pronunciation box on prominence so that students use correct intonation when practicing Exercise H.

H. COMPARE AND CONTRAST Talk to a partner and complete the diagram. Ask: *What things do you like?*

I. Introduce your partner to your classmates.

MULTILEVEL WORKSHEETS

Templates: Venn Diagram

Unit 1, Lesson 4, Worksheet 1: What do you and your partner like?

Unit 1, Lesson 4, Worksheet 2: Simple Present

INSTRUCTOR'S NOTES

_____
_____
_____
_____
_____
_____
_____
_____
_____
_____
_____
_____
_____
_____
_____
_____

F. Create sentences and repeat them to a partner. Answers will vary.

1. Carla likes restaurants _____.

2. _____.

3. _____.

4. _____.

G. CLASSIFY Write Silvia's and Roberto's information from Exercise A into the Venn diagram.

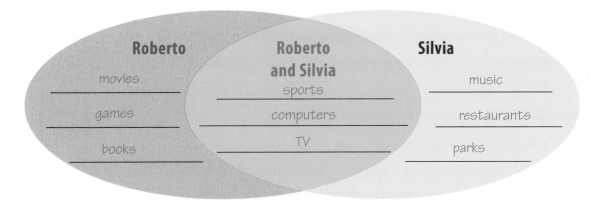

Roberto
movies
games
books

Roberto and Silvia
sports
computers
TV

Silvia
music
restaurants
parks

H. COMPARE AND CONTRAST Talk to a partner and complete the diagram. Ask: *What things do you like?* Answers will vary.

STRESS
➤ What **THINGS** do you like?

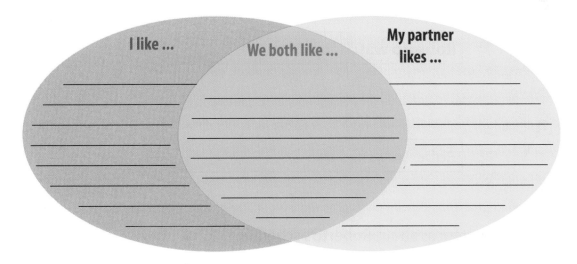

I like …

We both like …

My partner likes …

I. Introduce your partner to your classmates.

> **EXAMPLE:** This is my friend Roberto. He is from Mexico. He is married and has two children. Roberto likes movies and books.

WORKPLACE CONNECTION
Exercise G: Collect and organize information.
Exercise H: Interact appropriately with
team members; Interpret and communicate

information; Collect and organize
information; Complete tasks as assigned.
Exercise I: Interpret and communicate
information.

Lesson 4   25

LESSON **5** When do you study?

GOAL ■ Plan a schedule   WORKPLACE CONNECTION
Exercise B: Collect and organize information.

A. INTERPRET Complete the information about what Roberto does.

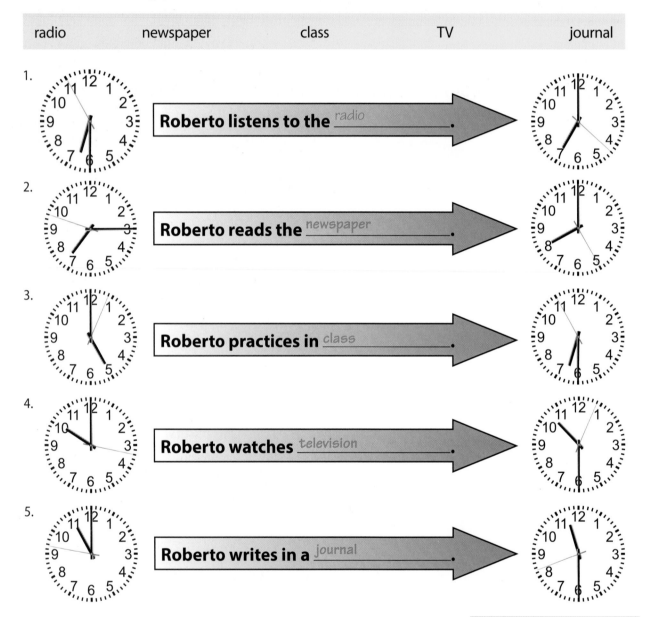

| radio | newspaper | class | TV | journal |

1. Roberto listens to the ___radio___.

2. Roberto reads the ___newspaper___.

3. Roberto practices in ___class___.

4. Roberto watches ___television___.

5. Roberto writes in a ___journal___.

B. Complete the sentences about Roberto's schedule.

START	FINISH
from 3:00	to 10:00

1. He reads the newspaper from ___7:15___ to ___8.00___.

2. He practices English in class from ___5:00___ to ___6:30___.

3. He watches TV from ___10:00___ to ___10:30___.

4. He writes in a journal from ___11:00___ to ___11:30___.

Goal: Plan a schedule
Grammar: *From . . . to* for describing duration
Academic Strategies: Focused listening
Vocabulary: Clock times

Agenda

- Review *likes* in a corners activity.
- Talk about schedules and times.
- Listen for information about schedules and times.
- Write your own schedule.
- Ask about your partner's schedule.

Resources

Multilevel Worksheets: Unit 1, Lesson 5, Worksheets 1–2
Workbook: Unit 1, Lesson 5
Audio: CD 1, Track 22
Heinle Picture Dictionary: Time, pages 4–5; Calendar, pages 6–7
Stand Out 1 Assessment CD-ROM with ExamView®

Pacing

- 1.5 hour classes
- 2.5 hour classes
- 3+ hour classes

CCRS: SL1, SL2, L1, RF2
CASAS: 2.3.1
SCANS: **Resources** Allocate time
Information Acquire and evaluate information, organize and maintain information, interpret and communicate information
Basic Skills Reading, writing, listening, speaking
Personal Qualities Self-management
EFF: **Communication** Read with understanding, convey ideas in writing, speak so others can understand, listen actively, observe critically
Decision Making Plan

Warm-up and Review   7–10 mins. ■■■

Do a corners activity to warm students up as well as to review Lesson 4. Take a class poll and ask students what they like to do in their free time based on the vocabulary they learned in the previous lesson. From the list, categorize the items into four groups. For example, you may choose outside activities, such as sports, or indoor activities, such as reading.

Next, assign a category to each corner of the room. Ask students to choose a corner and go there. Then, ask students to share with their new group what, specifically, they like to do. To facilitate this activity, write *What do you like?* on the board.

Introduction   5–7 mins. ■■■

With their books closed, ask students in groups to compile a list of what makes a good student. Then, discuss the lists with the class. If students didn't think of coming to school every day, add this. Suggest that a schedule will help them learn English. State the goal: *Today, we will learn how to plan a personal schedule.*

Presentation 1   15–20 mins. ■■■

Tell students what you do every day and write your schedule on the board. Include times. This schedule will be referred to throughout the entire lesson. Point to the clock in the room and ask students what it is. Then, do the same with your watch so students understand that we use two different words in English.

Write on the board: *When do we practice English?* Then, ask the question and see what students say. Write on the board: *We practice English in class from (the starting time) to (the ending time).*

A. INTERPRET Complete the information about what Roberto does.

Ask students to open their books and discuss the vocabulary in the word box. Ask for the times on each clock. Together fill in the information in the arrows.

Go over the grammar box and make sure students understand the function of *from* and *to*.

Practice 1   5–7 mins. ■■■

B. Complete the sentences about Roberto's schedule.

Have students complete this activity individually.

Evaluation 1   5–7 mins. ■■■

Ask students to practice the sentences with a partner. Observe as they practice. Write these questions on the board:
When does he read the newspaper?
When does he practice English in class?
When does he watch TV?
When does he write in a journal?

Presentation 2

15–20 mins. ■■■

Refer back to your personal schedule that you developed on the board. Ask students questions about it, for example: *When do I leave for work?*

C. Look at the clocks. Write the times.

Do this activity as a class. Then, ask students in the class how long they think Lidia reads the newspaper. Write on the board: *Lidia reads the newspaper from 6:45 to* _____. Ask students in groups to briefly discuss what time Lidia will stop reading the newspaper. Then, have the groups report and get a class consensus. Complete the sentence on the board. Do the same for the other activities Lidia does. When you finish, you will have four sentences on the board.

D. Write Lidia's schedule.

Do this activity as a class as well. Prepare students for the focused listening activity they will do in Exercise E by doing a quick practice with times in sentences. For example, you might say: *I drive to school from 7:45 to 8:00.*

Practice 2

5–7 mins. ■■

E. Listen and write Juan's schedule.

> **LISTENING SCRIPT** 🎧 CD 1 TR 22
>
> *Juan is a good student. He wants to learn English so he can get a better job. He has a regular schedule and follows it every day. He eats breakfast every morning from 6:00 to 6:30. He usually eats cereal, but sometimes he has eggs. Directly after he eats, he reads the newspaper. He usually reads in English from 6:30 to 6:45. He listens to the radio on the way to school from 7:00 a.m. to 7:25 a.m. He writes in his journal before class from 7:30 to 8:00. He practices English in class from 8:00 to 10:00 a.m. Monday through Friday.*

> **BEST PRACTICE**
>
> ## Focused listening
>
> *Stand Out* has a lot of listening at the beginning levels to improve students' developing listening skills. It is imperative that students don't get discouraged because most of the listening is in context. Stress to students that the tasks will help them begin to understand every word, but, for now, completing the tasks by picking out the target information is sufficient.
>
> In a discourse like the one in this particular activity, it is a good idea to play the recording once and ask students to listen for the information, but to refrain from writing anything down. At this level, when students are writing, many of them will not be able to listen to the information coming up. So, it is a good strategy to play it in five parts, isolating the five pieces of information. You may need to play the recording several times to help students hear what the task requires.

F. Write sentences about Juan's schedule.

Have students complete this activity individually.

Evaluation 2

7–10 mins. ■■

Ask volunteers to write the sentences on the board so that students can check their answers.

> **INSTRUCTOR'S NOTES**
>
> _____
>
> _____
>
> _____
>
> _____
>
> _____
>
> _____
>
> _____
>
> _____

WORKPLACE CONNECTION
Exercise D: Interpret and communicate information.
Exercise E: Collect and organize information.

C. Look at the clocks. Write the times.

1. Lidia reads the newspaper at ___6:45___.

2. Lidia listens to the radio at ___1:15___.

3. Lidia practices English in class at ___2:25___.

4. Lidia writes in a journal at ___7:50___.

D. Write Lidia's schedule.

Time	Activity
6:45	She reads the newspaper.
1:15	She listens to the radio.
2:25	She practices English in class.
7:50	She writes in a journal.

E. Listen and write Juan's schedule.

CD 1
TR 22

Start time	End time	Activity
6:00	6:30	Juan eats breakfast.
6:30	6:45	Juan reads the newspaper.
7:00	7:25	Juan listens to the radio.
7:30	8:00	Juan writes in a journal.
8:00	10:00	Juan practices English in class.

F. Write sentences about Juan's schedule.

1. Juan ___eats breakfast___ from ___6:00___ to ___6:30___.
2. Juan ___reads the newspaper___ from ___6:30___ to ___6:45___.
3. Juan ___listens to the radio___ from ___7:00___ to ___7:25___.
4. Juan ___writes in a journal___ from ___7:30___ to ___8:00___.
5. Juan ___practices English___ from ___8:00___ to ___10:00___.

WORKPLACE CONNECTION
Exercise H: Collect and organize information; Complete tasks as assigned; Interact appropriately
with team members.
Exercise I: Interpret and communicate information.

G. Write your schedule in the chart. Answers will vary.

	Start time	End time	Activity
in the morning			
in the afternoon			
at night			

H. Talk to a partner. Ask: _When do you practice English?_ Write the schedule in the chart. Answers will vary.

	Start time	End time	Activity
in the morning			
in the afternoon			
at night			

I. Report the information about your partner to a group.

Presentation 3

7–10 mins. ■■■

Write *morning, afternoon,* and *night* across the board. Then, under each one, write *from* _____ *to* _____. Ask students to come up to the board and write the information in the space provided.

CULTURAL NOTE

Time

Some cultures consider the starting time of morning, afternoon, and night differently. For example, many people from Spanish-speaking countries may consider 7:00 p.m. as the afternoon and translate it as *la tarde*. Elicit students' opinion and teach them the standard for the U.S.

Look back at the personal schedule you wrote on the board. Ask students what you do in the morning, in the afternoon, and at night. Show them that they can also say *in the evening*.

Practice 3

10–15 mins. ■

G. Write your schedule in the chart.

Have students work individually to complete the chart.

Evaluation 3

5–7 mins. ■

Check students' information. Ask them questions such as: *What do you do in the morning?*

Refer students to *Stand Out 1 Workbook,* Unit 1, Lesson 5 for more practice with *from* and *to*.

Go to the *Activity Bank* online for suggestions on promoting digital literacy and using the Internet to enhance this lesson.

Application

5–7 mins. ■■■

H. Talk to a partner. Ask: *When do you practice English?* Write the schedule in the chart.

Make sure that students ask for and listen to the information from their partner and do not merely copy from their partner's book.

I. Report the information about your partner to a group.

MULTILEVEL WORKSHEETS

Unit 1, Lesson 5, Worksheet 1: Study Habits
Unit 1, Lesson 5, Worksheet 2: When to Study

INSTRUCTOR'S NOTES

▶ Where are you from?

Before You Watch

- Read the title out loud.
- Have students ask the question and discuss their answers in pairs.
- Read the title again. Ask volunteers to share their answers with the class.

A. Look at the picture. Complete the sentences.

- Have students look at the pictures.
- Ask students to tell you how the pictures are related.
- Have students complete each sentence about the pictures.

While You Watch

B. Watch the video. Complete the dialog.

- Have students watch the video before they complete the dialog.
- Play the video once for understanding.
- Ask students to read and complete the dialog.
- Play the video again and have students check their answers.
- Have volunteers read the completed dialog to the class.

Check Your Understanding

C. Read the statements. Write *T* for True and *F* for False.

- Ask students to read the sentences and write *T* for True or *F* for False for each one.
- Have students check their answers with partners.
- Ask volunteers to share the correct answers with the class.

INSTRUCTOR'S NOTES

Where are you from?

Before You Watch

A. Look at the picture. Complete the sentences. Answers will vary; sample answers are given.

1. Picture 1 shows
   a mother and daughter.

2. In picture 2, we see a
   an old wedding photo.

3. The boy in picture 3 is a
   cousin.

While You Watch

B. ▶ Watch the video. Complete the dialog.

Naomi: Nice to meet you, too, Mrs. Sanchez. Hector was showing me some of the (1) _____family_____ photos.

Mrs. Sanchez: Oh, was he? Well, this is my (2) _____sister_____. She's married, and she has two kids.

Naomi: So, these are your (3) _____cousins_____?

Hector: Yes, (4) _____Aidan_____ and Marta.

Mrs. Sanchez: Aiden is 10, and Marta is 8. Aren't they (5) _____cute_____? Oh, and this is my brother, and these are my parents. They all live in New York.

Hector: (6) _____Ma_____, take it easy! Naomi doesn't need to know our whole family history.

Check Your Understanding

C. Read the statements. Write _T_ for True and _F_ for False.

1. Hector's mother is from Mexico. _____F_____

2. Hector's father is 50 years old. _____F_____

3. Mrs. Sanchez's sister is married. _____T_____

4. Hector has two cousins named Aida and Marta. _____F_____

5. Naomi is from Japan. _____F_____

Review

Learner Log

I can ask and give personal information.   I can describe people.
☐ Yes   ☐ No   ☐ Maybe   ☐ Yes   ☐ No   ☐ Maybe

A. **Complete the chart about Trinh, Duong, and Alan.**

WORKPLACE CONNECTION
Exercise A: Collect and organize information.

Trinh Hong
33 years old
Single
Cambodia

Duong Bui
33 years old
Married
Vietnam

Alan Hart
64 years old
Divorced
United States

Name	Marital status	Age	Country
1. Trinh Hong	single	33	Cambodia
2. Duong Bui	married	33	Vietnam
3. Alan Hart	divorced	64	United States

B. **Check the correct answer.**

1. My name _____ Duong.

   ☐ am   ☑ is   ☐ was

2. I _____ from Vietnam.

   ☑ am   ☐ is   ☐ are

3. Roberto _____ from Mexico.

   ☐ am   ☑ is   ☐ are

4. Roberto and Duong _____ students.

   ☐ am   ☐ is   ☑ are

5. Roberto and Duong _____ black hair.

   ☐ has   ☑ have   ☐ are

6. Roberto _____ one brother.

   ☑ has   ☐ have   ☐ is

7. Silvia _____ 23 years old.

   ☐ has   ☐ have   ☑ is

AT-A-GLANCE **PREP**

Goal: All unit goals
Grammar: All unit grammar
Academic Strategies: Reviewing, evaluating,
  developing study skills
Vocabulary: All unit vocabulary

Agenda

- ☐ Discuss unit goals.
- ☐ Complete the review.
- ☐ Evaluate and reflect on progress.

Resources

Stand Out 1 Assessment CD-ROM with ExamView®

Pacing

- ■ 1.5 hour classes
- ■ 2.5 hour classes
- ■ 3+ hour classes

STANDARDS CORRELATIONS

CCRS: RI1, R12, RI5, RI7, SL1, SL2, SL4, L1, L2, L5, RF2
CASAS: 0.1.2, 0.1.3, 0.2.1, 0.2.4, 1.1.4, 2.3.1, 4.8.1
SCANS: **Information** Acquire and evaluate information,
organize and maintain information
Personal Qualities Responsibility, self-management
EFF: **Communication** Speak so others can understand
Lifelong Learning Take responsibility for learning, reflect and
evaluate

Warm-up and Review   10–15 mins. ■■■

Ask students to write their schedule on a 3-by-5 index
card. Tell them not to put their name on it. Collect the
cards and pass them out again to different people.
Ask students to find the author of their cards by
asking questions. Write the questions on the board
and demonstrate how to do this activity by practicing
with a few students. The questions would be based
on the card: *When do you eat breakfast? What time do
you eat lunch?*

Introduction   2 mins. ■■■

Write all the goals on the board from Unit 1. Show
students the first page of the unit and say the
five goals. Explain that today they will review the
whole unit.

Note: Depending on the length of the term, you may
decide to have students do Practice for homework and

then review student work as either the warm-up or
another class activity.

Presentation   10–15 mins. ■■■

This presentation will cover the first three pages
of the review. Quickly go to the first page of each
lesson. Discuss the objective of each. Ask simple
questions to remind students of what they have
learned.

Practice   15–20 mins. ■■■

**A. Complete the chart about Trinh, Duong, and
Alan. (Lesson 1)**

B. Check the correct answer. (Lessons 1 and 2)

INSTRUCTOR'S NOTES

_____

_____

_____

_____

_____

_____

_____

_____

_____

_____

_____

_____

_____

_____

_____

_____

_____

_____

Practice *(continued)*

C. Read the sentences and complete Duong's license. (Lesson 2)

Recycling/Review

The review and the project that follows are part of the recycling/review process. Students at this level often need to be reintroduced to concepts to solidify what they have learned. Many concepts are learned and forgotten while learning other new concepts. This is because students learn but are not necessarily ready to acquire language concepts.

Therefore, it becomes very important to review and to show students how to review on their own. It is also important to recycle the new concepts in different contexts.

D. Match the questions and answers. Write the correct letter next to each number. (Lesson 2)

E. What is the relationship? Look at page 21 and fill in the missing words. (Lesson 3)

F. Unscramble the family words. (Lesson 3)

INSTRUCTOR'S NOTES

C. **Read the sentences and complete Duong's license.**

Duong's birth date is July 2, 1979.

His address is 23 South Street.

He lives in New York City, NY.

He is 5'6" tall.

He has brown eyes.

His zip code is 10038.

He is 165 pounds.

DRIVER'S LICENSE

Name: Duong
Age: will vary   Weight: 165
Height: 5'6"   Eyes: Brown
Address: 23 South St.
City: New York
State: NY   Zip Code: 10038

D. **Match the questions and answers.**
Write the correct letter next to each number.

1. _d_ What's your name?
2. _f_ Where are you from?
3. _b_ How old are you?
4. _e_ What is your weight?
5. _a_ How tall are you?
6. _c_ Are you married?

a. 6 feet, 2 inches.
b. 28.
c. Yes, I am.
d. Ernesto Gonzalez.
e. 195 pounds.
f. Colombia.

E. **What is the relationship? Look at page 21 and fill in the missing words.**

1. Silvia is Juan's mother, and Juan is Silvia's _____ son _____.

2. Juan is Carla's brother, and Carla is Juan's _____ sister _____.

3. Roberto is Carla's father, and Carla is Roberto's _____ daughter _____.

4. Roberto and Silvia are Juan and Carla's _____ parents _____.

5. Juan and Carla are Roberto and Silvia's _____ children _____.

F. **Unscramble the family words.**

1. tehrfa _____ father _____
2. nos _____ son _____
3. dlehcinr _____ children _____
4. htreaudg _____ daughter _____
5. tehrmo _____ mother _____

G. What does Silvia like? Fill in the missing words.

1. She likes _____TV_____.

2. She likes _____music_____.

3. She likes the _____park_____.

4. She likes the _____radio_____.

H. How does Roberto practice English? Fill in the missing verbs.

1. He _____listens_____ to the _____radio_____.

2. He _____watches_____ the _____TV_____.

3. He _____reads_____ the _____newspaper_____.

4. He _____writes_____ in a _____journal_____.

I. What time is it? Write the times.

1. It's _____11:30_____.

2. It's _____8:00_____.

3. It's _____10:15_____.

4. It's _____8:50_____.

J. Describe two of your classmates. Answers will vary.

John has short black hair and brown eyes.

_____

_____

Practice (continued)

G. What does Silvia like? Fill in the missing words. (Lesson 4)

H. How does Roberto practice English? Fill in the missing verbs. (Lesson 5)

I. What time is it? Write the times. (Lesson 5)

J. Describe two of your classmates. (Lesson 2)

Evaluation   10–15 mins. ■■■

Go around the room and check on students' progress. Help individuals when needed. If you see consistent errors among several students, interrupt the class and give a mini lesson or review to help students feel comfortable with the concept.

MULTILEVEL WORKSHEETS

Unit 1, Computer Worksheets

Unit 1, Internet Worksheets

Presentation   5 mins. ■■■

Learner Log

Review the concepts of the Learner Log. Make sure students understand the concepts and how to complete the log including circling the answers, finding page numbers where the concept is taught, and ranking favorite activities.

BEST PRACTICE

Learner Logs

Learner Logs function to help students in many different ways:

1. They serve as part of the review process.
2. They help students to gain confidence and to document what they have learned. Consequently, students see that they are progressing in their learning.
3. They provide students with a tool that they can use over and over to check and recheck their understanding of the target language. In this way, students become independent learners.

Practice   10–15 mins. ■

Ask students to complete the Learner Log.

Evaluation   2 mins. ■

Go over the Learner Log with students.

Application   5–7 mins. ■■■

Ask students to record their favorite lesson or page in the unit.

Assessment   ■■■

Use the Stand Out 1 Assessment CD-ROM with ExamView® to create a post-test for Unit 1.

Refer students to *Stand Out 1 Workbook*, Unit 1, Lesson 1 for more practice with possessive adjectives and Lesson 2 for more practice with possessive proper nouns.

INSTRUCTOR'S NOTES

_____

_____

_____

_____

_____

_____

_____

_____

_____

_____

_____

_____

_____

_____

_____

_____

STANDARDS CORRELATIONS

CCRS: SL1, SL2, W8

CASAS: 0.1.2, 0.1.3, 0.2.1, 0.2.4, 1.1.4, 2.3.1

SCANS: **Resources** Allocate time, allocate materials and facility resources, allocate human resources

Information Acquire and evaluate information, organize and maintain information, interpret and communicate information

Interpersonal Participate as a member of a team, teach others, exercise leadership, negotiate to arrive at a decision, work with cultural diversity

Systems Understand systems, monitor and correct performance

Basic Skills Reading, writing, listening, speaking

Thinking Skills Think creatively, make decisions, solve problems, see things in the mind's eye

Personal Qualities Responsibility, sociability, self-management

EFF: **Communication** Read with understanding, convey ideas in writing, speak so others can understand, listen actively, observe critically

Decision Making Solve problems and make decisions, plan

Interpersonal Cooperate with others, advocate and influence, resolve conflict and negotiate, guide others

Lifelong Learning Take responsibility for learning, reflect and evaluate

Introduction   5 mins.

TEAM PROJECT

Create a student profile

In this project, students will work in teams to create student profiles. These will be profiles about each individual student on the team. However, all students will work together on one profile at a time.

Stage 1   10–15 mins.

COLLABORATE Form a team with four or five students.

Refer to the Multilevel Worksheets CD-ROM for a profile template (Unit 1, Project, Worksheet 1).

Complete two or three example profiles with students as a class. Write the position responsibilities on the board as identified on the project page. Simulate a group activity by arbitrarily assigning positions. Help students understand the process.

Now, help students form groups and assign positions in their groups. On the spot, students will have to choose who will be the leader of their group. Review the responsibility of the leader and ask students to write the name of their leader in their books.

Do the same with the remaining positions: *secretary, the first student for profile,* and *host* or *hostess.* If there are five people in the group, double up on the position of host or hostess. Every member of each group should have a responsibility.

Stage 2   10–15 mins.

Create a student profile sheet.

Complete the student profile sheet for one student. Students obtain the information by asking questions. Write sample questions they can use on the board.

Stage 3   10–15 mins.

Choose one student in your group to create a profile for.

Practice introducing the student to the group. Again, give students samples of how this might be done.

Stage 4   30–50 mins.

Complete the student profile sheet by asking questions. Each student in the group asks three or more questions.

Do the same activity again with a different team member until all students have been interviewed and all profile sheets have been completed.

Stage 5   10–30 mins.

Practice introducing and describing the student to other groups. Use the profile sheet.

Have pairs from the groups go to a different group and introduce a partner.

BEST PRACTICE

Digital literacy

Projects are a perfect place to allow students opportunities to use other forms of presentations beyond pictures they create. Digital literacy is becoming more necessary as a life skill. Encourage students to create presentations using pictures from the Internet. They might also consider using other digital presentation tools.

MULTILEVEL WORKSHEETS

Unit 1, Project, Worksheet 1: Personal Profile Template

Unit 1, Project, Worksheet 2: Schedule

Unit 1, Extension, Worksheet 1: Application Forms

In this project, you will work together to create a student profile for one person on your team.

1. **COLLABORATE** Form a team with four or five students. Choose a position for each member of your team.

Position	Job description	Student name
Student 1: **Team Leader**	Check that everyone speaks English. Check that everyone participates.	
Student 2: **Secretary**	Complete the student profile with help from the team.	
Student 3: **Student for profile**	Give personal information for introductions.	
Students 4/5: **Hosts or Hostesses**	Introduce student to other groups.	

2. Create a student profile sheet. Write questions. See page 31 for help.

3. Choose one student in your group to create a profile for.

4. Complete the student profile sheet by asking questions. Each student in the group asks three or more questions.

5. Practice introducing and describing the student to other groups. Use the profile sheet.

6. Create more student profiles if you have time.

About the Explorer

Gordon Wiltsie is first and foremost a photographer; however, he is also a mountaineer and climber. Gordon grew up in Bishop, California, and taught himself the art of photography by taking pictures of the amazing scenery that surrounded his home. Primarily an outdoor adventure photographer, Gordon's photographs have appeared in many publications including *National Geographic* magazine. His assignments have taken him to places such as Antarctica, the Andes Mountains of Peru, and Mongolia.

About the Photo

This photo shows Gordon resting near some foothills after a camel trek through the Xinjiang autonomous region in China. The region borders Mongolia, Russia, Kazakhstan, Kyrgyzstan, Tajikistan, Afghanistan, Pakistan, and India. The region was once famous for having the most well-known Silk Road route; however, nowadays oil and mineral deposits are what the region is known for. The land in Xinjiang is varied with mountain ranges, lakes, rivers, and deserts spread across a large area of land.

Read the title out loud. Tell students they are going to read about Gordon Wiltsie, a photographer.

A. PREDICT Answer the questions about Gordon Wiltsie.

- Ask students why they think Gordon Wiltsie is called an *adventure photographer*. Discuss as a class.
- Read the quote to the class. Explain the meaning of *tactic* and *to blend in*.

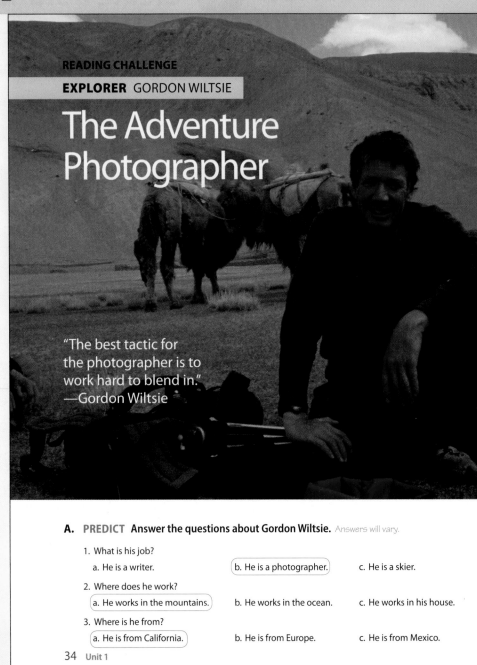

READING CHALLENGE

EXPLORER GORDON WILTSIE

The Adventure Photographer

"The best tactic for the photographer is to work hard to blend in."
—Gordon Wiltsie

A. PREDICT Answer the questions about Gordon Wiltsie. Answers will vary.

1. What is his job?
   a. He is a writer.   b. He is a photographer.   c. He is a skier.

2. Where does he work?
   a. He works in the mountains.   b. He works in the ocean.   c. He works in his house.

3. Where is he from?
   a. He is from California.   b. He is from Europe.   c. He is from Mexico.

34   Unit 1

CCRS FOR READING

RI1, RI2, RI5

B. PREDICT Look at the photograph. What can you say about Gordon? Answers will vary.

Name: _____

Age: _____

Height: _____

Marital Status: _____

Country: _____

Eye Color: _____

Hair Color: _____

C. Read the interview with Gordon Wiltsie. Then, check your predictions in Exercise B.

We meet with Gordon Wiltsie, a 63-year-old American photographer.

Interviewer: Gordon, it is great to meet with you. You are tall!

Gordon: Well, I'm 5'11".

Interviewer: We want to ask you a few questions about your work and your life.

Gordon: It is a pleasure. Please ask anything you would like.

Interviewer: Well, first, where are you from?

Gordon: I am from Bishop, California. It is a small town near beautiful mountains.

Interviewers: What do you do?

Gordon: I am a photographer. I go to mountains all over the world and study different cultures and people. I wake up very early in the morning before the sun and work through the day until it is dark.

Interviewer: Are you married?

Gordon: Yes, my wife's name is Meredith.

Interviewer: Well, it sounds like you have a wonderful life.

Gordon: Yes, I do.

D. APPLY Complete the information about you. Answers will vary.

Name: _____

Age: _____

Height: _____

Marital Status: _____

Country: _____

Eye Color: _____

Hair Color: _____

Reading Challenge   35

READING STRATEGIES

Making Predictions

Explain to students that they make predictions about many things every day. Tell them that making predictions largely depends on *prior knowledge* or things that they already know. Point out that students can also gather a lot of information from what they see. Explain that in Exercise B, they are able to make predictions about Gordon Wiltsie's personal information just by looking at a photograph.

- Have students look at the picture. Ask them to explain what Gordon Wiltsie means in the quote. Discuss as a class.

B. PREDICT Look at the photograph. What can you say about Gordon?

- Ask students to look at the photo and predict the correct answers for the information below.

- Have students cover up Exercise C. Read each point in the personal information out loud before students begin.

- Ask students to complete the exercise alone.

C. Read the interview with Gordon Wiltsie. Then, check your predictions in Exercise B.

Ask students to read the interview with Gordon Wiltsie and check their predictions in Exercise B.

D. APPLY Complete the information about you.

- Ask students to complete personal information about themselves.

- Complete the information for yourself on the board.

- Have students share their information in small groups.

- Share your own personal information with the class. Then, ask who has something in common with you.

Let's Go Shopping

About the Photo

Photojournalist David Yoder took this photo. It shows shoppers at the Grand Bazaar in Istanbul walking among brightly lit lamps. The Grand Bazaar is one of the world's largest marketplaces. It has over 3,000 stores that are spread over 61 streets. Over a quarter of a million people visit the bazaar each day. Many of the visitors to the market are tourists, who hope to buy exotic and traditional Turkish gifts. At many stores, there are no set prices. Tourists like the opportunity of haggling for purchases.

- Introduce the unit by reading the title out loud. Go over the unit outcomes.

- Ask the questions. Have students look at the photo and discuss their answers in pairs.

- Ask a volunteer to read the caption out loud. Then, explain to students that a bazaar is a shopping center or a part of the city dedicated to shopping with many different shops. Tell them that bazaars are usually located in the Middle East.

UNIT 2

Let's Go Shopping

Shoppers walk in the Grand Bazaar and look at brightly colored lamps and other things.

UNIT OUTCOMES	GRAMMAR	VOCABULARY	EL CIVICS
• Identify types of retail stores • Make purchases and read receipts • Identify articles of clothing • Describe clothing • Describe items in a store	• Simple present: *Shop* • Questions and answers with *Be* • Singular and plural nouns • Possessive adjectives • Adjectives • Simple present: *Want*	• Types of stores and products they sell • Money • Clothing • Colors, patterns • Adjectives of size, age, pattern	The skills students learn in this unit can be applied to the following EL Civics competency areas: • Banking • Community Resources

- Have students identify the shoppers and the sellers. Ask students to describe what the people are wearing.
- Ask students what different items they see for sale.

Life Skills Link

In this unit, students will learn the necessary skills for identifying and making purchases when shopping for goods. They will also learn how to interpret proof of their purchases.

Workplace Link

All lessons and units in *Stand Out* include basic communication skills and interpersonal skills important for the workplace. They are not individually identified. Other workplace skills are indicated. They include *collecting and organizing information, making decisions and solving problems,* and *combining ideas and information.*

UNIT OUTCOMES

☐ Identify types of retail stores
☐ Make purchases and read receipts
☐ Identify articles of clothing
☐ Describe clothing
☐ Describe items in a store

Look at the photo and answer the questions.

1. What do you see in the picture?
2. What are the people doing?
3. How much are the lamps?

CASAS	SCANS	CCRS
Lesson 1: 1.1.3, 1.3.7, 2.5.4 Lesson 2: 1.3.3, 1.3.8, 1.3.9, 1.6.4 Lesson 3: 1.2.1, 1.3.9 Lesson 4: 1.3.9 Lesson 5: 0.1.2, 1.1.9, 1.3.9 Review: 0.1.2, 1.1.9, 1.2.1, 1.3.3, 1.3.8, 1.3.9, 1.6.4 Team Project: 0.1.2, 1.1.9, 1.2.1, 1.3.3, 1.3.8, 1.3.9, 1.6.4, 4.8.1	Most SCANS are incorporated into this unit, with an emphasis on: • Allocating money • Serving customers • Organizing and maintaining information • Decision making (Technology is optional.)	RI1, RI2, RI5, RI7, SL1, SL2, SL4, L1, L2, RF2, RF3

LESSON **1** Shopping

GOAL Identify types of retail stores

A. Read about Van.

> Van starts school on Monday. She needs a dictionary, sneakers, new blouses, a digital music player, and food for lunches.

B. CLASSIFY Where can Van buy the items? Write the items from Exercise A under the stores below.

dictionary
music player

food for lunches
oranges, bread, cheese

food for lunches
oranges, bread, cheese

dictionary

sneakers

blouses
sneakers

blouses, sneakers
music player

Goal: Identify types of retail stores
Grammar: Simple present: *Shop*
Pronunciation: Stress and rhythm
Academic Strategies: Focused listening, categorizing, bar graphs
Vocabulary: Types of stores and products

Agenda

- Identify stores to purchase items.
- Identify places to shop.
- Listen for place names.
- Use the simple present.
- Make a bar graph.

Resources

Multilevel Worksheet: Unit 2, Lesson 1, Worksheet 1
Workbook: Unit 1, Lesson 1
Audio: CD 1, Track 23
Heinle Picture Dictionary: Shops and Stores, pages 48–49
Stand Out 1 Assessment CD-ROM with ExamView®

Pacing

- 1.5 hour classes ■ 2.5 hour classes
- 3+ hour classes

STANDARDS CORRELATIONS

CCRS: SL2, L1, L2, L5, RF2, RF3
CASAS: 1.1.3, 1.3.7, 2.5.4
SCANS: **Basic Skills** Listening, speaking
EFF: **Communication** Speak so others can understand, listen actively

Preassessment *(optional)*   ■■■

Use the Stand Out 1 Assessment CD-ROM with ExamView® to create a pretest for Unit 2.

Warm-up and Review   7–10 mins. ■■■

Write *$1,000,000* on the board. Ask students what they would buy with that much money. Tell them what you would buy. Write *shopping* on the board. Ask students what their favorite store is and write the stores on the board as students call them out.

Ask students to work in groups and add more stores to the list. Go over the list as a class.

Introduction   5–7 mins. ■■■

Ask students to open their books and look over the goals for the unit. Tell them that by the end of the unit, they will be able to do each of the skills listed. State the goal: *Today, we will identify places to make purchases.*

Presentation 1   10–15 mins. ■■■

With books closed, ask students what items they need at school. Start them off by saying they need a pencil or a pen. Show them your pencil or pen. Ask what else they need.

Now, ask students to open their books and look at Exercise A. Tell them that Van is preparing to start school.

A. Read about Van.

Read the paragraph as a class. Make sure students understand all of the vocabulary. Ask students to help you list other things Van might need. Write the class list on the board. This activity is similar to what you have already asked them to say about themselves.

B. CLASSIFY Where can Van buy the items? Write the items from Exercise A under the stores below.

Do this activity as a class. Ask students if they can think of similar stores in their community. Ask them to give the names of the stores.

Practice 1   10–15 mins. ■■■

C. DEBATE In a group, discuss the best place to buy each item in your neighborhood.

Ask students to form groups or assign groups. Then, ask them to discuss the question before they begin a list. To expand its list, a group might visit the other groups in the class and add one item from each group's list to their own.

Evaluation 1   3–5 mins. ■■■

Ask groups to write their lists on the board. Go over the vocabulary once more.

Presentation 2

15–20 mins. ■■■

D. What other things can you buy at each store? Make a list with a group.

Ask the question. Then, remind students that stores sometimes sell many different items. Have students make a list with a group.

Review focused listening with students. Write *department store*, *convenience store*, *clothing store*, and *supermarket* across the board. Ask students to point to each word as you say it. Then, ask students to point as you use the words in sentences and, finally, in a paragraph that you improvise.

Tell students that in the following exercise they will hear words that they may not understand. The object is to listen for the target vocabulary in the exercise. Teach students to look at the words in the chart before they listen.

E. PREDICT First, predict where Van buys the products. Then, listen and circle the correct place.

This is still part of the presentation, so stop and start the recording often. Help students hear what they are expected to hear.

LISTENING SCRIPT

CD 1
TR 23

Van: *I need some things for school. Do you want to shop for me?*
Nam: *No, not today. I have things here to do at home.*
Van: *OK, where can I go for these things?*
Nam: *What do you need?*
Van: *I need sneakers, shirts, bread, cheese, and fruit for lunches, a radio, and a bilingual dictionary.*
Nam: *Wow! That sounds like a lot.*
Van: *I know.*
Nam: *The best place for shoes is Martin's Department Store. You can buy shirts at Martin's also. You can also buy a good radio at Martin's.*
Nam: *All at Martin's?*
Van: *Yes, it's a good place for many things, but you need to go to Hero's Bookstore for the dictionary, and Sam's Supermarket around the corner has all you need for lunches.*

Go over the question students will ask in the example in Exercise G. Use this opportunity to do a short mini lesson on the pronunciation, intonation, and rhythm of the question and the answer.

Mini lessons

Within a lesson, there are opportunities to teach different concepts, either as an introduction to future concepts or as a quick review of concepts students have already been exposed to. Sometimes, students ask specific questions. If you can respond in a short explanation or mini lesson, it might be more beneficial than tabling the discussion for another time. Be careful not to allow the lesson plan to restrict you to the point where you are not meeting students' specific needs.

F. Practice pronouncing the sentences with a partner.

Practice 2

5–7 mins. ■■■

G. Use the information in Exercise E to practice the conversation. Use *shoes, shirts, a dictionary,* and *bread, cheese,* and *fruit* in new conversations.

Make sure students understand how to substitute the new information into the conversation. They should replace the underlined words with new words.

Evaluation 2

3–5 mins. ■■■

Ask students to demonstrate their conversations in front of the class.

Teaching the logic of the book

Take opportunities throughout the term to help students understand the logic of the textbook. Students who understand why they are doing different activities and how activities relate to one another will have more confidence in the process.

Near the beginning of the book, help students see how the goals relate to the lessons and that each lesson is a one-day activity. Soon students will be anticipating the next lesson and understanding the purpose of the goal. At the end of each lesson, ask students if they feel they have accomplished the goal and can do what is asked of them even outside of the classroom.

C. DEBATE In a group, discuss the best place to buy each item in your neighborhood.

D. What other things can you buy at each store? Make a list with a group.

Answers will vary.

_____   _____

_____   _____

_____   _____

CD 1
TR 23

E. PREDICT First, predict where Van buys the products. Then, listen and circle the correct place.

Product	Type of Store	
1. a radio	(a department store)	a convenience store
2. sneakers	a shoe store	(a department store)
3. shirts	a clothing store	(a department store)
4. a dictionary	(a bookstore)	a department store
5. bread, cheese, and fruit	(a supermarket)	a convenience store

---

STRESS AND INTONATION

➤ WHERE do VAN // and her HUSband // SHOP for a RADio?

➤ At a dePARTment store.

F. Practice pronouncing the sentences with a partner.

1. Van // shops at the department store // every Wednesday.

2. Her husband // likes to buy food // at the supermarket.

3. Where's // the convenience store?

4. The bookstore // has dictionaries.

G. Use the information in Exercise E to practice the conversation. Use *shoes, shirts, a dictionary,* and *bread, cheese,* and *fruit* in new conversations.

Student A: Where do Van and her husband shop for <u>a radio</u>?
Student B: <u>At a department store.</u>

H. **Study the chart with your classmates and teacher.**

Simple Present: *Shop*		
Subject	**Verb**	**Example sentence**
I, You, We, They	shop	I **shop** for shoes at a department store. You **shop** for bread at a convenience store. We **shop** for food at a supermarket. They **shop** for books at a bookstore.
He, She, It	shops	He **shops** for shoes at a shoe store. She **shops** for dresses at a clothing store.

I. **Complete the sentences with the correct form of *shop*.**

1. Van _____ shops _____ for a radio at a department store.

2. They _____ shop _____ for food at a supermarket.

3. We _____ shop _____ for sneakers at a shoe store.

4. He _____ shops _____ for soda at a convenience store.

5. I _____ shop _____ for a dictionary at a bookstore.

J. **SURVEY** **Make a bar graph. How many of your classmates shop in different types of stores?**

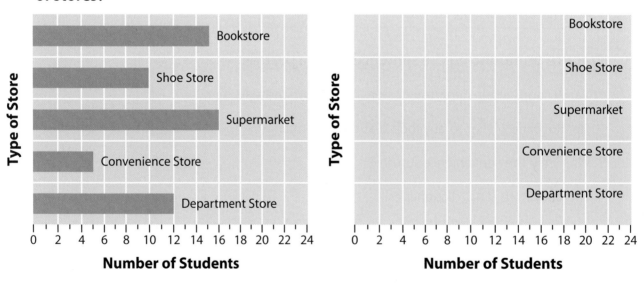

K. **Go to a mall or use the Internet. Find the names of three clothing stores that you like. Report them to the class.** Answers will vary.

Presentation 3

H. Study the chart with your classmates and teacher.

Remember that at this stage some students will have trouble understanding a chart like this one. Go over it together carefully.

BEST PRACTICE

Drills

Drills can be a good way to help students become familiar with vocabulary, grammar structures, and proper pronunciation. They also help students to gain confidence, especially when performing together with their classmates. However, drills should not be the sole practice or method used to help students memorize something or acquire a grammar structure. There are several ways to drill (choral repetition, substitution, build up, backward build up, etc.). If particular drills are overused, there is a risk of losing meaning for structure.

Practice 3

I. Complete the sentences with the correct form of *shop*.

Ask students to complete the sentences and then to copy them into a notebook. Show students how *look for* might work in place of *shop for* in these sentences.

Evaluation 3

Ask students to write the five sentences using *look for* instead of *shop for* on the board. Then, discuss their work.

Refer students to *Stand Out 1 Workbook,* Unit 2, Lesson 1 for more practice with the simple present and *shop*.

Go to the *Activity Bank* online for suggestions on promoting digital literacy and using the Internet to enhance this lesson.

Application

J. SURVEY Make a bar graph. How many of your classmates shop in different types of stores?

Look at the example of the graph and have students answer questions about the data presented. Write on the board: *How many students shop in a _____?* Ask students to decide in a group which stores they will ask the rest of the class about. Show them how to get the attention of the class, phrase a question, and ask for a vote. Each group should ask the class at least one question. If you would like, you can mention other types of graphs as well.

There are graph templates available on the Multilevel Worksheets Activity Bank if you wish to distribute blank graphs to students.

After all the groups have asked their questions, have them complete their graphs.

K. Go to a mall or use the Internet. Find the names of three clothing stores that you like. Report them to the class.

MULTILEVEL WORKSHEETS

Templates: Cluster Map

Templates: Bar Graph

Unit 2, Lesson 1, Worksheet 1: Shopping

INSTRUCTOR'S NOTES

_____

_____

_____

_____

_____

_____

_____

_____

AT-A-GLANCE PREP

Goal: Make purchases and read receipts
Grammar: *How much is . . . ? / How much are . . . ?*
Academic Strategy: Focused listening
Vocabulary: Money, amounts, bills, coins

Agenda

- Discuss neighborhood stores.
- Learn to make purchases.
- Read receipts and listen to amounts.
- Ask for amounts.
- Count U.S. money.
- Write checks.

Resources

Multilevel Worksheet: Unit 2, Lesson 2, Worksheet 1
Workbook: Unit 1, Lesson 2
Audio: CD 1, Tracks 24–25
Heinle Picture Dictionary: Money and Shopping,
pages 8–9
Stand Out 1 Assessment CD-ROM with ExamView®

Pacing

- 1.5 hour classes
- 2.5 hour classes
- 3+ hour classes

STANDARDS CORRELATIONS

CCRS: RI1, RI7, SL2, L1, L2, RF3

CASAS: 1.3.3, 1.3.8, 1.3.9, 1.6.4

SCANS: **Resources** Allocate money

Information Acquire and evaluate information, organize and maintain information

Basic Skills Listening, speaking

EFF: **Communication** Speak so others can understand, listen actively

Warm-up and Review   8–10 mins. ■■■

Write the names of several local stores on the board. Use high-end and lower-end department stores. Ask students which are more expensive. Use a money gesture or take out some bills to make the point. Then, ask students which store is their favorite.

Introduction   2 mins. ■■■

Write *How much?* on the board and ask students how much different items might cost at a store. State the goal: *Today, we will learn to make purchases and read receipts.*

Presentation 1   15–20 mins. ■■■

Write *item*, *price*, *tax*, and *total* on the board. Ask students what each word means. They might not be able to explain the words well, but allow them to try. Draw a receipt on the board. Ask students to help you fill it out. Then, ask students to open their books and read the receipts.

A. INTERPRET Look at the receipts. What are the totals? What is the tax?

Go over the receipts. Ask questions such as: *How much are the oranges? How much is the dictionary?*

B. How much is the total for the shirts, sneakers, bilingual dictionary, and food?

Work with the class to figure out the total. If you like, make it a competition where the first student to get the correct total is the winner. Do the math on the board to ensure that all students know how to do it. You might also ask for the total before taxes and the total of different quantities of the items.

Practice 1   15–20 mins. ■■■

C. Listen and circle the amounts you hear.

LISTENING SCRIPT   CD 1
                                       TR 24

EXAMPLE: *How much is it? It's $22.50.*

1. *That's $34.15.*
2. *Here's $33.00.*
3. *That comes to $15.70.*
4. *The total cost is $77.95.*

D. Listen and write the prices.

LESSON **2** **Van's purchases**

GOAL ▪ Make purchases and read receipts

A. INTERPRET **Look at the receipts. What are the totals? What is the tax?**

Martin's
Department Store

Date: 09-06-2015

Shirt .... 2@$17.98 - $35.96
Sneakers $22.99

Subtotal........................... $58.95
Tax.................................... $4.72

TOTAL $63.67

Customer Copy

HERO BOOKS

Date: 09-06-2015

Bilingual dictionary............ $21.95

Subtotal............................. $21.95
Tax....................................... $1.76

TOTAL $23.71

No Returns Without Receipt

Sam's
Food Mart

Date: 09-06-2015

Bread................................... $2.30
Cheese................................. $2.75
Oranges @.99 a pound......... $1.98
Potato Chips $2.60

TOTAL $9.63

THANK YOU for shopping at Sam's.

B. **How much is the total for the shirts, sneakers, bilingual dictionary, and food?**

$63.67 (clothes) + $23.71 (dictionary) + $ 9.63 (food) = _____ *$97.01*

C. **Listen and circle the amounts you hear.**

CD 1
TR 24

EXAMPLE: $12.50 $2.15 $22.50 $22.15

1. $12.95 $34.15 $34.50 $45.50

2. $13.00 $30.00 $33.00 $43.00

3. $ .57 $57.00 $15.70 $17.00

4. $19.75 $17.90 $79.00 $77.95

D. **Listen and write the prices.**

CD 1
TR 25

Lang's
DEPARTMENT STORE

VACUUM	WASHING MACHINE	CANDY BARS	PAPER	CELL PHONE
$89.99	$450.00	$1.25	$6.50	$199.00

E. Practice asking about prices. Look at Exercise D on page 41 for information.

Student A: Excuse me, how much is the <u>vacuum</u>?
Student B: $98.99.
Student C: Thank you.

> **BE VERB**
> How much *is* the vacuum?
> How much *are* the candy bars?

F. Write the words from the box under the pictures.

a nickel	a ten-dollar bill	a penny	a one-dollar bill
a twenty-dollar bill	a quarter	a five-dollar bill	a dime

1. _____a penny_____   2. _____a nickel_____   3. _____a dime_____   4. _____a quarter_____

5. _____a one-dollar bill_____   6. _____a five-dollar bill_____

7. _____a ten-dollar bill_____   8. _____a twenty-dollar bill_____

G. CALCULATE What bills and coins do you need for these items? Tell a partner.

$53.99
Bills: 2 $20 bills, 1 $10 bill, 3 $1 bills
Coins: 3 quarters, 2 dimes, 4 pennies

$75.50
Bills: 3 $20 bills, 1 $10 bill, 1 $5 bill
Coins: 2 quarters

$23.71
Bills: 1 $20 bill, 3 $1 bills
Coins: 2 quarters, 2 dimes, 1 penny

Practice 1 (continued)

LISTENING SCRIPT

CD 1
TR 25

1. **Customer:** *Excuse me. How much is the vacuum?*
   Salesperson: *It's $89.99 on sale.*
   Customer: *Thanks, I'll take it.*

2. **Customer:** *Excuse me, can you help me? I'm looking for a washing machine.*
   Salesperson: *This is a good brand.*
   Customer: *Is that right? OK, how much is it?*
   Salesperson: *It's four hundred and fifty dollars.*
   Customer: *Four hundred and fifty dollars? That much?*
   Salesperson: *I'm afraid so.*

3. **Customer:** *I just want this candy bar.*
   Salesperson: *That will be $1.25, please.*
   Customer: *Here you go—one dollar and twenty-five cents.*

4. **Customer:** *I want to buy a ream of white paper.*
   Salesperson: *The paper is over there. It's $6.50.*
   Customer: *Thank you.*

5. **Customer:** *Every time I buy a cell phone, I get a bad one. Maybe I should buy an expensive one.*
   Salesperson: *How about this one for $199?*

Go over the grammar box with students, reminding them of the singular and plural forms of the *be* verb. Say one of the objects from page 41, Exercise D. Ask students to form a question with *how much* and *is* or *are*. Help them with the pronunciation of dollars and make sure they pronounce the final *s*.

Show students how to substitute information in the conversation for Exercise E. This activity can also be expanded to include the items on the receipts in Exercise A.

E. Practice asking about prices. Look at Exercise D on page 41 for information.

Evaluation 1   7–10 mins. ■■■

Ask students to demonstrate their conversations in front of the class.

Presentation 2   7–10 mins. ■■■

F. Write the words from the box under the pictures.

Do this activity with the class. Review all the bills. If possible, display real bills and coins in the classroom. Be prepared to discuss who and what is pictured on each bill and coin if students are interested.

Practice 2   7–10 mins. ■■

G. CALCULATE What bills and coins do you need for these items? Tell a partner.

Ask students to work individually at first and then to compare items in pairs. Bring in real ads if you wish to extend the activity even more.

Evaluation 2   5–7 mins. ■■

Do an impromptu role-playing exercise with a few students. Write an amount on the board and ask individuals to decide what bills and coins they will need. You might extend this by writing some prices on the board and asking individuals to write the bills and coins they think would work.

INSTRUCTOR'S NOTES

_____

_____

_____

_____

Presentation 3

10–15 mins. ■■■

H. INTERPRET Read the check.

Study the check with students. Look at every part of the check to ensure that students can read it. Ask the questions in the boxes.

Practice 3

7–10 mins. ■

I. Look at the items in Exercises D and G. Which items do you want to buy? Write a check for one of the items.

Write the following chart on the board:

	Who is the check to?	What is the check for?	How much is the check for?
Check #1			
Check #2			

Have students do an information-gap activity. Divide the class into pairs and have Student A ask Student B about Check #1 with his or her book closed. Ask Student B to ask Student A about Check #2 with his or her book closed.

BEST PRACTICE

Information gap

Two students work together. Each student has a different piece of information needed to complete the task. The two students have to ask each other questions in order to get the information they each need. In most cases, one student is looking at one page while the other is looking at another page.

Evaluation 3

2–3 mins. ■

Look at students' written checks.

Refer students to *Stand Out 1 Workbook,* Unit 2, Lesson 2 for more practice with *How much is . . .* and *How much are . . . .*

Go to the *Activity Bank* online for suggestions on promoting digital literacy and using the Internet to enhance this lesson.

Application

5–7 mins. ■■■

J. INVESTIGATE Visit some banks or use the Internet. Find out how to open a checking account.

MULTILEVEL WORKSHEET

Unit 2, Lesson 2, Worksheet 1: Counting U.S. Money

INSTRUCTOR'S NOTES

_____

_____

_____

_____

_____

_____

_____

_____

_____

_____

_____

_____

_____

_____

_____

_____

_____

_____

_____

_____

_____

H. INTERPRET Read the check.

What is the account holder's name and address?

What is the date?

How much is the check for?

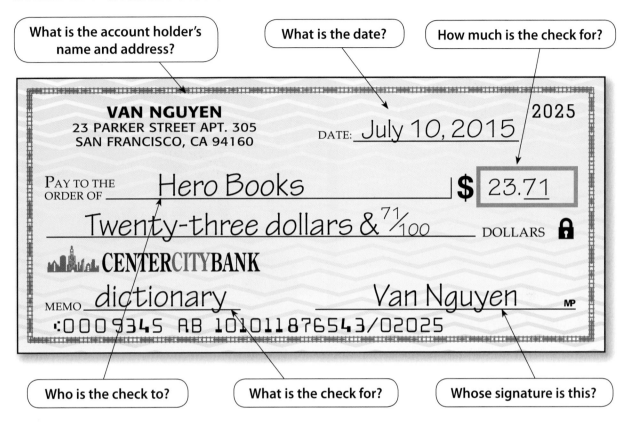

VAN NGUYEN
23 PARKER STREET APT. 305
SAN FRANCISCO, CA 94160

DATE: July 10, 2015

2025

PAY TO THE ORDER OF ___Hero Books___ $ 23.71

Twenty-three dollars & 71/100 DOLLARS

CENTERCITYBANK

MEMO _dictionary_   Van Nguyen   MP

⑆000934S AB 10101187654 3/02025

Who is the check to?

What is the check for?

Whose signature is this?

I. Look at the items in Exercises D and G. Which items do you want to buy? Write a check for one of the items. Answers will vary. Sample answer is given.

Juanita Gomez
47 Broadway
Dallas, TX 83471

DATE: March 10, 2017

2026

PAY TO THE ORDER OF ___Lang's Department Store___ $ 89.99

Eighty-nine dollars & 99/100 DOLLARS

CENTERCITYBANK

MEMO ___vacuum___   Juanita Gomez   MP

⑆000934S AB 10101187654 3/02026

J. INVESTIGATE Visit some banks or use the Internet. Find out how to open a checking account.

LESSON ③ Buying new clothes

GOAL ▪ Identify articles of clothing

A. INTERPRET Write the correct letter under each type of clothing. Then, listen for the missing prices.

CD 1
TR 26

a. suit

b. T-shirt

c. ties

d. hat

e. sweater

f. dress

g. socks

h. baseball cap

i. sneakers

j. blouse

k. coat

l. skirt

YOUR DEPARTMENT STORE

DRESS FOR LESS

g ONLY $12

k ONLY $84

d $ 38

f $ 48

h ONLY $12

c ONLY $22

l $ 35

a $285

e ONLY $36

i ONLY $33

b $17

j $24

B. CLASSIFY In a group, write clothing words from Exercise A in the chart. Add other clothing words that you know. Answers will vary. Sample answers are given.

Women's	Men's	Both
blouse	suit	sneakers
skirt	ties	socks
dress	shirt	T-shirt
hat	baseball cap	coat
high-heeled shoes	tuxedo	sweater

44   Unit 2

Goal: Identify articles of clothing

Grammar: *Be* verb: questions and answers

Academic Strategies: Predicting, classifying, focused listening

Vocabulary: Clothing

Agenda

- Practice with receipts.
- Learn clothing words.
- Classify clothing prices.
- Ask for prices.
- Read about Gabriela.

Resources

Multilevel Worksheets: Unit 2, Lesson 3, Worksheets 1–2

Workbook: Unit 1, Lesson 3

Audio: CD 1, Track 26

Heinle Picture Dictionary: Clothes, pages 104–105

Stand Out 1 Assessment CD-ROM with ExamView®

Pacing

- 1.5 hour classes
- 2.5 hour classes
- 3+ hour classes

STANDARDS CORRELATIONS

CCRS: RI1, RI7, SL1, SL2, L1, L2, L5

CASAS: 1.2.1, 1.3.9

SCANS: **Resources** Allocate money

Information Acquire and evaluate information

Basic Skills Reading, writing, listening, speaking

EFF: **Communication** Read with understanding, convey ideas in writing, speak so others can understand, listen actively

Warm-up and Review   15–20 mins. ■■■

Bring in some receipts and distribute them, or create one or two on the board with several different items on them. On the board, write: *How much is the _____?* Write five items on the board that students will recognize. Ask students in groups to come up with a price for each item. Then, have groups report their prices and see how close they got to the right amounts.

If you have time, consider playing a game where students guess the prices of items as on the popular TV show *The Price is Right*. Write the prices on 3-by-5 index cards in front of the items.

Introduction   5–7 mins. ■■■

Ask students again where they shop for clothing. Help them understand the words *cheap* and *expensive*. State the goal: *Today, we will identify articles of clothing*.

Presentation 1   15–20 mins. ■■■

With books closed, ask students to stand up. Ask them to point to items of clothing they are wearing as you say them. For example, you might say *socks* and students would point at their socks. Use colors, too if you feel your students are ready. This activity will help you to see what students already know.

Instruct the class to study the picture in Exercise A. Next, ask students to close their books and ask them the questions in the box.

Ask students to open their books and look at the clothing. Go over the vocabulary with the class. Point to students wearing articles of clothing similar to those in the picture.

A. INTERPRET **Write the correct letter under each type of clothing. Then, listen for the missing prices.**

Do this activity as a class, but elicit the information from students.

> ### LISTENING SCRIPT   🎧 CD 1 TR 26
> *We have many good deals at Dress for Less. Be sure to come in. Socks are $12, ties are $22, and suits are $285. Our dresses are $48, and our skirts are $35! We have great deals on sweaters at $36, and women's hats are $38. Don't miss our great deals!*

Practice 1   3–10 mins. ■■■

B. CLASSIFY **In a group, write clothing words from Exercise A in the chart. Add other clothing words that you know.**

Do one or two items as a class. Then, ask students to complete this activity in groups. When they finish, explain different ways to classify the same information. Ask the groups to reclassify the clothing words by casual and formal, above and below the waist, and singular and plural.

Evaluation 1   5 mins. ■■■

Ask group representatives to write their classifications on the board.

Presentation 2

C. Study the charts with your classmates and teacher.

Go over the charts as a class. Have students look back at the previous page. Ask questions about prices and show them how you use *How much is . . .* and *How much are . . . .* It is important that students know that money is implied in the question. This will help them better understand *How many . . .* when it is presented later.

Do a chain drill where Student A asks Student B a question. Student B responds and then asks Student C a new question, etc.

BEST PRACTICE

Drills

Drills can be a good way to help students become familiar with vocabulary, grammar structures, and proper pronunciation. They also help students to gain confidence, especially when performing together with their classmates. However, drills should not be the sole practice or method used to help students memorize something or acquire a grammar structure. There are several ways to drill (choral repetition, substitution, build up, backward build up, etc.) If particular drills are overused, there is a risk of losing meaning for structure.

D. Practice the conversation.

Practice 2

5–7 mins. ■■

E. Ask a partner about the prices. Use the conversation in Exercise D.

This is an information-gap activity, so be sure that students who are asking the questions refrain from looking at the previous page.

BEST PRACTICE

Facilitating information-gap activities

Information-gap activities are activities that allow one student to give new information to another. In the *Stand Out* approach, there are many opportunities to do this type of activity.

Sometimes the nature of the activity is difficult to understand for some students. There are several things to do to help students.

1. Model the activity several times with several different students.
2. Make sure students know who is A and who is B. To do this, ask all As to stand up. Check to make sure all students understand.
3. Monitor the practice. If a pair of students is having trouble, do the exercise with them.
4. Do the activity in groups of four with at least one student who can direct the others. In groups of four, one pair goes first and the other pair listens. Then, the other pair performs.

Evaluation 2

3–5 mins. ■■

Ask students to demonstrate the conversation in front of the class.

INSTRUCTOR'S NOTES

_____

_____

_____

_____

_____

_____

_____

_____

_____

_____

C. Study the charts with your classmates and teacher.

Be Verb (Questions)			
Question words	*Be*	**Singular or plural noun**	**Example question**
How much (money)	is	the dress the suit	How much **is** the dress? How much **is** the suit?
How much (money)	are	the socks the ties	How much **are** the socks? How much **are** the ties?

Be Verb (Answers)		
Singular or plural noun or pronoun	*Be*	**Example answer**
It	is	It **is** $48. It's $48. (The dress **is** $48.) It **is** $285. It's $285. (The suit **is** $285.)
They	are	They **are** $12. They're $12. (The socks **are** $12.) They **are** $22. They're $22. (The ties **are** $22.)

D. Practice the conversation.

Student A: How much <u>is the dress</u>?
Student B: <u>It's $48</u>.

E. Ask a partner about the prices. Use the conversation in Exercise D.

Student A asks Student B:

$ ___48___

$ ___36___

$ ___22___

Student B asks Student A:

$ ___285___

$ ___33___

$ ___35___

WORKPLACE CONNECTION

Exercise G, H, I: Perform basic computations; Interpret and communicate information.

F. **Look at the picture. Where is Gabriela? What is her problem?**

G. **INFER Read about Gabriela. What is her problem?**

> Gabriela shops at Dress for Less. It is a clothing store on Main Street. The prices are good, but she only has $75. She needs clothes for a party. She needs a new blouse, a skirt, and a hat. She has a problem.

H. **Circle *Yes* or *No*. Look at page 44 for prices.**

1. Gabriela shops at Lang's department store.	Yes	(No)
2. Gabriela has $75.	(Yes)	No
3. Gabriela can buy a shirt, a skirt, and a hat.	Yes	(No)

I. **Look at the ad on page 44. You have $75. What different items can you buy? Write the items and their prices. Then, talk in a group.** Answers will vary.

_____   _____   _____

_____   _____   _____

J. **INVESTIGATE Research clothing stores on the Internet. What can you buy for $100?**

Presentation 3 7–10 mins. ■■■

F. Look at the picture. Where is Gabriela? What is her problem?

Ask students to look at the picture, but avoid reading the information by covering Exercise G. Talk about the picture and encourage students to decide what the problem might be. Ask questions about specific items in the picture, such as: *How much is the blouse?* and *How much money do you think she has?* Explain to students that they are predicting in order to prepare themselves for reading.

Write any words that may be new to students on the board.

Practice 3 5–7 mins. ■

G. INFER Read about Gabriela. What is her problem?

H. Circle *Yes* or *No*. Look at page 44 for prices.

Evaluation 3 2 mins. ■
Observe students as they do Exercises G and H.

Refer students to *Stand Out 1 Workbook,* Unit 2, Lesson 3 for more practice with *It is . . .* and *They are . . . .*

Go to the *Activity Bank* online for suggestions on promoting digital literacy and using the Internet to enhance this lesson.

Application 5–7 mins. ■■■

I. Look at the ad on page 44. You have $75. What different items can you buy? Write the items and their prices. Then, talk in a group.

J. INVESTIGATE Research clothing stores on the Internet. What can you buy for $100?

MULTILEVEL WORKSHEETS

Unit 2, Lesson 3, Worksheet 1: Clothing Vocabulary

Unit 2, Lesson 3, Worksheet 2: Family Vocabulary

INSTRUCTOR'S NOTES

Goal: Describe clothing

Grammar: Singular and plural, possessive adjectives

Academic Strategy: Focused listening

Vocabulary: Clothing, colors

Agenda

- Decide what Gabriela can buy.
- Describe clothing.
- Identify colors.
- Use plurals.
- Use possessive adjectives.
- Describe classmates' clothing.

Resources

Multilevel Worksheets: Unit 2, Lesson 4,
Worksheets 1–2

Work book: Unit 1, Lesson 4

Audio: CD 1, Track 27

Heinle Picture Dictionary: Colors, pages 10–11;
Describing Clothes, pages 110–111

Stand Out 1 Assessment CD-ROM with ExamView®

Pacing

- 1.5 hour classes
- 2.5 hour classes
- 3+ hour classes

STANDARDS CORRELATIONS

CCRS: R3, SL1, SL2, SL4, L1, L2, L5

CASAS: 1.3.9

SCANS: **Basic Skills** Listening, speaking, writing

EFF: **Communication** Speak so others can understand,
listen actively, observe critically

Warm-up and Review   10–15 mins. ■■■

Look back at page 46. Ask students to do Exercise H
again in groups, but this time ask them to decide
what Gabriela can buy for $100. Ask the groups to
report to the class.

Introduction   5–7 mins. ■■■

Ask students to stand up. Do a modified *stand up and
share* activity. Ask students with various color items
of clothing to sit down. Observe how much students
know about colors. For example, you might say: *All
students wearing a white T-shirt, please sit down.* State
the goal: *Today, we will describe clothing.*

Presentation 1   10–12 mins. ■■■

With the students' books closed, write the items
that Roberto and Gabriela are wearing across the
board. Make sure students know what each word
means. Show examples from the class when possible.
Practice correct pronunciation of the words.

When identifying clothing that students in the class
are wearing, ask students what color the items are.
This activity will help you identify how much students
already know.

Ask students to open their books and discuss the
vocabulary as well as all the colors. Prepare students
for the listening by asking them to point to items as
you say them.

**A. Listen and point to the clothing you hear
about in the conversation.**

LISTENING SCRIPT   🎧 CD 1 TR 27

Roberto: *Gabriela, what are you wearing to class today?*

Gabriela: *I think I will wear my white blouse. How about you?*

Roberto: *I'll wear my red T-shirt. And I think I will go casual
and wear shorts.*

Gabriela: *Me, too. I want to go casual. I am wearing my
blue pants with a black belt.*

Roberto: *You won't miss me. I will be wearing a baseball cap.*

Ask students questions again, such as: *What color is
Roberto's T-shirt?* Encourage students to respond with
a complete sentence: *It's red.* Respond by reiterating
the vocabulary: *That's right. His shirt is red.* Write the
exchange on the board. Help students see when to
use *are* and *is.*

Remind students about plurals and work with their
pronunciation to prepare them for Exercise B.

Practice 1   10–20 mins. ■■■

**B. CLASSIFY Complete the chart with the
words from the picture. Then, add more
clothing words.**

Evaluation 1   7–10 mins. ■■■

Have students ask one another questions following
the exchange you wrote on the board. Observe their
conversations.

4 **What color is your shirt?**

GOAL ■ Describe clothing

🎧 **A.** **Listen and point to the clothing you hear about in the conversation.**
CD 1
TR 27

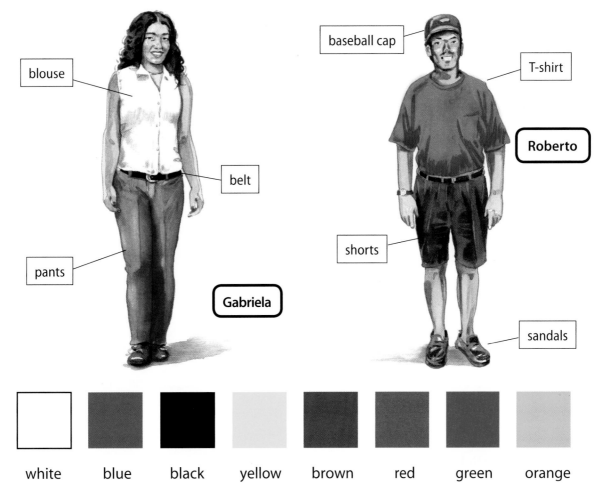

white	blue	black	yellow	brown	red	green	orange

B. **CLASSIFY** **Complete the chart with the words from the picture. Then, add more clothing words.** Answers will vary. Sample answers are given.

Singular	Plural
T-shirt	T-shirts
blouse	blouses
belt	belts
baseball cap	baseball caps
dress	dresses

Plural only
shorts
pants
shoes

Lesson 4   47

C. Study the chart. Complete the chart with words from the box.

His	Her
My	Our
Your	Their

Pronoun	Possessive Adjectives
I	_____My_____ shirt is blue.
	_____My_____ shoes are black.
You	_____Your_____ baseball cap is blue.
	_____Your_____ shorts are brown.
He	_____His_____ belt is black.
	_____His_____ sandals are brown.
She	_____Her_____ blouse is pink.
	_____Her_____ shoes are white.
We	_____Our_____ shirts are white.
	_____Our_____ pants are blue.
They	_____Their_____ dresses are red.
	_____Their_____ shoes are black.

D. Look at page 47. Answer the questions.

1. What color are Roberto's shorts?
   His shorts are brown.

2. What color is Gabriela's blouse?
   Her blouse is white.

3. What color are Gabriela and Roberto's belts?
   Their belts are black.

4. What color are Gabriela's pants?
   Her pants are blue.

5. What color is Roberto's T-shirt?
   His T-shirt is red.

6. What color are Gabriela and Roberto's shoes?
   Their shoes are brown.

Presentation 2

10–15 mins. ■■■

C. Study the chart. Complete the chart with words from the box.

Some students might be confused by the fact that the possessive adjective does not reflect whether the noun is singular or plural. Try to clarify. Also, make sure they understand that the form of the *be* verb is determined by the subject.

BEST PRACTICE

Contrastive analysis

Possessive adjectives are treated differently in different languages. For example, *his*, *her*, and *your* in English all translate to the same word in Spanish, which can be very confusing. In Portuguese, the adjectives reflect the gender and number of the noun instead of what it is referring to. In Korean, possessive adjectives are often avoided all together and names or titles are used. These differences can cause problems for students. If you are aware of language differences, sometimes it will prompt additional instruction. If the students in your class all speak the same language, knowledge of their first language can be even more useful.

Practice 2

10–15 mins. ■■■

D. Look at page 47. Answer the questions.

This activity is similar to what students did orally in Practice 1, except now they are using possessive adjectives.

You can turn this exercise into an information-gap activity by having students practice in pairs. One student asks the questions while the other looks at page 47 and answers the questions.

Evaluation 2

3–5 mins. ■■

Briefly quiz students on possessive adjectives.

INSTRUCTOR'S NOTES

_____
_____
_____
_____
_____
_____
_____
_____
_____
_____
_____
_____
_____
_____
_____
_____
_____
_____
_____
_____
_____
_____
_____
_____
_____
_____
_____
_____
_____
_____

Presentation 3
7–10 mins. ■■■

Ask a female and a male volunteer to come forward. Ask students to help you describe his and her clothes, and write sentences on the board. For example, you might write: *His shirt is red. Her pants are blue.*

Practice 3
10–15 mins. ■

E. **COMPARE AND CONTRAST** Talk to a partner and describe your classmates' clothes. Then, write sentences.

F. With a different partner, describe your classmates by their clothes. Let your partner guess who the classmates are.

An alternate activity would be to pass out 3-by-5 index cards and ask students to write their sentences from Exercise E on the cards, but not their names. Then, ask students to exchange their cards with a partner and see if the partner can identify the people.

Evaluation 3
10 mins. ■

Observe the activity.

Refer students to *Stand Out 1 Workbook*, Unit 2, Lesson 4 for more practice with possessive adjectives.

Go to the *Activity Bank* online for suggestions on promoting digital literacy and using the Internet to enhance this lesson.

Application
5–7 mins. ■■■

G. **CLASSIFY** Look around the classroom. In groups, make a list of clothes by color.

MULTILEVEL WORKSHEETS

Unit 2, Lesson 4, Worksheet 1: Clothing

Unit 2, Lesson 4, Worksheet 2: Possessive Adjectives

INSTRUCTOR'S NOTES

WORKPLACE CONNECTION
Exercises E, F: Interpret and communicate information; Interact appropriately with team members.
Exercise G: Collect and organize information.

E. COMPARE AND CONTRAST Talk to a partner and describe your classmates' clothes. Then, write sentences. *Answers will vary. Sample answers are given.*

My	**His**
My shirt is ___blue and white___.	His shirt is ___green___.
My shoes are ___grey___.	His pants are brown.
My ___pants are black___.	His socks are white.
Your	**Her**
Your shirt is ___purple___.	Her shirt is ___orange___.
Your shoes are black.	Her shorts are brown.
Your pants are blue.	Her shoes are red.
Our	**Their**
Our shirts are ___white___.	Their ___T-shirts are yellow___.
Our belts are brown.	Their pants are black.
Our socks are black.	Their baseball caps are blue.

F. With a different partner, describe your classmates by their clothes. Let your partner guess who the classmates are.

Student A: Her blouse is blue.
Student B: Amy?

G. CLASSIFY Look around the classroom. In groups, make a list of clothes by color.
Answers will vary.

Red	Blue	Green	Orange
Carolina's sweater			

A large TV or a small TV?

GOAL ■ Describe items in a store

A. Look at the pictures. Write a word under each picture.

1. Do you want a small laptop or a large
   desktop computer?

small

large

2. Do you want a new house or an
   old house?

new

old

3. Do you want a new car or a used car?

new

used

4. Do you want a striped shirt or a plaid shirt?

striped

plaid

5. Do you want a large blouse
   or a medium blouse?

large

medium

6. Do you want a small T-shirt or a medium
   T-shirt?

medium

small

B. CLASSIFY Complete the chart. Write the new words from Exercise A.

Size	Age	Pattern
large	used	striped
medium	new	plaid
small	old	

AT-A-GLANCE PREP

Goal: Describe items in a store
Grammar: Simple present: *Want*
Pronunciation: Emphasis
Academic Strategies: Focused listening, classifying
Vocabulary: Adjectives of size, age, and pattern

Agenda

▪ Find the student based on description of clothes.

▪ Describe store items.

▪ Use adjectives.

▪ Practice a conversation.

▪ Use the verb *want*.

▪ Practice new conversations.

Resources

Multilevel Worksheets: Unit 2, Lesson 5, Worksheets 1–2
Workbook: Unit 1, Lesson 5
Audio: CD 1, Tracks 28–32
Heinle Picture Dictionary: Opposites, pages 14–15
Stand Out 1 Assessment CD-ROM with ExamView®

Pacing

■ 1.5 hour classes ■ 2.5 hour classes
■ 3+ hour classes

STANDARDS CORRELATIONS

CCRS: SL1, SL2, L1, RF2
CASAS: 0.1.2, 1.1.9, 1.3.9
SCANS: **Resources** Allocate money, allocate materials and facility resources
Information Acquire and evaluate information
Basic Skills Reading, writing, listening, speaking
EFF: **Communication** Read with understanding, convey ideas in writing, speak so others can understand, listen actively, observe critically

Warm-up and Review   7–10 mins. ■■■

Ask students to write what they are wearing on an index card, for example, *blue shirt, black pants*. Tell students not to write their name on the card. Collect and redistribute the cards randomly. Ask students to find who the card was written by.

Introduction   5–7 mins. ■■■

Use items from the classroom, for example, a pencil, a book, a backpack, and a chair. Line the items up in the front of the classroom and, with the help of students, put them in order from the smallest to the largest. State the goal: *Today, we will describe things we can buy in a store.*

Presentation 1   15–20 mins. ■■■

Compare the items you used in the introduction. Don't use comparative adjectives here. Say: *The pencil is small and the book is big.* Make these comparisons until students can do them with you.

A. Look at the pictures. Write a word under each picture.

Do this activity with the class. Practice asking the questions after you fill in the words below the pictures. For example, ask: *Do you want a striped shirt or a plaid shirt?* Make sure you show students how adjectives come before the noun. Once they are comfortable with one-word answers, encourage them to answer with both the adjective and the noun.

PRONUNCIATION

Emphasis

For the questions in this activity, the adjectives get the emphasis because these descriptions are the items of information in question. *Do you want a STRIPED shirt or a PLAID shirt?* Help students to respond with emphasis on the adjective to show their preference: *a PLAID shirt.*

One way to practice emphasizing this information is to ask students to stand when they say the adjective and sit when they say the noun. Another idea is to have half of the class say the adjective and the other half of the class follow with a noun.

Ask students to ask and answer the questions in pairs, emphasizing the adjectives in both the questions and the answers. Finally, make sure they understand *size*, *age*, and *pattern* in preparation for the practice.

Practice 1   5–7 mins. ■■■

B. CLASSIFY Complete the chart. Write the new words from Exercise A.

Evaluation 1   5–7 mins. ■■■

Write the three categories on the board: *size*, *age*, and *pattern*. Have volunteers come up and fill in the categories. Discuss their answers as a class.

Presentation 2

C. Look at the picture. Where is Tatsuya? What does he want?

Look back at page 50. Ask students if there is anything on the page that they really want. Write the word *want* on the board. Then, ask students to look at page 51. Ask them to cover up everything under the picture with a piece of paper. Ask questions about details in the picture. For example, you could ask: *Are the TVs new or old?, small or large?, etc.*

D. Listen to the conversation with your books closed. What does Tatsuya want to buy?

With the lower half of the page still covered, ask students to listen to the conversation. Ask students again: *What does Tatsuya want to buy?* Have them call out the answers. Play the recording again and ask students to follow along. Go over the pronunciation and ask students to listen a final time to see if they can hear the emphasis.

LISTENING SCRIPT 🎧 CD 1 TR 28

Tatsuya: *Excuse me. I want a TV.*
Salesperson: *A big TV or a small TV?*
Tatsuya: *I want a small TV.*
Salesperson: *OK, how about this one?*
Tatsuya: *Yes, that's good. How much is it?*
Salesperson: *It's $135.*
Tatsuya: *I'll take it!*

E. Practice the conversation with a partner.

At this point, you want students to place emphasis on the appropriate words. Drill students as a class on the conversation, using correct emphasis.

Next, show students how to substitute information into the conversation.

BEST PRACTICE

Dialog preparation

There are many opportunities in *Stand Out* for students to do dialogs or conversational exchanges. The conversations help students manipulate new vocabulary, think critically about what to substitute, and practice pronunciation. To prepare students to do the substitutions and to help them with pronunciation, consider the following steps:

1. Do a choral drill where students repeat what you say.
2. Take the role of Student A and allow students in unison to take the role of Student B.
3. Reverse roles.
4. Ask part of the class to be A and part to be B.
5. You be A and ask a student to be B.
6. You be B and ask another student to be A.
7. Ask two or three pairs to demonstrate.

This may appear to be more than you think is needed; however, remember your goal is to help all of your students be successful. You don't want to start the practice before everyone understands exactly what to do.

Practice 2

F. Practice new conversations. Use the information below. Use the conversation in Exercise D as an example.

Evaluation 2

Ask students to demonstrate their conversations in front of the class.

INSTRUCTOR'S NOTES

_____

_____

_____

_____

_____

_____

C. Look at the picture. Where is Tatsuya? What does he want?

CD 1
TR 28

D. Listen to the conversation with your books closed. What does Tatsuya want to buy?

Tatsuya:	Excuse me. I want a <u>TV</u>.
Salesperson:	<u>A **big** TV</u> or <u>a **small** TV</u>?
Tatsuya:	I want <u>a **small** TV</u>.
Salesperson:	OK, how about this one?
Tatsuya:	Yes, that's good. How much is it?
Salesperson:	It's <u>$135</u>.
Tatsuya:	I'll take it!

STRESS
I want a **SMALL** TV.

E. Practice the conversation with a partner.

F. Practice new conversations. Use the information below. Use the conversation in Exercise D as an example.

Student A is the customer.
Student B is the salesperson.

1. blouse:	medium/small	$24
2. laptops:	large/small	$899
3. refrigerator:	new/used	$210
4. shirt:	small/medium	$18

Student B is the customer.
Student A is the salesperson.

1. car:	used/new	$12,000
2. house:	old/new	$300,000
3. sweater:	striped/ plaid	$42
4. dress:	large/medium	$33

G. **Study the chart with your classmates and teacher.**

Simple Present: *Want*		
Subject	**Verb**	**Example sentence**
I, You, We, They	want	I **want** a large TV.
He, She, It	wants	He **wants** a new house.

H. **Listen to the conversations and circle the correct answers.**

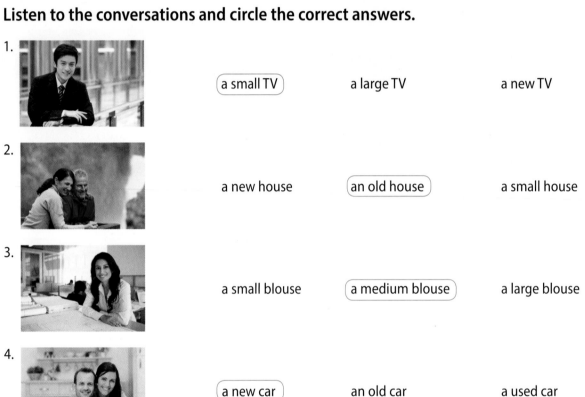

1. (a small TV) a large TV a new TV

2. a new house (an old house) a small house

3. a small blouse (a medium blouse) a large blouse

4. (a new car) an old car a used car

I. **Complete the sentences with the correct form of *want*. Use the information from Exercise H.**

1. Tatsuya _____ *wants* _____ a small TV.

2. Emily and Steve _____ *want an old house* _____.

3. Gabriela _____ *wants a medium blouse* _____.

4. Ivan and Natasha _____ *want a new car* _____.

J. **With a partner, write a conversation like the ones you heard in Exercise H. Present it to the class.** Answers will vary.

Presentation 3 7–10 mins. ■■■

Return to page 51 briefly and ask students again what they want from the page. Write sentences on the board using student names. For example, write: *Van wants a large CD player*. You might also write: *I want a large CD player*. Ask the students who responded to read the sentences from the board out loud.

Next, underline *want* and *wants*. Circle the third person singular *s* in *wants*.

G. Study the chart with your classmates and teacher.

After going over the chart, prepare students for focused listening in Exercise G.

Practice 3 10–15 mins. ■

H. Listen to the conversations and circle the correct answers.

After listening, go over the listening script in the back of the book and ask students to underline *want* and *wants*. Go over the answers with the class.

LISTENING SCRIPT
CD 1
TR 29–32

1. **Tatsuya:** *Excuse me. I want a TV.*
   Salesperson: *A big TV or a small TV?*
   Tatsuya: *I want a small TV.*
   Salesperson: *OK, how about this one?*
   Tatsuya: *Yes, that's good. How much is it?*
   Salesperson: *It's $135.*
   Tatsuya: *I'll take it!*

2. **Emily:** *We need to move.*
   Steve: *I know. What do you want? Do you want a new house or an old house?*
   Emily: *Well, I am not sure. They both have benefits. I guess I want an old house.*
   Steve: *OK, we want an old house, right?*

3. **Nancy:** *I am here to buy a blouse for my friend Gabriela.*
   Salesperson: *OK, do you know her size?*
   Nancy: *She wants a medium blouse, I think.*
   Salesperson: *Step over here, and we will see what we can find in a medium blouse.*

4. **Ivan:** *I want a new car.*
   Natasha: *I want a new car, too.*
   Ivan: *They are expensive.*
   Natasha: *How can we afford it?*
   Ivan: *I guess we want a new car, but we will have to wait to buy one.*

Evaluation 3 5–7 mins. ■

I. Complete the sentences with the correct form of *want*. Use the information from Exercise H.

Refer students to *Stand Out 1 Workbook*, Unit 2, Lesson 5 for more practice with adjectives.

Go to the *Activity Bank* online for suggestions on promoting digital literacy and using the Internet to enhance this lesson.

Application 5–7 mins. ■■■

J. With a partner, write a conversation like the ones you heard in Exercise H. Present it to the class.

Students can use Exercise H and the script as models.

MULTILEVEL WORKSHEETS

Unit 2, Lesson 5, Worksheet 1: Adjectives

Unit 2, Lesson 5, Worksheet 2: Receipts

INSTRUCTOR'S NOTES

_____

_____

_____

_____

_____

_____

_____

_____

_____

_____

_____

_____

LIFESKILLS ▶ Can I help you?

Before You Watch

- Read the title out loud.
- Ask students when or where they might hear this question.

A. PREDICT Look at the picture. Complete each sentence.

- Have students look at the picture.
- Ask students who might be saying, "Can I help you?"
- Have students complete each sentence. Then, discuss answers as a class.

While You Watch

B. Watch the video. Read the statements. Write *T* for True or *F* for False.

- Ask students to watch the video before they complete the exercise.
- Play the video once.
- Ask students to decide which statements are true and which statements are false. Tell them to write *T* or *F* on the line.
- Play the video again and ask students to check their answers.
- Have volunteers share their answers with the class.

Check Your Understanding

C. Put the sentences in order to make a conversation.

- Tell students that the sentences make a conversation between a sales clerk and a customer.
- Ask students to put the sentences in the correct order.
- Have students check their answers and practice the conversation in pairs.
- Ask for two volunteers to demonstrate the conversation in front of the class.

Before You Watch

A. PREDICT Look at the picture. Complete each sentence.

1. Hector is talking to

   _____a customer_____.

2. They are in a(n)

   _____clothing store_____.

3. Hector is holding a

   _____blue sweater_____.

While You Watch

B. ▶ Watch the video. Read the statements. Write *T* for True or *F* for False.

1. A customer comes to the store. ___T___

2. The customer wants a dress. ___F___

3. The customer sees three pairs of jeans. ___F___

4. The green sweater is the cheapest. ___F___

5. The customer is happy. ___T___

6. Hector helps the customer. ___T___

Check Your Understanding

C. Put the sentences in order to make a conversation.

a. __5__ **Sales Clerk:** Please follow me to the men's department.

b. __2__ **Customer:** I'm looking for a sweater.

c. __1__ **Sales Clerk:** Can I help you?

d. __4__ **Customer:** No, it's for my brother.

e. __3__ **Sales Clerk:** Is the sweater for you?

f. __6__ **Customer:** Thank you.

g. __7__ **Sales Clerk:** You're welcome.

Review

Learner Log

I can name different kinds of stores.   I can read receipts and write checks.
■ Yes   ■ No   ■ Maybe   ■ Yes   ■ No   ■ Maybe

A. Listen and write the prices in Column 1.

CD 1
TR 33

WORKPLACE CONNECTION

Exercise A: Collect and organize information.

Prices match CD 1, Track 33. Other answers will vary. Sample answers are given.

Item	How much is it?	Where can you buy it?	Describe it.
	$899.00	department store	black and white
	$168.00	department store	upright
	$18.95	bookstore	black
	$28.98	shoe store	brown leather
	$456.78	department store	large flat-screen
	$33.99	department store	red
	$17.00	department store	black
	$24.50	department store	striped

B. Complete Columns 2 and 3 in the table above with your ideas.

54   Unit 2

AT-A-GLANCE PREP

Goal: All unit goals

Grammar: All unit grammar

Academic Strategies: Focused listening, reviewing, evaluating, developing study skills

Vocabulary: All unit vocabulary

Agenda

◻ Discuss unit goals.

◻ Complete the review.

◻ Evaluate and reflect on progress.

Resources

Audio: CD 1, Track 33

Stand Out 1 Assessment CD-ROM with ExamView®

Pacing

◼ 1.5 hour classes ◼ 2.5 hour classes

◼ 3+ hour classes

STANDARDS CORRELATIONS

CCRS: RI1, RI2, RI5, RI7, SL1, SL2, SL4, L1, L2, RF2, RF3

CASAS: 0.1.2, 1.1.9, 1.2.1, 1.3.3, 1.3.8, 1.3.9, 1.6.4

SCANS: **Information** Acquire and evaluate information, organize and maintain information

Basic Skills Reading, writing, speaking, listening

Personal Qualities Responsibility, self-management

EFF: **Communication** Speak so others can understand

Lifelong Learning Take responsibility for learning, reflect and evaluate

Warm-up and Review   10–15 mins. ◼◼◻

Ask additional students to perform their conversations from the previous lesson in front of the class.

Introduction   2–5 mins. ◼◼◻

Write all the goals on the board from Unit 2. Show students the first page of the unit and mention the five goals. Explain that today they will review the whole unit.

Note: Depending on the length of the term, you may decide to have students do Practice for homework and then review students' work as either the warm-up or another class activity.

Presentation   10–15 mins. ◼◼◻

This presentation will cover the first three pages of the review. Quickly go to the first page of each lesson. Discuss the goal of each. Ask simple questions to remind students of what they have learned.

Practice   15–20 mins. ◼◼◻

A. Listen and write the prices in Column 1. (Lesson 2)

> ### LISTENING SCRIPT   🎧 CD 1 TR 33
>
> *The TV is $456.78.*
> *The shoes are $28.98.*
> *The laptop is $899.*
> *The dictionary is $18.95.*
> *The shirt is $24.50.*
> *The sweater is $33.99.*
> *The vacuum is $168.*
> *The shorts are $17.00.*

B. Complete Columns 2 and 3 in the table above with your ideas. (Lessons 1, 2, and 5)

BEST PRACTICE

Recycling/Review

The review and the project that follows are part of the recycling/review process. Students at this level often need to be reintroduced to concepts to solidify what they have learned. Many concepts are learned and forgotten while learning other new concepts. This is because students learn but are not necessarily ready to acquire language concepts.

Therefore, it becomes very important to review and to show students how to review on their own. It is also important to recycle the new concepts in different contexts.

INSTRUCTOR'S NOTES

_____

_____

_____

_____

_____

Practice *(continued)*

C. Look at the receipts. What is the total of all three receipts? (Lesson 2)

D. Write a check for the first receipt. (Lesson 2)

E. Write the word under each picture. (Lesson 3)

INSTRUCTOR'S NOTES

C. **Look at the receipts. What is the total of all three receipts?**

WORKPLACE CONNECTION
Exercise C: Perform basic computations.

Martin's
Department Store

Date: 09-06-2015

Shirt ....2@$27.98

Subtotal $55.96
Tax $4.48
_____
TOTAL $60.44

Customer Copy

ELECTRONICS SURPLUS

Date: 09-26-2015

Magi big screen TV $789.55

Subtotal..........................$789.55
Tax..................................$63.16
_____
TOTAL $852.71

Customer Copy

SHOE EMPORIUM

Date: 09-26-2015

Black Loafers $44.95

Subtotal..........................$44.95
Tax $3.60
_____
TOTAL $48.55

Customer Copy

$961.70

D. **Write a check for the first receipt.**

(Your Name) _____

(Your Street Address) _____

(City, State, Zip Code) _____

2026

DATE: _____ 9/06/2015 _____

PAY TO THE ORDER OF _____ Martin's Department Store _____ **$** 60.44

_____ Sixty and 44/100 _____ **DOLLARS** 🔒

CENTERCITYBANK

MEMO _two shirts_ _____ (Your signature) _____ MP

⑆000 9345 AB 10101187654 3/02026

E. **Write the word under each picture.**

1. _____ blouse _____

2. _____ sandals _____

3. _____ skirt _____

F. **Describe the pictures. Use** *his, her,* **or** *their.*

WORKPLACE
CONNECTION
Exercise H: Interpret and
communicate information;
Interact appropriately with
team members.

Eva

Duong

1. What color is Eva's hat? _Her hat is blue._

2. What color is Duong's cap? _His cap is red._

3. What color is Duong's shirt? _His shirt is white._

4. What color are Eva's pants? _Her pants are green._

5. What color are Eva and Duong's shoes? _Their shoes are brown._

6. What color is Duong's belt? _His belt is black._

G. **Write sentences about things you want in Unit 2.** Answers will vary.

1. _I want a vacuum._

2. _____

3. _____

4. _____

5. _____

H. **Talk to a partner. Write sentences about things your partner wants in Unit 2.**

Answers will vary.

1. _Eduardo wants a car._

2. _____

3. _____

4. _____

5. _____

Practice (continued)

F. Describe the pictures. Use *his*, *her*, or *their*. (Lesson 4)

G. Write sentences about things you want in Unit 2. (Lessons 1–5)

H. Talk to a partner. Write sentences about things your partner wants in Unit 2. (Lessons 1–5)

Evaluation   15–20 mins. ■■■

Go around the room and check on students' progress. Help individuals as needed. If you see consistent errors among several students, interrupt the class and give a mini lesson or review to help students feel comfortable with the concept.

MULTILEVEL WORKSHEETS

Unit 2, Computer Worksheets

Unit 2, Internet Worksheets

Presentation   5 mins. ■■■

Learner Log

Review the concepts in the Learner Log. Make sure students understand the concepts and how to complete the log including circling the answers, finding page numbers where the concept is taught, and ranking favorite activities.

BEST PRACTICE

Learner Logs

Learner Logs function to help students in many different ways.

1. They serve as part of the review process.
2. They help students to gain confidence and to document what they have learned. Consequently, students see that they are progressing in their learning.
3. They provide students with a tool that they can use over and over to check and recheck their understanding of the target language. In this way, students become independent learners.

Practice   10–15 mins. ■

Ask students to complete the Learner Log.

Evaluation   2 mins. ■

Go over the Learner Log with students.

Application   5–7 mins. ■■■

Ask students to record their favorite lesson in the unit.

Assessment   ■■■

Use the Stand Out 1 Assessment CD-ROM with ExamView® to create a post-test for Unit 2.

Refer students to *Stand Out 1 Workbook*, Unit 2, Lesson 1 for more practice with singular and plural and Lesson 2 for more practice with the negative simple present.

Go to the *Activity Bank* online for suggestions on promoting digital literacy and using the Internet to enhance this lesson.

INSTRUCTOR'S NOTES

_____

_____

_____

_____

_____

_____

_____

_____

_____

_____

_____

_____

_____

Combine ideas and information; Make decisions; Exercise leadership roles; Complete tasks as assigned; Interact appropriately with team members; Interpret and communicate information.

STANDARDS CORRELATIONS

CCRS: RI7, SL1, SL2

CASAS: 0.1.2, 1.1.9, 1.2.1, 1.3.3, 1.3.8, 1.3.9, 1.6.4, 4.8.1

SCANS: **Resources** Allocate time, allocate materials and facility resources, allocate human resources

Information Acquire and evaluate information, organize and maintain information, interpret and communicate information

Interpersonal Participate as a member of a team, teach others, exercise leadership, negotiate to arrive at a decision, work with cultural diversity

Systems Understand systems, monitor and correct performance

Basic Skills Reading, writing, listening, speaking

Thinking Skills Think creatively, make decisions, solve problems, see things in the mind's eye

Personal Qualities Responsibility, sociability, self-management

EFF: **Communication** Read with understanding, convey ideas in writing, speak so others can understand, listen actively, observe critically

Decision Making Solve problems and make decisions, plan

Interpersonal Cooperate with others, advocate and influence, resolve conflict and negotiate, guide others

Lifelong Learning Take responsibility for learning, reflect and evaluate

Introduction   5 mins.

TEAM PROJECT

Plan a department store

In this project, students will work in teams to plan a department store and present it to the class.

Stage 1   10–15 mins.

COLLABORATE **Form a team with four or five students.**

Help students form groups and assign positions in their groups. On the spot, students will have to choose who will be the leader of their group. Review the responsibility of the leader and ask students to write the name of their leader in their books.

Do the same with the remaining positions: *architect*, *sales manager*, and *writers*. Every member of the group should have a responsibility.

Stage 2   5 mins.

Choose a name for your department store.

Ask each group to choose a name for their department store and write it on the board.

Stage 3   10 mins.

Draw a floor plan of your store in your notebook.

Templates are available on the Multilevel Worksheets Activity Bank that teams may use (Unit 2, Project, Worksheets 1 and 2).

Stage 4   10–15 mins.

Make a list of ten things you sell. Include their prices. Where are the items located on your floor plan?

Ask students to make a list of items they will sell. Make sure that they choose at least ten items and that the items are from more than one department.

Stage 5   30–50 mins.

Prepare a role-play in which a person in your group talks to a salesperson and buys some things. You can also make checks and receipts. Students in your group can take on the roles of a salesperson, a cashier, a customer or customers, and a manager.

Help students understand how they are going to prepare a role-play. Show them different conversations from the unit that they can use as models. There are models for receipts, checks, and bills on the Multilevel Worksheets Activity Bank (Unit 2, Project, Worksheet 3).

Stage 6   10–30 mins.

Practice the role-play and present it to the class.

Ask teams to perform their role-plays in front of the class.

MULTILEVEL WORKSHEETS

Unit 2, Project, Worksheet 1: Department Store Floor Plan

Unit 2, Project, Worksheet 2: Department Store Information

Unit 2, Project, Worksheet 3: Handwritten Checks and Receipts

Unit 2, Extension, Worksheet 1: Checks and Ledgers

Unit 2, Extension, Worksheet 2: Checks

57a   Unit 2

✓ # Plan a department store

In this project, you will plan a department store and present it to the class.

1. **COLLABORATE** Form a team with four or five students. In your team, you need:

Position	Job desciption	Student name
Student 1: **Team Leader**	Check that everyone speaks English. Check that everyone participates.	
Student 2: **Architect**	With help from the team, draw the floor plan.	
Student 3: **Sales Manager**	With help from the team, list the prices of the items in your store.	
Students 4/5: **Writers**	With help from the team, prepare a role-play to present to the class.	

2. Choose a name for your department store.

_____

3. Draw a floor plan of your store in your notebook.

4. Make a list of ten things you sell. Include their prices. Where are the items located on your floor plan?

Answers will vary.

_____   _____

_____   _____

_____   _____

5. Prepare a role-play in which a person in your group talks to a salesperson and buys some things. You can also make checks and receipts. Students in your group can take on the roles of a salesperson, a cashier, a customer or customers, and a manager.

6. Practice the role-play and present it to the class.

About the Explorer

Andrew Skurka is an adventurer. Also considered a professional backpacker, he was named as National Geographic's Adventurer of the Year in 2008 for his 6,785-mile hike, known as the Great Western Loop. For this particular adventure, Andrew hiked around nine states in the western United States over seven months. Andrew completed a longer hike two years earlier called the Sea-to-Sea Route. On this route, he covered 7,778 miles from Quebec, Canada to Washington State in the western United States.

About the Photo

Brent Humphreys took this photo. It shows Andrew in Salida, Colorado during his 7,778-mile Sea-to-Sea hike. The hike took Andrew 11 months to complete. The trip also involved close to 1,500 miles of snowshoeing. Andrew travels lightly on his hikes. The contents of his backpack rarely exceed 12 pounds as he only carries the essentials for daily life on the road. These include a tent, cooking supplies, a journal, and a camera.

- Introduce the explorer and read the title.
- Have students look at the photo. Ask what they think Andrew Skurka is doing. Discuss as a class.
- Have a volunteer read the quote out loud. Ask students what they think Andrew Skurka means. Discuss as a class.

A. Complete Column 1. Make a list of the clothing Andrew is wearing in the picture.

- Ask students to look at what Andrew is wearing in the photo.
- Tell them to make a list of Andrew's clothing and write the items in the chart under Column 1.
- Ask students to check their answers with a partner.

READING CHALLENGE

EXPLORER ANDREW SKURKA

Relationships With Nature

"Relationships are the most important things in life, specifically relationships with nature, others, and self."
—Andrew Skurka

A.   Complete Column 1. Make a list of the clothing Andrew is wearing in the picture.
Some answers will vary.

Clothing	Types of Stores
shirt	department store
shorts	department store
sneakers	shoe store
socks	department store
watch	department store

58   Unit 2

CCRS FOR READING

RI1, RI2, RI3, RF4

READING STRATEGIES

Thinking Aloud

After completing a reading, students can usually recall key details or apply newly acquired knowledge by thinking aloud. Ask students to talk through an exercise in groups or pairs before going directly back to the reading to find an answer. Tell students to get in the habit of speaking their responses and then checking the answers against the reading once they have completed an exercise.

B. **PREDICT** Where do you think Andrew shops for the clothing? Complete Column 2 in Exercise A.

C. Read about Andrew.

National Geographic Explorer Andrew Skurka is a speaker and an author. He is also an adventurer and a guide. He is the author of a book for campers and hikers. Campers stay in one place and hikers walk from one place to another. Campers need different clothing than hikers.

Before a trip, Andrew goes shopping for important items. He shops for hiking boots at the shoe store. He shops for sweaters, shirts, and pants at the clothing store or the department store. Sometimes he shops at sporting goods stores for clothing, too. Andrew travels for a long time, so he also shops for a few interesting books to read at the bookstore.

D. What are Andrew's four jobs?

adventurer   author   guide   speaker

E. **ANALYZE** Look at the list of clothing and supplies. Write *speaker, author, adventurer,* or *guide* next to each item. You can write more than one job next to the items.

Answers may vary.

Clothing	Andrew's Job
boots	adventure / guide
cap or hat	adventurer/guide
computer	author/adventurer/guide
dictionary	author
jacket or coat	adventurer/guide
paper	speaker/author
suit	speaker
sunglasses	adventurer/guide
tent	adventurer/guide

F. **APPLY** What do you need for school or work? Make a list with a partner.

Answers will vary. Sample answers are given.

dictionary	vacuum cleaner
suit	ties
computer	dress

B. **PREDICT** Where do you think Andrew shops for the clothing? Complete Column 2 in Exercise A.

Ask students to predict where Andrew shops for clothes and then complete Column 2 in Exercise A.

C. **Read about Andrew.**

- Ask students to read about Andrew.
- Have students underline or circle each clothing item mentioned in the passage.
- Ask students what Andrew shops for.

D. **What are Andrew's four jobs?**

Ask students what Andrew's four jobs are.

E. **ANALYZE** Look at the list of clothing and supplies. Write *speaker, author, adventurer,* or *guide* next to each item. You can write more than one job next to the items.

- Have students carefully look at the list of clothing and supplies.
- Ask students to write Andrew's job (speaker, author, adventurer, or guide) next to each item in the list. Explain that students can write more than one job next to the item.
- Have students compare their answers in small groups.
- Write the list on the board in a chart. Then, have volunteers from the groups complete the column about Andrew's job.

F. **APPLY** What do you need for school or work? Make a list with a partner.

Ask students to think about what they need for school or work and make a list with a partner.

Food

About the Photo

Henry Sudarman took this photo. It shows a busy market in southern Jakarta early in the morning. This particular market only sells food until eight o'clock in the morning, so buyers need to wake up early. After eight, the food sellers pack up, and the stalls are handed over to clothes vendors for the remainder of the day. Various fruits and vegetables are on display, as well as exotic spices used in Indonesian cooking.

- Introduce the unit. Have students look at the photo. Then, ask the questions. Discuss as a class.

- Ask a volunteer to read the caption out loud. Ask students if they have ever bought their food in a busy food market like the one in the photo. Discuss as a class.

- Go over the unit outcomes. Then, ask more questions about the photo: *What foods are for sale in the market? What else is sold in the market? What do you think some of the prices are for the items in the photo?* Discuss as a class.

UNIT **3**

Food

People walk and buy their food in a busy food market.

UNIT OUTCOMES	GRAMMAR	VOCABULARY	EL CIVICS
• Identify common meals and foods • Interpret food advertisements • Express needs • Compare prices • Take and place orders	• Simple present: *Like* • *How much is…? / How much are…?* • Simple present • Comparative adjectives • Questions and *yes/no* answers	• Meals • Foods • Quantities and containers • *Expensive, cheap* • Menu sections	The skills students learn in this unit can be applied to the following El Civics competency areas: • Consumer Economics • Health and Nutrition

Life Skills Link

In this unit, students will learn how to identify various foods and interpret advertisements and menus. They will also learn how to compare prices and to become informed consumers.

Workplace Link

All lessons and units in *Stand Out* include basic communication skills and interpersonal skills important for the workplace. They are not individually identified. Other workplace skills are indicated. They include *collecting and organizing information, making decisions and solving problems,* and *combining ideas and information.*

UNIT OUTCOMES

- Identify common meals and foods
- Interpret food advertisements
- Express needs
- Compare prices
- Take and place orders

Look at the photo and answer the questions.

1. What do you see in the photo?
2. Where are the people?
3. What are the people doing?

CASAS	SCANS	CCRS
Lesson 1: 1.3.8, 7.2.3	Most SCANS are incorporated into this unit, with an emphasis on:	RI1, RI2, RI5, RI7, SL1, SL2, SL4, L1, L2, L5, RF2, RF3
Lesson 2: 1.2.1, 1.2.4, 1.3.8		
Lesson 3: 0.1.2, 1.1.7, 1.3.8, 7.2.6	• Allocating money	
Lesson 4: 1.1.3, 1.2.1, 1.2.2, 1.3.8	• Understanding systems	
Lesson 5: 1.3.8, 2.6.4, 7.2.3	• Creative thinking	
Review: 0.1.2, 1.1.3, 1.1.7, 1.2.1, 1.2.2, 1.2.4, 2.6.4	• Seeing things in the mind's eye	
Team Project: 0.1.2, 1.1.3, 1.1.7, 1.2.1, 1.2.2, 1.2.4, 2.6.4, 4.8.1	(Technology is optional.)	

GOAL ■ Identify common meals and foods

WORKPLACE CONNECTION
Exercise C: Collect and organize information.

A. **Look at the photo. Where is Dave? What food will he eat? Then, read about Dave.**

> I'm Dave Chen. I'm an English teacher in Florida. I like to eat! I eat a big breakfast in the morning at around seven, a small lunch at noon, and a big dinner at about six o'clock.

B. **Practice the conversation.**

Mario: Dave, what time do you eat <u>breakfast</u>?

Dave: Oh, at about <u>7:00 a.m.</u> How about you, Mario?

Mario: I eat breakfast at <u>8:00 a.m.</u>

C. **SURVEY** **Ask four students:** *What time do you eat breakfast, lunch, and dinner?*

Answers will vary.

Name	Breakfast	Lunch	Dinner
Dave	7:00 a.m.	12:00 p.m.	6:00 p.m.
You			

Goal: Identify common meals and foods

Grammar: Simple present: *Like*

Academic Strategies: Brainstorming, classifying, predicting

Vocabulary: Food vocabulary

Agenda

- Talk about favorite meals.
- Identify meals and common foods.
- Learn new food vocabulary.
- Write what you like to eat.

Resources

Multilevel Worksheet: Unit 3, Lesson 1, Worksheet 1

Workbook: Unit 3, Lesson 1

Audio: CD 1, Track 34

Heinle Picture Dictionary: Food, pages 82–103

Stand Out 1 Assessment CD-ROM with ExamView®

Pacing

- 1.5 hour classes
- 2.5 hour classes
- 3+ hour classes

STANDARDS CORRELATIONS

CCRS: RI1, RI7, W2, SL2, SL4, L1, L2

CASAS: 1.3.8, 7.2.3

SCANS: **Resources** Allocate materials and facility resources

Information Acquire and evaluate information, organize and maintain information, interpret and communicate information

Interpersonal Participate as a member of a team

Basic Skills Listening, speaking

Thinking Skills Make decisions

EFF: **Communication** Speak so others can understand, listen actively, observe critically

Interpersonal Cooperate with others

Preassessment *(optional)*

Use the Stand Out 1 Assessment CD-ROM with ExamView® to create a pretest for Unit 3.

Warm-up and Review   10–15 mins.

Write the word *favorite* on the board. Tell students what your favorite meal is. Write the words *breakfast, lunch,* and *dinner* on the board and above them write *meals.* Ask students what their favorite meal is and take a class poll. You may need to explain in more detail what each meal is. You might do this by using a clock or drawing clock faces on the board to indicate the approximate time each meal is usually eaten.

Introduction   5 mins.

Present the title of the unit and show students the unit goals. Explain them briefly. State the goal: *Today, we will identify common meals and foods.*

BEST PRACTICE

Stating the goal

We always suggest that you state the goal and write it on the board for all students to see. It is also important to revisit the goal at the end of the class period so students can see that they learned something new. This will give them confidence. Revisiting the goals in the review and in the project is also important.

Presentation 1   10–15 mins.

Ask students to open their books and to cover up the reading about Dave. Discuss the picture with them. Write *food* on the board as a heading for the information students will give you. Ask students to identify any foods they can. If they are unable to tell what the foods are, ask them to make guesses. Make a list on the board in no particular order.

A. Look at the photo. Where is Dave? What food will he eat? Then, read about Dave.

Ask students to look at the picture Then, ask where Dave is and and what he is eating. Next, ask a volunteer to read the paragraph. Discuss any new words with the class. Review again the names for meals that students learned in the warm-up.

Practice 1   7–10 mins.

B. Practice the conversation.

Ask students to practice the conversation with a partner. Have students take turns practicing each role.

C. SURVEY Ask four students: *What time do you eat breakfast, lunch, and dinner?*

Have students complete the survey with information for themselves and four of their classmates. Then, draw the survey form on the board. Next, ask volunteers to share some of their information with the class by filling in the survey. Now, add information that is true for you.

Evaluation 1

3–5 mins. ■■■

Go over their charts and, as a class, discuss differences in meal schedules.

Presentation 2

10–15 mins. ■■■

D. Read the foods in the box with your classmates and teacher.

Take another class poll and find out about students' preferences. Ask which food they like best. Take the top four choices and do a corners activity. Each corner is one of the four top choices. Once students have formed groups in the different corners, ask them to make a list of foods that go along with the food that they chose. Students may use dictionaries or rely on other members of the group to make the list.

BEST PRACTICE

Corners

A corners activity is a cooperative-learning technique where the instructor assigns the four corners in the room with different attributes or qualities. For example, in this case, the instructor might assign each corner one of the following: *hamburger, spaghetti, roast beef,* and *toast.* Then, the teacher asks students to go to the corner of their choice and perform some kind of task. Dictation helps students remember the new vocabulary, more so than if they were to merely listen, recognize, and repeat it.

Remind students again about the three meals. Ask individuals what they eat for breakfast, lunch, and dinner.

BEST PRACTICE

Asking individuals

Educators debate whether or not to call on individuals who have not volunteered to speak in class. Some feel that students could be intimidated and leave the course.

One of the most important things the instructor can do is to develop a community in the class where students are comfortable about participating and not afraid to make mistakes. It should be a place where students feel they will get help from the instructor and other students and won't be left embarrassed or unsatisfied.

Calling on individuals serves several purposes. First, students who ordinarily are timid about participating get more comfortable and may become more likely to volunteer in the future. Second, students don't know when they will be asked to participate, so they stay alert in the class. Third, students get a better sense of their classmates' abilities and personalities, which promotes community. Fourth, the information in the class should come from many different sources. Finally, the instructor gets a better feel for the students' level and how much the group as a whole understands and can produce.

Practice 2

10–15 mins. ■■

E. PREDICT AND CLASSIFY What do you think Dave eats for breakfast, lunch, and dinner? Complete the diagram with the foods from the box.

Ask students in groups of three or four to do this activity. Help students understand that at this point all answers are acceptable, but ultimately, students will be listening to what Dave actually eats and checking their answers.

Evaluation 2

■■

F. Listen to Dave and check the information in Exercise E.

Play the recording two or three times and allow students to check their work by putting a checkmark by each item in the cluster diagram. Ask which groups predicted correctly.

LISTENING SCRIPT

CD 1
TR 34

Hello, my name is Dave. I am a teacher at Alexander Adult School. I eat lunch here. They have a cafeteria. I teach all day so I can eat here for all three meals. For breakfast before class, I eat eggs, cereal, and toast. For lunch after my first class, I eat a hamburger and french fries. Sometimes, I eat a sandwich for lunch instead of a hamburger. For dinner, I either have spaghetti, roast beef, or fried chicken. Spaghetti is my favorite.

D. **Read the foods in the box with your classmates and teacher.**

| a hamburger | spaghetti | toast | french fries | cereal |
| a sandwich | roast beef | eggs | fried chicken | |

E. **PREDICT AND CLASSIFY** **What do you think Dave eats for breakfast, lunch, and dinner? Complete the diagram with the foods from the box.**

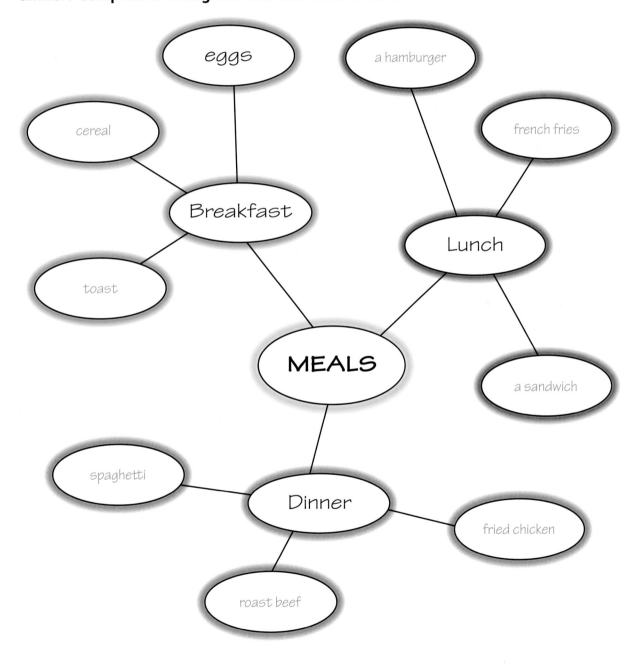

F. **Listen to Dave and check the information in Exercise E.**

CD 1
TR 34

G. **Practice the conversation. Make new conversations with the food words.**

Mario: What do you like for lunch?

Jim: I like egg rolls. How about you?

Mario: I like tacos.

roast beef and potatoes

rice and beans

pasta

egg rolls

H. **Practice in groups of four or five.**

Student A: What do you like for lunch?

Student B: I like hamburgers.

Student C: He likes hamburgers, and I like sandwiches.

Student D: He likes hamburgers, she likes sandwiches, and I like soup.

> **SIMPLE PRESENT**
> I like . . .
> He/She likes . . .

I. **CLASSIFY** **What do you eat for breakfast, lunch, and dinner?** Answers will vary.

Breakfast	Lunch	Dinner

J. **APPLY** **Write sentences about what you like for breakfast, lunch, and dinner.**

Answers will vary.

1. I like _____ for breakfast.

2. _____ for lunch.

3. _____.

Presentation 3

10–15 mins. ■■■

Ask different individuals what they like for breakfast, lunch, and dinner again. Make a chart on the board for *like* in the simple present, or ask students to go back to page 24 in Unit 1 and study the chart. Show them how the third person singular form of the verb has an *s*.

Look over the pictures on the page with students and discuss the meals. Ask students to tell you what their first, second, and third choice would be for lunch.

G. Practice the conversation. Make new conversations with the food words.

Go over the conversation as a class. Practice the intonation of the question. Ask students to briefly practice it with a partner to get the feel of the exchange. Show students how they will do the building game for Exercise H. Do it first as a class and see how far students can go before they forget what the previous students have said. Then, start over.

Practice 3

10–15 mins. ■

H. Practice in groups of four or five.

In this activity, Student A asks the question. After all the members of the group finish the circle, start over. This time, however, Student B becomes Student A and asks the question. Do the activity four or five times so each person in the group can ask the question. Remind students throughout the activity to clearly pronounce the third-person singular *s* when appropriate.

Evaluation 3

5–7 mins. ■

Observe groups doing the activity.

Application

10–15 mins. ■■■

I. **CLASSIFY** What do you eat for breakfast, lunch, and dinner?

J. **APPLY** Write sentences about what you like for breakfast, lunch, and dinner.

Refer students to *Stand Out 1 Workbook*, Unit 3, Lesson 1 for more practice with the simple present and *like*.

Go to the *Activity Bank* online for suggestions on promoting digital literacy and using the Internet to enhance this lesson.

MULTILEVEL WORKSHEET

Unit 3, Lesson 1, Worksheet 1: Favorite American Food

INSTRUCTOR'S NOTES

Goal: Interpret food advertisements

Grammar: *How much are …? / How much is …?*

Academic Strategies: Critical thinking, focused listening

Vocabulary: Food, quantities, and containers

Agenda

☐ Talk about fruits and vegetables.

☐ Read food advertisements.

☐ Listen to Duong and Minh.

☐ Learn quantities and containers.

☐ Ask *How much?*

☐ Make an advertisement.

Resources

Multilevel Worksheets: Unit 3, Lesson 2, Worksheets 1–2

Audio: CD 1, Track 35

Heinle Picture Dictionary: Measurements and Containers, pages 96–97; Fruits and Nuts, pages 82–83; Vegetables, pages 84–85.

Stand Out 1 Assessment CD-ROM with ExamView®

Pacing

■ 1.5 hour classes   ■ 2.5 hour classes

■ 3+ hour classes

STANDARDS CORRELATIONS

CCRS: SL1, SL2, SL4, L1, L2, L4, RF3

CASAS: 1.2.1, 1.2.4, 1.3.8

SCANS: **Information** Acquire and evaluate information, interpret and communicate information

Interpersonal Participate as a member of a team, teach others, exercise leadership, negotiate to arrive at a decision

Basic Skills Reading, writing, listening, speaking

Thinking Skills Think creatively, make decisions, solve problems, see things in the mind's eye

EFF: **Communication** Read with understanding, convey ideas in writing, speak so others can understand, listen actively, observe critically

Decision Making Solve problems and make decisions, plan

Interpersonal Cooperate with others, advocate and influence, resolve conflict and negotiate, guide others

Warm-up and Review
10–15 mins. ■■■

Ask students in groups to list on the board all the fruits and vegetables they know. Make sure they don't use a picture dictionary because then they will include fruits and vegetables they wouldn't ordinarily think of. Make sure that the list includes *tomatoes, carrots,* and *avocados.*

Introduction
2 mins. ■■■

Refer to the list on the board and ask students how much they think items cost. Help them by guessing a few of the prices yourself. Use the phrase *a pound* when appropriate. State the goal: *Today, we will interpret food advertisements.*

Presentation 1
20–30 mins. ■■■

Go over the fruits and vegetables on the board in more detail. Ask groups to come up with a price for each item. Then, come to a class consensus. Finally, ask questions, such as: *How much are the apples?* Accept one-word answers for now.

A. INTERPRET Read the advertisement with your classmates and teacher.

Show how we shorten *advertisement* to *ad.* Compare the prices you assigned to *avocados, tomatoes,* and *carrots* with the prices at Puente Market.

In Exercise B, students will listen for the vocabulary from Exercise A. To prepare for the focused listening, ask questions about the ad: *How much are the carrots? What costs $3.20?*

Practice 1
10–15 mins. ■■■

B. Listen to Duong and his wife make a shopping list. What do they need to buy? Check *Yes* or *No*.

Play the recording several times. Ask students to discuss their answers in groups or pairs between listenings.

Note: Listening Script and Evaluation 1 (Exercise C) appear on next page.

LESSON ② It's in the newspaper

GOAL ■ Interpret food advertisements

WORKPLACE CONNECTION
Exercise B: Collect and organize information.

A. INTERPRET Read the advertisement with your classmates and teacher.

B. Listen to Duong and his wife make a shopping list. What do they need to buy? Check (✓) *Yes* or *No*.

CD 1
TR 35

Do they need . . .	Yes	No
ground beef?	✓	
spaghetti?		✓
milk?		✓
carrots?	✓	
tomatoes?	✓	
peanut butter?		✓
soda?	✓	
avocados?	✓	

C. Write sentences about what Duong and Minh need. Answers will vary.

1. *They need ground beef.* _____

2. _____

3. _____

D. INTERPRET Study the advertisement with your classmates and teacher.

E. ANALYZE Scan the advertisement. Complete the chart with information from Exercise D.

Product	Container or Quantity	Price
cookies	box	$2.75
potato chips	bag	$2.75
soda	bottle	$.99
orange	each	$.69
yogurt	each	$.79
avocado	each	$1.25
cucumber	each	$.68
milk	gallon	$3.25
mustard	jar	$1.89
peanut butter	jar	$3.25
bread	loaf	$1.98
spaghetti	package	$2.20
carrots	one pound package	$1.00
tomatoes	pound	$.68
apples	pound	$1.49
ground beef	pound	$3.75

LISTENING SCRIPT

Duong: *We need to go shopping. We are out of everything.*
Minh: *You're right. Let's make a shopping list.*
Duong: *Well, I know we need ground beef.*
Minh: *That's not all. We really need carrots and tomatoes, too.*
Duong: *OK, I'll write that down—carrots and tomatoes.*
Minh: *Let's buy some soda, too.*
Duong: *OK, I'll add it to the list.*
Minh: *Wow! Avocados are expensive. Let's just buy two.*
Duong: *OK, two it is. Anything else?*
Minh: *No, I think that is it.*
Duong: *OK. I have ground beef, carrots, tomatoes, soda, and avocados on the list.*

CD 1
TR 35

Evaluation 1
10–15 mins.

C. Write sentences about what Duong and Minh need.

Ask students to write their sentences on the board.

Presentation 2
10–15 mins.

In this presentation, students will scan information in the newspaper and continue to learn quantity and container vocabulary. The practice will be for students to engage in a process of elimination to complete a chart. They will need to use all the vocabulary to do it. Therefore, spend some time making sure students understand the new vocabulary.

D. INTERPRET Study the advertisement with your classmates and teacher.

Ask questions about the items: *How much are the apples? What costs $2.75?* At this point, encourage students to say the price and the container or quantity in their answers.

Practice 2
10–15 mins.

E. ANALYZE Scan the advertisement. Complete the chart with information from Exercise D.

Students will use the clues to complete the chart. Do the first two or three items with them so they get the idea. Encourage students to work in pairs or groups to do this activity so they have an opportunity to speak.

Critical thinking

It is important to help students to think critically about topics. It gives them more of an ability to apply learning and serves as a "hook" to future learning. Students who think critically will develop better organizational and academic skills and presumably learn better and faster. There are many ways to provide this kind of activity. Below is a list of activities that develop critical thinking skills:

- using graphic organizers—students complete charts and graphs based on given information
- categorizing and classifying information
- reading charts and graphs
- doing projects with no one correct answer
- applying instruction to their daily lives
- problem solving

Many cooperative-learning techniques will stimulate critical thinking skills.

Evaluation 2
7–10 mins. ■■■

Review students' book work.

INSTRUCTOR'S NOTES

_____

_____

_____

_____

_____

_____

_____

_____

_____

_____

_____

_____

_____

Presentation 3

15–20 mins. ■■□

Go over the advertisements again. Ask: *How much is the milk? How much are the carrots?* Write the questions on the board and ask students why in the first question you used *is* and in the second you used *are*. Draw a three-column chart on the board. Write all the new food vocabulary in the first column. You may also want to distribute a three-column chart template from the Multilevel Worksheets for students to copy what you are starting on the board. The second column will be labeled *Question,* and students must decide whether to use *How much are* or *How much is*. The third column will contain the subject and the verb of the answer.

F. Read the chart.

Read the chart to students. Ask students to go over the advertisements in Exercise A and D to find the answers to the questions. Then, write the questions on the board

Item	Question	Answer
carrots	How much are	They are
milk	How much is	It is

Ask students in groups to complete the chart and then go over it as a class. Prepare students to do the practice in Exercises G and H.

Practice 3

10–15 mins. ■

Exercises G and H are information-gap activities. Only the student giving the answers should look at page 66. Ask students to record their answers on another sheet of paper.

G. Practice the conversation. Student A asks questions. Student B looks at the advertisement on page 66 to answer. Ask about *peanut butter, tomatoes, milk,* and *cookies*.

H. Practice the conversation. Student B asks questions. Student A looks at the advertisement on page 66 to answer. Ask about *bread, potato chips, soda,* and *apples*.

Evaluation 3

7–10 mins. ■

Observe students as they do the activity.

Application

15–20 mins. ■■■

I. **DESIGN** In a group, make your own food advertisement.

J. Look at a food advertisement in a local newspaper or search on an online store. Are the prices in your advertisement in Exercise I more expensive or cheaper?

MULTILEVEL WORKSHEETS

Templates: Two-Column Chart

Templates: Three-Column Chart

Unit 3, Lesson 2, Worksheet 1: Reading Advertisements

Unit 3, Lesson 2, Worksheet 2: Advertisements and Quantities

Refer students to *Stand Out 1 Workbook*, Unit 3, Lesson 2 for more practice with *How much …* and *How many ….*

Go to the *Activity Bank* online for suggestions on promoting digital literacy and using the Internet to enhance this lesson.

INSTRUCTOR'S NOTES

_____

_____

_____

_____

_____

_____

_____

_____

_____

_____

_____

F. Read the chart.

Be Verb	
How much **is** the	bread? peanut butter?
How much **are** the	tomatoes? potato chips?

G. Practice the conversation. Student A asks questions. Student B looks at the advertisement on page 66 to answer. Ask about *peanut butter, tomatoes, milk,* and *cookies.*

Student A: How much is the peanut butter?   **Student A:** How much are the tomatoes?
Student B: It's $3.25 a jar.   **Student B:** They are $.68 a pound.

H. Practice the conversation. Student B asks questions. Student A looks at the advertisement on page 66 to answer. Ask about *bread, potato chips, soda,* and *apples.*

Student A: How much is the bread?   **Student A:** How much are the potato chips?
Student B: It's $1.98 a loaf.   **Student B:** They are $2.75 a bag.

I. DESIGN In a group, make your own food advertisement. Answers will vary.

News Observer		Sunday, October 1

J. Look at a food advertisement in a local newspaper or search on an online store. Are the prices in your advertisement in Exercise I more expensive or cheaper?

LESSON ③ What do we need?

GOAL ■ Express needs

A. **INTERPRET** Look at the picture. Where is Doung? What is Doung eating? Then, read Duong's story.

> **EAT OUT**
> eat out = eat at a restaurant

> My name is Duong. I'm from Vietnam. I study at North Creek Adult School. It is very expensive to eat out every day, so I bring my lunch to school. My wife and I go to the store every Saturday. We buy bread and meat for my sandwiches.

B. Answer the questions. Check (✓) *True* or *False*.

	True	False
1. Duong buys his lunch at school.	☐	☑
2. Duong and his son go to the store every Saturday.	☐	☑
3. Duong and his wife buy bread and meat for sandwiches.	☑	☐

C. Listen to the conversation between Duong and Minh. Check (✓) the foods they need from the supermarket.

CD 1
TR 36

Shopping List

_____ ham	_____ turkey
✓ tuna fish	✓ chicken
✓ peanut butter	_____ salami
✓ jelly	

Goal: Express needs
Grammar: Simple present
Pronunciation: /z/ and /iz/
Academic Strategy: Focused listening
Vocabulary: Food vocabulary, containers

Agenda

◻ Talk about sandwiches.

◻ Express needs.

◻ Read about Duong.

◻ Learn food container vocabulary.

◻ Use the simple present tense.

◻ Read a shopping list.

Resources

Multilevel Worksheets: Unit 3, Lesson 3,
Worksheets 1–2
Audio: CD 1, Track 36
Heinle Picture Dictionary: Measurements
and Containers, pages 96–97
Stand Out 1 Assessment CD-ROM with ExamView®

Pacing

■ 1.5 hour classes   ■ 2.5 hour classes
■ 3+ hour classes

STANDARDS CORRELATIONS

CCRS: RI1, SL2, SL4, L1, RF2

CASAS: 0.1.2, 1.1.7, 1.3.8, 7.2.6

SCANS: **Resources** Allocate materials and facility resources

Information Acquire and evaluate information, organize and maintain information, interpret and communicate information

Interpersonal Participate as a member of a team, teach others

Basic Skills Reading, writing, listening, speaking

Thinking Skills Make decisions, solve problems

EFF: **Communication** Read with understanding, convey ideas in writing, speak so others can understand, listen actively, observe critically

Decision Making Solve problems and make decisions

Interpersonal Cooperate with others

Warm-up and Review   10–15 mins. ■■■

Write *sandwich* on the board. Ask groups to list on the board as many types of sandwiches they can. It is OK for students to use a bilingual or picture dictionary. Take a class poll. Find out what sandwich is the class favorite.

Introduction   7–10 mins. ■■■

Make a two-column chart on the board. Label the first *needs* and the second *wants*. Say: *I want ice cream for breakfast.* Write *ice cream* in the *wants* column. Then say: *I need three meals a day.* Write *three meals a day* in the *needs* column. As another example, say something and ask students if you *need* it or just *want* it. Ask them to figure out which column to write it in. State the goal: *Today, we will express needs.*

Presentation 1   30–40 mins. ■■■

Ask students what they eat for lunch. Write their answers on the board. Ask students to open their books and cover up the reading in Exercise A. Look at the picture and ask questions.

A   INTERPRET   Look at the picture. Where is Doung? What is Doung eating? Then, read Duong's story.

Ask volunteers to take turns reading sentences in the story. Clarify any words as necessary.

B.   Answer the questions. Check (✓) *True* or *False*.

Do this as a class. Ask students to correct the false sentences and make them true. Then, ask volunteers to write the new true sentences on the board. Compare the list in Exercise C to the list students created in the warm-up.

Practice 1   5–7 mins. ■■■

C.   Listen to the conversation between Duong and Minh. Check (✓) the foods they need from the supermarket.

Play the recording two or three times. Allow students to compare answers between listenings.

Evaluation 1   5–7 mins. ■■■

Go over students' answers.

LISTENING SCRIPT   🎧 CD 1 TR 36

Duong: *It is too expensive to buy food at school every day. I have the same sandwiches every week. Maybe we should buy something different, but I need something healthy.*
Minh: *OK. What did you have in mind?*
Duong: *Well, I thought I might try tuna fish. It is delicious.*
Minh: *Yes, they say fish is good for you, too. What about chicken?*
Duong: *Chicken is OK, but I don't have time to prepare it.*
Minh: *We can buy it in slices. You don't need to prepare it.*
Duong: *Great. I also need peanut butter and jelly.*
Minh: *Yes, we do need both. We are completely out.*

Presentation 2   15–20 mins. ■■■

This presentation will further reinforce the new vocabulary and prepare students to express their needs.

D. Study the words for food containers. Write the correct word under each picture.

Do this activity with the class and make sure students understand the vocabulary.

E. In a group, discuss what other foods go into each container.

Ask students to brainstorm in a group. Give them a brief time frame such as three minutes. You may also suggest that they look back at the advertisements on pages 65 and 66 to help them. Ask the groups for their answers and suggest they respond in sentences, such as: *We have a can of soup and a bottle of oil.*

Ask students to brainstorm in a group. Give them a brief time frame such as three minutes. You may also suggest that they look back at the advertisements on pages 65 and 66 to help them.

PRONUNCIATION

/z/, /iz/

The final /s/ is sometimes omitted by students, especially if final consonants are not emphasized in their native languages. Show students how the final *s* in these words is voiced by asking them to put two fingers on their voice box and feeling the vibration.

Show them how often the words are followed by *of*. When they are followed by *of*, the /z/ links to the *o* in *of*. So, for example, students should practice pronouncing: *bottle-zof* and *boxe-zof*.

Overemphasizing a sound is OK for demonstration as long as you also demonstrate the sound in context with appropriate emphasis.

Remember that most students need to be exposed several times to pronunciation and grammar concepts before they acquire them.

Practice 2   7–10 mins. ■■

F. Create sentences by adding words from Exercise E. Then, read your sentences to a partner.

Evaluation 2   10–15 mins. ■■

After completing the sentences, ask students to close their books. Write *Duong* on the board and then give students a dictation on the sentences they just wrote. Then, ask volunteers to write the sentences on the board.

BEST PRACTICE

Dictation

Dictation can be a very good activity for encouraging writing accuracy and developing listening skills. At this level, students have a limited vocabulary, so it often makes sense to give a dictation of a passage or sentences that students have already seen.

When doing a dictation activity, be aware that, at this level, students have difficulty listening and writing at the same time. And yet they will try to do it. The minute you start speaking, students will probably start writing. After writing one or two words, they will ask for more. This is not a productive way to do dictation and it can be frustrating for the instructor.

Teach students to listen to the sentence, repeat the sentence, and then write the sentence. The first time you read the dictation passage, have students put their pencils down to listen and then ask them to repeat the passage in unison. Finally, ask them to write what they have heard and repeated. After they are confident that they understand the passage, ask students to repeat the passage to themselves silently instead of out loud.

INSTRUCTOR'S NOTES

_____

_____

_____

_____

_____

_____

_____

_____

WORKPLACE CONNECTION

Exercise E, F: Interpret and communicate information; Interact appropriately with team members.

D. Study the words for food containers. Write the correct word under each picture.

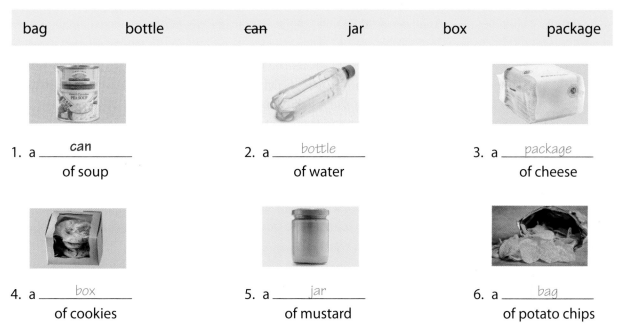

| bag | bottle | ~~can~~ | jar | box | package |

1. a ___can___
   of soup

2. a ___bottle___
   of water

3. a ___package___
   of cheese

4. a ___box___
   of cookies

5. a ___jar___
   of mustard

6. a ___bag___
   of potato chips

E. In a group, discuss what other foods go into each container. Answers will vary.

Container	Food
can / cans	beans, coffee
bottle / bottles	
package / packages	
box / boxes	
jar / jars	
bag / bags	

PLURALS

/z/	/iz/
jar**z**	packag**iz**
bag**z**	box**iz**
can**z**	

F. Create sentences by adding words from Exercise E. Then, read your sentences to a partner. Answers will vary depending on responses to Exercise E.

1. Alicia needs three cans of _____coffee_____.

2. She needs four bottles of _____.

3. She needs two packages of _____.

4. _____ three boxes of _____.

5. _____.

6. _____.

G. **Study the chart with your classmates and teacher.**

Simple Present		
Subject	**Verb**	**Example sentence**
I, You, We, They	eat like need want make	I **eat** tacos for lunch. You **like** eggs for breakfast. We **need** three cans of corn. They **want** three boxes of cookies. I **make** sandwiches for lunch.
He, She, It	eats likes needs wants makes	He **eats** pizza for dinner. She **likes** tomato soup. He **needs** three pounds of tomatoes. She **wants** two bottles of water. She **makes** sandwiches for Duong.

H. **Read the shopping list.**

Shopping List

6 bottles of water

3 cans of soup

1 jar of jelly

3 packages of cheese

I. **Complete the sentences with the correct form of the verbs in parentheses and the correct containers.**

1. Duong _____ needs _____ (need) one _____ jar _____ of jelly.

2. They _____ like _____ (like) soup at night.

3. Duong _____ eats _____ (eat) sandwiches at school.

4. Minh _____ makes _____ (make) sandwiches for Duong.

5. They _____ want _____ (want) three _____ packages _____ of cheese.

J. **Make a list of things you need at the store. Tell your partner what you need.**

Presentation 3

15–20 mins. ■■■

Rewrite the sentences on the board from the dictation. For the first one, use the first-person singular: *I need three cans of beans*. For the next ones, use *you, we,* and *they*.

Underline the third-person singular *s* in the original dictation sentences and show students how the verbs in the new sentences don't take an *s*.

G. Study the chart with your classmates and teacher.

Go over the chart carefully.

H. Read the shopping list.

Briefly go over the shopping list.

Practice 3

10–15 mins. ■

I. Complete the sentences with the correct form of the verbs in parentheses and the correct containers.

Make sure students see that the sentences they are completing directly relate to the shopping list.

Evaluation 3

10–15 mins. ■

Ask students to write the words on the board.

Application

10–15 mins. ■

J. Make a list of things you need at the store. Tell your partner what you need.

Ask students at the completion of the activity to share their partner's list with a group. In other words, Student A gives the information to Student B, Student B writes down the information, and then Student B shares the information with a group. In the final step, Student B might say: *He needs two jars of peanut butter.*

Refer students to *Stand Out 1 Workbook*, Unit 3, Lesson 3 for more practice using the simple present.

Go to the *Activity Bank* online for suggestions on promoting digital literacy and using the Internet to enhance this lesson.

MULTILEVEL WORKSHEETS

Unit 3, Lesson 3, Worksheet 1: Simple Present

Unit 3, Lesson 3, Worksheet 2: Shopping List

INSTRUCTOR'S NOTES

Goal: Compare prices
Grammar: Comparative adjectives
Pronunciation: Rhythm
Academic Strategies: Graphs, focused listening
Vocabulary: Food items, *cheaper, more expensive*

Agenda

- List foods.
- Compare prices.
- Complete a graph.
- Listen for prices.
- Discuss stores.

Resources

Multilevel Worksheet: Unit 3, Lesson 4, Worksheet 1
Audio: CD 1, Track 37
Heinle Picture Dictionary: Supermarket, pages 98–99
Stand Out 1 Assessment CD-ROM with ExamView®

Pacing

- 1.5 hour classes
- 2.5 hour classes
- 3+ hour classes

STANDARDS CORRELATIONS

CCRS: SL1, SI2, SL4, L1, L2
CASAS: 1.1.3, 1.2.1, 1.2.2, 1.3.8
SCANS: **Resources** Allocate money
Information Acquire and evaluate information, organize and maintain information, interpret and communicate information
Basic Skills Reading, listening, speaking
Thinking Skills Make decisions, solve problems, see things in the mind's eye
EFF: **Communication** Read with understanding, speak so others can understand, listen actively, observe critically
Decision Making Solve problems and make decisions

Warm-up and Review   15–20 mins. ■■■

On the board, list all the vocabulary used in this unit thus far. Make sure students know what each word means. Make a four-column chart on the board with the following headings: *fruit, vegetables, meat,* and *drinks*. Students in groups should make a similar chart. Ask students to work in groups and put all the items in the appropriate columns. You can make this a competition if you wish. You may also use the four-column chart template on the Multilevel Worksheets Activity Bank.

BEST PRACTICE

Group participation

There are many ways to encourage all students to participate in groups. It helps when students are working on a written task if they work on one chart for the entire group and not their own individual ones. One student is chosen as the secretary and the others offer suggestions.

Ask representatives from the groups to put the information in the chart on the board. Erase the board and do a dictation with a few words.

Introduction   5–7 mins. ■■■

Ask students to look at pages 65 and 66. Ask which store they think is better and why. Students may determine that the prices at one store are cheaper than at the other. State the goal: *Today, we will compare prices.*

Presentation 1   10–15 mins. ■■■

A. **EVALUATE** **Look at Duong's shopping list. Look at the advertisement on page 65 for Puente Market and the advertisement on page 66 for Food City. Which store is cheaper for Duong?**

B. **Study the graph. Fill in the missing information.**

Study the graph as a class and help students understand how to read it. Make sure they are referring to the two stores on pages 65 and 66. Ask questions, such as: *Where is ground beef cheaper? How much are the carrots at Puente Market?*

Ask students to complete the graph. Ask again which store they think is better for Duong. Talk about the completed graph. You may want to recreate the graph on the board.

Practice 1   10–15 mins. ■■■

C. **Complete the chart and calculate the totals.**

Ask students to complete the chart based on the information in the graph and calculate the totals. Then, ask which store is cheaper for Duong.

Evaluation 1   5–7 mins. ■■■

Go over the completed charts and totals as a class.

LESSON **4** What's cheaper?

GOAL ▨ Compare prices

WORKPLACE CONNECTION
Exercise B: Collect and organize information; Combine ideas and information; Exercise C: Perform basic computations; Manage money.

A. EVALUATE Look at Duong's shopping list. Look at the advertisement on page 65 for Puente Market and the advertisement on page 66 for Food City. Which store is cheaper for Duong?

Puente Market will be cheaper for Duong.

> Shopping List
>
> 2 pounds of ground beef
>
> 3 pounds of tomatoes
>
> avocados
>
> carrots

B. Study the graph. Fill in the missing information.

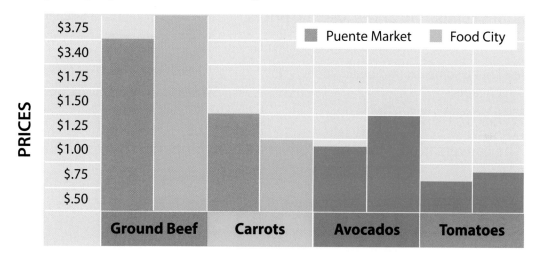

C. Complete the chart and calculate the totals.

	Puente Market	Food City
Ground beef	$3.40	$3.75
Carrots	$1.25	$1.00
Avocados	$.99	$1.25
Tomatoes	$.60	$.68
Total	$6.24	$6.68

D. Study the charts with your classmates and teacher.

Cheaper		
	Question	**Answer**
Singular	Where is ground beef cheaper?	It's **cheaper** at Puente Market.
Plural	Where are carrots cheaper?	They're **cheaper** at Food City.

More Expensive		
	Question	**Answer**
Singular	Where is ground beef more expensive?	It's **more expensive** at Food City.
Plural	Where are carrots more expensive?	They're **more expensive** at Puente Market.

E. Practice the conversation. Make new conversations comparing prices. Use the prices on page 71.

> **STRESS**
>
> **WHERE** is ground **beef CHEAPER**?
> **WHERE** is ground **beef** more **EXPENSIVE**?
>
> **WHERE** are **carrots CHEAPER**?
> **WHERE** are **carrots** more **EXPENSIVE**?

Student A: I need some ground beef. Where is it cheaper?
Student B: It's cheaper at Puente Market.

F. Practice the conversation. Make new conversations comparing prices. Use the prices on page 71.

Student A: I buy ground beef at Puente Market.
Student B: Why?
Student A: It's more expensive at Food City.

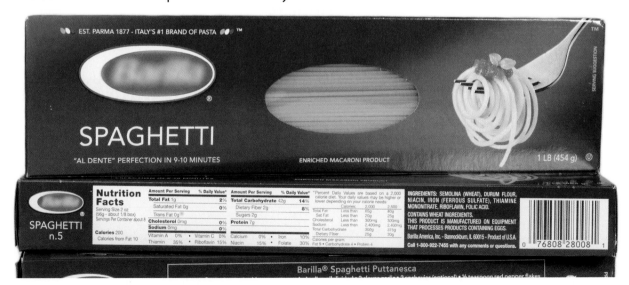

Presentation 2

10–15 mins. ■■■

Review the difference between questions that start with *How much is* and *How much are*. Ask when to use each phrase with the words on the shopping list on the previous page. Also, remind students of *it is* and *they are*.

Now, write *cheap* and *cheaper* on the board. Also, write *expensive* and *more expensive* on the board. Explain these new words by talking about the prices on the previous page. Also, point out the word *at* (as in *at* Puente Market). Ask questions and see how much students understand before they open their books. It is helpful to work with students and allow them to think about the concepts before you give them all the information in a chart. In this way, students will understand the charts better.

D. Study the charts with your classmates and teacher.

PRONUNCIATION

Rhythm

There is a rhythm to English that is similar to some languages and very distinct from others. Speakers of different languages vary which words they emphasize to show rhythm in discourse. However, important words are given emphasis regularly, and words that answer a specific question are also given emphasis. Syllables with less emphasis are generally spoken quickly; whereas, words with more emphasis are lengthened.

For people who understand music notation, English loosely has the feel of an eighth note followed by a sixteenth note. In stressing rhythm, an instructor might have students clap along with this pattern several times before they attempt to produce an utterance so they have a general feel for the rhythm.

Ask students to say only the syllables that receive more emphasis. In this case, they might say: *Where-car-cheap*.

Once students are comfortable with the rhythm, say the question and ask them to repeat it.

Prepare students for the practice. Go over the two exchanges in Exercises E and F. Pay special attention to the rhythm.

Practice 2

10–15 mins. ■■

E. Practice the conversation. Make new conversations comparing prices. Use the prices on page 71.

F. Practice the conversation. Make new conversations comparing prices. Use the prices on page 71.

Evaluation 2

5–10 mins. ■■

Ask for volunteers to demonstrate for the class.

INSTRUCTOR'S NOTES

_____

_____

_____

_____

_____

_____

_____

_____

_____

_____

_____

_____

_____

_____

_____

_____

_____

_____

_____

Presentation 3

15–20 mins. ■■■

G. INTERPRET Read the paragraph about Sebastian.

Read the paragraph with students. If you have time, you might make this paragraph into a cloze activity on the board. Ask students to close their books and attempt to complete the paragraph on the board. Your cloze paragraph might look like this:

I shop at Food City. I _____ the bananas and oranges there. The _____ is more expensive, but I like _____ store. They have good specials, _____. Food City is near my home.

Then, read the paragraph out loud to students and ask them to orally fill in the correct words.

H. Answer the questions. Check (✓) *True* or *False*.

Do this exercise as a class.

Prepare students for focused listening by having them look at the charts. Ask them to predict what information they will listen for.

Practice 3

10–15 mins. ■

I. COMPARE Listen to Sebastian ask about prices. Complete the charts.

You may need to play this recording several times. Allow students to discuss their answers with a group between listenings.

LISTENING SCRIPT

CD 1
TR 37

Sebastian: *Excuse me. I see that you have a special deal where if a customer finds a cheaper price at a different store, you will give him the same deal. Is that right?*
Salesperson: *That's right. Do you have a newspaper ad?*
Sebastian: *Yes. It says right here that at Puente Market, bananas are ninety-two cents a pound. Here at Food City, they are ninety-eight cents.*
Salesperson: *That looks right. We will give you the deal.*
Sebastian: *Here are more examples. Puente Market is always cheaper.*
Salesperson: *Let's see. You're right. Oranges at Puente Market are $2.20 a pound and at Food City, they cost $2.39 a pound. Pears at Puente Market are $1.29 a pound. Here at Food City, they are $1.39.*
Sebastian: *Look at this! Apples are $2.00 at Food City and only $1.49 at Puente Market.*
Salesperson: *Wow. It looks like we need to change a lot of prices!*

Evaluation 3

5–10 mins. ■

J. CREATE Complete the bar graph about the two markets. Use the information from Exercise I.

Ask students to complete the graph. This activity can also be done on the board as a class.

Application

20–30 mins. ■■■

K. APPLY What store do you shop at? Why? Tell the group.

L. As a class, choose one food item. Choose two stores in your neighborhood or go online. Compare prices of the food item. Which store is cheaper?

Refer students to *Stand Out 1 Workbook*, Unit 3, Lesson 4 for more practice with comparative adjectives.

Go to the *Activity Bank* online for suggestions on promoting digital literacy and using the Internet to enhance this lesson.

MULTILEVEL WORKSHEETS

Templates: Four-Column Chart

Unit 3, Lesson 4, Worksheet 1: Comparison Shopping

INSTRUCTOR'S NOTES

_____

_____

_____

_____

_____

_____

_____

_____

G. **INTERPRET** Read the paragraph about Sebastian.

> I shop at Food City. I like the bananas and oranges there. The fruit is more expensive, but I like the store. They have good specials, too. Food City is near my home.

H. Answer the questions. Check (✓) *True* or *False*.

	True	False
1. Sebastian shops at Puente Market.	☐	☑
2. The fruit at Puente Market is cheaper.	☑	☐
3. Food City has bananas and oranges.	☑	☐

I. **COMPARE** Listen to Sebastian ask about prices. Complete the charts.

CD 1
TR 37

Puente Market	
Fruit	**Price**
bananas	$.92
oranges	$2.20
pears	$1.29
apples	$1.49

Food City	
Fruit	**Price**
bananas	$.98
oranges	$2.39
pears	$1.39
apples	$2.00

J. **CREATE** Complete the bar graph about the two markets. Use the information from Exercise I.

	Puente Market	Food City	Puente Market	Food City	Puente Market	Food City	Puente Market	Food City
$2.50								
$2.00								
$1.75								
$1.50								
$1.25								
$1.00								
$ .75								
	bananas		oranges		pears		apples	

K. **APPLY** What store do you shop at? Why? Tell the group.

L. As a class, choose one food item. Choose two stores in your neighborhood or go online. Compare prices of the food item. Which store is cheaper?

LESSON **5** Buying lunch

GOAL ■ Take and place orders

WORKPLACE CONNECTION
Exercise B: Collect and organize information; Exercise C: Interpret
and communicate information.

A. Study the menu on the lunch truck with your classmates and teacher.

B. CLASSIFY Write the information from the menu in the chart below.

Sandwiches	Beverages	Side orders
cheese	milk	french fries
burgers / cheeseburgers	orange juice	fruit cup
hot dog	soda	green salad
ham	water	

C. Practice the conversation. Make new conversations. Change the underlined words. Use the words from Exercise B.

SINGULAR	PLURAL
a burger	two burger**s**
a salad	three salad**s**
	french frie**s**

Sebastian: Hi! I want a <u>ham sandwich</u>, please.

Server: Do you want a side order?

Sebastian: Yes, a <u>salad</u>.

Server: Great! Do you want a drink?

Sebastian: <u>Milk</u>, thanks.

74 Unit 3

Goal: Take and place orders
Grammar: Questions and *yes/no* answers
Academic Strategies: Focused listening, classifying
Vocabulary: Foods, menu sections

Agenda

- Read a menu.
- Place an order.
- Listen to restaurant orders.
- Ask and answer questions.
- Place your own lunch order.

Resources

Multilevel Worksheets: Unit 3, Lesson 5, Worksheets 1–2
Workbook: Unit 3, Lesson 5
Audio: CD 1, Tracks 38–40
Heinle Picture Dictionary: Order, Eat, Pay, pages 102–103
Stand Out 1 Assessment CD-ROM with ExamView®

Pacing

- 1.5 hour classes
- 2.5 hour classes
- 3+ hour classes

STANDARDS CORRELATIONS

CCRS: SL2, L1, L2, L5
CASAS: 1.3.8, 2.6.4, 7.2.3
SCANS: **Resources** Allocate money
Information Acquire and evaluate information, interpret and communicate information
Basic Skills Reading, writing, listening, speaking
EFF: **Communication** Read with understanding, convey ideas in writing, speak so others can understand, listen actively

Warm-up and Review   5–7 mins. ■■■

Play a game. Write the items from pages 65 and 66 on the board in random order under a heading for each store. Split the class into two teams. Team 1 guesses a price of an item. Team 2 guesses if the item is cheaper than what Team 1 has said or more expensive. If the price is exactly right, Team 1 receives a point. If Team 2 successfully determines that the price is cheaper or more expensive than what Team 1 guessed, they get a point.

Introduction   5–7 mins. ■■■

Ask students what restaurants they like. Ask what their favorite foods to order are. Ask if they order in English. State the goal: *Today, we will learn to place orders in restaurants.*

Presentation 1   15–20 mins. ■■■

A. Study the menu on the lunch truck with your classmates and teacher.

Ask students what they would like from the lunch truck. Discuss the foods and when students might eat them. Talk about breakfast, lunch, and dinner. Work on the pronunciation of each item.

B. CLASSIFY Write the information from the menu in the chart below.

Do this activity as a class on the board and have students write the information in their books. Go over the conversation. Work on the rhythm by asking students to clap it out as they practice. Ask students to identify the most important words that might be given emphasis.

Practice 1   10–15 mins. ■■■

C. Practice the conversation. Make new conversations. Change the underlined words. Use the words from Exercise B.

Ask students to work in pairs.

BEST PRACTICE

Inside/Outside circle

At this level, students are asked to do short dialogs often to provide practice. This is necessary because they don't have an extended vocabulary to discuss things yet. It is a good idea to provide different ways to approach pair practice. In the previous unit, students used conversation or substitution cards. This can work again here. Another approach is *inside/outside circle.* Students stand in two circles, one circle inside the other. Both circles contain the same number of students. The students in the outer circle face the students in the inner one. They do the dialog once, and then one of the circles rotates so each student has a new conversation with another student. This activity continues until you feel students have gotten enough practice.

Evaluation 1   3–5 mins. ■■■

Ask volunteers to demonstrate in front of the class.

Presentation 2

10–15 mins. ■■■

D. Look at the menu in Exercise A. Talk to your classmates and teacher. What do you like to eat? What is cheap?

Go over the menu one last time. Tell students that they will take your order. Ask a volunteer to do the conversation on the previous page with you. Ask the other students to write down your order. Do several orders this way in preparation for the upcoming practice.

Practice

10–15 mins. ■■

E. Listen to the orders. Write each student's order in the chart below. Write the prices from Exercise A.

Ask students to only complete the first column of the three charts.

LISTENING SCRIPT

CD 1
TR 38–40

1. **Manny's Order**
   Manny: *I want a cheeseburger, a green salad, and an orange juice, please.*
   Server: *No orange juice today. Would you like milk or soda?*
   Manny: *A soda please.*
   Server: *OK, two minutes. Next.*

2. **Tran's Order**
   Tran: *What sandwiches do you have?*
   Server: *Ham or cheese.*
   Tran: *I'll have a ham sandwich.*
   Server: *OK.*
   Tran: *And a green salad, too.*
   Server: *Of course. What about a drink?*
   Tran: *No, thanks.*
   Server: *OK. That's a ham sandwich and a green salad, right?*
   Tran: *That's right. Thanks.*

3. **Miyuki's Order**
   Miyuki: *I want some milk, please, and a hot dog.*
   Server: *Do you want mustard?*
   Miyuki: *No, thanks. Just french fries.*
   Server: *That's fine. Hot dog, no mustard, french fries, and a milk coming up.*

Evaluation 2

7–10 mins. ■■

Ask students to complete the second and third columns of the chart and to compute the totals. Check to see that everyone got the same totals.

WORKPLACE CONNECTION

Exercise D: Interact appropriately with team members; Exercise E: Combine ideas and information;
Collect and organize information.

D. Look at the menu in Exercise A. Talk to your classmates and teacher. What do you like to eat? What is cheap?

E. Listen to the orders. Write each student's order in the chart below. Write the prices from Exercise A.

CD 1
TR 38-40

1. Manny's order

Selection	Section	Price
soda	beverages	$1.99
cheeseburger	sandwiches	$2.70
green salad	side orders	$2.00
	Total	$6.69

2. Tran's order

Selection	Section	Price
ham	sandwiches	$2.70
green salad	side order	$2.00
	Total	$4.70

3. Miyuki's order

Selection	Section	Price
hot dog	sandwiches	$2.25
milk	beverages	$2.00
french fries	side orders	$1.60
	Total	$5.85

F. **Study the chart with your classmates and teacher.**

Questions and *Yes/No* Answers		
Question	**Yes**	**No**
Do you want a hamburger?	Yes, I do.	No, I don't.
Do they want sandwiches?	Yes, they do.	No, they don't.
Does he want a sandwich?	Yes, he does.	No, he doesn't.
Does she want a hot dog?	Yes, she does.	No, she doesn't.

G. **Read the orders.**

Sebastian
Sandwich: ham sandwich
Side order: salad
Beverage: milk

Tri
Sandwich: cheeseburger
Side order: french fries
Beverage: milk

Natalia
Sandwich: hot dog
Side order: french fries
Beverage: orange juice

H. **Answer the questions.**

1. Does Sebastian want a salad? _____ Yes, he does. _____

2. Does Natalia want orange juice? _____ Yes, she does. _____

3. Do Sebastian and Tri want orange juice? _____ No, they don't. _____

4. Do Sebastian and Tri want milk? _____ Yes, they do. _____

5. Do Tri and Natalia want ham sandwiches? _____ No, they don't. _____

6. Does Natalia want a cheeseburger? _____ No, she doesn't. _____

I. **Look at the menu on page 74. Write your order. Then, practice taking an order with a partner. Use the conversation in Exercise C as a model.** Answers will vary.

Selection	Section	Price

J. **Go to a lunch truck or cafeteria and order your lunch in English.**

Presentation 3

8–10 mins. ■■■

Practice role-playing with individuals in front of the class. Use the menu on page 74. Then, ask students questions about what they may want.

BEST PRACTICE

Conversations in *Stand Out*

In the lower levels of *Stand Out*, there are various things that might be considered conversation.

1. There are controlled dialogs where students merely read and repeat what is on the page. The purpose of these types of activities is to help students with pronunciation features and to help them become accustomed to new vocabulary. It is not necessary for students to memorize the dialogs.
2. Similarly, conversations with substitutions can be useful to help students think critically and manipulate the conversation.
3. Role-play activities should not be scripted. Students use the language they know and take on the roles of different characters. It is controlled in that the context is controlled.
4. Finally, we have open-ended discussions. These discussions can be difficult at this level, but students will find that in groups they can convey ideas with limited vocabulary.

F. Study the chart with your classmates and teacher.

Help students with pronunciation and intonation. Explain the different ways to answer the same *yes/no* questions in the affirmative and in the negative.

Practice 3

10–15 mins. ■

G. Read the orders.

H. Answer the questions.

I. Look at the menu on page 74. Write your order. Then, practice taking an order with a partner. Use the conversation in Exercise C as a model.

Evaluation 3

5–7 mins. ■

Go over the students' answers in their books. Consider having volunteers write the questions and answers on the board.

Application

10–15 mins. ■■■

J. Go to a lunch truck or cafeteria and order your lunch in English.

Refer students to *Stand Out 1 Workbook*, Unit 3, Lesson 5 for more practice with short answers.

Go to the *Activity Bank* online for suggestions on promoting digital literacy and using the Internet to enhance this lesson.

MULTILEVEL WORKSHEETS

Unit 3, Lesson 5, Worksheet 1: Reading Menus

Unit 3, Lesson 5, Worksheet 2: Taking Orders

INSTRUCTOR'S NOTES

_____

_____

_____

_____

_____

_____

_____

_____

_____

_____

_____

_____

_____

_____

_____

_____

_____

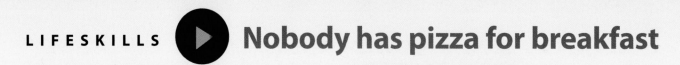
Before You Watch

- Read the title out loud. Then, ask students if they agree with the statement.
- Ask students what types of foods people eat for breakfast in the United States. Then, ask students what types of foods people eat for breakfast in their own countries. Have volunteers share individual answers with the class.

A. Look at the picture. Complete each sentence.

- Ask students to look at the picture.
- Have volunteers describe what they see.
- Tell students to complete each sentence. Then, have them share their answers with a partner.

While You Watch

B. Watch the video. Complete the dialog. Use the words in the box.

- Read each word in the box out loud.
- Tell students they will watch a video and then complete the conversation between Mr. and Mrs. Sanchez and Hector with the words in the box.
- Read the example sentence out loud. Then, play the video and ask students to watch and listen.
- Play the video two more times in order for students to (1) complete the dialog and (2) check their answers.
- Have three volunteers act out the conversation in front of the class.

Check Your Understanding

C. Watch the video. Read the statements. Write *T* for True or *F* for False.

- Tell students they will watch the video again and answer true or false for each of the statements. Ask them to write *T* or *F* on the line.
- Have students read the statements. Then, play the video once again.
- Ask students to write their answers. Then, have them share their answers with one or more students.
- Check answers as a class.

INSTRUCTOR'S NOTES

Before You Watch

A. Look at the picture. Complete each sentence.

1. Hector is holding vegetables and
   cheese and eggs.

2. It's time for _breakfast_.

3. The family is in _the kitchen_.

While You Watch

B. ▶ **Watch the video. Complete the dialog. Use the words in the box.**

~~eggs~~	make	milk	sugar	vegetables

Mrs. Sanchez: You should have *real* food for breakfast: (1) _____eggs_____, milk, fruit. Please, let me make something for you.

Hector: How about some cake? Cake has eggs and (2) _____milk_____ and fruit!

Mrs. Sanchez: It also has sugar in it. Lots and lots of (3) _____sugar_____. Isn't there anything else in the refrigerator besides pizza and cake?

Hector: There's… Well, there's (4) _____vegetables_____, cheese, and eggs.

Mr. Sanchez: Why don't you (5) _____make_____ an omelet?

Check Your Understanding

C. Watch the video. Read the statements. Write *T* for True or *F* for False.

1. Hector eats pizza for breakfast. _F_

2. Mr. Sanchez wants cake for breakfast. _F_

3. Hector takes vegetables out of the refrigerator. _T_

4. Mrs. Sanchez adds milk to the eggs. _F_

5. Hector puts sugar on his omelet. _F_

Review

A. Write the names of the foods and drinks in the chart. Are they for breakfast, lunch, or dinner? Add more foods to each list. Answers will vary.

Breakfast	Lunch	Dinner
eggs orange juice, milk, cereal pancakes	hamburger, hot dog, french fries, salad, soda, sandwich, egg roll, taco	spaghetti, taco, soup, salad, beans, rice, rice, hamburger

B. Talk to a partner about what he or she eats. Write the information. Answers will vary.

1. What do you eat for breakfast? _____

2. What do you eat for lunch? _____

3. What do you eat for dinner? _____

C. Write what you like to eat. Answers will vary.

Breakfast	Lunch	Dinner

D. Complete the sentences. Answers will vary.

1. I _____ like toast _____ for breakfast.

2. My partner _____ for breakfast.

3. I _____ for lunch.

4. My partner _____ for lunch.

5. I _____ for dinner.

6. My partner _____ for dinner.

AT-A-GLANCE PREP

Goal: All unit goals
Grammar: All unit grammar
Academic Strategies: Reviewing, evaluating, developing study skills
Vocabulary: All unit vocabulary

Agenda

☐ Discuss unit goals.
☐ Complete the review.
☐ Evaluate and reflect on progress.

Pacing

■ 1.5 hour classes   ■ 2.5 hour classes
■ 3+ hour classes

STANDARDS CORRELATIONS

CCRS: RI1, RI7, RI9, L4, RF3
CASAS: 0.1.2, 1.1.3, 1.1.7, 1.2.1, 1.2.2, 1.2.4, 2.6.4
SCANS: **Information** Acquire and evaluate information, organize and maintain information
Basic Skills Reading, writing, speaking
Personal Qualities Responsibility, self-management
EFF: Speak so others can understand
Lifelong Learning Take responsibility for learning, reflect and evaluate

Warm-up and Review   7–10 mins. ■■■

Ask individuals what they like to eat. Make a list on the board of all the vocabulary students can come up with from the unit.

Introduction   5 mins. ■■■

Write all the goals on the board from Unit 3. Show students the first page of every lesson so they understand that today will be review of the entire unit. Complete the agenda.

Note: Depending on the length of the term, you may decide to have students do Practice for homework and then review student work as either the warm-up or another class activity.

Presentation   10–15 mins. ■■■

This presentation will cover the first three pages of the review. Quickly go to the first page of each lesson. Discuss the goal of each. Ask simple questions to remind students of what they have learned.

Practice   15–20 mins. ■■

A. Write the names of the foods and drinks in the chart. Are they for breakfast, lunch, or dinner? Add more foods to each list. (Lessons 1–5)

B. Talk to a partner about what he or she eats. Write the information. (Lessons 1–5)

C. Write what you like to eat. (Lessons 1–5)

D. Complete the sentences. (Lesson 1)

BEST PRACTICE

Recycling/Review

The review and the project that follows are part of the recycling/review process. Students at this level often need to be reintroduced to concepts to solidify what they have learned. Many concepts are learned and forgotten while learning other new concepts. This is because students learn but are not necessarily ready to acquire language concepts.

Therefore, it becomes very important to review and to show students how to review on their own. It is also important to recycle the new concepts in different contexts.

INSTRUCTOR'S NOTES

_____

_____

_____

_____

_____

_____

_____

Practice *(continued)*

E. Read the advertisement. (Lesson 2)

F. Complete the chart. Use the information from Exercise E. (Lesson 2)

G. Ask a partner questions about the advertisement in Exercise E. Ask: *How much is …?* or *How much are …?* (Lesson 2)

H. Look at Sebastian's shopping list. What does he need? Write sentences. (Lesson 3)

Learner Log

I can express needs and quantities.   I can compare prices.

☐ Yes   ☐ No   ☐ Maybe   ☐ Yes   ☐ No   ☐ Maybe

E. Read the advertisement.

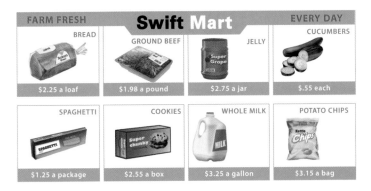

F. Complete the chart. Use the information from Exercise E.

Product	Container or Quantity	Price
bread	a loaf	$2.25
ground beef	a pound	$1.98
jelly	a jar	$2.75
cucumbers	each	$.55
spaghetti	a package	$1.25
cookies	a box	$2.55
milk	a gallon	$3.25
potato chips	a bag	$3.15

G. Ask a partner questions about the advertisement in Exercise E. Ask: *How much is . . . ?* **or** *How much are . . . ?*

H. Look at Sebastian's shopping list. What does he need? Write sentences.

Shopping List

6 bottles of water

1 jar of peanut butter

2 pounds of tomatoes

1 gallon of milk

1. Sebastian _____needs_____ six bottles of water.

2. _____He needs a jar of peanut butter._____

3. _____He needs two pounds of tomatoes._____

4. _____He needs a gallon of milk._____

Rudolf's Café

Lunch Menu

SANDWICHES

Ham.. $2.75
Tuna... $2.75
Hamburger................................... $3.50

SIDE ORDERS

Salad.. $1.98
Soup... $1.75
French fries................................. $1.50

BEVERAGES

Soda... $1.50
Milk.. $1.00
Coffee... $1.50

ALLEN'S Home Cooking

Lunch Menu

SANDWICHES

Turkey.. $3.50
Cheese.. $2.25
Hamburger................................... $3.95

SIDE ORDERS

Salad.. $2.75
French fries................................. $1.95

BEVERAGES

Soda... $2.00
Milk.. $1.25
Coffee... $2.00

I. Read the menu. Circle *R* for Rudolf's Café or *A* for Allen's Home Cooking.

1. Which is cheaper—a hamburger at Rudolf's Café or at Allen's Home Cooking?   Ⓡ   A

2. Which is more expensive—a salad at Rudolf's or at Allen's?   R   Ⓐ

3. Which is cheaper—coffee at Rudolf's or at Allen's?   Ⓡ   A

4. Which is more expensive—soda at Rudolf's or at Allen's?   R   Ⓐ

J. Answer the questions about you and a partner. *Answers will vary.*

1. Do you like pizza? _____Yes, I do._____

2. Do you eat hamburgers? _____

3. Do you eat egg rolls? _____

4. Do you make tuna fish sandwiches? _____

5. Does your partner like pizza? _____

6. Does your partner eat hamburgers? _____

7. Does your partner eat egg rolls? _____

8. Does your partner make tuna fish sandwiches? _____

Practice (continued)

I. Read the menu. Circle *R* for Rudolf's Café or *A* for Allen's Home Cooking. (Lessons 4 and 5)

J. Answer the questions about you and a partner. (Lesson 5)

Evaluation   15 mins. ■■■

Go around the room and check on students' progress. Help individuals when needed. If you see consistent errors among several students, interrupt the class and give a mini lesson or review to help students feel comfortable with the concept.

MULTILEVEL WORKSHEETS

Unit 3, Computer Worksheets

Unit 3, Internet Worksheets

Presentation   5 mins. ■■■

Learner Log

Review the concepts in the Learner Log. Make sure students understand the concepts and how to do the log including circling the answers, finding page numbers where the concept is taught, and ranking favorite activities.

BEST PRACTICE

Learner Logs

Learner Logs function to help students in many different ways.

1. They serve as part of the review process.
2. They help students to gain confidence and to document what they have learned. Consequently, students see that they are progressing in their learning.
3. They provide students with a tool that they can use over and over to check and recheck their understanding of the target language. In this way, students become independent learners.

Practice   10–15 mins. ■

Ask students to do the Learner Log.

Evaluation   2 mins. ■

Go over the Learner Log with students.

Application   5–7 mins. ■■■

Use the Stand Out 1 Assessment CD-ROM with ExamView® to create a post-test for Unit 3.

Refer students to *Stand Out* 1 Workbook, Unit 3, Lesson 1 for more practice with the negative simple present and Lesson 4 for more practice with comparative adjectives.

Go to the *Activity Bank* online for suggestions on promoting digital literacy and using the Internet to enhance this lesson.

INSTRUCTOR'S NOTES

Combine ideas and information; Manage money; Make decisions; Exercise leadership roles; Complete tasks as assigned; Interact appropriately with team members; Interpret and communicate information.

STANDARDS CORRELATIONS

CCRS: RI7, SL1, SL2

CASAS: 0.1.2, 1.1.3, 1.1.7, 1.2.1, 1.2.2, 1.2.4, 2.6.4, 4.8.1

SCANS: **Resources** Allocate time, allocate materials and facility resources, allocate human resources

Information Acquire and evaluate information, organize and maintain information, interpret and communicate information

Interpersonal Participate as a member of a team, teach others, exercise leadership, negotiate to arrive at a decision, work with cultural diversity

Systems Understand systems, monitor and correct performance

Basic Skills Reading, writing, listening, speaking

Thinking Skills Think creatively, make decisions, solve problems, see things in the mind's eye

Personal Qualities Responsibility, sociability, self-management

EFF: **Communication** Read with understanding, convey ideas in writing, speak so others can understand, listen actively, observe critically

Decision Making Solve problems and make decisions, plans

Interpersonal Cooperate with others, advocate and influence, resolve conflict and negotiate, guide others

Lifelong Learning Take responsibility for learning, reflect and evaluate

Introduction
5 mins.

TEAM PROJECT

Create a menu for a new restaurant

In this project, students will create a menu and an advertisement for a new restaurant.

Stage 1
15–20 mins.

COLLABORATE **Form a team with four or five students.**

Help students form groups and assign positions in their groups. On the spot, students will have to choose who will be the leader of their group. Review the responsibility of a leader and ask students to write the name of their leader in their books. Do the same with the remaining positions: advertising agent, chef, and trainers. Every member of each group should have a responsibility.

Stage 2
10–15 mins.

Choose a name for your restaurant.

Tell students that their group is a family and that they have a family restaurant. Ask them to choose a name for their restaurant and the foods that they might serve.

Stages 3 and 4
30–40 mins.

Make a list of foods your restaurant serves and design a menu.

The team works together to choose foods and design a menu. Make sure that groups divide their menus into sections. There is a worksheet that can serve as a template for this activity on the Multilevel Worksheets Activity Bank. (Unit 3, Project, Worksheet 2)

Stages 5 and 6
40–60 mins.

Create an advertisement for your restaurant, giving some prices. Then, create a conversation.

Ask teams to make an advertisement with their restaurant's prices. There is a worksheet that can serve as a template for this activity on the Multilevel Worksheets Activity Bank (Unit 3, Project, Worksheet 1). Have them prepare a conversation to present to the class. All members need to participate in the presentation.

Stage 7
30–40 mins.

Present your conversation and menu to the class.

Consider videotaping the presentations. Students will prepare better if they know they will be videotaped. Another approach would be to have students videotape themselves and polish their presentations after they have viewed the recorded presentation.

Stage 8
5–10 mins.

Compare prices on your menu with prices from other teams' menus.

Ask teams to compare and contrast the prices of items on their menus.

MULTILEVEL WORKSHEETS

Unit 3, Project, Worksheet 1: Restaurant Advertisement

Unit 3, Project, Worksheet 2: Menu Template

Unit 3, Extension, Worksheet 1: Recipes

Unit 3, Extension, Worksheet 2: Count and Noncount Nouns

BEST PRACTICE

Digital literacy

Projects are a perfect place for students to use other forms of presentations beyond pictures they create. Digital literacy is more necessary now as a life skill. Encourage students to create presentations using pictures from the Internet. They might also consider using other digital presentation tools.

✔ # Create a menu for a new restaurant

In this project, you will create a menu for a new restaurant (including foods and prices) and an advertisement for your restaurant. You will also write a conversation between a server and customers in your restaurant as the server takes their orders.

1. **COLLABORATE** Form a team with four or five students. In your team, you need:

Position	Job description	Student name
Student 1: **Team Leader**	Check that everyone speaks English. Check that everyone participates.	
Student 2: **Advertising Agent**	With help from the team, make an advertisement for your restaurant with a few prices.	
Student 3: **Chef**	With help from the team, write a list of foods for the menu. Design the menu.	
Students 4/5: **Trainers**	With help from the team, write a conversation between a server and customers in a restaurant.	

2. Choose a name for your restaurant.

3. Make a list of foods your restaurant serves.

4. Design a menu.

5. Create an advertisement for your restaurant, giving some prices.

6. Create a conversation.

7. Present your conversation and menu to the class.

8. Compare prices on your menu with prices from other teams' menus.

READING CHALLENGE

About the Explorer

Tristram Stuart is an author and campaigner. Through his various campaigns, he is raising awareness about the amount of food that is wasted by supermarkets and restaurants. Tristram claims that companies waste food because of the way it looks. This food—one-third of what the world produces—can be used to feed the one billion hungry people in the world. Tristram has started a number of different campaigns to bring this issue to people's attention.

About the Photo

This photo was taken during a Feeding the 5000 event in London's Trafalgar Square. During the event, 5000 people were given a free lunch, which was made entirely from food wasted by supermarkets. Since the first Feeding the 5000 event in 2009, people in different cities all around the world have had a free lunch. At some events, celebrity chefs have helped prepared the food. These mass feedings have not only fed people, but also brought together local businesses to help highlight the global problem of food waste.

- Write the title, *Eat What You Buy,* on the board. Then, have students discuss as a class what they think this means.
- Ask students to look at the photo and introduce the explorer, Tristram Stuart.
- Ask volunteers to describe what they see in the photo. Then, ask students what they can tell you about Tristram from what they see.
- Ask a volunteer to read the quote out loud. Then, have the class discuss how they think this quote relates to the title.

READING CHALLENGE

EXPLORER TRISTRAM STUART

Eat What You Buy

"Use your power as customer and citizen to demand that the businesses you buy from also stop wasting food."
—Tristam Stuart

A. ANALYZE Study the charts and answer the questions.

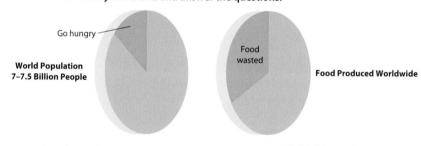

Go hungry

World Population 7–7.5 Billion People

Food wasted

Food Produced Worldwide

1. According to the graphs, how many people are in the world? <u>7–7.5 billion people</u>
2. According to the graphs, how many people need food but don't have it? <u>one seventh</u>
3. According to the graphs, what percentage of food is wasted?
   a. one quarter is wasted   (b. one third is wasted)   c. one half is wasted

82 Unit 3

CCRS FOR READING

RI1, RI2, RI7, RI10

B. **PREDICT** What do you think Tristram Stuart talks about? *Answers will vary.*

C. **Read about Tristram Stuart.**

> Tristram Stuart is an author. He wants people to know that food is important in the world. He says one third of fresh food is wasted every year. Supermarkets don't sell some food because it doesn't look perfect. People throw away food every day, too.
>
> One billion people go hungry every day. Tristram works hard to help people understand that wasting food is very serious. For example, in Portugal, a project called *"Ugly Fruit"* sells fruit that supermarkets don't want. In London and many other places, *"Feeding the 5000"* is a large community party where everyone eats good food that supermarkets don't sell. Tristram wants to help people have food to eat everywhere in the world.

D. **Circle *True* or *False*.**

1. Wasting food is not serious.	True	(False)
2. 5000 people go hungry every day.	True	(False)
3. Some supermarkets only sell food that looks perfect.	(True)	False

E. **CREATE** In a group, create a plan. What comes first? Number the ideas 1–4.

Plan to Avoid Food Waste

_4_ Eat leftovers.

_1_ Carefully plan meals.

_2_ Go shopping more and buy less food.

_3_ Cook only what you need.

F. **APPLY** As a class, add other ideas to avoid waste. *Answers will vary.*

_____

_____

_____

_____

_____

Reading Challenge 83

A. **ANALYZE** Study the charts and answer the questions.

Ask students to answer the questions based on the information they study in the charts.

B. **PREDICT** What do you think Tristram Stuart talks about?

Ask students to guess what Tristram Stuart talks about.

C. **Read about Tristram Stuart.**

Have students read the passage about Tristram.

D. **Circle *True* or *False*.**

- Ask students to read each sentence and then circle *true* or *false*.
- Tell students to refer back to the reading to check their answers.
- Review answers as a class.

E. **CREATE** In a group, create a plan. What comes first? Number the ideas 1–4.

- Have students form small groups. Tell them they will work together to create a plan.
- Read the section title, *Plan to Avoid Food Waste,* to the class. Ask, *What comes first?*
- Explain to students that they will discuss and number the ideas 1–4 for their plan.
- Have groups share their plans with other groups.

F. **APPLY** As a class, add other ideas to avoid waste.

Ask groups to add other ideas to avoid waste to their plans. Discuss as a class.

READING STRATEGIES

Visualization

A reader always uses a fair amount of imagery. In order for the reading to be understood, it needs us to create pictures in our minds. Visualization is not just what our eyes see, but how we imagine something smells, tastes, or sounds, and our feelings about what we are reading as well. These elements personalize and make the reading more engaging.

Housing

About the Photo

This photo was taken by landscape and travel photographer Francesco Riccardo Lacomino. It shows the famous Painted Ladies of San Francisco. The term *Painted Lady* is given to Victorian- and Edwardian-style homes that are painted in three different colors. This particular row of houses, located on Steiner Street, attracts many tourists who visit the area because of the view of the city behind the houses. Many US tourists know the houses from a popular TV show.

- Introduce the unit by reading the title. Ask students to look at the photo. Tell them that this is the city of San Francisco.

- Ask students if San Francisco is a large city. Then, have students discuss the different kinds of housing we might find in large cities.

- Ask a volunteer to read the caption out loud. Ask students to look at the photo again and answer the questions. Discuss as a class.

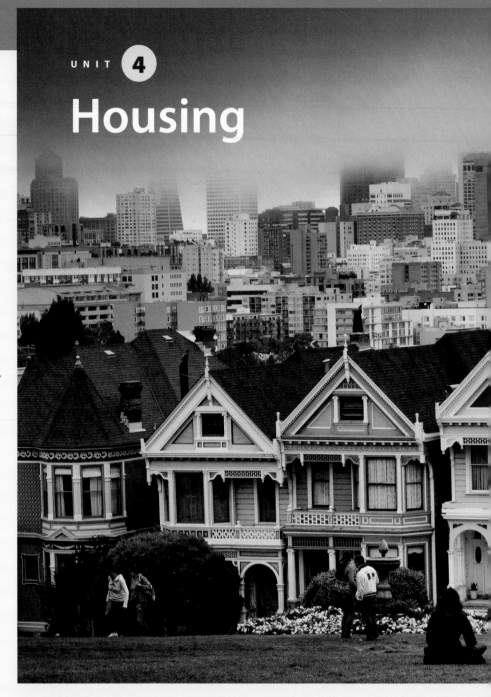

UNIT 4

Housing

UNIT OUTCOMES	GRAMMAR	VOCABULARY	EL CIVICS
• Identify types of housing • Describe parts of a home • Interpret classified ads • Use the telephone and make appointments • Identify furniture in a house	• Simple present: *live* • *a/an* • Simple present: have • *Yes/No* questions • Present continuous • Prepositions of location	• Housing • Parts of a home • Classified ads • Appointments • Furniture	The skills students learn in this unit can be applied to the following EI Civics competency areas: • Consumer Economics • Housing

People in San Francisco call these houses the "painted ladies". They are colorful and make the city look pretty.

Life Skills Link

In the unit, students will learn how to identify different types of housing and different parts of a house. They will also learn how to research homes, look at classified ads, and make appointments for viewing homes.

Workplace Link

All lessons and units in *Stand Out* include basic communication skills and interpersonal skills important for the workplace. They are not individually identified. Other workplace skills are indicated. They include *collecting and organizing information, making decisions and solving problems,* and *combining ideas and information.*

UNIT OUTCOMES

- Identify types of housing
- Describe parts of a home
- Interpret classified ads
- Use the telephone and make appointments
- Identify furniture in a house

Look at the photo and answer the questions.

1. What kind of buildings are in the picture?
2. Do you want to live in a big city?
3. Who lives in these houses?

CASAS	SCANS	CCRS
Lesson 1: 1.1.3, 1.4.1	Most SCANS are incorporated into this unit, with an emphasis on:	RI1, RI2, RI5, RI7, W2, SL1, SL2, SL4, L1, L2, L4, L5, RF2, RF3
Lesson 2: 1.1.3, 1.4.1, 4.8.1, 7.2.3	• Acquiring and evaluating information	
Lesson 3: 1.4.2	• Creative thinking	
Lesson 4: 1.4.2	• Seeing things in the mind's eye	
Lesson 5: 1.4.1, 1.4.2, 2.2.1	(Technology is optional.)	
Review: 1.4.1, 1.4.2		
Team Project: 1.4.1, 1.4.2, 4.8.1		

LESSON A house or an apartment?

GOAL ▮ Identify types of housing

A. INTERPRET Read the web page and underline the information.

1. name of the real estate company

2. phone number

3. name of the salesperson

4. type of housing

Corbin Real Estate
Find your dream home in one week!

Find the perfect home in beautiful Corbin. We can help you move in to the home that fits your budget. We deal with <u>large homes</u>, <u>small starters</u>, <u>condominiums</u>, and <u>mobile homes</u>. Stop by our offices today or call for an appointment.

John Green
Sales Associate

Phone: 555-3726
Visit us: 7821 Main Street
Corbin, CA 97811

B. INTERPRET Study the pie chart about housing in Corbin. Listen and write the numbers.

CD 1
TR 41

Housing Statistics: Corbin, CA

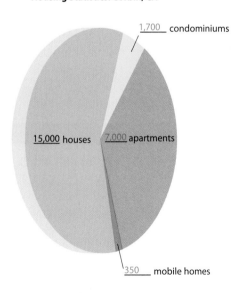

1,700 condominiums

15,000 houses   7,000 apartments

350 mobile homes

C. Complete the chart with the information from Exercise B.

Type of housing	Number of units
	15,000
	1,700
	7,000
	350
Toal number of housing units:	24,050

AT-A-GLANCE PREP

Goal: Identify types of housing
Grammar: Simple present: *live, a/an*
Pronunciation: /v/
Academic Strategies: Pie charts, focused listening
Vocabulary: Housing vocabulary

Agenda

- Give personal information.
- Read a pie chart.
- Use the simple present.
- Talk about housing.
- Write a paragraph.
- Complete a pie chart.

Resources

Multilevel Worksheets: Unit 4, Lesson 1,
  Worksheets 1–2
Workbook: Unit 4, Lesson 1
Audio: CD 1, Track 41
Heinle Picture Dictionary: Housing, pages 62–81
Stand Out 1 Assessment CD-ROM with ExamView®

Pacing

- 1.5 hour classes ■ 2.5 hour classes
- 3+ hour classes

STANDARDS CORRELATIONS

CCRS: RI1, RI7, W2, SL2, SL4, L1, L2
CASAS: 1.1.3, 1.4.1
SCANS: **Information** Acquire and evaluate information, interpret and communicate information
Basic Skills Reading, writing, listening, speaking
Thinking Skills See things in the mind's eye
EFF: **Communication** Read with understanding, convey ideas in writing, speak so others can understand, listen actively

Preassessment *(optional)* ■■■

Use the Stand Out 1 Assessment Activity Bank with ExamView® to create a pretest for Unit 4.

Warm-up and Review   10–15 mins. ■■■

Ask students what city they live in. Pass out index cards to every student. Have them write their address, city, and native country on the card. Make sure they don't write their names on the cards.

Explain that students who don't want to write their addresses may write *Private Information*.

Collect the cards and randomly pass them out to all students. Ask students to find the author of the card by asking the *yes/no* questions that you have written on the board:

1. *Is your address (address)?*
2. *Do you live in (city)?*
3. *Are you from (native country)?*

Show students how to answer the *yes/no* questions:
1. *Yes, it is.* or *No, it's not.* 2. *Yes, I do.* or *No, I don't.*
3. *Yes, I am.* or *No, I'm not.*

Introduction   5 mins. ■■■

Survey students to find out who lives in an apartment, a house, or a condominium. State the goal: *Today, we will identify types of housing.*

Presentation 1   30–45 mins. ■■■

Ask students how many people live in your town or city. Ask if it is a big or little city or town. Then, ask about the size of their city or town in their native country.

Help students understand the pie chart. Make a simplified pie chart on the board. Draw a line through the middle to indicate 50% and then another to show 25%. If time permits, make a more complex pie chart that shows 10%, 20%, 30%, and 40%.

Make sure students understand what houses, condominiums, apartments, and mobile homes are.

Students need to understand that they will listen for specific words (*house, condominium, apartment,* or *mobile home*) and the numbers associated with the words. They don't need to understand all the vocabulary in the listening.

A. INTERPRET **Read the web page and underline the information.**

B. INTERPRET **Study the pie chart about housing in Corbin. Listen and write the numbers.**

Note: Listening script CD 1 TR 41 is on page 87a.

Evaluation 1   5 mins. ■■■

C. Complete the chart with the information from Exercise B.

Presentation 2   20–30 mins. ■■■

D. Study the chart with your classmates and teacher.

Review the simple present tense with students. Focus on the third-person singular *s*. First, do a choral drill where students repeat what you say. Next, do a transformation drill where you say a sentence, perhaps in the first person, and then give students a different pronoun to use in place of the pronoun you used.

When you feel comfortable with the students' grasp of the structure, introduce the pronunciation.

PRONUNCIATION

/v/

There are many ways to teach /v/. Remember that many languages don't have this sound. Some have similar sounds but are not written with the letter *v*, which often causes confusion.

One approach is to teach the articulation points. Use the diagram in the book, which shows the top teeth over the bottom lip. This is not completely sufficient, however, because the same articulation points are used to create /f/.

Many students will already be able to pronounce an /f/ because many languages have this sound. Also, romance languages write it the same way. Ask students to pronounce an /f/ sound and attach a word to it such as *Frank*, *farm*, or even *pharmacy*. Ask students to put two fingers on their voice boxes and have them vibrate it as when they pronounce /m/. Then, ask them to do the same with /f/.

E. Read about the students and their homes.

Continue your presentation of the verb chart in Exercise D by asking specific questions about the three students in this exercise.

Prepare students to practice the conversation in Exercise F by using the steps mentioned in previous lessons:

1. Teacher reads; students repeat.
2. Teacher is Saud; students are Tien.
3. Teacher is Tien; students are Saud.
4. Teacher is Saud; student volunteer is Tien.
5. Teacher is Tien; student volunteer is Saud.
6. Student volunteer is Saud; another student volunteer is Tien.

Also, work on the rhythm of the sentences and questions. Remind students about the use of indefinite articles.

Practice 2   15–20 mins. ■■

F. Practice the conversation. Then, make new conversations with information from Exercise E.

BEST PRACTICE

Conversation

In *Stand Out*, we have suggested a few ways to do these substitution practices, including the following:

- Students work in pairs.
- Students use conversation or substitution cards.
- Students practice the conversation in an inside/outside circle activity.

Sometimes inside/outside circle activities take up too much room in the class. If this is the case, try forming two lines in the class that face one another. Students pair up with the person across from them. After students have practiced the conversation at least one time, ask one line to shift. The student at one end of the line will go to the other end of the line.

Evaluation 2   5–7 mins. ■■

Ask volunteers to demonstrate the conversation in front of the class.

D. Study the chart with your classmates and teacher.

Simple Present: *Live*		
Subject	**Verb**	**Example sentence**
I, You, We, They	live	I **live** in a house. You **live** in an apartment. We **live** in a condominium. They **live** in a mobile home.
He, She, It	lives	He **lives** in a house. She **lives** in an apartment.

NOTICE

/v/   live

E. Read about the students and their homes.

Saud

Housing: house

Address: 2323 Hartford Rd.

City: Corbin

State: California

Silvia

Housing: mobile home

Address: 13 Palm Ave.

City: Corbin

State: California

Tien

Housing: apartment

Address: 15092 Arbor Lane #22

City: Corbin

State: California

F. Practice the conversation. Then, make new conversations with information from Exercise E.

Saud: Do you live in a house, an apartment, or a condominium?

Tien: I live in <u>an apartment</u>.

Saud: Where do you live?

Tien: My address is <u>15092 Arbor Lane #22</u>.

Saud: Where does Silvia live?

Tien: She lives at <u>13 Palm Ave.</u>

Saud: That's close by.

A /AN

a house

an apartment

WORKPLACE CONNECTION
Exercise I: Interpret and communicate information.
Exercise J: Interact appropriately with team members; Combine ideas and information.

G. INTERPRET Read the paragraph.

> Felipe and his sister are from Argentina. Felipe lives in a condominium in Corbin, California. His sister also lives in Corbin. She lives in an apartment. Felipe's brothers live in a small house in Los Angeles. Their parents live in a condominium in Argentina.

H. Write your own paragraph. Use the paragraph in Exercise G as a model. Then, talk with a partner. Write a new paragraph about your partner.

I. SURVEY Ask four classmates what type of housing they live in. Share your information with the class. Answers will vary.

Name	Type of housing
Saud	Saud lives in a house.

J. CREATE Combine your information from Exercise I with the rest of the class and create a pie chart. Answers will vary depending on answers to Exercise I.

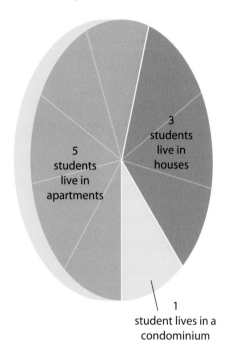

5 students live in apartments

3 students live in houses

1 student lives in a condominium

Presentation 3
10–15 mins. ■■■

Write a paragraph about yourself or someone you know on the board. Here is an example:

Mary is from Portugal. She lives in an apartment. Her parents live in Lisbon, Portugal. They live in a condominium.

Study the paragraph with students. Show them the third-person singular *s* and the third-person plural with no *s*.

G. INTERPRET Read the paragraph.

You may choose to have student volunteers read this paragraph out loud to the class.

Practice 3
20–30 mins. ■

H. Write your own paragraph. Use the paragraph in Exercise G as a model. Then, talk with a partner. Write a new paragraph about your partner.

Students will mostly use the format you have given them on the board and from the book. It will take some students a long time to do this activity.

BEST PRACTICE

Student writing

Depending on your personal preference and purpose, you may want to do one of two things with student writing in a practice like this one.

One idea would be to give students a certain amount of time. Once that time is up, collect all work whether students have finished or not. This method will provide you with a sense of the true level of students' writing and you can adjust your teaching appropriately.

Another way would be to ask all students to take time at home to do the activity and turn it in the next class period. This will get you more polished work and students may learn a lot laboring over it. However, unless you give grades, you may not get a writing sample back from each student.

Evaluation 3
5–7 mins. ■

Ask a few students who have completed their work to read their paragraphs out loud, or collect the paragraphs and look them over.

Application
10–15 mins. ■■■

I. SURVEY Ask four classmates what type of housing they live in. Share your information with the class.

After they complete the chart for four classmates, ask students to talk to more classmates or to look at someone else's chart to get the information for other classmates.

J. CREATE Combine your information from Exercise I with the rest of the class and create a pie chart.

Refer students to *Stand Out 1 Workbook,* Unit 4, Lesson 1 for more practice with the simple present and prepositions.

Go to the *Activity Bank* online for suggestions on promoting digital literacy and using the Internet to enhance this lesson.

MULTILEVEL WORKSHEETS

Lesson 1, Worksheet 1: Housing

Lesson 1, Worksheet 2: Simple Present: *Live*

INSTRUCTOR'S NOTES

_____

_____

_____

_____

_____

_____

_____

_____

_____

_____

_____

_____

Goal: Describe parts of a home
Grammar: Simple present: *have*
Academic Strategies: Focused listening, classifying
Vocabulary: Parts of a home

Agenda

☐ Make a pie chart.

☐ Listen for number of bedrooms and bathrooms.

☐ Describe what people do.

☐ Learn about the parts of a home.

☐ Ask questions about your partner's home.

Resources

Multilevel Worksheets: Unit 4, Lesson 2, Worksheets 1–2
Reading and Writing Challenge: Unit 4
Workbook: Unit 4, Lesson 2
Audio: CD 1, Tracks 42–45
Heinle Picture Dictionary: Housing, pages 68–75
Stand Out 1 Assessment CD-ROM with ExamView®

Pacing

■ 1.5 hour classes ■ 2.5 hour classes
■ 3⁺ hour classes

STANDARDS CORRELATIONS

CCRS: SL1, SL2, SL4, L1, L2, L4, RF3

CASAS: 1.1.3, 1.4.1, 4.8.1, 7.2.3

SCANS: **Resources** Allocate materials and facility resources

Information Acquire and evaluate information, organize and maintain information

Interpersonal Participate as a member of a team, teach others

Basic Skills Listening, speaking

Thinking Skills See things in the mind's eye

EFF: **Communication** Speak so others can understand, listen actively

Decision Making Solve problems and make decisions

Interpersonal Cooperate with others, advocate and influence, resolve conflict and negotiate

Warm-up and Review   15–20 mins. ■■■

Make a pie chart on the board or distribute the pie chart template from the Multilevel Worksheets Activity Bank. Take a class poll and make a pie chart of the housing everyone in the class lives in.

Introduction   10–15 mins. ■■■

Ask students to write all the rooms in a home they can think of. Don't allow dictionary use; the idea is

to see what students already know. State the goal: *Today, we will describe parts of a home.*

Presentation 1   30–45 mins. ■■■

A. PREDICT Look at the picture. Where is Saud? Why is he there?

Look at the picture with students. Ask the questions in the direction line.

B. Look at the floor plan. Answer the questions.

Ask students how many bathrooms and bedrooms they see.

Practice 1   5–7 mins. ■■■

C. Listen and take notes. Complete the chart.

Play the recording a few times. If students have trouble, play each conversation separately and check the answers together. Review the principles of focused listening. Students only need to listen for the number of *bedrooms* and *bathrooms* that are needed.

LISTENING SCRIPT   CD 1 TR 42–45

1. **Saud:** *I'm looking for a house to rent for my family.*
   Agent: *Would you please sit down?*
   Saud: *Thank you.*
   Agent: *How many bedrooms do you need?*
   Saud: *I need three bedrooms and one bathroom.*
   Agent: *I think we can help you.*
2. **Silvia:** *We're interested in a nice apartment in the city.*
   Agent: *I'm sure we can help you. This one has two bedrooms and two bathrooms. Is that OK?*
   Silvia: *Maybe. What's the rent?*
   Agent: *It's only $850 a month.*
   Silvia: *$850 a month? This is going to be more difficult than I thought.*
3. **Tien:** *Do you have any properties for a big family?*
   Agent: *Well, let's see.*
   Tien: *I think I need a house with four bedrooms.*
   Agent: *To buy or rent?*
   Tien: *To rent, I think. How much are the rentals here?*
   Agent: *We have one here with two bathrooms for $1,300 a month.*
   Tien: *Can we go out and look at it?*
   Agent: *Yes, of course.*
4. **Felipe:** *What do you have in terms of one-bedroom apartments?*
   Agent: *We have a one-bedroom apartment on Sycamore Street.*
   Felipe: *That looks great. How much is the rent?*
   Agent: *It's $750 a month, plus utilities.*
   Felipe: *Is it one bathroom, too?*
   Agent: *That's right, one bathroom and one bedroom.*

LESSON ② Does it have a yard?

GOAL ▢ Describe parts of a home

WORKPLACE CONNECTION
Exercise C: Collect and organize information.

A. PREDICT Look at the picture. Where is Saud? Why is he there?

B. Look at the floor plan. Answer the questions.

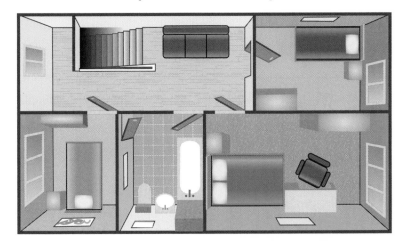

1. How many bedrooms are there? _____3_____

2. How many bathrooms are there? _____1_____

C. Listen and take notes. Complete the chart.

CD 1
TR 42-45

Name	Bedrooms	Bathrooms
1. Saud	3	1
2. Silvia	2	2
3. Tien	4	2
4. Felipe	1	1

D. Study the words with your classmates and teacher.

| bedroom | bathroom | kitchen | dining room | living room |

E. Where in a home do people do these things? With a group, write the names of the rooms. Use the words from the box above.

Activity		Room
People sleep in this room.		bedroom
People take showers in this room.		bathroom
People watch TV in this room.		living room
People eat dinner in this room.		dining room
People make dinner in this room.		kitchen

F. IDENTIFY Practice the conversation. Make new conversations. Talk with a partner.

Student A: Where do people make breakfast?
Student B: People make breakfast in the kitchen.

1. Where do people sleep?
2. Where do people take showers?
3. Where do people watch TV?
4. Where do people eat dinner?
5. Where do people make dinner?

Evaluation 1

3–5 mins. ■■■

Go over the answers as a class.

Presentation 2

10–15 mins. ■■■

In Presentation and Practice 2, you will go over the principle vocabulary. In Presentation and Practice 3, you will expand the vocabulary.

Write on the board: *I have two bedrooms and one bathroom.* Then, ask students to guess how many kitchens, living rooms, and dining rooms you have. Write *I have one kitchen.*

PRONUNCIATION

Distinguishing words

Sometimes comparing one word with another word with only one or two distinguishing factors can help students hear the difference between two words. One way to drill students is to write the two words on opposite ends of the board. Ask students to point at each word when they hear it. Say the words randomly and see how many students have caught on. Then, say the words in sentences and, finally, in a paragraph. Try this with *bedroom* and *bathroom*.

D. **Study the words with your classmates and teacher.**

E. **Where in a home do people do these things? With a group, write the names of the rooms. Use the words from the box above.**

Students should work in groups to complete this activity because it may be too challenging for individual work. After the groups have finished the task, discuss the vocabulary, including *sleep*, *shower*, *watch*, *oven*, *dining room set*, etc.

Next, go over the questions in Exercise F and help students to prepare to do the activity. Ask the questions and help students answer.

Practice 2

15–20 mins. ■■

F. **IDENTIFY Practice the conversation. Make new conversations. Talk with a partner.**

BEST PRACTICE

Conversation

We have now suggested four ways to do these substitution practices including:

• Students work in pairs.
• Students use conversation or substitution cards.
• Students practice the conversation in an inside/outside circle activity.
• Students work in two lines, which face each other.

Sometimes, it works to do a conversation chain. Do this activity in a group of four. Ask Student A to ask one question of Student B. Everyone will listen as Student B responds. Then, Student B asks Student C the next question, and so on.

Evaluation 2

■■

At some point during the activity, ask students to cover the top part of the page so they can't see the answers to the questions. Observe how students do.

INSTRUCTOR'S NOTES

_____

_____

_____

_____

_____

_____

_____

_____

_____

_____

_____

_____

_____

_____

_____

Presentation 3

15–20 mins. ▪▪▪

G. Work in groups. Match the letters to the words.

Ask students to first try doing this activity on their own. Give them only five minutes. Then, ask them to work with a partner for five more minutes. Then, ask them to work in a group and complete the task.

Practice 3

10–15 mins. ▪

Write the words *inside* and *outside* on the board. Ask students to identify which items are inside the house and which items are outside. Have students in pairs classify the items on another sheet of paper. You can give students a two-column chart template from the Multilevel Worksheets Activity Bank if you wish.

Evaluation 3

7–10 mins. ▪

Draw the columns on the board and ask volunteers to come to the board and complete the chart.

Application

10–15 mins. ▪▪▪

Before doing this activity, remind students about the forms of *have*.

H. APPLY Ask your partner about his or her home. Then, share what you learned with a group.

Alternative Activity: Ask students to make a Venn diagram with a partner about their rooms at home. Show them how this is done. A template for a Venn diagram is available on the Multilevel Worksheets Activity Bank.

Refer students to Stand *Out 1 Workbook*, Unit 4, Lesson 2 for more practice with have and the simple present.

Go to the *Activity Bank* online for suggestions on promoting digital literacy and using the Internet to enhance this lesson.

MULTILEVEL WORKSHEETS

Templates: Pie Chart

Templates: Two–Column Chart

Templates: Venn Diagram

Unit 4, Lesson 2, Worksheet 1: Do you have a yard?

Unit 4, Lesson 2, Worksheet 2: Rooms in a House

INSTRUCTOR'S NOTES

G. Work in groups. Match the letters to the words.

<u>d</u> stairs   <u>m</u> swimming pool   <u>a</u> bathroom   <u>f</u> family room

<u>g</u> kitchen   <u>j</u> garage   <u>e</u> hall   <u>c</u> balcony

<u>b</u> bedroom   <u>l</u> deck   <u>h</u> front porch   <u>i</u> front yard

<u>n</u> backyard   <u>k</u> driveway

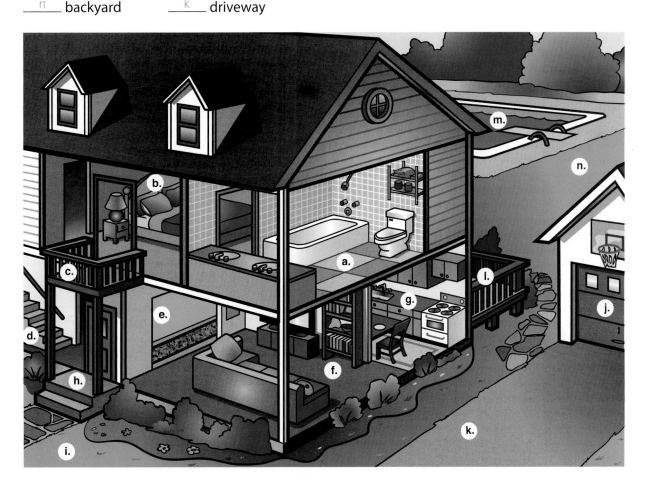

H. APPLY Ask your partner about his or her home. Then, share what you learned with a group.

1. What kind of home do you have?

2. How many bedrooms do you have?

3. How many bathrooms do you have?

4. Do you have a front yard or backyard?

5. Do you have a garage or parking?

6. Do you have a balcony?

> **HAVE**
> I **have** . . .
> He/She **has** . . .

garage

LESSON ③ Look in the newspaper

GOAL ▮ Interpret classified ads   WORKPLACE CONNECTION
Exercises B,C,D: Collect and organize information.

A. PREDICT Look at the picture. What is Saud reading? Why?

B. INTERPRET Read the ads and label each *house, apartment,* or *condominium*.

a.
AVAILABLE

2 bed, 3 bath condo, nr
schools and parks, gated.
Call 454-7899.

___condominium___

b.
HOME FOR RENT

3 bdrm, 2 bath hse,
Cherry Tree Lane,
a/c, garage, pool,
nice neighborhood, utls pd.,
lease $q, 550. Call 995-5555.

___house___

c.
APT. FOR RENT

2br, 2ba apt.,
818 Sundry Cir. #19
2nd fl, furn, balcony.
No pets.
Call 824-7744.

___apartment___

C. Read the classified ads. Write the abbreviations for bedroom and bathroom in the chart.

Bedroom	Bathroom
bed	bath
bdrm	ba
br	

D. Complete the sentences about the classified ads above with information about the number of bedrooms and bathrooms.

1. The house *has* _____three_____ bedrooms and _____two_____ bathrooms.

2. The apartment *has* _____two bedrooms and two bathrooms_____.

3. The condominium _____has two bedrooms and three bathrooms_____.

4. The house _____has_____ two _____bathrooms_____.

Goal: Interpret classified ads
Grammar: *Yes/No* questions
Pronunciation: Intonation: *Yes/No* questions
Academic Strategy: Focused listening
Vocabulary: Classified ads, utilities

Agenda

▢ Complete a Venn diagram.

▢ Interpret classified ads.

▢ Listen to identify ads.

▢ Answer questions about classified ads.

Resources

Multilevel Worksheets: Unit 4, Lesson 3, Worksheets 1–3
Audio: CD 1, Track 46
Reading and Writing Challenge: Unit 4
Workbook: Unit 4, Lesson 3
Heinle Picture Dictionary: Finding a place to live, pages 64–65
Stand Out 1 Assessment CD-ROM with ExamView®

Pacing

■ 1.5 hour classes   ■ 2.5 hour classes
■ 3⁺ hour classes

STANDARDS CORRELATIONS

CCRS: RI1, SL2, SL4, L1, RF2
CASAS: 1.4.2
SCANS: **Information** Acquire and evaluate information, organize and maintain information, interpret and communicate information
Basic Skills Reading, listening, speaking
Thinking Skills Think creatively
EFF: **Communication** Read with understanding, speak so others can understand, listen actively

Warm-up and Review   10–15 mins. ■■■

Ask students to do the application from the previous lesson using the questions on page 91. Provide a blank Venn diagram and ask them to complete it with a different partner than in the previous lesson.

Introduction   5 mins. ■■■

Tell students that you are looking for a new place to live. Ask them where you might go to find housing. Answers might include the newspaper, the Internet, friends, and an agency. State the goal: *Today, we will interpret classified ads.*

Presentation 1   30–40 mins. ■■■

Ask students if they read the newspaper. Write *classified ads* on the board. Ask students if they recognize the words. Tell them that classified ads help people to find jobs, housing, automobiles, and other goods and services. Bring in copies of local classified ads if possible.

BEST PRACTICE

Realia

Using realia is always effective in the ESL classroom. The Lesson Planner doesn't mention realia very often because many teachers are limited in preparation time and resources; however, whenever real objects can be brought to class to help students understand and associate them with target vocabulary, they can be very beneficial.

A. **PREDICT** **Look at the picture. What is Saud reading? Why?**

Ask students to open their books and look at the picture at the top of the page. Answer the questions with students.

B. **INTERPRET** **Read the ads and label each** *house*, *apartment*, **or** *condominium*.

Go over the classified ads with students. Help them to see that they can guess at the meanings of abbreviations.

C. **Read the classified ads. Write the abbreviations for bedroom and bathroom in the chart.**

Practice 1   5–7 mins. ■■■

D. **Complete the sentences about the classified ads above with information about the number of bedrooms and bathrooms.**

Students can do this activity alone or in pairs.

Evaluation 1   7–10 mins. ■■■

Ask volunteers to write the sentences on the board. Insist on uppercase letters at the beginning of sentences and periods at the end.

Presentation 2

12–15 mins. ■■■

Read through the ads with students. Ask pertinent comprehension questions, such as: *Is it a house or an apartment? How many bedrooms does it have?* Write *bed* on the board and ask students what it means. Students may reply that it is what you sleep on. Help them see that, in the ad, *bed* serves as an abbreviation for bedroom. Write *utilities* on the board. Ask students what the word means. Clarify the definition after they answer by discussing the box on the page.

E. Read the classified ad and match the word to its abbreviation.

Ask students to do this activity in pairs. Explain that abbreviations in classified ads are not standard. Show students that both *bed* and *bdrm* can mean *bedroom*.

Then, ask volunteers to read the ads out loud, replacing the abbreviation with the complete word. Ask additional questions to see what students know and understand.

Prepare students for focused listening by giving them clues and seeing if they can identify which ad you are talking about.

BEST PRACTICE

Presentation and practice

There is a distinct difference between presenting new material and practicing it. In the presentation stage, the instructor explains the new material and walks students through all the information they will need later in the practice stage. It is certainly teacher-directed. The classroom can be both student-centered and teacher-directed.

In the practice stage, the instructor allows students to "try out" the new structures and vocabulary, while often making mistakes. The activities are teacher-guided because the teacher prepared and initiated the activity, but they are not totally controlled by the teacher as in the presentation stage.

Practice 2

10–12 mins. ■■

F. Read the classified ads. Then, listen and write the letter.

Play the recording several times. Ask students to list the abbreviations that they see in the ads on a separate sheet of paper. Then, ask them to write out what the abbreviations stand for without looking at the previous page.

LISTENING SCRIPT

🎧 CD 1 TR 46

1. *This apartment is a large three-bedroom apartment with lots of good features. There is a pool. All utilities are paid, and it's near a school. Come and see. You won't be sorry.*
2. *Apartments come and go, but this is the best. It has three bedrooms, and it's only $800 a month. It's on the second floor so you can enjoy a beautiful balcony.*
3. *This great apartment is far from city traffic. Hot summers are no problem. We have air-conditioning, and we pay the electricity. Call Margaret at 555–2672.*
4. *This is a bargain! Seven hundred dollars a month to lease this one-bedroom, one-bath apartment. No pets, please! Call our manager, Fred. He will get you in today! 555–7164.*

If possible, provide students with authentic newspapers. Ask students to find the classified section and then the housing section. Finally, ask them to look at three or four ads and report the content to the class.

Evaluation 2

3 mins. ■■

Go over the answers in Exercise F.

INSTRUCTOR'S NOTES

_____

_____

_____

_____

_____

_____

_____

E. Read the classified ad and match the word to its abbreviation.

APT. FOR RENT

2 bed, 1 bath apt,
818 Sundry Ave., #13
$900, furn, a/c,
all utls pd, 1 mo dep.
Call 555-6294.

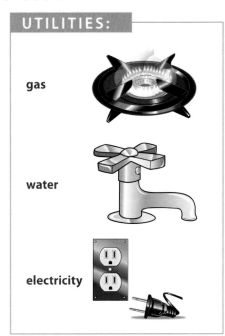

UTILITIES:

gas

water

electricity

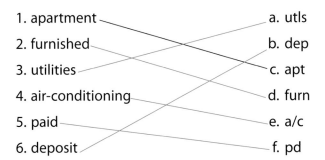

1. apartment   a. utls
2. furnished   b. dep
3. utilities   c. apt
4. air-conditioning d. furn
5. paid   e. a/c
6. deposit   f. pd

F. Read the classified ads. Then, listen and write the letter.

CD 1
TR 46

a.

FOR RENT

3 bed, 2 bath apt,
a/c, balcony,
$800. Call Lien
at 555-1734.

b.

APT. FOR RENT

$700/MONTH
1 bed, 1 bath apt.
No pets.
Call Fred at 555-7164.

c.

FOR RENT

2 bed, 3 bath apt.
a/c, elect. pd.
Call Margaret for
more information-
555-2672.

d.

AVAILABLE

3 bed, 3 bath apt.
w/pool, utls pd.,
nr school.
Call 555-5987.

1. _d_   2. _a_   3. _c_   4. _b_

G. Study the chart with your classmates and teacher.

Yes/No Questions	
Question	Answer
Does it have three bedrooms?	Yes, it does. No, it doesn't.
Does it have air conditioning?	Yes, it does. No, it doesn't.

INTONATION

Yes/No **Questions**

Does it have three bedrooms?

Does it have air conditioning?

H. INTERPRET Read the classified ad and answer the questions.

FOR RENT-CONDO

3 bed, 2 bath condo,
22954 Kensington Place,
a/c, utls pd., lrg yard,
$1,500 a month.
Call Margaret: 555-3452

1. Does the home have four bedrooms? _____No, it doesn't._____

2. Does it have a yard? _____Yes, it does._____

3. Does it have two bathrooms? _____Yes, it does._____

4. Does it have furniture? _____No, it doesn't._____

5. Does it have a balcony? _____No, it doesn't._____

I. Put a check (✓) by things in your home. Share the information with a partner.

Answers will vary.

_____ pets allowed   _____ utilities paid   _____ balcony   _____ garage

_____ air-conditioning   _____ near a school   _____ near a park

J. CREATE Write a classified ad for your home. Use abbreviations.

K. Look in a newspaper or on the Internet to find a home that is good for you.

Presentation 3

15–20 mins. ■■■

Look at the classified ads in Exercise F once again. Ask *yes/no* questions similar to the questions in Exercise H, but don't let students know that you are asking those particular questions. Accept short and long answers.

G. Study the chart with your classmates and teacher.

Review the short answers and ask similar questions about the classified ads on the previous page. Go over the intonation of *yes/no* questions and answers as described in the pronunciation box.

Practice 3

5–7 mins. ■

H. INTERPRET Read the classified ad and answer the questions.

Ask students to do this activity on their own.

Evaluation 3

7–10 mins. ■

Ask volunteers to write their sentences on the board. Be sure to ask other students for help correcting capitalization errors and pointing out where periods are missing.

Have students work with partners and peer-edit their work.

Application

10–15 mins. ■■■

I. Put a check (✓) by things in your home. Share the information with a partner.

Lead students through this activity.

J. CREATE Write a classified ad for your home. Use abbreviations.

K. Look in a newspaper or on the Internet to find a home that is good for you.

Refer students to *Stand Out 1 Workbook*, Unit 4, Lesson 3 for more practice with *yes/no* questions.

Go to the *Activity Bank* online for suggestions on promoting digital literacy and using the Internet to enhance this lesson.

MULTILEVEL WORKSHEETS

Unit 4, Lesson 3, Worksheet 1: Read Classified Ads

Unit 4, Lesson 3, Worksheet 2: Daily News Classifieds

Unit 4, Lesson 3, Worksheet 3: Abbreviations and Ads

INSTRUCTOR'S NOTES

Goal: Use the telephone and make appointments
Grammar: Present continuous
Academic Strategies: Focused listening
Vocabulary: Appointments

Agenda

◼ Ask questions about classified ads.

◼ Learn the steps to finding a home.

◼ Listen and ask for information.

◼ Use the present continuous tense.

Resources

Multilevel Worksheet: Unit 4, Lesson 4, Worksheet 1
Audio: Unit 4, Lesson 4
Audio: CD 1, Tracks 47–50
Heinle Picture Dictionary: Finding a Place to Live, pages 64–65
Stand Out 1 Assessment CD-ROM with ExamView®

Pacing

◼ 1.5 hour classes   ◼ 2.5 hour classes
◼ 3⁺ hour classes

STANDARDS CORRELATIONS

CCRS: SL1, SI2, SL4, L1, L2
CASAS: 1.4.2
SCANS: **Information** Acquire and evaluate information, interpret and communicate information
Basic Skills Writing, listening, speaking
EFF: **Communication** Convey ideas in writing, speak so others can understand, listen actively

Warm-up and Review   10–15 mins. ◼◼◼

Ask students to come up with questions to ask when calling about renting an apartment. Write on the board: *How much is the rent?* Students most likely won't construct such questions correctly, but encourage them to try. Then, write your corrected versions of their questions on the board. Ask students to turn back to Exercise H on page 94 and look at the questions again. Write each question on the board.

Introduction   5 mins. ◼◼◼

Write *classified ads* on the board. Ask students what they should do after they find a home in the classified ads. Accept all answers. State the goal: *Today, we will learn how to use the telephone and make appointments.*

Presentation 1   30–45 mins. ◼◼◼

A. PREDICT Look at the picture. What is Saud doing? Who is he talking to? Then, read about Saud's plan to find a new home.

Look at the picture at the top of the page with students. Ask them what Saud is doing. If they don't say that he is talking to a rental agent, write *rental agent* on the board. Ask students what they think a rental agent is. Help them understand the concept.

B. RESEARCH Read different ideas you can use to find a new home.

Have volunteers read the different ideas used to find a new home out loud. Go over vocabulary and/or expressions students are not familiar with.

Practice 1   5–7 mins. ◼◼◼

C. CREATE In a group, make a plan to find a new home. Use the ideas from Exercise B.

Ask students to work in small groups and make a plan to find a new home. Have them use the ideas from Exercise B.

Evaluation 1   5 mins. ◼◼◼

Have volunteers share which ideas they think are best to find a new home. Ask the class to discuss why they think each idea is important.

Group responses

An interesting approach to getting the whole class involved in discussions is to have students give a group response. Ask students to form small groups of no more than three or four. Assign each group a name or number. Write each group name or number on a small piece of paper and place all the pieces in a bowl or small box. When you ask a question, instruct groups to first discuss on their own and come up with a group response. Then, select a name or number to signal that it is that group's turn to give their response. Repeat this action randomly giving groups a chance to share with the class.

LESSON ④ When can I see it?

GOAL ■ Use the telephone and make appointments

WORKPLACE CONNECTION
Exercise C: Combine ideas and information.

A. PREDICT Look at the picture. What is Saud doing? Who is he talking to? Then, read about Saud's plan to find a new home.

Saud's Plan

1. Talk to a rental agent.
2. Read classified ads.
3. Call for appointments.
4. Look at homes.

B. RESEARCH Read different ideas you can use to find a new home.

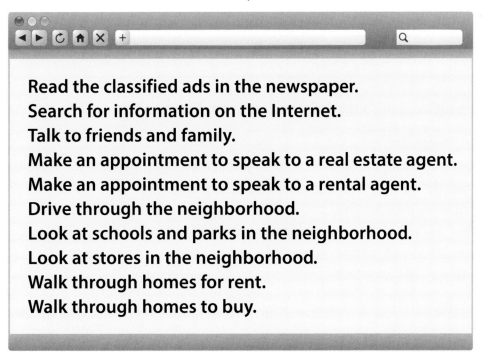

Read the classified ads in the newspaper.
Search for information on the Internet.
Talk to friends and family.
Make an appointment to speak to a real estate agent.
Make an appointment to speak to a rental agent.
Drive through the neighborhood.
Look at schools and parks in the neighborhood.
Look at stores in the neighborhood.
Walk through homes for rent.
Walk through homes to buy.

C. CREATE In a group, make a plan to find a new home. Use the ideas from Exercise B.

D. Practice the conversation.

Owner: Hello, can I help you?

Saud: Yes, I am calling about the condominium for rent.

Owner: How can I help you?

Saud: How much is the rent?

Owner: It's $1,200 a month.

Saud: When can I see it?

Owner: How about today at 3:00?

Saud: Great! Thank you.

E. Listen to the conversations. Take notes and complete the chart.

CD 1
TR 47-50

	How much is the rent?	What time is the appointment?
1.	$1,200	3:00
2.	$1,450	10:00
3.	$2,000	3:30
4.	$900	2:00

F. Complete Conversation 2 with the information from Exercise E.

Owner: Hello. Can I help you?

Saud: Yes, I am calling about the apartment for rent that I saw in the paper. Is it still available?

Owner: Yes, we are renting it for _____ $1,450 _____.

Saud: Wow! That sounds expensive.

Owner: Maybe, but it is a beautiful and new apartment.

Saud: OK, when can I see it?

Owner: You can stop by at _____ 10:00 _____.

G. Practice Conversations 3 and 4 with the information from Exercise E. Use the model in Exercise F.

Presentation 2　　15–20 mins. ■■■□

D. Practice the conversation.

Go over the conversation with students. Discuss any words that might be unfamiliar to them. Work with the rhythm of the conversation. Remind students of how English is similar to the musical notation, a dotted eighth followed by a sixteenth feel. (This was discussed in the Lesson Planner, Unit 03, page 72a.)

E. Listen to the conversations. Take notes and complete the chart.

Remember that this is still the presentation stage, so you can direct the listening more than you might in the practice stage.

LISTENING SCRIPT
CD 1
TR 47–50

1. **Owner:** *Hello. Can I help you?*
   Saud: *Yes, I am calling about the condominium for rent.*
   Owner: *How can I help you?*
   Saud: *How much is the rent?*
   Owner: *It's $1,200 a month.*
   Saud: *When can I see it?*
   Owner: *How about today at 3:00?*
   Saud: *Great! Thank you.*
2. **Owner:** *Hello. Can I help you?*
   Saud: *Yes, I am calling about the apartment for rent that I saw in the paper. Is it still available?*
   Owner: *Yes, we are renting it for $1,450.*
   Saud: *Wow! That sounds expensive.*
   Owner: *Maybe, but it is a beautiful and new apartment.*
   Saud: *OK, when can I see it?*
   Owner: *You can stop by at 10 a.m.*
3. **Owner:** *Hello.*
   Saud: *Hi. I am calling about the house for rent. Are you the owner?*
   Owner: *Yes, I am. What would you like to know?*
   Saud: *How much is the rent?*
   Owner: *It's $2,000. It's a four-bedroom.*
   Saud: *I don't know if I need something that big. When can I see it?*
   Owner: *Come by at 3:30.*
   Saud: *OK, see you then.*
4. **Saud:** *Hello.*
   Owner: *Hello. Is this Saud?*
   Saud: *Yes, that's me.*
   Owner: *I am returning your call about the two-bedroom apartment.*
   Saud: *Oh, yes. How much is the rent?*
   Owner: *It's $900 a month.*
   Saud: *Great. Can I come by today.*
   Owner: *Of course. Come by around 2:00.*
   Saud: *Thanks, I will.*

F. Complete Conversation 2 with the information from Exercise E.

This is a writing activity to help students prepare for Exercise G.

Practice 2　　10–15 mins. ■■□

G. Practice Conversations 3 and 4 with the information from Exercise E. Use the model in Exercise F.

Make sure students use proper rhythm as they practice.

Evaluation 2　　5–7 mins. ■■

Ask volunteers to demonstrate the conversations in front of the classroom.

BEST PRACTICE

Demonstrating conversations

Many students are shy about demonstrating conversations in front of the class. They may be shy or concerned about their English pronunciation. When assigning conversations to demonstrate, give students a few minutes to prepare and, if time allows, have students practice with another pair or group before presenting to the class.

INSTRUCTOR'S NOTES

_____

_____

_____

_____

_____

_____

_____

_____

_____

_____

Presentation 3 15–20 mins. ■■■

Write and present the following conversation on the board. Use this conversation to help students see when they might use the present continuous.

Ms. Rollings: Hello.
Carmen: Hello. My name is Carmen. <u>I'm calling about the house</u> you have for rent.
Ms. Rollings: Of course. It's still available.
Carmen: Great. When can I see it?
Ms. Rollings: <u>What are you doing right now?</u>
Carmen: Right now, <u>I'm watching my niece.</u>
Ms. Rollings: Oh, can you come tomorrow about this time?
Carmen: I think so.
Ms. Rollings: The house is beautiful. <u>I'm painting the inside</u> right now.
Carmen: That's great. I'll see you tomorrow. Goodbye.
Ms. Rollings: OK, goodbye.

H. Study the chart with your classmates and teacher.

BEST PRACTICE

Grammar presentations

This lesson is intended to help students become more familiar with the present continuous and when to use it.

Remember that students throughout the beginning of their English learning experience will be introduced again and again to the structure. At some point, they will be ready to acquire the structure instead of merely learning it. This means they will be able to produce it correctly without thinking about it. Until then, be prepared to repeat this presentation in later lessons in new or different contexts.

I. Write sentences in the present continuous. What is Saud doing?

Practice 3 5–7 mins. ■

J. Complete the sentences with the present continuous.

Evaluation 3 5–7 mins. ■

Check students' work. Ask volunteers to write the information on the board.

Application 10–15 mins. ■■■

K. RANK In a group, rank the steps from easy to difficult. 1 is easiest.

Refer students to *Stand Out 1 Workbook*, Unit 4, Lesson 4 for more practice with the present continuous.

Go to the *Activity Bank* online for suggestions on promoting digital literacy and using the Internet to enhance this lesson.

MULTILEVEL WORKSHEET

Unit 4, Lesson 4, Worksheet 1: Present Continuous

INSTRUCTOR'S NOTES

H. Study the chart with your classmates and teacher.

Present Continuous			
Subject	*Be* **verb**	**Base** + *ing*	**Example sentence**
I	am	talk + *ing*	I **am talking** on the phone.
You, We, They	are	read + *ing* make + *ing*	We **are making** an appointment.
He, She, It	is	move + *ing*	She **is moving** into a new apartment.

I. Write sentences in the present continuous. What is Saud doing?

1. Saud _____ is talking _____ to a rental agent.

2. He _____ is making an appointment _____.

3. He _____ is reading the classified ads _____.

J. Complete the sentences with the present continuous.

~~read~~	talk	look	move	make

1. I _____ am reading _____ the classified ads.

2. They _____ are moving _____ into a new home.

3. We _____ are looking _____ at a condominium.

4. Silvia _____ is making _____ an appointment.

5. You _____ are talking _____ on the phone.

K. RANK In a group, rank the steps from easy to difficult. 1 is easiest. Answers will vary.

_____ He talks to a rental agent.   _____ He calls for appointments.

_____ He reads classified ads.   _____ He looks at homes.

LESSON ⑤ Where do you want the sofa?

GOAL ▢ Identify furniture in a house

WORKPLACE CONNECTION
Exercise B: Complete tasks as assigned; Interact appropriately with team members.

A. Write the words under the correct room. Share your ideas with a partner.

a. bed   b. car   c. chair   d. refrigerator   e. bathtub   f. sofa

1. bedroom _____bed_____

2. kitchen _____refrigerator_____

3. dining room _____chair_____

4. bathroom _____bathtub_____

5. garage _____car_____

6. living room _____sofa_____

B. CLASSIFY In a group, list the other things you see in the rooms above. Use a dictionary or ask your teacher for help. Answers will vary.

Bedroom	Kitchen	Dining room	Bathroom	Garage	Living room

AT-A-GLANCE PREP

Goal: Identify furniture in a house
Grammar: Prepositions of location
Academic Strategies: Focused listening
Vocabulary: Furniture

Agenda

- Write a classified ad.
- Identify furniture in a house.
- Match furniture and rooms.
- Use prepositions.
- Describe your classroom.

Resources

Multilevel Worksheet: Unit 4, Lesson 5,
  Worksheet 1
Workbook: Unit 4, Lesson 5
Audio: CD 1, Track 51
Heinle Picture Dictionary: Living Room,
  pages 73–74
Stand Out 1 Assessment CD-ROM with ExamView®

Pacing

- 1.5 hour classes
- 2.5 hour classes
- 3+ hour classes

STANDARDS CORRELATIONS

CCRS: SL2, L1, L2, L5
CASAS: 1.4.1, 1.4.2, 2.2.1
SCANS: **Resources** Allocate material and facility resources
Information Acquire and evaluate information, organize and maintain information, interpret and communicate information
Basic Skills Reading, writing, listening, speaking
EFF: **Communication** Read with understanding, convey ideas in writing, speak so others can understand, listen actively

Warm-up and Review   15–20 mins.

Ask students to form groups of four or five. Ask each group to choose one student from their group and design a classified ad around that student's home. Ask groups to share their classified ads with the rest of the class.

Introduction   7–10 mins.

Ask students in groups to make a list of furniture without using a dictionary or their books. This will tell you how much students already know. Ask one

group to put its list on the board. Then, ask the other groups to add to the list. State the goal: *Today, we will identify furniture in a house.*

Presentation 1   30–40 mins.

Go over the pictures in Exercise A. Help students with pronunciation. Make sure students understand what it means by asking questions about things in the classroom, such as: *Where does the trash go?*

A. Write the words under the correct room. Share your ideas with a partner.

Ask students to do this exercise quickly by themselves and then explain to their partners what they did and why.

Continue this presentation by asking students to number the pictures from 1 to 6. Describe different pictures and ask students to identify the pictures by raising the correct number of fingers.

Practice 1   5–7 mins.

B. CLASSIFY In a group, list the other things you see in the rooms above. Use a dictionary or ask your teacher for help.

BEST PRACTICE

Limiting vocabulary

Each student will have a different idea of which vocabulary items are the most important. In a lesson like this one, students may identify so much vocabulary that individual learners become overwhelmed. It is the instructor's job to clarify for students which words they are responsible for.

Evaluation 1   5 mins.

Ask groups to report to the class.

Presentation 2 10–15 mins. ■■■

C. Study the prepositions with your classmates and teacher.

Quiz students by asking them where various items are located in the classroom. Go back to the pictures in Exercise A and ask about items there as well.

On this page, students will see more furniture that they may need help identifying. Ask students to form groups and briefly discuss which room of the house they believe each item belongs in.

Practice 2 15–20 mins. ■■■

D. Practice the conversation. Make new conversations. Ask a partner where things are in the pictures above. Ask about *the lamp, the cat, the nightstand, the sofa,* and *the clock*.

Observe students as they practice the exchange.

E. Use prepositions to say the location of things in your classroom. Your partner will guess which thing you are talking about.

Evaluation 2 5–7 mins. ■

Observe students as they do this activity.

BEST PRACTICE

Prepositions of place

Teaching prepositions of place is not that difficult. They must simply be practiced, and there are many different ways to give students the practice they need. Start off by presenting the prepositions with easy-to-understand examples; for instance, *The trash can **is next to** the door.* You can check students' understanding of prepositions by asking questions, such as: *Where is the bed? Where is the book?*

Some approaches to practicing prepositions of place include the following:
a. Ask students to write their own example sentences.
b. Have students create their own conversations in pairs asking where something is located.
c. Command students to move objects in the classroom to different locations using prepositions. For example, *Put your book **on** the desk. Put a piece of paper **under** your book.*

C. **Study the prepositions with your classmates and teacher.**

in	on
under	over
next to	between

D. **Practice the conversation. Make new conversations. Ask a partner where things are in the pictures above. Ask about *the lamp, the cat, the nightstand, the sofa*, and *the clock*.**

Student A: Where's the trash?
Student B: It's in the trash can.

E. **Use prepositions to say the location of things in your classroom. Your partner will guess which thing you are talking about.**

Student A: It's next to the window.
Student B: The door?

F. Study the words with your classmates and teacher.

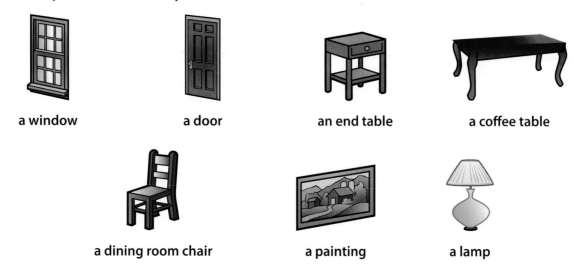

| a window | a door | an end table | a coffee table |

| a dining room chair | a painting | a lamp |

CD 1
TR 51

G. Listen to the instructions and add objects to the room below. *Sample placements shown.*

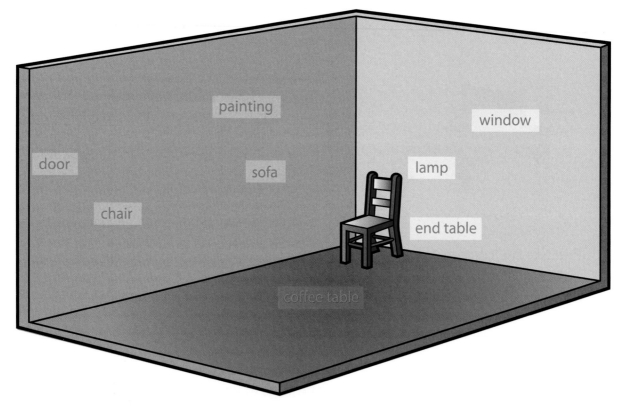

H. **APPLY** Show your partner where the furniture is in your classroom. Walk around the room and talk about it.

I. Find a picture of a room with furniture from a magazine or online. Show the picture to the class and describe it.

Presentation 3

15–20 mins.

Take an inventory of the furniture in the classroom. Ask students to help you do this. Ask: *How many chairs are there? How many desks are there?*

F. Study the words with your classmates and teacher.

Make sure that students understand the meaning of each word. Quiz them a bit on the new vocabulary. You might want to use the technique described in Exercise A where you number the items and have students show fingers to identify each one. In this case, you would practice the words in isolation, then within a sentence, and finally in discourse.

BEST PRACTICE

Monitoring student responses

An easy way to monitor responses is to have students simply respond verbally with a word. Say: *bed*. Students respond: *bedroom*.

With the above method, however, the stronger students sometimes overwhelm the students who need more time to think when asked for a verbal response. You may choose other ways for students to respond where students are less likely to "go along with the crowd." One such response could be to use 3-by-5 index cards with different answers on them. Students hold up the card with their answer on it. Each card could have different rooms. If you choose to use this method, have students create the actual cards themselves so they also get writing practice.

Another way is described in this lesson. Students respond by showing the number of fingers that correspond to each picture you describe. They will be listening for target vocabulary words.

Practice 3

10–15 mins. ■

G. Listen to the instructions and add objects to the room below.

LISTENING SCRIPT

CD 1
TR 51

1. *Draw a window and a door.*
2. *Put a painting on the wall.*
3. *Put a sofa under the painting.*
4. *Put a chair between the sofa and the door.*
5. *Put a coffee table in the middle of the room.*
6. *Draw an end table next to the chair in the corner.*
7. *Draw a lamp on the end table.*

Evaluation 3

3 mins. ■

Look at the students' drawings. Find a good example and display it for the class.

Application

10–15 mins. ■■■

H. APPLY Show your partner where the furniture is in your classroom. Walk around the room and talk about it.

Alternative idea: Ask students to draw diagrams of their own living rooms on a sheet of paper. They should identify the location of their furniture using prepositions and describe the furniture's location to a partner.

I. Find a picture of a room with furniture from a magazine or online. Show the picture to the class and describe it.

Refer students to *Stand Out 1 Workbook*, Unit 4, Lesson 5 for more practice with prepositions.

Go to the *Activity Bank* online for suggestions on promoting digital literacy and using the Internet to enhance this lesson.

MULTILEVEL WORKSHEET

Unit 4, Lesson 5, Worksheet 1: Prepositions of Location

Before You Watch

- Write the title on the board and read it out loud. Underline the word *utilities*.
- Ask students the meaning of *utilities*. Then, ask them how much utilities cost. Discuss as a class.

A. Look at the picture. Complete each sentence.

- Have students look at the picture carefully, reading the information they see.
- Ask students to complete each sentence with the correct word from the picture.
- Go over answers with volunteers.

While You Watch

B. Watch the video. Complete the dialog. Use the words in the box.

- Review the words in the box.
- Tell students they will watch the video and then complete the dialog between Naomi and her apartment manager with the words from the box.
- Ask a volunteer to read the example sentence out loud. Then, play the video once for understanding.
- Play the video again. Ask students to complete the dialog.
- Have students review their answers in pairs.
- Play the video once more. Then, ask students to act out the dialog with their partners.
- Have volunteers act out the dialog in front of the class.

Check Your Understanding

C. Match the questions and answers.

- Ask students to look at the questions and answers in the columns below. Tell them to match each question with the correct answer.
- Ask a volunteer to read a question out loud. Then, have another volunteer give the correct answer.

INSTRUCTOR'S NOTES

_____
_____
_____
_____
_____
_____
_____
_____
_____
_____
_____
_____
_____
_____
_____
_____
_____
_____
_____
_____
_____
_____
_____
_____
_____
_____
_____
_____
_____

LIFESKILLS ▶ Are the utilities included?

Before You Watch

A. Look at the picture. Complete each sentence.

1. The sign is for

   _____*an apartment*_____ for rent.

2. The rent is

   _____*$850*_____ a month.

3. _____*Electricity*_____ is included in the rent.

APARTMENT FOR RENT

$850/month

swimming pool

electricity included

near bus route

call 555-6768

ROUTE 11- BRAND
EXPRESS S

While You Watch

B. ▶ Watch the video. Complete the dialog. Use the words in the box.

electricity	garbage	parking	rent	~~utilities~~

Naomi: That's good. What about electricity and water? Are the (1) ____*utilities*____ included in the rent?

Apartment Manager: Yes, some utilities are included. Water and (2) ____*garbage*____ are included, but you have to pay for the electricity. Do you want to make an appointment to come look at the apartment? It has a very nice view. I'm sure you'll like it.

Naomi: Well… How much is the (3) ____*rent*____?

Apartment Manager: It's only $900 a month—plus electricity. But the (4) ____*parking*____ is free!

Naomi: Um, I don't have a car. Well, let's see… $900 a month, plus (5) ____*electricity*____…

Check Your Understanding

C. Match the questions and answers.

1. Do you have any apartments for rent?
2. How much is the rent?
3. Are the utilities included?
4. Do you allow any pets?
5. Does the building have a garage?

a. Water is included, but you have to pay for electricity.
b. Dogs are allowed, but cats aren't.
c. Yes, we have two apartments for rent.
d. No, you have to park on the street.
e. The rent is $900 a month.

Review

A. **Read the classified ads.**

WORKPLACE CONNECTION
Exercise B: Collect and organize information.

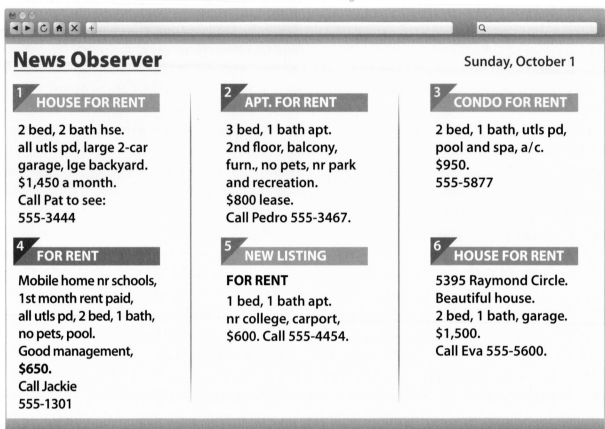

News Observer   Sunday, October 1

1 | HOUSE FOR RENT

2 bed, 2 bath hse.
all utls pd, large 2-car
garage, lge backyard.
$1,450 a month.
Call Pat to see:
555-3444

2 | APT. FOR RENT

3 bed, 1 bath apt.
2nd floor, balcony,
furn., no pets, nr park
and recreation.
$800 lease.
Call Pedro 555-3467.

3 | CONDO FOR RENT

2 bed, 1 bath, utls pd,
pool and spa, a/c.
$950.
555-5877

4 | FOR RENT

Mobile home nr schools,
1st month rent paid,
all utls pd, 2 bed, 1 bath,
no pets, pool.
Good management,
$650.
Call Jackie
555-1301

5 | NEW LISTING

FOR RENT
1 bed, 1 bath apt.
nr college, carport,
$600. Call 555-4454.

6 | HOUSE FOR RENT

5395 Raymond Circle.
Beautiful house.
2 bed, 1 bath, garage.
$1,500.
Call Eva 555-5600.

B. **Cover the ads above so you can't see them. Ask your partner questions about the ads and write the information below. Then, your partner covers the ads and asks questions.**

What kind of housing is it?	How many bedrooms are there?	How many bathrooms are there?	Is it near anything?	How much is the rent?
1. house	2	2		$1,450
2. apartment	3	1	park	$800
3. condominium	2	1		$950
4. mobile home	2	1	schools	$650
5. apartment	1	1	college	$600
6. house	2	1		$1,500

Goal: All unit goals

Grammar: Reviewing, evaluating, developing study skills

Academic Strategies: All unit grammar

Vocabulary: All unit vocabulary

Agenda

☐ Discuss unit goals.

☐ Complete the review.

☐ Evaluate and reflect on progress.

Pacing

■ 1.5 hour classes   ■ 2.5 hour classes

■ 3+ hour classes

STANDARDS CORRELATIONS

CCRS: RI1, RI2, RI5, L4, L5

CASAS: 1.4.1, 1.4.2

SCANS: **Information** Acquire and evaluate information, organize and maintain information

Basic Skills Reading, writing, speaking

Personal Qualities Responsibility, self-management

EFF: Speak so others can understand

Lifelong Learning Take responsibility for learning, reflect and evaluate

Warm-up and Review   7–10 mins. ■■■

Ask students about their homes. Make a list on the board of all the vocabulary students can come up with from the unit.

Introduction   5 mins. ■■■

Write all the goals on the board from Unit 4. Show students the first page of every lesson so they understand that today will be review. Complete the agenda.

Presentation   10–15 mins. ■■■

This Presentation and Practice will cover the first three pages of the review. Quickly go to the first page of each lesson. Discuss the goal of each lesson. Ask simple questions to remind students of what they have learned.

Practice   15–20 mins. ■■

A. Read the classified ads. (Lesson 3)

B. Cover the ads above so you can't see them. Ask your partner questions about the ads and write the information below. Then, your partner covers the ads and asks questions. (Lessons 1–3)

BEST PRACTICE

Recycling/Review

The review and the project that follows are part of the recycling/review process. Students at this level often need to be reintroduced to concepts to solidify what they have learned. Many concepts are learned and forgotten while learning other new concepts. This is because students learn but are not necessarily ready to acquire language concepts.

Therefore, it becomes very important to review and to show students how to review on their own. It is also important to recycle the new concepts in different contexts.

INSTRUCTOR'S NOTES

_____

_____

_____

_____

_____

_____

_____

_____

_____

_____

_____

Practice *(continued)*

C. Study the words. Complete the chart with the words. (Lessons 2 and 5)

D. Look at the picture and complete the sentences. (Lesson 5)

INSTRUCTOR'S NOTES

C. **Study the words. Complete the chart with the words.**

kitchen	pool	hall	sofa	bathtub
balcony	porch	driveway	deck	refrigerator

Inside	Outside
kitchen	pool
hall	balcony
sofa	porch
bathtub	driveway
refrigerator	deck

D. **Look at the picture and complete the sentences.**

1. The cat is _____ under _____ the sofa.

2. The lamp is _____ next to _____ the sofa.

3. The sofa is _____ between _____ the end table and the lamp.

4. The book is _____ on _____ the _____ end table _____ .

5. The painting is _____ over _____ the sofa.

E. Describe the pictures with sentences in the present continuous.

Carmen

Saud

Saud

1. Carmen _is calling for an appointment_____.

2. Saud _is reading the classified ads_____.

3. Saud _is talking to the rental agent_____.

F. Write a conversation about finding a home. Make an appointment to see
the home.   Answers will vary.

Owner: _____

You: _____

Owner: _____

You: _____

Owner: _____

You: _____

Owner: _____

You: _____

G. List furniture for each room.   Answers will vary.

Bedroom	Kitchen	Dining room	Bathroom	Garage	Living room

Practice (continued)

E. Describe the pictures with sentences in the present continuous. (Lesson 4)

F. Write a conversation about finding a home. Make an appointment to see the home. (Lesson 4)

G. List furniture for each room. (Lesson 5)

Evaluation
15 mins. ■■□

Go around the room and check on students' progress. Help individuals when needed. If you see consistent errors among several students, interrupt the class and give a mini lesson or review to help students feel comfortable with the concept.

Presentation
5 mins. ■■□

Learner Log

Review the concepts of the Learner Log. Make sure students understand the concepts and how to complete the log including circling the answers, finding page numbers where the concept is taught, and ranking favorite activities.

BEST PRACTICE

Learner Logs

Learner Logs function to help students in many different ways:

1. They serve as part of the review process.
2. They help students to gain confidence and to document what they have learned. Consequently, students see that they are progressing in their learning.
3. They provide students with a tool that they can use over and over to check and recheck their understanding of the target language. In this way, students become independent learners.

Practice
10–15 mins. ■

Ask students to complete the Learner Log.

Evaluation
2 mins. ■

Go over the Learner Log with students.

Application
5–7 mins. ■■□

Ask students to record their favorite lesson in the unit.

Assessment
■■□

Use the Stand Out 1 Assessment Activity Bank with ExamView® to create a post-test for Unit 4.

Refer students to *Stand Out 1 Workbook*, Unit 4, Lesson 5 for more practice with prepositions.

Go to the *Activity Bank* online for suggestions on promoting digital literacy and using the Internet to enhance this lesson.

MULTILEVEL WORKSHEETS

Unit 4, Computer Worksheets

Unit 4, Internet Worksheets

INSTRUCTOR'S NOTES

Make decisions and solve problems; Collect and organize information; Combine ideas and information; Exercise leadership roles; Manage time; Complete tasks as assigned; Interact appropriately with team members; Interpret and communicate information.

STANDARDS CORRELATIONS

CCRS: SL1, SL2, L1, RF3

CASAS: 1.4.1, 1.4.2, 4.8.1

SCANS: **Resources** Allocate time, allocate materials and facility resources, allocate human resources

Information Acquire and evaluate information, organize and maintain information, interpret and communicate information

Interpersonal Participate as a member of a team, teach others, exercise leadership, negotiate to arrive at a decision, work with cultural diversity

Systems Understand systems, monitor and correct performance

Basic Skills Reading, writing, listening, speaking

Thinking Skills Think creatively, make decisions, problems, see things in the mind's eye

Personal Qualities Responsibility, sociability, self-management

EFF: **Communication** Read with understanding, convey ideas in writing, speak so others can understand, listen actively, observe critically

Decision Making Solve problems and make decisions, plan

Interpersonal Cooperate with others, advocate and influence, resolve conflict and negotiate, guide others

Lifelong Learning Take responsibility for learning, reflect and evaluate

Introduction   5 mins.

TEAM PROJECT

Plan a dream home

In this project, students will work in groups to make a floor plan for a dream home and design a classified ad for it. Then, they will present both to the class.

Stage 1   15–20 mins.

COLLABORATE Form a team with four or five students.

Set the scene and form teams of four or five. Show students examples of the project if you have one.

On the spot, students will have to choose the leader and other positions of their groups. Review the responsibilities of the positions and ask students to write the names in their books.

Stage 2   5 mins.

Choose a kind of home. Is it an apartment, house, condominium, or mobile home?

Ask students to decide how many bedrooms and bathrooms their dream home will have after they have chosen what kind of home it is.

Stage 3   20–30 mins.

Make a floor plan of the home.

Supply students with paper and other materials as needed.

Stage 4   20–30 mins.

Make a list of furniture for your home.

Stage 5   20–30 mins.

Decide where to put the furniture.

Ask students to discuss where furniture should go using prepositions.

Stage 6   10–15 mins.

Write a classified ad for your home.

Stage 7   10–30 mins.

Plan a presentation for the class and present your dream home.

Consider videotaping the presentations. Students will prepare better for formal presentations if they know they will be videotaped. Another approach would be to have students videotape themselves and polish their presentations after they have viewed the recorded presentation.

MULTILEVEL WORKSHEETS

Unit 4, Project, Worksheet 1: Home Design Worksheet
Unit 4, Project, Worksheet 2: Floor Plan
Unit 4, Project, Worksheet 3: Furniture List
Unit 4, Extension, Worksheet 1: Reading Budgets
Unit 4, Extension, Worksheet 2: Family Budget

BEST PRACTICE

Digital literacy

Projects are a perfect place to allow students opportunities to use other forms of presentations beyond pictures they create. Digital literacy is becoming more necessary as a life skill. Encourage students to create presentations using pictures from the Internet. They might also consider using other digital presentation tools.

✓ **Plan a dream home**

In this project, you will make a floor plan of a dream home, write a classified ad for the home, and present both to the class.

1. **COLLABORATE** Form a team with four or five students. In your team, you need:

Position	Job description	Student name
Student 1: **Team Leader**	Check that everyone speaks English. Check that everyone participates.	
Student 2: **Architect**	With help from the team, draw the floor plan.	
Student 3: **Decorator**	With help from the team, place furniture in your plan.	
Students 4/5: **Spokespeople**	With help from the team, organize a presentation.	

2. Choose a kind of home. Is it an apartment, house, condominium, or mobile home?

3. Make a floor plan of the home.

4. Make a list of furniture for your home.

5. Decide where to put the furniture.

6. Write a classified ad for your home.

7. Plan a presentation for the class and present your dream home.

About the Explorer

Ben Horton is a photographer whose work has been featured in the *National Geographic* magazine. He was the first person to be awarded the National Geographic Young Explorers Grant. He received the grant for the work he did exposing shark poaching in Costa Rica. Since then, he has been involved in a number of conservation projects in Costa Rica and involved in various projects with the National Geographic Society.

About the Photo

This photo shows Ben in the Arctic region of Canada with sled dogs in the background. In 2008, Ben spent 60 days sledding across Ellesmere Island with Arctic explorer Will Steger to document the issue of global warming. During the two months, the entire team traveled by dog sled and crossed frozen seas, ice shelves, and mountain ranges. Ben described this experience as his first major photography expedition.

- Tell students they are going to read about an explorer named Ben Horton.
- Read the title out loud and ask students if they think Ben Horton is a photographer.

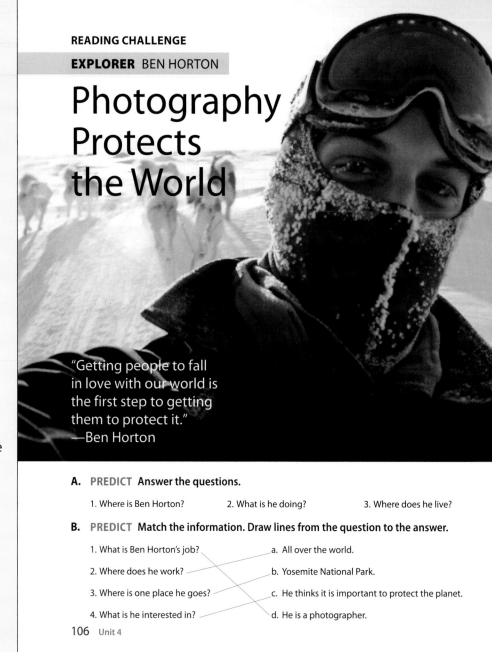

READING CHALLENGE

EXPLORER BEN HORTON

Photography Protects the World

"Getting people to fall in love with our world is the first step to getting them to protect it."
—Ben Horton

A. PREDICT Answer the questions.

1. Where is Ben Horton?   2. What is he doing?   3. Where does he live?

B. PREDICT Match the information. Draw lines from the question to the answer.

1. What is Ben Horton's job?   a. All over the world.
2. Where does he work?   b. Yosemite National Park.
3. Where is one place he goes?   c. He thinks it is important to protect the planet.
4. What is he interested in?   d. He is a photographer.

106   Unit 4

CCRS FOR READING

SL1, SL2, L1, RF3

C. Read about Ben Horton.

Ben Horton is a photographer. He lives in an apartment in California, but he doesn't stay at his apartment for long. Ben goes on lots of adventures. For example, he often visits Yosemite National Park. He takes pictures to remind people of the beauty in the world. On his adventures he doesn't sleep in a home, but he sleeps in a tent. Does it have a living room? No, it doesn't. Does it have a dining room? No, it doesn't. It's one small, portable room!

D. Answer the questions about Ben Horton's story.

1. In the story, it says Ben Horton *doesn't stay home for long*. What do you think this means?
   a. He is home a lot.
   b. He is not home a lot.
   c. He doesn't like his home.

2. What do you think *adventure* means in the story?
   a. an exciting experience
   b. a portable room
   c. a photographer

3. What do you think *remind* means in the story?
   a. sleeping in a tent
   b. help people remember
   c. beauty

E. CLASSIFY Discuss the words in the box with your teacher and complete the chart.

bed	dining room	fire	ice chest
picnic table	refrigerator	sleeping bag	stove

Home	Away from home
dining room	picnic table
refrigerator	ice chest
stove	fire
bed	sleeping bag

READING STRATEGIES

Use Word-Attack Strategies

Explain to students that when they encounter new vocabulary in a reading, they may use a word attack strategy to understand the meaning of the word. Tell them that this means looking for a prefix in the word, looking at the word's root, or looking for a suffix. Point out that a word-attack strategy might also include looking to see if the vocabulary is a compound (two separate words that carry the meaning of a single word; e.g., *picnic table* and *living room*).

A. PREDICT Answer the questions.

- Ask and have students discuss the answers to the questions in Exercise A.
- Ask a volunteer to read the quote in the photo to the class. Then, ask students what they think Ben Horton means. Discuss as a class.

B. PREDICT Match the information. Draw lines from the question to the answer.

- Ask students to match the questions in the left column to the correct answers in the right column.
- Remind students that they are making predictions, so their answers are just guesses or based on what they see in the photo and on what Ben Horton says.
- Review and discuss answers as a class.

C. Read about Ben Horton.

Have students read about Ben Horton.

D. Answer the questions about Ben Horton's story.

- Ask students if their predictions in Exercises A and B were correct.
- Ask students to answer the questions about Ben Horton's story.
- Have students check their answers with a partner.
- Ask volunteers to share their answers with the class.

E. CLASSIFY Discuss the words in the box with your teacher and complete the chart.

Discuss the words in the box as a class. Then, complete the chart by writing the words in the correct columns.

Before You Watch

A. Look at the picture. What do you see? Tell a partner. Then read about cotton.

Ask students to look at the picture and tell a partner what they see. Then, have them read the paragraph.

B. In groups, look at everyone's clothes. What is cotton? Make a list of the items of clothing.

- Ask students to get into small groups. Then, ask them to look at everyone's clothes in their groups.
- Ask students if the clothes are made of cotton. Have them discuss.
- Ask students to make a list of the clothing. Then, have them complete the chart writing the items under Men's or Women's.

There are many ways to use video in the classroom. Students should rarely watch a video without some kind of task. You might introduce comprehension questions before they watch so they know what they are looking for. Below are a few techniques that you may try for variety beyond the comprehension checks and other ideas already presented in this lesson.

Freeze Frame: Pause the video during viewing and use it like a picture dictionary, identifying and expanding on the vocabulary.

Silent Viewing: Show the video in segments without sound so students can guess at the story line. This helps them to understand that listening is more than just the words people say.

Prediction Techniques: Show portions of the video and ask students to predict what will come next.

Listening without Viewing: This helps students create their own image of what is happening. After

---

▶ VIDEO CHALLENGE

How Your T-Shirt Can Make a Difference

Before You Watch

A. Look at the picture. What do you see? Tell a partner. Then read about cotton.

> Cotton is a plant. It makes cloth. We make clothes and many other things from cotton. It is light and easy to wear. People usually wear cotton when the weather is hot.

B. In groups, look at everyone's clothes. What is cotton? Make a list of the items of clothing.

Women's	Men's
Answers will vary.	Answers will vary.

108   How Your T-Shirt Can Make a Difference

C. Describe your favorite T-shirt? What color is it? What size is it? Is it cotton? How many times do you wash it? Use the phrases in the box. Tell a partner.

My favorite T-shirt is (color).	I wash it every week.	My T-shirt is made from cotton.
It is large.	I wash it every day.	It is medium.
It is nice.	It is small.	

D. Read the list. Check each item that you think has cotton in it. Compare your list with a partner. *Answers will vary.*

_____ paper money   _____ bed sheets   _____ living room curtains

_____ towels   _____ a bookbag   _____ a bed

_____ pillows   _____ a sofa   _____ a rug

E. Read the words and their definitions. Then complete the paragraph.

manufacture	to make something with machines
carbon footprint	things you do that affect the environment
transport	to carry or move something from one place to another
loads of washing	amounts of clothes put into a washing machine
buy	use money to pay for something

My family has a clothing business. We (1) _____ manufacture _____ cotton T-shirts. We (2) _____ transport _____ our T-shirts to stores all over the United States. We want our business to do well. However, we make choices that don't hurt the environment. For example, we only (3) _____ buy _____ from farmers who use less water to grow cotton. This is important because we want our (4) _____ carbon footprint _____ to be smaller. We want our customers to do the same. We tell them to do fewer (5) _____ loads of washing _____.

APPLICABLE STRATEGIES

***True/ False* statements.** Explain to students that there are strategies for correctly answering *true/false* statements.

1. Look for extreme modifiers that might make the question or statement false, such as *all, always, never, only, none,* and *nobody.*
2. Look for qualifying word that might make the question or statement true, such as *usually, probably, often, most,* and *sometimes.*
3. Look for negative words and prefixes, such as *not* or *un-.*

---

a discussion, allow students to watch the video and the sound together.

Back-to-Back: In pairs, one student faces the video and the other faces away. Play the video without sound and ask the student viewing to report to the student who is facing away what is happening.

Summary Strips: Create strips of sentences that describe the events. Have students watch the video and then put the strips in the correct order, or ask students to predict the story line before watching and then check their answers. The Activity Bank has summary strips for each video in *Stand Out.*

C. Describe your favorite T-shirt? What color is it? What size is it? Is it cotton? How many times do you wash it? Use the phrases in the box. Tell a partner.

- Ask students to describe their favorite T-shirt. Ask them what color and size it is. Then, ask them if the T-shirt is made of cotton.
- Ask students how many times they wash the T-shirt.
- Go over the phrases in the box. Then, ask students to tell a partner about the T-shirt using the phrases.

D. Read the list. Check each item that you think has cotton in it. Compare your list with a partner.

Tell students to read the list and check each item they think has cotton in it. Then, ask them to compare their list with a partner.

E. Read the words and their definitions. Then complete the paragraph.

Ask students to read the words and their definition. Then, complete the paragraph.

▶ VIDEO CHALLENGE

While You Watch

F. Watch the video. Read each question. Write an amount.

- Ask students to watch the video.
- Read each question out loud. Then, tell students to write an amount. Play the video again.
- Ask students to check their answers with a partner.

G. Watch the video. Then read each sentence. Circle T for *True* or F for *False*.

- Have students watch the video again. Then, ask them to read each sentence and circle T for *True* and F for *False*.

H. Watch the video. Then look at the pie chart. Complete the information with the correct words and numbers.

- Play the video once again.
- Ask students to look at the pie chart. Then, have them complete the information with the correct words and numbers.
- Check answers as a class.

While You Watch

F. Watch the video. Read each question. Write an amount.   Answers will vary.

1. How many T-shirts are in your closet? _____

2. How many T-shirts do you really need? _____

3. How often do you wash and dry your T-shirts? _____

4. How often do you need to wash and dry your T-shirt? _____

G. Watch the video. Then read each sentence. Circle T for *True* or F for *False*.

1. It takes eight cups of water to make one T-shirt.   T   (F)

2. It takes a lot of energy to grow and care for cotton.   (T)   F

3. One load of washing uses more energy than one load of drying.   T   (F)

4. One load of washing uses 40 gallons of water.   (T)   F

5. It takes more water to make one T-shirt than one person drinks in a day.   (T)   F

H. Watch the video. Then look at the pie chart. Complete the information with the correct words and numbers.

1	salty	human use
snow	2	97

Earth's Water

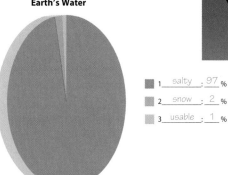

1 _salty_ : _97_ %

2 _snow_ : _2_ %

3 _usable_ : _1_ %

110   How Your T-Shirt Can Make a Difference

After You Watch

I. Read each question. Choose the answer that is true for you. *Answers will vary.*

a. Yes = 0 points	b. No = 1 point	

Total points

1. Do you buy a new t-shirt every three months? _____
2. Do you do a load of washing every day? _____
3. Do you use a dryer to dry your clothes? _____
4. Do you use public transportation? _____
5. Do you walk or use a bicycle to go places? _____
6. Do you turn off the lights when you leave a room? _____

J. Compare your answers from Excercise I with a partner. Decide who has the smaller *carbon footprint*.

> I think I have a smaller carbon footprint. I only have two points.

> I think I have a larger carbon footprint. I have five points!

K. Read the question. Then read the list. Check the correct answers.

How can you make your carbon footprint smaller?

✓ Use cold water to wash clothes
_____ Drive to work and school
_____ Wash three loads of clothing every day
✓ Wear less cotton
✓ Ride a bicycle or walk

✓ Plant a tree
✓ Eat food from your garden
_____ Leave all the lights on in your home
_____ Use more paper
✓ Hang your clothes outside to dry

L. Complete the columns and the total amount. Discuss the amount of water you use in a day in small groups. *Answers will vary.*

Activity	Times (per day)	Water (gallons)	Total (gallons)
Washing machine		40 per load	
Bath		35	
Five minute shower		10	
Brushing teeth		2	
Flushing toilet		3	
Dishwasher		10	

Total number of gallons of water you use per day: _____

Video Challenge 111

After You Watch

I. **Read each question. Choose the answer that is true for you.**

- Ask students to read each question. Then, have them choose the answer that is true for them. Ask them to write *0* for *Yes* and *1* for *No* on the line.
- Ask students to add these numbers to get the total.

J. **Compare your answers from Exercise I with a partner. Decide who has the smaller *carbon footprint*.**

Ask students to compare their answers from Exercise I with a partner. Then, ask them who has the smaller carbon footprint.

K. **Read the question. Then read the list. Check the correct answers.**

- Read the question out loud.
- Ask students to read the list and check the correct answers.
- Have volunteers share their answers with the class. Discuss answers as necessary.

L. **Complete the columns and the total amount. Discuss the amount of water you use in a day in small groups.**

Ask students to complete the columns and the total amount. Then, have them discuss the amounts of water they use per day in small groups.

APPLICABLE STRATEGIES

Completing pie charts. Tell students that pie charts can help them visualize percentages. Point out that percentages are portions or parts of a whole. Explain to students that each portion or part in the pie chart is usually represented by different colors. Add that the percentages in a pie chart are written in numbers.

Our Community

UNIT **5**

Our Community

Crowds are waiting for the fireworks at Arlington National Cemetery.

About the Photo

Annie Griffiths took this photo. Annie was one of the first women photographers to work for the National Geographic Society. A lot of her work is with charitable organizations. The photo shows a crowd of people gathered in the Arlington National Cemetery sitting awaiting Independence Day fireworks. The cemetery, across the Potomac River from Washington, D.C., is a popular place for people to watch the fireworks from the nation's capital on July 4th.

- Introduce the unit. Ask students to look at the photo. Then, ask students what a *community* is. Discuss as a class.

- Go over the unit outcomes. Then, ask the questions about the photo. Have students share their answers with the class.

- Ask a volunteer to read the caption out loud. Then, ask students if they ever do activities in their own communities like they see in the photo.

UNIT OUTCOMES	GRAMMAR	VOCABULARY	EL CIVICS
• Identify locations and services • Give and follow street directions • Give and follow directions in a mall • Leave a phone message • Write an e-mail	• Imperatives and *in/on* • Prepositions of location • Questions with *can* • Present continuous • Simple present • Adverbs of frequency	• Places in your community • Directions • Stores • Prepositions • Social language	The skills students learn in this unit can be applied to the following El Civics competency area: • Community Resources

Life Skills Link

In this unit, students will learn how to identify places in their community as well as find their way and express how to get around these places. Students will also learn how to inquire about services through different communication methods.

Workplace Link

All lessons and units in *Stand Out* include basic communication skills and interpersonal skills important for the workplace. They are not individually identified. Other workplace skills are indicated. They include *collecting and organizing information, making decisions and solving problems,* and *combining ideas and information.*

UNIT OUTCOMES

- ☐ Identify locations and services
- ☐ Give and follow street directions
- ☐ Give and follow directions in a mall
- ☐ Leave a phone message
- ☐ Write an e-mail

Look at the photo and answer the questions.

1. What are the people doing in the picture?
2. Where do you think they are?
3. Are they all facing the same way for a reason?

CASAS	SCANS	CCRS
Lesson 1: 1.1.3, 2.5.1, 2.5.3, 7.4.4	Most SCANS are incorporated into this unit, with an emphasis on:	RI1, RI2, RI5, RI7, W2, SL1, SL2, SL4, L1, L2, L4, L5, RF3
Lesson 2: 1.1.3, 1.9.1, 1.9.4, 2.2.1, 2.2.2, 2.2.5	• Acquiring and evaluating information	
Lesson 3: 1.3.7, 2.2.1, 2.5.4	• Reading	
Lesson 4: 2.1.7, 2.1.8	• Seeing things in the mind's eye	
Lesson 5: 0.2.3	• Sociability	
Review: 0.2.3, 1.1.3, 2.1.7, 2.1.8, 1.9.1, 2.2.2	(Technology is optional.)	
Team Project: 0.2.3, 1.1.3, 2.1.7, 2.1.8, 1.9.1, 2.2.2, 4.8.1		

LESSON ❶ Places and services

GOAL ▮ Identify locations and services

A. INTERPRET Look at the web page with your classmates and teacher. Talk about the different sections.

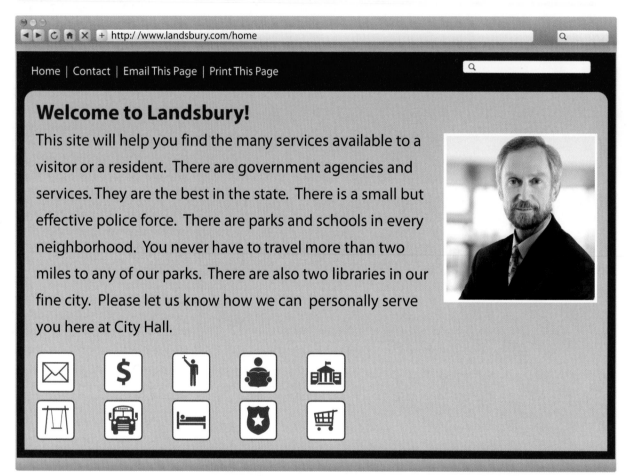

B. INFER Make a list of government agencies and services in Landsbury based on the reading.

> ### ONE OR MORE
> There **is** a police station.
> There **are** parks and schools.

1. public libraries

2. post offices

3. city hall

4. parks

5. schools

6. police force

114   Unit 5

Goal: Identify locations and services
Grammar: Imperatives
Academic Strategies: Focused listening, classifying
Vocabulary: Community vocabulary, government agencies and services

Agenda

☐ Do a corners activity.
☐ Identify locations and services.
☐ Read a web page.
☐ Identify agencies.
☐ Make a bar graph.

Resources

Multilevel Worksheets: Unit 5, Lesson 1, Worksheets 1–3
Workbook: Unit 5, Lesson 1
Audio: CD 2, Tracks 1–2
Heinle Picture Dictionary: Places Around Town, pages 46–47; City Square, pages 58–59
Stand Out 1 Assessment CD-ROM with ExamView®

Pacing

■ 1.5 hour classes   ■ 2.5 hour classes
■ 3+ hour classes

STANDARDS CORRELATIONS

CCRS: RI1, RI7, SL1, SL2, SL4, L1, L2, L5, RF3
CASAS: 1.1.3, 2.5.1, 2.5.3, 7.4.4
SCANS: **Information** Acquire and evaluate information, organize and maintain information, interpret and communicate information
Basic Skills Reading, listening, speaking
Thinking Skills See things in the mind's eye
EFF: **Communication** Read with understanding, speak so others can understand, listen actively

Preassessment (optional)   ■■■

Use the Stand Out 1 Assessment CD-ROM with ExamView® to create a pretest for Unit 5.

Warm-up and Review   7–10 mins. ■■■

Ask students where they live. Help them use the preposition *in* before the name of the city. Ask students what they like to do in their city. Tell them what you like to do. Write *entertainment* on the board and list under it various activities you do for entertainment. Ask students for their ideas to add to the list. Choose four types of entertainment and do a corners activity where each corner represents a different activity. For example, the corners might consist of *movies, restaurants, sports,* and *shopping.* Ask students to go to the corner that represents the activity they prefer. When they find their corner, ask them to discuss with their group what they like about the area they have chosen.

Introduction   7–10 mins. ■■■

Ask students to help you brainstorm different places to obtain services in your community. Write them on the board. Start them off with a few, such as *post office* and *hospital.* State the goal: *Today, we will identify locations and services in our community.*

Presentation 1   20–30 mins. ■■■

Take the list that students helped you make on the board about services in the community and see if you can classify each item. Some classifications might include *health, transportation, protection,* etc. Write *neighborhood* on the board and state that you live in a neighborhood. Explain to students that a neighborhood is a small area of people who live near each other. Ask students again where they live and explain how a community can be made up of a few or several neighborhoods.

With books closed, ask students about different aspects of their community. For example, ask: *Where do you keep your money? Where do you go if you are ill? Where can you buy clothes? Where do you mail letters?* Their answers will tell you how much students already know.

A. INTERPRET Look at the web page with your classmates and teacher. Talk about the different sections.

Ask students to open their books. Discuss the different buttons on the web page. Ask students to match the symbols and section headings. They will probably need examples for some categories.

Note: Practice 1 (Exercise B) and Evaluation 1 appear on next page.

Practice 1

7–10 mins. ■■■

B. INFER Make a list of government agencies and services in Landsbury based on the reading.

Ask students to work in groups to make their lists.

Evaluation 1

7–10 mins. ■■■

Go over students' answers and write them on the board. Review the new vocabulary as you are doing this.

Presentation 2

15–20 mins. ■■■

Ask students to close their books. Write the following terms on the board: *lodging, parks and recreation, medical care,* and *residential area.* Make sure that students understand each of the phrases. Start with *residential area.* Ask students about the kinds of housing they discussed in the previous unit.

C. CLASSIFY Work in a group. Write the words from the box under the correct pictures below.

Don't go over the words at first. Allow students to do the activity and struggle a bit with the language. Encourage students to ask one another before you give them all the information.

After students have done their best completing the activity on their own, review each word in the box with the class by asking questions in a focused-listening fashion. For example: *Where do you go to play with your children?* You can provide more context: *You and your family have a free day and….* Help students listen for clues to determine which words you are targeting. Then, as a class, complete putting all the words in the appropriate categories.

Go over the places in Exercise D with students. Check their understanding by asking questions.

Practice 2

7–10 mins. ■■

D. Listen. Write the number under the correct picture.

LISTENING SCRIPT

CD 2
TR 1

1. *This is a place where people mail letters and packages, and they buy stamps.*
2. *This is a place with trained workers who help the community when there is an emergency such as a fire.*
3. *This is a place where very sick people go for surgery and other problems. Sometimes people go here in an emergency. They sometimes come by ambulance.*
4. *This is a place where people go to get a driver's license and identification.*
5. *This is a place where people put their money. Sometimes they get a checking account and sometimes they get credit cards and loans.*
6. *This is a place where police officers work. It is the police officers' office.*

You will probably have to play this recording several times. To make it easier, pause after each item and allow students to think about what they have heard.

Evaluation 2

5–7 mins. ■■

Check students' work in their books. Further test students by describing the places in Exercise D and seeing if students can tell you the name of each object.

INSTRUCTOR'S NOTES

_____

_____

_____

_____

_____

_____

_____

_____

_____

_____

_____

C. CLASSIFY Work in a group. Write the words from the box under the correct pictures below.

apartment	hostel	hotel	dentist's office
tennis court	hospital	motel	doctor's office
mobile home	playground	house	park

a. Lodging

hostel

hotel

motel

b. Parks and Recreation

tennis court

playground

park

c. Medical Care

hospital

dentist's office

doctor's office

d. Residences

apartment

mobile home

house

 D. Listen. Write the number under the correct picture.

CD 2
TR 1

4

1

3

5

2

6

E. PREDICT Look at the picture. What are they doing? Who are they calling?

Fire 911
Police 911
Jefferson Memorial Bank 555-3232
Landsbury Hospital 555-7665
Post Office 555-8444
DMV 555-3722

F. Listen to the conversation. Practice the conversation with new information.

CD 2
TR 2

Emanuela: I need to call the <u>hospital</u>.
Lisa: Why?
Emanuela: <u>My sister is very sick.</u>
Lisa: The number is <u>555-7665</u>.

Place	Problem	Phone number
hospital	My sister is very sick.	555-7665
bank	I need to get some money from my account.	555-4856
DMV	I need a driver's license.	555-7698
post office	I need to send a letter.	555-2047

G. SURVEY Make a bar graph for your class. How many students go to these places?

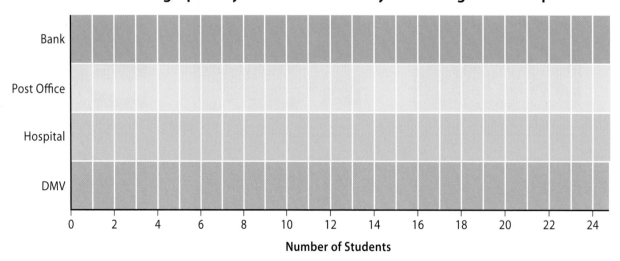

Number of Students

H. APPLY Find a telephone directory or look on the Internet. Make a list of important numbers to put on your phone at home.

Presentation 3

15–20 mins. ■■■

E. PREDICT Look at the picture. What are they doing? Who are they calling?

Look at the picture with the class and ask the questions. Ask additional questions about the phone numbers on the notepad. Ask students if they have special numbers that they keep close to the phone.

Present the conversation. Go over the rhythm by clapping it out. Try to make a chant out of it by making a big pause after *why*. Play the recording to help students hear the rhythm.

PRONUNCIATION

Intonation and rhythm

Singing or chanting is a good way to teach intonation and rhythm. In this case, students are given the rhythm in the first example, and they will try to fit all the words in the substitutions into the same framework. Keeping the rhythm can be challenging, but it will help them sound more natural in their speech. Do just the first three lines.

I NEED to CALL the HOSpital.

WHY? (pause)

My SISter is very SICK.

I NEED to CALL the BANK.

WHY? (pause)

I NEED to GET some MONey from my acCOUNT.

(The words *from my* are spoken very quickly.)

I NEED to CALL the DMV.

WHY? (pause)

I NEED a DRIver's LIcense.

I NEED to CALL the POSToffice.

WHY? (pause)

I NEED to SEND a LETter.

Practice 3

7–10 mins. ■

F. Listen to the conversation. Practice the conversation with new information.

LISTENING SCRIPT

The listening script matches the conversation in Exercise F.

🎧 CD 2 TR 2

Evaluation 3

5–7 mins. ■

Ask volunteers to demonstrate the conversation in front of the class.

Application

10–15 mins. ■■■

G. SURVEY Make a bar graph for your class. How many students go to these places?

Survey the class and put the results on the board. Ask student groups to discuss the results before each student fills in the graph shown in his or her book.

H. APPLY Find a telephone directory or look on the Internet. Make a list of important numbers to put on your phone at home.

Refer students to *Stand Out 1 Workbook*, Unit 5, Lesson 1 for more practice with *need to*.

Go to the *Activity Bank* online for suggestions on promoting digital literacy and using the Internet to enhance this lesson.

MULTILEVEL WORKSHEETS

Unit 5, Lesson 1, Worksheet 1: Places in your Community
Unit 5, Lesson 1, Worksheet 2: Community Cluster
Unit 5, Lesson 1, Worksheet 3: Public Agencies and Services

INSTRUCTOR'S NOTES

_____

_____

_____

_____

_____

_____

_____

_____

Goal: Give and follow street directions

Grammar: Imperatives and *in/on*

Academic Strategies: Focused listening, map reading

Vocabulary: Directions

Agenda

☐ Do a cluster activity.

☐ Give and follow street directions.

☐ Read a map and write locations.

☐ Listen for directions.

☐ Ask other students for information.

Resources

Multilevel Worksheets: Unit 5, Lesson 2, Worksheets 1–3

Workbook: Unit 5, Lesson 2

Audio: CD 2, Tracks 3–7

Heinle Picture Dictionary: Places Around Town, pages 46–47

Stand Out 1 Assessment CD-ROM with ExamView®

Pacing

■ 1.5 hour classes   ■ 2.5 hour classes

■ 3+ hour classes

STANDARDS CORRELATIONS

CCRS: R7, SL2, L1, L2, RF3

CASAS: 1.1.3, 1.9.1, 1.9.4, 2.2.1, 2.2.2, 2.2.5 (See CASAS Competency List on pages 169–175.)

SCANS: **Information** Acquire and evaluate information, interpret and communicate information

Basic Skills Listening, speaking

EFF: **Communication** Speak so others can understand, listen actively

Warm-up and Review   10–12 mins. ■■■

Make a big circle on the board. Write *Community* inside the circle. Draw lines out from the circle and make four secondary circles. Label one of them *Lodging*. Make lines from this circle to additional circles. Label these *Hotels, Motels,* and *Hostels.*

Ask students to close their books and help you complete the cluster. Use *Medical Care, Parks and Recreation,* and *Residential Areas* for the remaining three secondary circles.

In the Multilevel Worksheets CD-ROM template folder, there are cluster diagrams that can be duplicated for each student.

Introduction   7–10 mins. ■■■

Identify well-known places in your community and ask students where they are located. Accept any answer. They may give you street names or use prepositions to say what they are next to. State the goal: *Today, we will give and follow street directions.*

Presentation 1   30–40 mins. ■■■

Ask students where something is in the classroom; for example, the door. Encourage students to point to the door. Start walking in the opposite direction and ask if what you are doing is right. If students haven't caught on, ask them where the door is again and go through the same process until they do. Encourage students to give a direction such as: *Turn around.* Write it on the board and ask students to repeat.

Ask students to open their books and look at the picture.

A. Discuss the phrases with your teacher.

Explain the phrases by referencing the map to the right.

Then, explain to students that a *block* is the buildings next to each other between crossing streets or the distance from one street to the next in a city or town.

Point out the block on the map.

B. Look at the picture. Where is Gabriela? What is she doing? Then, practice the conversation.

Ask students to look at the picture on the right. Then, ask the questions.

Prepare students to practice the conversation by modeling it to the class. Choose a student volunteer to read the part of Alma or Gabriela.

Review any new or unfamiliar vocabulary. Then, ask students to practice the conversation with a partner.

Practice 1   7–10 mins. ■■■

C. Make new conversations. Use the information below. Use Exercise B as a model.

This activity can be beneficial both as an oral exercise and as a written exercise.

Evaluation 1   3–7 mins. ■■■

Ask volunteers to demonstrate their conversations in front of the class.

LESSON **2** Where is City Hall?

GOAL ■ Give and follow street directions

A. **Discuss the phrases with your teacher.**

turn left

go straight ahead

It's on the left.

turn right

turn around

It's on the right.

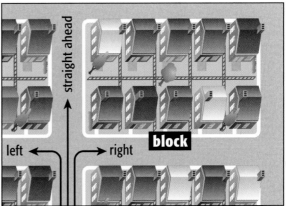

B. **Look at the picture. Where is Gabriela? What is she doing? Then, practice the conversation.**

Alma:	I need to find <u>City Hall.</u>
Gabriela:	Of course. <u>Go straight ahead one block and turn right.</u>
Alma:	Can you repeat that slowly for me?
Gabriela:	Sure. That's straight ahead one block... Turn right... It's on the left.
Alma:	Thanks.
Gabriela:	No problem.

C. **Make new conversations. Use the information below. Use Exercise B as a model.**

Place	Directions
1. bus station	Go straight ahead one block and turn right. Go one block and turn right. Go one block. It's on the left.
2. City Hall	Go straight ahead one block and turn right. It's on the left.
3. Rosco's Buffet Restaurant	Go straight ahead two blocks and turn left. It's on the right.
4. post office	Go straight ahead one block and turn right. Go one more block and turn left. It's on the right.
5. zoo	Go straight ahead two blocks and turn right. It's on the right.
6. high school	Go straight ahead two blocks and turn right. Go one more block and turn right. It's on the left.

D. **Look at the map. Read the directions from Exercise C on page 117. Number the places 1–6 in the squares on the map.**

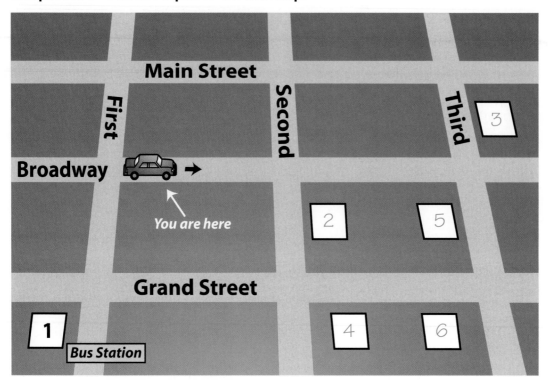

E. **ANALYZE** **Where are the places? Look at the map and complete the table.**

Place	Location
1. bus station	The bus station is on Grand Street.
2. City Hall	City Hall is on Second.
3. Rosco's Buffet Restaurant	Rosco's Buffet Restaurant is on Third.
4. post office	The post office is on Grand Street.
5. zoo	The zoo is on Third.
6. high school	The high school is on Grand Street.

F. **Practice the conversation with information from Exercise E.**

Student A: Where is the bus station?
Student B: It's on Grand Street in Landsbury.

> **IN / ON**
>
> **in** the city
>
> **on** the street
>
> It's **on** Main Street **in** Landsbury.

Presentation 2

15–20 mins. ■■■

Study the map with students by asking questions, such as: *What street is next to First Street? Where is the car?* Review the direction vocabulary with the class again as you did in Exercise B on the previous page.

Draw a similar map on the board. Find City Hall with students by following the directions in Exercise C on the previous page. Ask students where each place is. Emphasize that they use *on* with a street name and *in* with a city.

D. Look at the map. Read the directions from Exercise C on page 117. Number the places 1–6 in the squares on the map.

Walk students through the directions.

At this level, it is difficult for students to give complete directions, but check their understanding by asking them to cover page 117 and listen as you give directions.

Practice 2

7–10 mins. ■■□

Ask volunteers to demonstrate the conversation in front of the class.

BEST PRACTICE

Demonstrations

Student demonstrations often help you to evaluate what students have learned. They also provide a model for the other students. Sometimes it becomes necessary to correct students as they demonstrate to ensure that no faulty learning is occurring. Be careful to only correct where the error directly relates to the lesson goal. If a lot of correction is necessary, more practice is needed.

E. ANALYZE Where are the places? Look at the map and complete the table.

Ask students to follow the example. Make sure they understand that they need to use the word *on*, not *in*. Also, explain that we don't always use the word *street,* but just the proper noun in the street's name.

Evaluation 2

5–7 mins. ■■□

F. Practice the conversation with information from Exercise E.

Go over the exchange quickly and observe as students do the activity.

Presentation 3

10–15 mins. ■■■

G. Write the phrases under the signs.

Go over the vocabulary once again. This time, stand up and ask students to play *Simon Says*. In this activity, you give students simple instructions. For example, you may ask students to turn right and left, have them raise their right or left hand, and lower their right or left hand. You may ask them to turn around and to go straight ahead two or three steps. However, students should only follow your directions when you preface the command with *Simon says*. When you don't say *Simon says* and students perform the action anyway, they are required to sit down. The winner is the student who remains standing the longest.

Prepare students for focused listening.

LISTENING SCRIPT

CD 2
TR 3–7

1. **A:** *Can you give me directions, please?*
   B: *Maybe. Where do you want to go?*
   A: *I am looking for the mall.*
   B: *It's on Broadway. Turn around and go straight for two blocks. Turn right on Hamilton Ave. You will see it.*
   A: *Thanks!*

2. **A:** *Excuse me. Do you know the way to the post office?*
   B: *Yes, of course. Go straight ahead two miles. Turn left on Maple.*

3. **A:** *I am totally confused. Where is the movie theater from here?*
   B: *It is very close.*
   A: *Can you give me directions?*
   B: *Sure. Turn left on First Street. Then, go straight ahead three blocks.*
   A: *Thanks so much.*

4. **A:** *Can I help you find something?*
   B: *Yes, I am looking for the museum. I hear there is a great dinosaur exhibit there.*
   A: *Yes, that's right. It is on Main Street.*
   B: *Where is Main Street?*
   A: *Turn right and go three blocks.*
   B: *Thank you.*

5. **A:** *Where is the park?*
   B: *Turn around and go straight for six blocks. You can't miss it.*
   A: *Are you sure?*
   B: *I am absolutely positive.*

Practice 3

5 mins. ■

H. Listen and check (✓) the boxes for the phrases you hear.

Play the recording a few times and give students some time between listenings to discuss what they have written down.

Evaluation 3

3–5 mins. ■

Go over the listening as a class and check answers.

Application

5–7 mins. ■■■

I. Ask four classmates and complete the chart.

BEST PRACTICE

Student interaction

Students often select people who they know or are comfortable with in activities such as Exercise I. To encourage students to talk to different classmates, you can set up the activity as an inside/outside circle. You can also divide the class into four parts or quadrants. Then, require that students talk to people outside of their own quadrant.

Refer students to *Stand Out 1 Workbook,* Unit 5, Lesson 2 for more practice with imperatives.

Go to the *Activity Bank* online for suggestions on promoting digital literacy and using the Internet to enhance this lesson.

MULTILEVEL WORKSHEETS

Templates: Cluster

Unit 5, Lesson 2, Worksheet 1: Follow Directions

Unit 5, Lesson 2, Worksheet 2: Following Directions

Unit 5, Lesson 2, Worksheet 3: Giving Directions

INSTRUCTOR'S NOTES

_____

_____

_____

_____

G. **Write the phrases under the signs.**

Turn right	Turn left	Turn around	Go straight

Turn left	Go straight	Turn right	Turn around

H. **Listen and check (✓) the boxes for the phrases you hear.**

CD 2
TR 3-7

	Turn right	Turn left	Turn around	Go straight
1. Directions to the mall	✓		✓	✓
2. Directions to the post office		✓		✓
3. Directions to the movie theater		✓		✓
4. Directions to the museum	✓			
5. Directions to the park			✓	✓

I. **Ask four classmates and complete the chart.**

Student A: Where do you live, Herman?
Student B: I live in Landsbury on Maple Avenue.   Answers will vary.

Student name	City	Street
1. Herman	Landsbury	Maple Avenue
2.		
3.		
4.		
5.		

LESSON **3** Let's go to the mall!

WORKPLACE CONNECTION
Exercise B: Interact appropriately
with team members.

GOAL ■ Give and follow directions in a mall

A. INTERPRET Answer the questions about the directory.

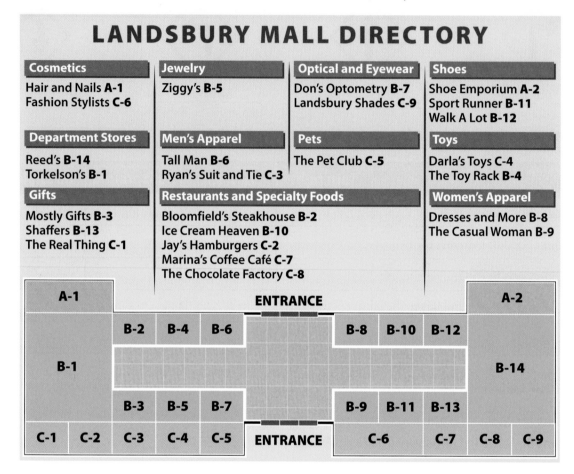

1. What store is next to Tall Man? _The Toy Rack_

2. What store is next to Dresses and More? _Sport Runner_

3. What store is between The Pet Club and Ryan's Suit and Tie? _Darla's Toys_

4. What store is between Landsbury Shades and Marina's Coffee Café? _The Chocolate Factory_

B. SCAN Scan the directory. Take turns asking and answering the questions with a partner.

1. Where can you buy a dog?

2. Where can you buy a suit for a man?

3. Where can you buy ice cream?

4. Where can you buy sneakers?

5. Where can you eat a steak?

120   Unit 5

Goal: Give and follow directions in a mall
Grammar: Prepositions of location
Academic Strategy: Focused listening, scanning for information
Vocabulary: Stores, prepositions

Agenda

☐ Talk about stores and malls.

☐ Give directions.

☐ Read a directory.

☐ Use prepositions of location.

☐ Ask about locations and give directions.

☐ Create a mall directory and floor plan.

Resources

Multilevel Worksheet: Unit 5, Lesson 3, Worksheet 1
Workbook: Unit 5, Lesson 3
Audio: CD 2, Track 8
Heinle Picture Dictionary: Shops and Stores, pages 48–49
Stand Out 1 Assessment CD-ROM with ExamView®

Pacing

■ 1.5 hour classes   ■ 2.5 hour classes
■ 3+ hour classes

STANDARDS CORRELATIONS

CCRS: RI1, RI7, SL1, SL2, L1
CASAS: 1.3.7, 2.2.1, 2.5.4
SCANS: Allocate materials and facility resources
Information Acquire and evaluate information
Interpersonal Participate as a member of a team
Basic Skills Reading, writing, listening, speaking
Thinking Skills Think creatively
EFF: **Communication** Read with understanding, convey ideas in writing, speak so others can understand, listen actively
Interpersonal Cooperate with others

Warm-up and Review   10–15 mins. ■■■

Write *mall* on the board and ask students if they know the word. Define it for them. Ask them in groups to quickly make a list of the kinds of stores they're likely to find in a mall. After they have finished, ask groups to send representatives to other groups to try to add three or four more types of stores to their lists.

Introduction   5–7 mins. ■■■

Review the prepositions of location the students have already learned. They should know *in, on, between,* and *next to.* State the goal: *Today, we will give directions and follow directions in a mall.*

Presentation 1   15–20 mins. ■■■

Ask students to look at the mall directory and briefly discuss each kind of store with them. As a class, compare the lists they made in the warm-up with the directory. Make sure students understand the directory's numbering system. Ask them to point to locations when you give them the names of various stores. Also, go over the categories. Ask questions, such as: *Where can you eat? Where can you buy a birthday present? Where can you buy a dog?*

Practice 1   10–15 mins. ■■■

A. INTERPRET Answer the questions about the directory.

Ask students to do this exercise in pairs.

B. SCAN Scan the directory. Take turns asking and answering the questions with a partner.

Go over the pronunciation of the questions with the class before students begin to practice. Make sure that they use correct rising and falling intonation on the information questions.

BEST PRACTICE

Step-by-Step

At this level, it is important that when there are several tasks to perform, you only ask students to do one at a time. Carefully model the target activity for students. Let students know how much time they have to complete each task as you give it to them, but monitor them to make sure they don't complete early and lose interest before the allotted time.

Evaluation 1   3–5 mins. ■■■
Go over students' work.

Presentation 2   20–30 mins. ■■■

C. Study the information with your teacher. Listen for the prepositions.

Go over the vocabulary in the box. Use each item several times in the context of the mall to ensure students know the words.

Prepare students to listen by giving a few sentences. When students hear a preposition—use one from the box—they are to stand up and then sit down again.

Play the recording. The prepositions are spread out enough in the recording that students will have time to stand up and sit down again before the next one. Play the recording once through and see how many students stand up. The second time, play it and stop after every sentence with a preposition. Ask students to identify each preposition.

LISTENING SCRIPT

CD 2
TR 8

A: *Well, it's time to go to the mall.*
B: *I love shopping.*
A: *What do you need?*
B: *I want a new dress.*
A: *Oh, you should go to the Casual Woman. It's next to Sport Runner.*
B: *Sounds good. Do you want to eat?*
A: *Yes, I do. Where would you suggest we go?*
B: *I don't know. Maybe Jay's Hamburgers around the corner.*
A: *Great! I will meet you there. First, I need to go to Landsbury Music and buy a CD.*
B: *Where is that?*
A: *It's on the corner outside.*
B: *Oh, that's right. I remember.*
A: *OK, I'll see you at Jay's. Where is it again?*
B: *It's between The Real Thing and Ryan's Suit and Tie.*
A: *OK. See you later.*

Teach students the difference between *in the corner* and *on the corner*. Use *in the corner* for things inside and *on the corner* for things outside.

D. Listen again and complete the sentences.

Ask students to listen and complete each sentence. Play the recording again.

Practice 2   7–10 mins. ■■

E. Write sentences about the mall diagram in Exercise C.

Ask students to write their sentences independently.

Evaluation 2   3–5 mins. ■■

Ask students to peer-edit each other's sentences and then call on volunteers to write their sentences on the board. Don't overcorrect, but make sure students spell and use the prepositions correctly. Also, make sure they use the complete form of *across from*.

BEST PRACTICE

Error correction

There is sometimes the temptation to overcorrect students. Students will make errors, but too much correcting without explanation can intimidate students so they are afraid to respond or, in this case, write. We suggest that you correct students on the concept you are teaching or have already taught. It is often more desirable to encourage peer-correcting over teacher-correcting because it can be less intimidating. It may be useful also to wait until you hear the error several times and explain the error to the class instead of identifying the students who are making the error.

Finally, be careful to limit correcting in application stages and team projects. In these activities, students are taking ownership of their own language and overcorrecting can inhibit this process.

INSTRUCTOR'S NOTES

_____

_____

_____

_____

_____

C. Study the information with your teacher. Listen for the prepositions.

around the corner	next to	on the corner	between	across from

D. Listen again and complete the sentences.

1. The Casual Woman is _____ next to _____ Sport Runner.

2. Jay's Hamburgers is _____ around _____ the corner.

3. Jay's Hamburgers is _____ between _____ the Real Thing and Ryan's Suit and Tie.

E. Write sentences about the mall diagram in Exercise C.   *Answers will vary.*

1. Jay's Hamburgers / Ryan's Suit and Tie
   Jay's Hamburgers is next to Ryan's Suit and Tie.

2. Ziggy's / The Pet Club
   _____

3. The Casual Woman / Dresses and More
   _____

4. Landsbury Shades
   _____

5. Sport Runner / Shaffers / The Casual Woman
   _____

6. Fashion Stylists / Marina's Coffee Café
   _____

WORKPLACE CONNECTION

Exercises F, G, H: Interpret and communicate information; Complete tasks as assigned.

F. Student A looks at page 121 and Student B looks at page 122. Student B asks where Ice Cream Heaven, Shoe Emporium, and the Pet Club are. Write the information on the diagram.

Student B: Where's Ice Cream Heaven?

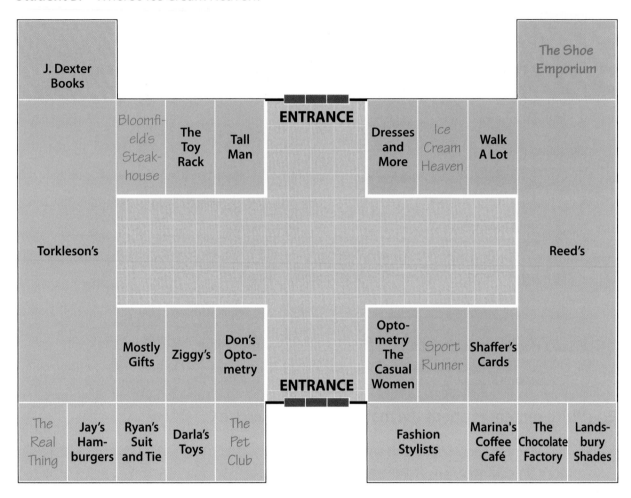

G. Student B looks at page 121 and Student A looks at page 122. Student A asks where Sport Runner, The Real Thing, and Bloomfield's Steakhouse are. Write the information on the diagram.

Student A: Where is Sport Runner?

H. **DESIGN** In groups, create a mall directory and floor plan. Then, share with the class. Answers will vary.

Presentation 3

10–15 mins. ■■■

Go over the picture of the mall again with students. Then, ask students to cover page 121. Show them how some of the stores are missing and explain that they will ask their partner where these stores are located.

BEST PRACTICE

Information gap

In an information-gap activity, two students work together. Each student has a different piece of information needed to complete the task. The two students have to ask each other questions in order to get the information they each need. In most cases, one student is looking at one page while the other is looking at another page. In this case, one student will be looking at page 121 while the other will be looking at page 122 and asking the questions.

Help students understand what they are to do in Exercises F and G by modeling it for them with a volunteer.

Practice 3

7–10 mins. ■

F. **Student A looks at page 121 and Student B looks at page 122. Student B asks where Ice Cream Heaven, Shoe Emporium, and the Pet Club are. Write the information on the diagram.**

G. **Student B looks at page 121 and Student A looks at page 122. Student A asks where Sport Runner, The Real Thing, and Bloomfield's Steakhouse are. Write the information on the diagram.**

Evaluation 3

3–7 mins. ■

Observe students as they practice.

Application

10–15 mins. ■■■

H. **DESIGN In groups, create a mall directory and floor plan. Then, share with the class.**

Encourage students to work together, speaking only English, to complete this activity. When they decide where stores should go, make sure they use prepositions of location. Supply paper and additional materials if necessary.

Refer students to *Stand Out 1 Workbook,* Unit 5, Lesson 3 for more practice with prepositions of location.

Go to the *Activity Bank* online for suggestions on promoting digital literacy and using the Internet to enhance this lesson.

MULTILEVEL WORKSHEET

Unit 5, Lesson 3, Worksheet 1: Prepositions of Location

INSTRUCTOR'S NOTES

_____
_____
_____
_____
_____
_____
_____
_____
_____
_____
_____
_____
_____
_____
_____
_____
_____
_____
_____
_____

Goal: Leave a phone message

Grammar: Questions with *can*

Academic Strategies: Focused listening, classifying

Vocabulary: Social language

Agenda

☐ List favorite stores.

☐ Take a class poll.

☐ Listen to answering machine messages.

☐ Use *can* to ask questions.

☐ Leave a phone message.

Resources

Multilevel Worksheets: Unit 5, Lesson 4, Worksheets 1–3

Workbook: Unit 5, Lesson 4

Audio: CD 2, Track 9

Heinle Picture Dictionary: The Telephone, pages 16–17

Stand Out 1 Assessment CD-ROM with ExamView®

Pacing

■ 1.5 hour classes ■ 2.5 hour classes

■ 3+ hour classes

STANDARDS CORRELATIONS

CCRS: RI1, SL1, SL2, L1, L2

CASAS: 2.1.7, 2.1.8

SCANS: **Information** Acquire and evaluate information, organize and maintain information, interpret and communicate information

Basic Skills Writing, listening, speaking

EFF: **Communication** Convey ideas in writing, speak so others can understand, listen actively

Warm-up and Review   15–20 mins. ■■■

Ask students in groups to make a list of their favorite stores and businesses in the community or neighborhood. Ask them to classify the list by restaurants, services, clothing stores, etc. After each group has finished its list, have a group representative share it with the class.

Introduction   3–5 mins. ■■■

Take a class poll. Ask: *Who is nervous when you answer the phone here in the United States? Who likes to call agencies to get information? Who doesn't like*

to leave messages on voicemail? Who has problems understanding messages on voicemail? State the goal: *Today, we will learn how to leave phone messages.*

Presentation 1   15–20 mins. ■■■

Look at the picture on this page and ask the questions. Ask additional questions, including questions about the mailing address and return address on the package.

A. INTERPRET Look at the package. Who is the package from? Who is the package to? Then, read about Gabriela's problem.

Read the short passage as a class. Ask some comprehension questions to make sure students understand.

B. EVALUATE What can Gabriela do? Who can help her? Talk in a group and complete the sentences below.

Have students discuss these questions in groups before completing the sentences in their books. Prepare students for focused listening by previewing the questions in Exercise C before you play the recording.

Practice 1   7–10 mins.

C. Listen to Gabriela leave a message. Circle the answers.

Play the recording. Write the following questions on the board: *What does Gabriela say she needs? When will David get back to her?* Ask additional questions if you wish. You may need to play the recording several times.

LISTENING SCRIPT   🎧 CD 2 TR 9

Machine: *Hello, this is David. I can't come to the phone right now, but your call is very important. Please leave a message after the tone and I will get back to you right away.*

Gabriela: *This is Gabriela. I want to go to the post office tomorrow. Can you go with me? I hope so. I need some help from a friend. Call me back at 555-3765.*

Evaluation 1   3–5 mins. ■■■

Go over the answers to Exercise C with students.

LESSON **4** **Please call**

GOAL █ Leave a phone message

A. INTERPRET Look at the package. Who is the package from? Who is the package to? Then, read about Gabriela's problem.

From | Gabriela Ramirez
37 Main Street
Landsbury, WA
99037

CLEARED

9781304568791

TO | Familia Ramirez
Av. Callao 423
1022 Buenos Aires,
Argentina

FRAGILE

Gabriela has a problem. She needs to go to the post office. She wants to send a package to her family in Buenos Aires, Argentina. She doesn't know what to say at the post office.

B. EVALUATE What can Gabriela do? Who can help her? Talk in a group and complete the sentences below. *Answers will vary. Sample answers are given.*

1. She can ask *a friend for help* .

2. She can call *the post office* .

3. She can go *to the post office* .

C. Listen to Gabriela leave a message. Circle the answers.

CD 2
TR 9

1. Who does she talk to?
   (a. her friend David)
   b. a machine
   c. David, her brother

2. When does she want to go to the post office?
   a. today
   (b. tomorrow)
   c. Saturday

D. There are three important parts of a message. Read the chart with your classmates and teacher.

Your name	Reason for calling	Your phone number
Gabriela	I have a question.	My number is 555-2344.
	I want to talk.	Call me at 555-2344.
	I need some information.	Can you call me back at 555-2344?

E. **EVALUATE** Look at the messages. Talk in a group. Circle the good messages.

1. This is Gabriela. I need help. I want to send a package. Please call me at 555-2344. Thanks.

2. Call me. OK?

3. I am Gabriela. My phone number is 555-2344.

4. This is your friend Gabriela from school. My number is 555-2344. Please call me. I have a question for you. Thanks.

5. This is Gabriela. My number is 555-2344. I have a small problem. Can you call me back? Thanks.

F. Practice leaving a message with two classmates.

Student A: Hello, this is Gabriela. I can't come to the phone right now.
Please leave a message.

Student B: This is Ramon. I have a question. My number is 555-2125.   *Answers will vary.*

Name: _____

Phone number: _____

Reason for calling: _____

_____

_____

Name: _____

Phone number: _____

Reason for calling: _____

_____

_____

Presentation 2   20–30 mins. ■■□

Ask students about Gabriela's call. Play the recording again to refresh their memories. Write *name, reason for calling,* and *phone number* on the board. Ask students what Gabriela's phone number is. Have them listen again. Ask why she is calling. Write answers as students give them to you on the board.

BEST PRACTICE

Listening

Most of the listening exercises in *Stand Out* are focused-listening activities. This strategy helps students to listen for important words and to guess at meaning using context clues. Many standardized assessment tests also use focused-listening exercises. Exercise C is an example of this type of test. Another example at this level is when students look at a series of pictures and listen to a description. Then, students choose the picture that the recording or listening excerpt best describes.

In focused listening, students always have a task. The task determines what they are listening for. Therefore, on tests, students should learn to prepare to listen by determining what they are listening for. We suggest students read the questions before they listen. If students are choosing from a series of pictures, they should first look at the pictures and try to determine the context and guess at what to listen for.

D. There are three important parts of a message. Read the chart with your classmates and teacher.

As you look at the chart with the students, number each column 1–3. Tell students that a good message has all three parts. Use this information as a reference for when you are working on Exercise E.

E. EVALUATE Look at the messages. Talk in a group. Circle the good messages.

Show students how to do this exercise by doing the first item with them. Write 1–3 above the message where appropriate to highlight the necessary parts of the message.

This activity is still part of the presentation stage, so it is expected that the teacher help students when necessary. Go over the answers and make sure students understand how to identify all three aspects of a message.

Practice 2   7–10 mins. ■■□

F. Practice leaving a message with two classmates.

Evaluation 2   7–10 mins. ■■□

Ask volunteers to read the messages they have written down in their books. Ask the class to confirm that the messages contain all of the necessary information.

INSTRUCTOR'S NOTES

Presentation 3

10–15 mins. ■■■

Ask a few students to help you do some things around the room. For example, ask students to help you move the teacher's desk and move it back again. Ask: *Can you help me?* Write the question on the board and ask students to repeat it. Show students how their reason for calling might be expressed by one of the questions in the chart in Exercise G.

G. Study the chart with your classmates and teacher.

Go over the chart carefully. Show students how word order makes a difference in English.

H. Match the questions with the responses. There may be more than one correct response.

Do this exercise as a class. Notice that there are two answers that are the same.

Write the following information on the board: *see / can / I / tomorrow / you*. Ask students to help you unscramble the question. Make sure you add a question mark once the question is complete. Also, briefly explain to students the difference between *me* and *I* (object vs. subject). Your explanation doesn't need to be lengthy at this level.

Practice 3

7–10 mins. ■

I. Write questions. Put the words in the correct order.

Evaluation 3

7–10 mins. ■

Ask student volunteers to write their questions on the board.

Application

7–10 mins. ■■■

J. APPLY Write a message you can leave for a friend on an answering machine for each situation.

Refer students to *Stand Out 1 Workbook*, Unit 5, Lesson 4 for more practice with *can* and questions.

Go to the *Activity Bank* online for suggestions on promoting digital literacy and using the Internet to enhance this lesson.

MULTILEVEL WORKSHEETS

Unit 5, Lesson 4, Worksheet 1: Reasons for Calling

Unit 5, Lesson 4, Worksheet 2: Phone Messages

Unit 5, Lesson 4, Worksheet 3: Message Pad

INSTRUCTOR'S NOTES

_____

_____

_____

_____

_____

_____

_____

_____

_____

_____

_____

_____

_____

_____

_____

_____

_____

_____

_____

_____

G. Study the chart with your classmates and teacher.

Questions with *Can*			
Can	**Subject**	**Base verb**	**Example question**
Can	I you	help ask talk answer call	**Can** I help you? **Can** I ask you a question? **Can** I talk to you? **Can** you answer a question? **Can** you call me?

H. Match the questions with the responses. There may be more than one correct response.

1. Can you help me?
2. Can I ask you a question?
3. Can I talk to you?
4. Can you answer a question?
5. Can you call me?

a. Yes. What's the question?
b. I can call you tomorrow.
c. Sure. What can I do for you?
d. OK. What can we talk about?
e. Yes. What's the question?

I. Write questions. Put the words in the correct order.

1. help / can / I / you
   Can I help you?

2. answer / the question / I / can
   Can I answer the question?

3. I / talk / to you / can / tomorrow
   Can I talk to you tomorrow?

4. I / can / you / see / tomorrow
   Can I see you tomorrow?

J. **APPLY** Write a message you can leave for a friend on an answering machine for each situation. *Answers will vary.*

I am very sick. _____

I have a problem. _____

I don't understand. _____

GOAL ▮ Write an e-mail

A. INTERPRET Read Gabriela's e-mail to her family.

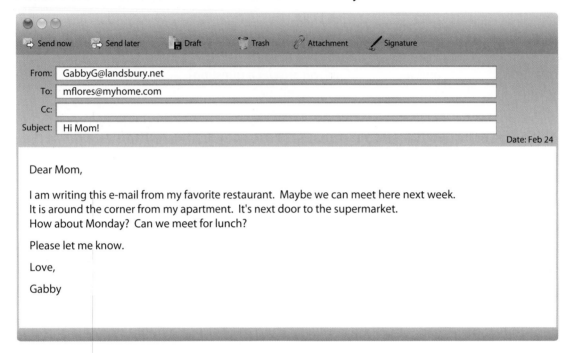

B. Answer the questions about the e-mail.

1. What is Gabriela's e-mail address?

   Gabriela's e-mail address is GabbyG@landsbury.net.

2. What is her mother's e-mail address?

   Her mother's e-mail address is mflores@myhome.com.

3. Where is the supermarket?

   The supermarket is next to Gabriela's favorite restaurant.

4. When did she write the e-mail?

   Gabriela wrote the e-mail on February 24.

5. Who is the e-mail to?

   The e-mail is to Gabriela's mother.

6. Where is Gabriela writing the e-mail from?

   Gabriela is writing the e-mail from her favorite restaurant.

Goal: Write an e-mail

Grammar: Present continuous, simple present, adverbs of frequency

Vocabulary: Community vocabulary

Agenda

- Review family relationships.
- Read an e-mail.
- Use the present continuous and the simple present.
- Use adverbs of frequency.
- Answer questions about an e-mail.
- Write an e-mail.

Resources

Multilevel Worksheet: Unit 5, Lesson 5, Worksheet 1

Workbook: Unit 5, Lesson 5

Audio: CD 2, Track 10

Heinle Picture Dictionary: Post Office, pages 52–53

Stand Out 1 Assessment CD-ROM with ExamView®

Pacing

- 1.5 hour classes
- 2.5 hour classes
- 3+ hour classes

STANDARDS CORRELATIONS

CCRS: RI1, W2, SL2, L1, L2

CASAS: 0.2.3

SCANS: **Information** Communicate information

Basic Skills Reading, writing, listening, speaking

Thinking Skills Think creatively

EFF: **Communication** Read with understanding, convey ideas in writing, speak so others can understand, listen actively, observe critically

Warm-up and Review   10–15 mins. ■■■

Ask students where their family members live and how they are related. If needed, review family relationship words. Ask students to list relatives on a sheet of paper. See how many they can write in two minutes.

Introduction   5 mins. ■■■

Ask students to choose one of the people on their list who lives in a different city or country and whom they would like to speak to or write an e-mail to. State the goal: *Today, we will write an e-mail.*

Presentation 1   5–7 mins. ■■■

Before students open their books, ask them if they know how to start and close an e-mail. Write *Dear...,* on the board and different words they can use to end a letter such as *sincerely, love,* etc. Tell students that they will read an e-mail by themselves. Explain to them that reading an e-mail with unfamiliar words is similar to focused listening—they don't have to understand every word.

A. INTERPRET Read Gabriela's e-mail to her family.

Suggest that students read through Gabriela's e-mail without stopping and then answer the questions in Exercise B without using a dictionary.

Practice 1   7–10 mins. ■■■

B. Answer the questions about the e-mail.

Students should try to answer every question even if they are unsure. This activity is designed for students to do on their own, not with help from other students or the teacher. Walk around the room and make sure students have written something on each line.

BEST PRACTICE

Independent learners

Some students are intimidated by writing tasks. A few may refuse to write or wait until you or another student gives them the answers. The only way such students will gain confidence is if they try to do activities and discover by so doing that they can do at least part of the activities on their own. Part of the *Stand Out* mission statement is to help students be independent learners. Strongly encourage students to do this activity and to guess when they need to.

Evaluation 1   5–7 mins. ■■

Ask students to check their work in pairs and then go over the answers as a class.

Presentation 2

20–30 mins. ■■■

C. Study the charts with your classmates and teacher.

Give students examples of the present continuous. Base the examples on classroom actions so students grasp that the present continuous refers to what is happening at the moment. Contrast this with the simple present, which is used for things we do regularly. Since the first sentence of Gabriela's e-mail is in the present continuous, point it out and contrast it with the second sentence in the simple present.

In the chart, help students see how the contractions work. Finally, explain that regular activities are often associated with adverbs of frequency. There is no need to use metalanguage here to explain it. Ask *yes/no* questions about what students do that will help explain these adverbs. For example: *Do you always drive to school?*

BEST PRACTICE

Metalanguage

Students don't need metalanguage to speak English well or to understand grammar. Some English speakers may never know what the third-person singular is. However, sometimes when working with adults, some identification of grammar structures can help them to identify things they have learned earlier and to apply them to new structures.

In this case, students have not learned about adverbs yet, and describing what an adverb is may confuse them in this activity. We suggest that you wait to delve into a description of what adverbs are at a more appropriate time.

Practice 2

10–12 mins. ■■

D. Complete the sentences with the present continuous form of the verb in parentheses.

E. Complete the sentences with the simple present form of the verb in parentheses.

Evaluation 2

5–7 mins. ■■

Ask students to write their answers on the board.

INSTRUCTOR'S NOTES

C. Study the charts with your classmates and teacher.

Present Continuous				
Subject	*Be*	**Base + *ing***	**Time**	**Example sentence**
I	am (I'm)	writing	right now today	I'**m writing** a letter right now.
He, She, It	is (she's)	eating		She'**s eating** a sandwich.
You, We, They	are (they're)	reading		They'**re reading** a book today.

D. Complete the sentences with the present continuous form of the verb in parentheses.

1. She _____ **is eating** _____ (eat) at a restaurant.

2. They _____ **are writing** _____ (write) e-mail.

3. We _____ **are reading** _____ (read) e-mail.

> **SPELLING**
> write → writing

4. I _____ **am going** _____ (go) to the hospital. I am very sick.

5. Gabriela _____ **is buying** _____ (buy) a book at the bookstore right now.

Simple Present			
Subject	**Adverb**	**Verb**	**Example sentence**
I	always	write	I always **write** e-mails.
He, She, It	often sometimes	eats	He rarely **eats** here.
You, We, They	rarely never	read	They never **read** the newspaper.

Adverbs of Frequency

0%		50%		100%
never	rarely	sometimes	usually	always

E. Complete the sentences with the simple present form of the verb in parentheses.

1. She _____ **lives** _____ (live) in Landsbury.

2. I never _____ **read** _____ (read) classified ads.

> **SPELLING**
> study → stud**ies**

3. We rarely _____ **study** _____ (study) on Saturday.

4. They often _____ **write** _____ (write) e-mails or texts at lunchtime.

5. You _____ **go** _____ (go) to school at the Orangewood School for Adults.

F. Listen and answer the questions. Answers will vary.

1. Where do you go to school? _I go to_ _____.

2. Where do you live? _I live_ _____.

3. Where is a restaurant nearby? _A restaurant is_ _____.

4. What do you sometimes do? _I sometimes_ _____.

G. Ask a partner questions and write his or her answers. Answers will vary.

1. Where do you go to school?

   He (She) goes to _____

2. Where do you live?

   _____

3. Where is a restaurant nearby?

   _____

4. What do you sometimes do?

   _____.

H. COMPOSE Write the text for an e-mail to a family member about your city. Use the information about yourself and your partner from this page. Answers will vary.

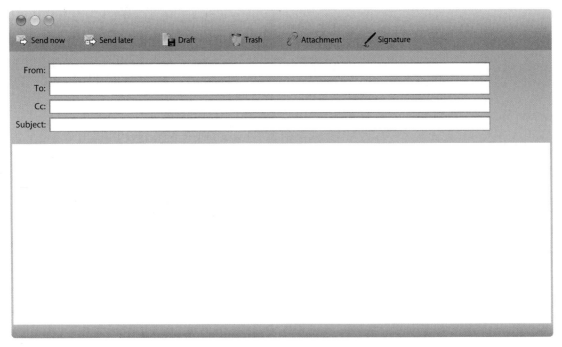

I. APPLY Write a real e-mail to friends or family. Get an e-mail account if necessary.

Presentation 3

7–10 mins. ■■■

F. Listen and answer the questions.

Do this activity first orally with the books closed. Play each question on the recording and ask individuals for answers. Play the recording two or three times. Then, ask students to open their books and write the answers.

Make sure students understand the meaning of each question and can answer it in complete sentences. This will help them do Exercise G as well as the application. Prepare students for Exercise G further by reminding them to use the third-person singular *s*.

> ### LISTENING SCRIPT
> *The listening script matches the questions in Exercise F.*
>
> CD 2
> TR 10

Practice 3

5–10 mins. ■

G. Ask a partner questions and write his or her answers.

This exercise will be used in the application stage, so encourage students to answer in complete sentences.

Evaluation 3

5–7 mins. ■

Ask students to tell the class about students they interviewed.

Application

20–30 mins. ■■■

H. COMPOSE Write the text for an e-mail to a family member about your city. Use the information about yourself and your partner from this page.

Remind students that images can be sent along with text in an actual e-mail. Encourage them to describe things pictured in the photos such as the inside of their apartments or a nearby restaurant.

I. APPLY Write a real e-mail to friends or family. Get an e-mail account if necessary.

Suggest to students that many local libraries offer the use of computers and Internet access at no cost.

MULTILEVEL WORKSHEETS

Unit 5, Lesson 5, Worksheet 1: Simple Present

Unit 5, Lesson 5, Worksheet 2: Present Continuous

Refer students to *Stand Out 1 Workbook*, **Unit 5, Lesson 5 for more practice with the present continuous and the simple present.**

Go to the *Activity Bank* **online for suggestions on promoting digital literacy and using the Internet to enhance this lesson.**

INSTRUCTOR'S NOTES

_____

_____

_____

_____

_____

_____

_____

_____

_____

_____

_____

_____

_____

_____

_____

_____

_____

LIFESKILLS ▶ How do I get there?

Before You Watch

- Read the title out loud.
- Ask students if anyone in the photo looks lost. Ask them how they know. Discuss as a class.

A. Look at the picture. Complete each sentence.

- Have students look at the picture and complete each sentence.
- Ask volunteers to share their answers with the class.

While You Watch

B. Watch the video. How do you get from the bookstore to the diner? Write numbers to show the correct order.

- Tell students they will watch the video. Then, ask them how you get from the bookstore to the diner.
- Ask students to write numbers to show the correct order.
- Go over the sentences. Then, play the video and ask students to watch and listen carefully.
- Play the video two more times in order for students to (1) complete the exercise and (2) check their answers.
- Check answers as a class.

Check Your Understanding

C. Complete the dialog. Use the words in the box.

- Read each word in the box out loud.
- Tell students they will complete the dialog with the words in the box. Read the example sentence to the class.
- Ask students to work individually. Then, ask them to share their answers in pairs.
- Ask students to practice the dialog with their partners. Then, ask for volunteers to demonstrate the dialog to the class.

INSTRUCTOR'S NOTES

▶ # How do I get there?

Before You Watch

A. Look at the picture. Complete each sentence.

1. Naomi, Hector, and Mateo are in a ___restaurant___.

2. Hector and Mateo are ___talking___.

3. Mateo is ___lost___.

While You Watch

B. ▶ **Watch the video. How do you get from the bookstore to the diner? Write numbers to show the correct order.**

a. __3__ Then turn right.

b. __2__ Go toward City Hall.

c. __5__ The diner is on the left.

d. __4__ Walk one block.

e. __1__ Walk down Atlantic for two blocks.

Check Your Understanding

C. Complete the dialog. Use the words in the box.

on the corner of	~~in front of~~	on	signs	straight

Mateo: I'm (1) ___in front of___ the bookstore. The bookstore is next to a coffee shop.

Naomi: Ask him what street he's (2) ___on___.

Hector: What street are you on? Do you see any street (3) ___signs___?

Mateo: Yeah, I'm (4) ___on the corner of___ Atlantic and Broadway.

Hector: He's on the corner of Atlantic and Broadway.

Naomi: Tell him to walk (5) ___straight___ for two blocks.

Review

A. **Look at the map. Ask a partner for directions to these places.**

the motel	the mobile homes	the hospital
the park	the apartments	the hotel
the public pool	the post office	

Student A: Where are the tennis courts?

Student B: They are on Second Street, next to the post office.

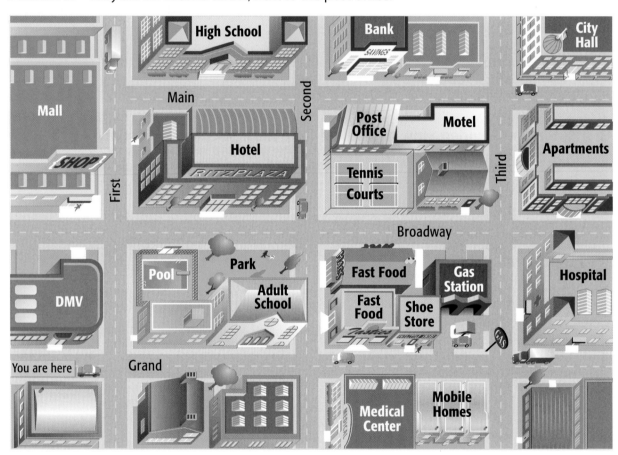

B. **Give directions to a partner to each location.**

the hotel	the apartments	City Hall
the hospital	the high school	the bank
the motel	the DMV	

Student A: Can you give me directions to the medical center?

Student B: Yes, go straight ahead on Grand. Go one block. It's on the right.

130 Unit 5

Goal: All unit goals

Grammar: All unit grammar

Academic Strategies: Reviewing, evaluating, developing study skills

Vocabulary: All unit vocabulary

Audio: CD 2, Track 11

Agenda

- Discuss unit goals.
- Complete the review.
- Evaluate and reflect on progress.

Pacing

- ■ 1.5 hour classes
- ■ 2.5 hour classes
- ■ 3+ hour classes

STANDARDS CORRELATIONS

CCRS: 0.2.3, 1.1.3, 2.1.7, 2.1.8, 1.9.1, 2.2.2

CASAS: 0.2.3, 1.1.3, 1.9.1, 2.1.7, 2.1.8, 2.2.2

SCANS: **Information** Acquire and evaluate information, organize and maintain information

Basic Skills Writing, listening, speaking

Personal Qualities Responsibility, self-management

EFF: Speak so others can understand

Lifelong Learning Take responsibility for learning, reflect and evaluate

Warm-up and Review
7–10 mins. ■■■

With their books closed, ask students to help you make a list on the board of all the vocabulary they can come up with from the unit. Then, have a competition where students in groups will look back in their books and write page numbers for each item on the list. The first group to find the correct page number for each item wins.

Introduction
5 mins. ■■■

Write all the goals on the board from Unit 5. Show students the first page of the unit and mention the five goals. Explain that today is review and that they will review the whole unit.

Presentation
10–15 mins. ■■■

This presentation and practice will cover the first three pages of the review. Quickly go to the first page of each lesson. Discuss the goal of each. Ask simple questions to remind students of what they have learned.

Practice
15–20 mins. ■■■

A. Look at the map. Ask a partner for directions to these places. (Lessons 1 and 2)

B. Give directions to a partner to each location. (Lesson 2)

BEST PRACTICE

Recycling/Review

The review and the project that follows are part of the recycling/review process. Students at this level often need to be reintroduced to concepts to solidify what they have learned. Many concepts are learned and forgotten while learning other new concepts. This is because students learn but are not necessarily ready to acquire language concepts.

Therefore, it becomes very important to review and to show students how to review on their own. It is also important to recycle the new concepts in different contexts.

INSTRUCTOR'S NOTES

_____

_____

_____

_____

_____

_____

_____

_____

_____

Practice *(continued)*

C. Listen to the messages. Complete the chart. (Lesson 4)

> ### LISTENING SCRIPT
>
> CD 2
> TR 11
>
> 1. **Machine:** *This is Herman. I can't come to the phone right now. Please leave a message.*
>   **Nadia:** *This is Nadia. I have a question. My number is 555-2344.*
>
> 2. **Machine:** *This is Herman. I can't come to the phone right now. Please leave a message.*
>   **Vien:** *This is Vien. I want to talk. Can you call me? My number is 555-7798.*
>
> 3. **Machine:** *This is Herman. I can't come to the phone right now. Please leave a message.*
>   **David:** *David here. I need information. Please call 555-1234.*
>
> 4. **Machine:** *This is Herman. I can't come to the phone right now. Please leave a message.*
>   **Ricardo:** *My name is Ricardo. I need a phone number. My number is 555-7343.*

D. Write sentences about yourself. (Lesson 5)

E. With a group, list the types of stores you can find at a mall. (Lesson 3)

🎧 **C. Listen to the messages. Complete the chart.**

CD 2
TR 11

Name	Reason for calling	Phone number
1. Nadia	I have a question.	555-2134
2. Vien	I want to talk.	555-7798
3. David	I need information.	555-1234
4. Ricardo	I need a phone number.	555-7343

D. Write sentences about yourself. Answers will vary.

I always _____.

I often _____.

Sometimes I _____.

I rarely _____.

I never _____.

E. With a group, list the types of stores you can find at a mall. Answers will vary.

_____   _____

_____   _____

_____   _____

_____   _____

_____   _____

_____

F. **Read the services in the box. Then, write them under the correct places below.**

| a. Delivers mail | b. Helps sick people | c. Keeps your money safe | d. Gives licenses |

1.

Gives licenses

2.

Helps sick people

3.

Delivers mail

4.

Keeps your money safe

G. **Write a new e-mail. Use the model on page 126.** _Answers will vary._

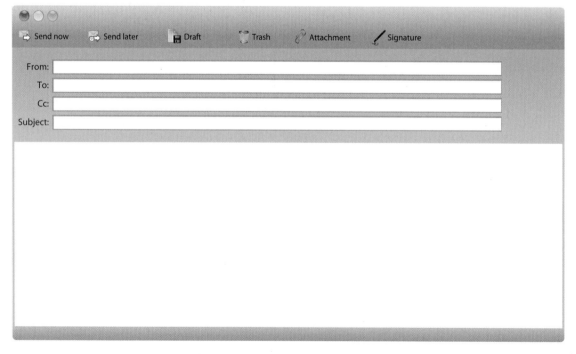

✓ **Make a brochure of a new city**

In this project, you will make a brochure of a new city and present it to the class.

1. **COLLABORATE** Form a team with four or five students. In your team, you need:

Position	Job description	Student name
Student 1: **Team Leader**	Check that everyone speaks English. Check that everyone participates.	
Student 2: **City Planner**	With help from the team, draw a map of your city.	
Student 3: **Artist**	With help from the team, make a brochure of your city.	
Students 4/5: **Spokespeople**	With help from the team, organize a presentation to give to the class.	

2. Choose a name for your city.

3. Make a list of important places in your city and put them in alphabetical order.

4. Make a map of your city and mark where the important places are.

5. Make a brochure. On the brochure, write one paragraph about the city, write the names of your team's members, and draw a picture that represents the city.

6. Prepare a presentation for the class.

About the Explorer

Maritza Morales Casanova is an environmentalist from Mérida in Yucatan, Mexico. Her aim is to raise environmental awareness among children with the hope of shaping future leaders. Maritza has been trying to raise awareness from a very young age. When she was ten years old, she founded HUNAB (Humanity United to Nature in Harmony for Beauty, Welfare, and Goodness). Her project grew and now, at the Ceiba Pentandra Park, children learn how to care for the environment.

About the Photo

This photo was taken at the Ceiba Pentandra Park. It shows Maritza and a group of children. They are learning about how to care for the environment. Each section of the park focuses on a different environmental issue. As Maritza believes in shaping the future leaders, she empowers some of the children as teachers at the park.

- Introduce the explorer. Ask students which person in the photo is Maritza Morales Casanova.

- Ask students what *environment* means. Then, ask them what *environmental education* is. Discuss as a class.

A. PREDICT Before you read about Maritza, look at the title and photo above. Answer the questions.

- Ask volunteers to describe what they see in the photo. Then, ask students what the children are doing. Discuss as a class.

- Ask a volunteer to read the quote out loud. Then, have the class discuss how they think this relates to the title.

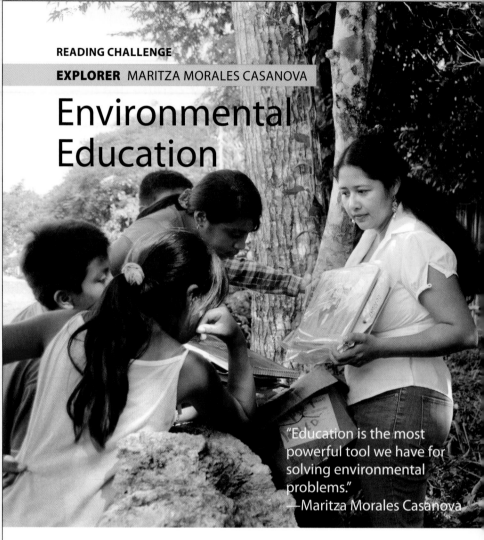

READING CHALLENGE

EXPLORER MARITZA MORALES CASANOVA

Environmental Education

"Education is the most powerful tool we have for solving environmental problems."
—Maritza Morales Casanova

A. PREDICT Before you read about Maritza, look at the title and photo above. Answer the questions.

1. What does *environment* mean?
   a. the natural world around us
   b. people in a country
   c. children

2. What are the children in the picture doing?
   a. They are eating lunch.
   b. They are learning about the environment.
   c. They are hiking.

134   Unit 5

CCRS FOR READING

RI1, RI2, RI7

B. Look at the blueprints of an environmental park in Yucatan, Mexico. Describe to a partner where things are located.

- Ask students to look at the blueprints of an environmental park in Yucatan, Mexico. Then, ask them to practice telling a partner where things are located.

Practice (continued)

F. Read the services in the box. Then, write them under the correct places below. (Lesson 1)

G. Write a new e-mail. Use the model on page 126. (Lesson 5)

Evaluation   15 mins. ■■■

Go around the room and check on students' progress. Help individuals when needed. If you see consistent errors among several students, interrupt the class and give a mini lesson or review to help students feel comfortable with the concept.

MULTILEVEL WORKSHEETS

Unit 5, Computer Worksheets

Unit 5, Internet Worksheets

Presentation   5 mins. ■■■

Learner Log

Review the concepts of the Learner Log. Make sure students understand the concepts and how to complete the log including circling the answers, finding page numbers where the concept is taught, and ranking favorite activities.

BEST PRACTICE

Learner Logs

Learner Logs function to help students in many different ways.

1. They serve as part of the review process. They help students to gain confidence and to document what they have learned.
2. Consequently, students see that they are progressing in their learning.
3. They provide students with a tool that they can use over and over to check and recheck their understanding of the target language. In this way, students become independent learners.

Practice   10–15 mins. ■

Ask students to complete the Learner Log.

Evaluation   2 mins. ■

Go over the Learner Log with students.

Application   5–7 mins. ■■■

Ask students to record their favorite lesson or page in the unit.

Assessment   ■■■

Use the Stand Out 1 Assessment CD-ROM with ExamView® to create a post-test for Unit 5.

Refer students to Stand Out 1 Workbook, Unit 5, Lesson 1 for more practice with in/on/at and Lesson 4 for more practice with the modal can.

Go to the Activity Bank online for suggestions on promoting digital literacy and using the Internet to enhance this lesson.

INSTRUCTOR'S NOTES

_____

_____

_____

_____

_____

_____

_____

_____

_____

_____

_____

_____

_____

_____

_____

_____

Make decisions and solve problems; Collect and organize information; Combine ideas and information; Exercise leadership roles; Manage time; Complete tasks as assigned; Interact appropriately with team members; Interpret and communicate information.

STANDARDS CORRELATIONS

CCRS: RI7, W2, SL1, SL2

CASAS: 0.2.3, 1.1.3, 1.9.1, 2.1.7, 2.1.8, 2.2.2, 4.8.1

SCANS: Resources Allocate time, allocate materials and facility resources, allocate human resources

Information Acquire and evaluate information, organize and maintain information, interpret and communicate information

Interpersonal Participate as a member of a team, teach others, exercise leadership, negotiate to arrive at a decision, work with cultural diversity

Systems Understand systems, monitor and correct performance

Basic Skills Reading, writing, listening, speaking

Thinking Skills Think creatively, make decisions, solve problems, see things in the mind's eye

Personal Qualities Responsibility, sociability, self-management

EFF: Communication Read with understanding, convey ideas in writing, speak so others can understand, listen actively, observe critically

Decision Making Solve problems and make decisions, plan

Interpersonal Cooperate with others, advocate and influence, resolve conflict and negotiate, guide others

Lifelong Learning Take responsibility for learning, reflect and evaluate

Introduction   5 mins.

TEAM PROJECT

Make a brochure of a new city

In this project, students will make a brochure of a new city and present it to the class.

Stage 1   15–20 mins.

COLLABORATE Form a team with four or five students.

Form teams with four or five students in each one. Show students examples of the project if you have one or discuss the photo on the student book page.

Help students to assign positions in their groups. On the spot, students will have to choose who will be the leader of their group. Review the responsibility of a leader and ask students to write the name of their leader in their books. Do the same with all positions.

Stage 2   5 mins.

Choose a name for your city.

Make sure students understand that this is an imaginary city, so they should not use the name of a real city.

Stage 3   15–20 mins.

Make a list of important places in your city and put them in alphabetical order.

Stage 4   20–30 mins.

Make a map of your city and mark where the important places are.

Supply paper and art materials. Make sure that all students work on map production. During this activity, encourage students to use prepositions of location.

Stage 5   20–30 mins.

Make a brochure. On the brochure, write one paragraph about the city, write the names of your team's members, and draw a picture that represents the city.

Ask students to make a brochure that describes the city. This project segment can be done on the template provided on the Multilevel Worksheets CD-ROM (Unit 5, Project, Worksheet 1). Ask students to write one paragraph about their city. Be careful not to overcorrect students' writing.

Stage 6   10–30 mins.

Prepare a presentation for the class.

Consider videotaping the presentations. Students will prepare better for formal presentations if they know they will be videotaped. Another approach would be to have students videotape themselves and polish their presentations after they have viewed the recorded presentation.

Display maps and brochures in the classroom if possible.

MULTILEVEL WORKSHEETS

Unit 5, Project, Worksheet 1: City Brochure

Unit 5, Extension, Worksheet 1: Read a Bus Schedule

Unit 5, Extension, Worksheet 2: Addressing Envelopes

BEST PRACTICE

Digital literacy

Projects are a perfect place to allow students opportunities to use other forms of presentations beyond pictures they create. Digital literacy is becoming more necessary as a life skill. Encourage students to create presentations using pictures from the Internet. They might also consider using other digital presentation tools.

B. Look at the blueprints of an environmental park in Yucatan, Mexico. Describe to a partner where things are located.

Student 1: Where are <u>the offices</u>?
Student 2: They are <u>on the right</u>.

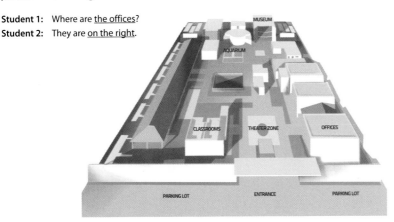

C. Read about Maritza Morales Casanova and her community.

Maritza Morales Casanova is <u>working</u> hard to teach children about the environment. On July 24th, 2013, she opened an environmental park in Yucatan, Mexico, called Ceiba Pentandra Park. The park is a little community. The plan for the park shows the different areas. The classrooms are <u>on the left</u>. The offices are <u>on the right</u>. The Theatre Zone is <u>between</u> the classrooms and the offices. At the school, children are the teachers. They teach other children how to take care of the planet.

D. Answer the questions about the paragraph.

1. **What** is the name of the park? _____Ceiba Pentandra Park_____

2. **Where** is the park? _____Yucatan, Mexico_____

3. **When** did the park open? _____July 24th, 2013_____

4. **Who** are the teachers? _____children are the teachers_____

E. **RANK** In a group, rank ways to save the environment. 1 is for the best way.

Answers will vary.

_____ Walk or ride a bike instead of driving.   _____ Don't use the heater too much.

_____ Use recycled paper.   _____ Take showers not baths.

_____ Don't use the air conditioner too much.   _____ Take short showers.

Reading Challenge **135**

- Tell students to follow the model conversation and demonstrate for them. Ask students if they can spot the offices on the blueprints.
- Have volunteers demonstrate their conversations to the class.

C. **Read about Maritza Morales Casanova and her community.**

Ask students to read about Maritza Morales Casanova and her community.

D. **Answer the questions about the paragraph.**

- Point out each interrogative word: *What, Where, When*, and *Who*? Then, ask students to answer the questions about the paragraph they read.
- Have students compare their answers with the person sitting next to them. Then, review answers as a class.

E. **RANK** In a group, rank ways to save the environment. 1 is for the best way.

- Tell students they will rank ways to save the environment. Explain to students that *rank* means putting things in order of importance. Point out that 1 is the best way.
- Ask students to read the statements and rank each from 1 to 6.
- Have students discuss their answers within their groups. Then, review and discuss as a class.

READING STRATEGIES

Re-read the Text

Students will often need to re-read the text to accurately recall specific details. It is not necessary that students memorize everything they read. This strategy is also useful when students need to rank content from a reading in order of importance. Students re-read the text to get a better sense of the importance for each item conveyed by the writer.

Health and Fitness

About the Photo

Benjamin Norman, a photojournalist and editorial photographer from New York City, took this photo. It shows participants in the New York City Marathon running over the Verrazano-Narrows Bridge to the south of Manhattan. The bridge connects the two New York boroughs of Staten Island and Brooklyn. The New York City Marathon takes place on the first Sunday in November each year. It is the largest marathon in the world with over 50,000 runners taking part in the event over the last few years.

- Introduce the unit. Read the title out loud. Ask students to form small groups.

- Ask students to look at the photo and answer the questions in their groups.

- Read the caption out loud and review answers as a class.

- Go over each unit outcome.

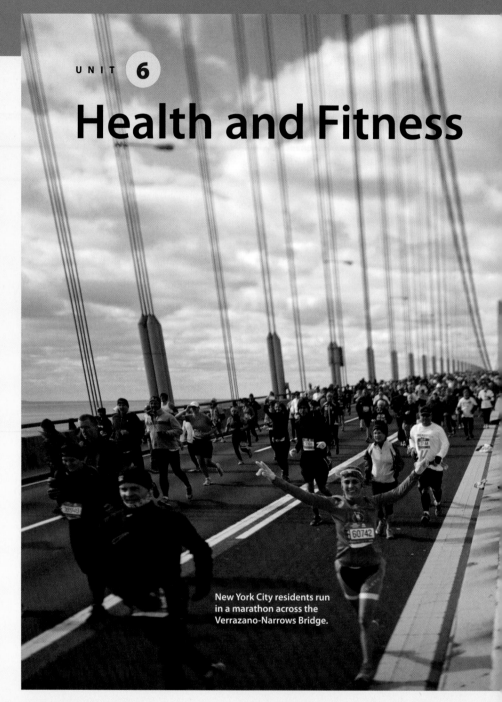

UNIT **6**

Health and Fitness

New York City residents run in a marathon across the Verrazano-Narrows Bridge.

UNIT OUTCOMES	GRAMMAR	VOCABULARY	EL CIVICS
• Identify parts of the body • Identify illnesses and health problems • Give advice • Ask for information • Develop an exercise plan	• Simple present • Simple present and negative: *have* • Modal: *should* • Prepositions of location • Question words • Infinitives	• Symptoms and illnesses • Medications • Hospital • Exercise, healthy, flexibility	The skills students learn in this unit can be applied to the following El Civics competency areas: • Health – Pharmacy • Health – Healthcare

UNIT OUTCOMES
- ☐ Identify parts of the body
- ☐ Identify illnesses and health problems
- ☐ Give advice
- ☐ Ask for information
- ☐ Develop an exercise plan

Look at the photo and answer the questions.
1. Where are the people?
2. What are they doing?
3. Do you think they are healthy? Why?

Life Skills Link

In this unit, students will learn how to identify body parts and explain ailments related to them. They will also learn how to give health advice and develop exercise plans.

Workplace Link

All lessons and units in *Stand Out* include basic communication skills and interpersonal skills important for the workplace. They are not individually identified. Other workplace skills are indicated. They include *collecting and organizing information, making decisions and solving problems,* and *combining ideas and information.*

CASAS	SCANS	CCRS
Lesson 1: 3.1.1 Lesson 2: 3.1.1, 6.6.5 Lesson 3: 0.1.3, 3.3.1, 3.3.2, 3.3.3 Lesson 4: 0.1.2, 2.5.1 Lesson 5: 1.1.3, 3.5.9, 7.1.1 Review: 2.5.1, 3.1.1, 3.3.1, 3.3.2, 3.3.3, 3.5.9 Team Project: 2.5.1, 3.1.1, 3.3.1, 3.3.2, 3.3.3, 3.5.9, 4.8.1	Most SCANS are incorporated into this unit, with an emphasis on: • Interpreting and communicating information • Understanding systems • Decision making • (Technology is optional.)	RI1, RI2, RI5, RI7, SL1, SL2, SL4, L1, L2, L4, L5, RF2, RF3

GOAL ▪ Identify parts of the body

A. PREDICT Look at the picture. Who is Victor talking to? What is the problem? Then, read about Victor.

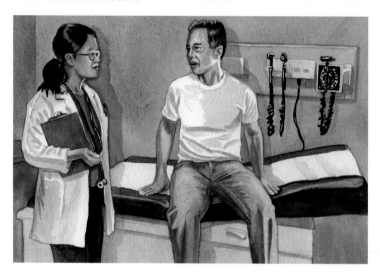

> Victor is sick. He visits the doctor. The doctor asks, "What is the problem?" Victor answers, "I hurt all over. I think I have a fever. My head hurts and my muscles ache." The doctor checks Victor for the flu. The doctor gives him some medicine for the pain.

B. Circle *True* or *False*.

1. Victor needs medicine.   (True)   False

2. Victor's head hurts.   (True)   False

3. Victor doesn't have a problem.   True   (False)

C. INFER Victor says, "I hurt all over." Make a list of body parts that you think he means:

_____*head*_____

_____

_____

_____

_____

_____

Goal: Identify parts of the body
Grammar: Simple present
Academic Strategies: Focused listening, ranking
Vocabulary: Parts of the body

Agenda

- Discuss visits to the doctor.
- Identify parts of the body.
- Read about Victor's visit to the doctor.
- Practice talking to the doctor.
- Use the simple present tense.
- Rank parts of the body.

Resources

Multilevel Worksheet: Unit 6, Lesson 1, Worksheet 1
Workbook: Unit 6, Lesson 1
Audio: CD 2, Tracks 12–14
Heinle Picture Dictionary: The Human Body, pages 132–133
Stand Out 1 Assessment CD-ROM with ExamView®

Pacing

- 1.5 hour classes
- 2.5 hour classes
- 3+ hour classes

STANDARDS CORRELATIONS

CCRS: RI1, SL1, SL2, L1, L2, RF3
CASAS: 3.1.1
SCANS: **Basic Skills** Listening, speaking
EFF: **Communication** Speak so others can understand, listen actively

Preassessment *(optional)* ■■■

Use the Stand Out 1 Assessment Activity Bank with ExamView® to create a pretest for Unit 6.

Warm-up and Review   7–10 mins. ■■■

Ask students if they like going to the doctor. Ask where they go if they have a medical problem. Write prompts on the board, such as *the emergency room*, *the doctor's office*, and *a clinic*. Ask students why they go to the doctor. They may suggest ailments or illnesses that are generally related to specific body parts. Write the body parts they mention on the board. Then, ask them to point to these parts on their bodies as you say them.

Introduction   10–15 mins. ■■■

Write *healthy* on the board and see if students can tell you some healthy things to do. Say *exercise* and write it on the board. State the goal: *Today, we will identify parts of the body.*

Presentation 1   20–25 mins. ■■■

Ask students how often they go to the doctor. Take a class poll. Then, ask students to open their books. As a class, look at the picture of Victor. Ask the questions in the direction line and any other questions you consider appropriate. As you do this, ask students to cover up Exercise A so they don't read ahead. Ask students to predict what the problem might be or decide if Victor is just there for a checkup.

Practice 1   7–10 mins. ■■■

Ask students to read the paragraph about Victor and answer the *true / false* questions. Give them a limited time to do this, perhaps one minute.

A. PREDICT Look at the picture. Who is Victor talking to? What is the problem? Then, read about Victor.

B. Circle *True* or *False*.

BEST PRACTICE

Timed tasks

Sometimes giving students a limited time to do a task will help them to stay focused and on task. It is good practice to regularly give students a time limit for tasks.

In reading, some students may have the false impression that reading slowly is better than reading quickly. This activity forces them to work quickly.

Evaluation 1   3–5 mins. ■■■

Read the paragraph together as a class. Check for unfamiliar words and go over the answers in Exercise B.

Presentation 2   15–20 mins. ■■■

C. INFER Victor says, "I hurt all over." Make a list of body parts that you think he means:

Ask students to make their lists individually. Have volunteers share their answers with the class.

D. Label the parts of the body. Use the words from the boxes.

Point out the singular and plural forms of the body parts, but only use the singular forms at this time in this presentation. Go over each word and its pronunciation. You may want to give a mini lesson on the *th* sound.

Final /θ/

The /θ/ is the symbol for voiceless *th*, as in *mouth* and *teeth*. This sound is problematic for many students. Some languages, for example, Spanish, have similar sounds but are represented by different letters. Often, students have problems making the connection between the sounds they make in their languages and the /θ/ in English because they are represented differently orthographically.

To produce this sound properly, the instructor needs to teach two things. First, teach the point of articulation. An easy way to do this is to exaggerate the articulation by asking students to bite their tongue. Most students won't have trouble with this. The second part is often not taught but will make a significant difference in student production. Ask students to attempt to blow air out of their mouths before releasing the tongue. They should build up air pressure and then release the tongue.

Note: Final consonants are very important in English. When speaking words in isolation and at the end of phrases or sentences, the point of articulation is released and, in most cases, the mouth is open. In other languages where the final consonant isn't as important, the final point of articulation is not immediately released and the mouth is closed. Help students see that it is important to release the tongue to finish the sound of the /θ/.

E. Listen to the patients talk to the doctor. What are their problems? Complete the sentences.

Go over the listening with students. If needed, pause the recording after each conversation and discuss it before you go on to the next one.

LISTENING SCRIPT

CD 2
TR 12–14

1. **Karen:** *Doctor, thank you for seeing me on such short notice.*
   Doctor: *What seems to be the trouble?*
   Karen: *Well, I'm having trouble with my hand.*
   Doctor: *What do you mean, trouble?*
   Karen: *My hand is very stiff in the morning. I work at a computer, and it is getting very difficult to do my work.*

2. **Doctor:** *How are you today, Roberto?*
   Roberto: *I'm fine except my leg hurts all the time.*
   Doctor: *I see. Let's check it out. Where does it hurt?*
   Roberto: *My leg hurts right here near the knee.*
   Doctor: *We probably should take some X-rays.*

3. **Doctor:** *Well, Tino, it seems like you are here every week these days.*
   Tino: *I guess so, doctor. My foot is killing me.*
   Doctor: *I know that you were here last week because of your elbow. Did the prescription help?*
   Tino: *Not at all. It seems to be getting worse.*

Prepare students by going over the conversation. Note that students are learning clarification skills as well as new vocabulary. Show them how the intonation rises on this clarification strategy.

Practice 2   7–10 mins. ◼◼◻

F. Read the conversation. Practice new conversations using the words in Exercise D.

Evaluation 2   5–7 mins. ◼◼◻
Ask volunteers to present their conversations in front of the class.

INSTRUCTOR'S NOTES

_____

_____

_____

_____

_____

_____

_____

D. Label the parts of the body. Use the words from the boxes.

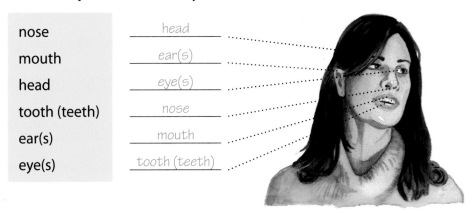

nose
mouth
head
tooth (teeth)
ear(s)
eye(s)

head

ear(s)

eye(s)

nose

mouth

tooth (teeth)

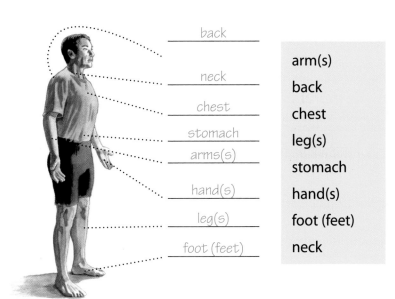

back

neck

chest

stomach

arms(s)

hand(s)

leg(s)

foot (feet)

arm(s)
back
chest
leg(s)
stomach
hand(s)
foot (feet)
neck

E. Listen to the patients talk to the doctor. What are their problems? Complete the sentences.

CD 2
TR 12-14

1. **Karen:**   Doctor, my _____ _hand_ _____ hurts.

2. **Roberto:** Doctor, my _____ _leg_ _____ hurts.

3. **Tino:**   Doctor, my _____ _foot_ _____ and _____ _elbow_ _____ hurt.

F. Read the conversation. Practice new conversations using the words in Exercise D.

Doctor: What is the problem today?
Patient: My leg hurts.
Doctor: Your leg?
Patient: Yes, my leg.

WORKPLACE CONNECTIONS
Exercises G, H: Collect and organize information.
Exercise I: Interact appropriately with team members.

G. Study the chart with your classmates and teacher.

Simple Present		
Subject	**Verb**	**Example sentence**
It My leg My arm My foot My head	hurts	My leg **hurts.** My arm **hurts.** My head **hurts.**
They My legs My arms My feet My ears	hurt	My legs **hurt.** My feet **hurt.** My ears **hurt.**

H. Write sentences for singular and plural subjects.

Part of body	Singular	Plural
leg	My leg hurts.	My legs hurt.
arm	My arm hurts.	My arms hurt.
head	My head hurts.	
foot	My foot hurts.	My feet hurt.
back	My back hurts.	
eye	My eye hurts.	My eyes hurt.
nose	My nose hurts.	
ear	My ear hurts.	My ears hurt.

I. **APPLY** In a group, create a list of body parts from the lesson. Discuss what hurts more often.

Presentation 3

10–15 mins. ■■■

G. Study the chart with your classmates and teacher.

Some students might be confused by *my*. Review the possessive adjective and help students to see that the noun is the word that follows.

Do a role-play with a few students where you are the patient and they are the doctors. Ask the class to help you finish sentences you begin with *My leg . . .* or *My feet . . . .*

Practice 3

7–10 mins. ■

H. Write sentences for singular and plural subjects.

Point out to students that the plural space for the words *head*, *back*, and *nose* are shaded in because we don't use the words in the plural with **my**.

BEST PRACTICE

Conversations

Some techniques to add variety to conversations that we have discussed include the following:

- Working with a partner
- Conversation chaining in a group
- Conversation cards
- Inside/outside circle
- Two lines with students moving one space after each rotation

---

Evaluation 3

7–10 mins. ■

Ask students to make a short conversation with a partner using sentences they learned in this lesson.

Application

7–10 mins. ■■■

Remind students how to rank things. It is easiest to do this with food preferences.

I. APPLY In a group, create a list of body parts from the lesson. Discuss what hurts more often.

Refer students to *Stand Out 1 Workbook*, Unit 6, Lesson 1 for more practice with the simple present.

Go to the *Activity Bank* online for suggestions on promoting digital literacy and using the Internet to enhance this lesson.

MULTILEVEL WORKSHEET

Templates: Venn Diagram

Unit 6, Lesson 1, Worksheet 1: Parts of the Body

INSTRUCTOR'S NOTES

AT-A-GLANCE **PREP**

Goal: Identify illnesses and health problems

Grammar: Simple present and negative: *have*

Pronunciation: Intonation: information and clarification questions; rhythm

Academic Strategies: Focused listening, clarification strategies, Venn diagram

Vocabulary: Symptoms and illnesses

Agenda

▪ Practice identifying body parts.

▪ Identify illnesses and health problems.

▪ Discuss colds and the flu.

▪ Describe symptoms.

▪ List ailments.

Resources

Multilevel Worksheets: Unit 6, Lesson 2, Worksheets 1–2

Workbook: Unit 6, Lesson 2

Audio: CD 2, Tracks 15–19

Heinle Picture Dictionary: Hurting and Healing, pages 136–137; Illnesses, Injuries, Symptoms, and Disabilities, pages 134–135

Stand Out 1 Assessment CD-ROM with ExamView®

Pacing

▪ 1.5 hour classes ▪ 2.5 hour classes
▪ 3⁺ hour classes

STANDARDS CORRELATIONS

CCRS: RI1, RI7, SL2, SL4, L1, L2, L5, RF2, RF3

CASAS: 3.1.1. 6.6.5

SCANS: **Information** Acquire and evaluate information, interpret and communicate information

Basic Skills Reading, writing, listening, speaking

Thinking Skills See things in the mind's eye

EFF: **Communication** Read with understanding, convey ideas in writing, speak so others can understand, listen actively

Warm-up and Review   7–10 mins. ▪▪▪

Ask students to quiz one another on body parts. In a group, have one person stand up and point to different parts of his or her body. The other students in the group call out the body part. Stop after a few minutes and ask the person standing to call out the name of a body part. Ask the other students to point to the body part on their own bodies.

BEST PRACTICE

Group drills

Group drills like the one described here can be very effective practice. Have the "teacher" stand up so that you can easily see that all groups are on task, even those across the room. Ask the teacher in the group to do five or six items and sit down. Continue with another student standing and becoming the teacher. Repeat this activity until all students have taken the role of the teacher.

Introduction   5–7 mins. ▪▪▪

Write *cold* and *flu* on the board. Ask individuals how many times a year they catch colds. Ask them why they get colds and what symptoms they get. Write the word *symptoms* on the board. Give some examples, such as *runny nose*. State the goal: *Today, we will identify illnesses and health problems.*

Presentation 1   15–20 mins. ▪▪▪

A. Label the picture with the words from the box.

Make sure students understand each word. Pay close attention to how students pronounce *stomachache*. Some will try to pronounce the *ch* as it is usually pronounced. Also, some students may have trouble pronouncing the initial *s* because their language doesn't have the sound without a vowel before it.

B. Listen and practice the conversation.

Help students with the intonation and rhythm of the questions. Use this conversation as a model and ask students to practice briefly with a partner as they add other symptoms. Also, review the clarification strategy. This conversation will be used again with Exercise E.

Prepare students for focused listening. See the listening script on page 139a.

> **LISTENING SCRIPT**
> *The listening script matches the conversation in Exercise B.*
> 🎧 CD 2 TR 15

Practice 1   7–10 mins. ▪▪▪

C. Listen to each conversation. Circle the problem.

Evaluation 1   3–5 mins. ▪▪▪

Go over the answers with the class.

GOAL ▦ Identify illnesses and health problems

A. **Label the picture with the words from the box.**

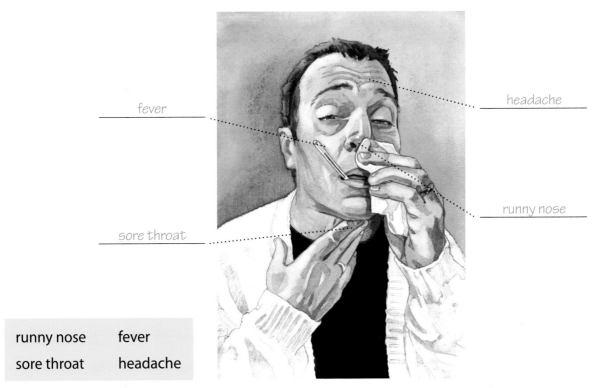

fever

headache

runny nose

sore throat

runny nose	fever
sore throat	headache

B. **Listen and practice the conversation.**

CD 2
TR 15

Doctor:	What's the matter?
Miguel:	Doctor, I feel very sick. I have a terrible sore throat.
Doctor:	You have the flu.
Miguel:	The flu?
Doctor:	Yes, the flu!

INTONATION

Intonation: Information Questions

What's the matter?

Intonation: Clarification Questions

The flu?

C. **Listen to each conversation. Circle the problem.**

CD 2
TR 16-19

(1. sore throat)	runny nose	fever	headache
2. sore throat	runny nose	(fever)	headache
3. sore throat	runny nose	fever	(headache)
4. sore throat	(runny nose)	fever	headache

D. ANALYZE Read about colds and flu. Then, complete the chart.

Every year people have both colds and the flu. What is the difference? Usually a person with a cold or the flu has a headache and a sore throat. A person with a cold sometimes has a low fever, and a person with the flu has a high fever and muscle aches. Cold symptoms also include a runny nose. Flu symptoms include a dry cough.

Common cold symptoms	Common flu symptoms
low fever	high fever
sore throat	sore throat
headache	headache
runny nose	muscle aches
	dry cough

E. COMPARE Complete the diagram using the information in Exercise D.

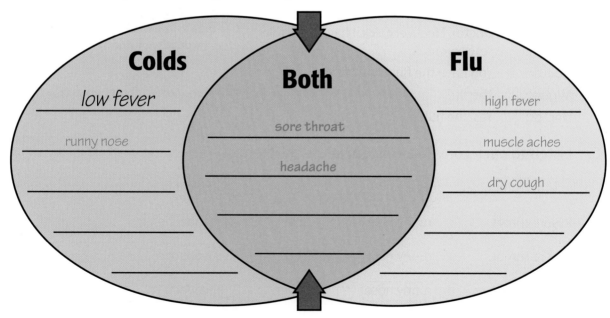

Colds

Both

Flu

low fever

runny nose

sore throat

headache

high fever

muscle aches

dry cough

LISTENING SCRIPT

CD 2
TR 16–19

1. **Doctor:** *What's the matter?*
   Miguel: *Doctor, I feel very sick. I have a terrible sore throat.*
   Doctor: *You have the flu.*
   Miguel: *The flu?*
   Doctor: *Yes, the flu!*

2. **Doctor:** *What's the matter?*
   Patient: *I don't know. I am terribly tired.*
   Doctor: *Do you have any other symptoms?*
   Patient: *Yes, I have a fever.*
   Doctor: *Well, let's examine you. Open up and say, "Aahh."*

3. **Doctor:** *What's the matter?*
   Patient: *I have a headache.*
   Doctor: *How long have you had it?*
   Patient: *I have had this headache for one week.*
   Doctor: *This could be serious. Please sit down.*

4. **Doctor:** *What's the matter?*
   Patient: *I have a cold.*
   Doctor: *Maybe I can give you some medicine for that runny nose.*
   Patient: *Yes, I have a terrible runny nose.*

Presentation 2   10–15 mins.

Ask students to close their books. Write *cold* and *flu* as headings for two columns on the board. Ask students if they know what the difference is. Talk about some related vocabulary. For example, remind them what a fever is. Draw a thermometer on the board and ask them what a normal temperature is. Mark it on your thermometer at 98.6°. Discuss what might be dangerous levels for children and adults without being too specific.

D. ANALYZE Read about colds and flu. Then, complete the chart.

Go over the chart with students and compare it to what you have on the board. Once again, go over any new vocabulary and review the vocabulary students have already learned.

Review how to complete a Venn diagram. You may wish to turn to page 24 for an example.

Practice 2   10–15 mins. ■■

E. COMPARE Complete the diagram using the information in Exercise D.

After students complete the Venn diagram, have them go back to the previous page and practice Exercise B with a partner, inserting the symptoms and diagnosing the problem.

Evaluation 2   5–7 mins. ■■

Ask volunteers to demonstrate the conversation in front of the class.

BEST PRACTICE

More ideas for using Venn diagrams

Use Venn diagrams on occasion as an icebreaker. Randomly arrange students in small groups and have them make a three-circle Venn diagram. Ask students to talk about themselves and things they like. Then, have students write ways they are like other members of their group and ways that they are unique.

Use Venn diagrams to introduce a lesson. Randomly organize students in groups and have them use a Venn diagram to discuss opinions about the topic at hand. Ask a key topic-related question. Then, ask students to organize opinions they share or do not share (similarities and differences). Have students move about the classroom and make new groups comparing and contrasting information.

INSTRUCTOR'S NOTES

_____

_____

_____

_____

_____

_____

_____

_____

_____

Presentation 3

10–15 mins. ■■■

Pantomime illnesses or symptoms. Start by holding your hands to your head in pain. Write on the board: *What's the matter?* Encourage students to ask you the question. Your response will be: *I have a headache.* Do this with all the symptoms and then ask students to open their books.

F. Study the charts with your classmates and teacher.

Go over the simple present again. Review the verb *have*. Concentrate on the negative form. Pantomime an illness or symptom again. Divide the class into halves. One side of the class will ask what your problem is. The other side will say what you don't have. Allow other students to pantomime something and extend the practice to the third-person singular.

Practice 3

7–10 mins. ■

G. Complete the sentences with the correct form of the verb.

Evaluation 3

7–10 mins. ■

Ask volunteers to write their completed sentences on the board.

Application

10–15 mins. ■■■

H. What other illnesses do you know? Use a dictionary and list illnesses and symptoms in your notebook.

BEST PRACTICE

Dictionaries

At times, we need to be careful to not bombard students with too much vocabulary at this level. This is not one of those occasions. This vocabulary will be very meaningful for students and they may need to use it without much notice.

Refer students to *Stand Out 1 Workbook,* Unit 6, Lesson 2 for more practice with the simple present.

Go to the *Activity Bank* online for suggestions on promoting digital literacy and using the Internet to enhance this lesson.

MULTILEVEL WORKSHEETS

Unit 6, Lesson 2, Worksheet 1: Conversations

Unit 6, Lesson 2, Worksheet 2: What's the matter?

INSTRUCTOR'S NOTES

F. **Study the charts with your classmates and teacher.**

Simple Present: *Have*		
Subject	*Have*	**Example sentence**
I, You, We, They	have	I **have** a headache. You **have** a sore throat.
He, She, It	has	She **has** a stomachache. He **has** a fever.

Negative Simple Present: *Have*			
Subject	**Negative**	*Have*	**Example sentence**
I, You, We, They	do not (don't)	have	I **don't have** a headache. You **don't have** a sore throat.
He, She, It	does not (doesn't)	have	She **doesn't have** a stomachache. He **doesn't have** a fever.

G. **Complete the sentences with the correct form of the verb.**

Armando

headache,
stomachache, fever

Yusuf

headache,
sore throat, cough

Lien

sore throat,
stomachache, backache

1. Armando _____ *has* _____ a headache.

2. Armando and Yusuf _____ *don't have* _____ backaches.

3. Yusuf _____ *has* _____ a cough.

4. Lien _____ *doesn't have* _____ a fever.

5. Armando and Lien _____ *have* _____ stomachaches.

6. Yusuf and Lien _____ *have* _____ sore throats.

H. **What other illnesses do you know? Use a dictionary and list illnesses and symptoms in your notebook.**

GOAL   ▊ Give advice

A. **Look at the pictures. Study the words and phrases with your classmates and teacher.**

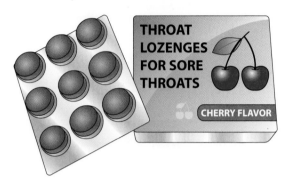

pain reliever   cough syrup   throat lozenges

rest	go to the doctor	take throat lozenges
take pain relievers	take cough syrup	

B.   **EVALUATE**   **What do you do when you have these symptoms? Complete the chart.**

Answers will vary.

Symptom	Take pain relievers	Rest	Take cough syrup	Take throat lozenges	Go to the doctor	Other
fever						
cough						
headache	✓					✓
sore throat						
stomachache						
backache						
feel tired						

C. **Practice the conversation. Then, use information from Exercise B to make new conversations.**

Patient: I have <u>a headache</u>.
Doctor: <u>Take pain relievers</u>.
Patient: Thanks.

Presentation 3

10–15 mins. ■■■

Using pantomime, cue students to give you advice about headaches, sore throats, and coughs.

H. Study the charts with your classmates and teacher.

In some languages, the modal *should* is a verb. This may confuse students. Make sure they understand that the base is the pure form of the verb before changes. Help them with the negative.

BEST PRACTICE

Grammar exposure

Students at this level are not always ready to acquire certain grammar points. *Stand Out* is designed to allow students to use the structures throughout their language-learning experience. At this level, students will learn structures, but they will often forget them until the structures are brought up in another context. This recycling process prepares students for the time they are ready to acquire the structures, meaning that they use them correctly in speech and in writing without thinking about the forms themselves.

Prepare students for the practice by going over the example in Exercise I.

Practice 3

10–15 mins. ■

I. Read each problem and give advice. Use *should* and *shouldn't*.

Evaluation 3

10–15 mins. ■

Ask students to write their sentences on the board.

Application

15–20 mins. ■■■

J. APPLY In a group, make a list of medications you have in your home and what they are good for.

Refer students to *Stand Out 1 Workbook,* Unit 6, Lesson 3 for more practice with *should*.

Go to the *Activity Bank* online for suggestions on promoting digital literacy and using the Internet to enhance this lesson.

MULTILEVEL WORKSHEETS

Unit 6, Lesson 3, Worksheet 1: Modal: *Should*

Unit 6, Lesson 3, Worksheet 2: Warning Labels

Unit 6, Lesson 3, Worksheet 3: Warnings with *Should*

INSTRUCTOR'S NOTES

Goal: Ask for information
Grammar: Prepositions of location, *is/are*
Academic Strategy: Focused listening
Vocabulary: Hospital vocabulary

Agenda

- Review symptoms and medicines.
- Ask for information at a hospital.
- Ask and answer information questions.

Resources

Multilevel Worksheets: Unit 6, Lesson 4, Worksheets 1–2
Workbook: Unit 6, Lesson 4
Audio: CD 2, Tracks 21–25
Heinle Picture Dictionary: Hospital, pages 138–139
Stand Out 1 Assessment CD-ROM with ExamView®

Pacing

- 1.5 hour classes
- 2.5 hour classes
- 3+ hour classes

STANDARDS CORRELATIONS

CCRS: RI1, SL1, SL2, SL4, L1, L2
CASAS: 0.1.2, 2.5.1
SCANS: **Information** Acquire and evaluate information
Interpersonal Participate as a member of a team, teach others
Basic Skills Reading, writing, listening, speaking
EFF: **Communication** Read with understanding, convey ideas in writing, speak so others can understand, listen actively, observe critically
Interpersonal Cooperate with others

Warm-up and Review   10–15 mins. ■■■

Ask students what illnesses and symptoms they take medicine for. List them on the board.

Name:	
Illness	**Medicine**
Headache	
Stomachache	
Backache	
Cold	
Sore throat	
Fever	

Then, ask students to complete the chart above about themselves and four of their classmates.

Introduction   15–20 mins. ■■■

Ask students if they have been to a hospital before. Ask if anyone has had to stay overnight and if they liked the food. Ask what questions they might ask in a hospital. State the goal: *Today, we will learn how to ask for information at a hospital.*

Presentation 1   30–40 mins. ■■■

Write *911* on the board. Ask when you should call 911. Give hypothetical situations to elicit discussion; for example:

- You have a cold.
- A cat is in a tree.
- A friend is not breathing.
- You had a car accident.

With books closed, play the recording of the conversation in Exercise A. Ask questions and play the recording again.

A. PREDICT Look at the picture. What is the problem? What is Victor doing? Then, listen and practice the conversation.

Answer the questions in the direction line. Help students to practice the conversation with appropriate rhythm and intonation.

> LISTENING SCRIPT 🎧 CD 2 TR 21
> *The listening script matches the conversation in Exercise A.*

B. Answer the questions.

After walking students through the activity, ask them to underline the part of the conversation that tells what has happened and the information that tells where the situation occurred.

Practice 1   15–20 mins. ■■■

C. INTERPRET With a partner, make a new conversation. Use one of the ideas in the chart below.

Have students use the chart as a guide. Students may also substitute their own ideas and addresses.

LESSON **4** There's an emergency!

GOAL ▦ Ask for information

🎧
CD 2
TR 21

A. PREDICT Look at the picture. What is the problem? What is Victor doing? Then, listen and practice the conversation.

Operator:	What is the emergency?
Victor:	There is a car accident.
Operator:	Where is the accident?
Victor:	It's on Fourth and Bush.
Operator:	What is your name?
Victor:	It's Victor Karaskov.
Operator:	Is anyone hurt?
Victor:	Yes. Please send an ambulance.

B. Answer the questions.

1. Who is calling about the emergency? _Victor Karaskov is calling about the emergency._

2. What is the emergency? _There is a car accident._

3. Where is the emergency? _The car accident is on Fourth and Bush._

C. INTERPRET With a partner, make a new conversation. Use one of the ideas in the chart below.

Who	What	Where
Antonio	A man is having a heart attack.	Broadway and Nutwood
Karen	There is a car accident.	First and Grand
Tran	A house is on fire.	234 Jones Avenue

D. **INTERPRET** **Write the letters next to the correct symbols.**

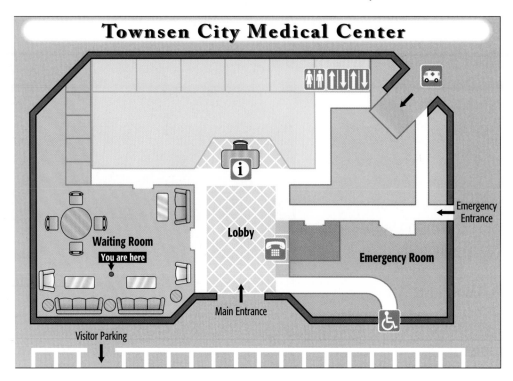

a. the wheelchair entrance   b. the restrooms   c. the elevators

d. Information   e. the pay phones   f. the ambulance entrance

1.  _____b_____

2. _____a_____

3. _____d_____

4. _____f_____

5. _____e_____

6. _____c_____

IS / ARE
Where **is** Information?
It is here.
Where **are** the restrooms?
They are here.

E. **Practice the conversations. Ask questions about places in the directory.**

Student A: Excuse me, where is Information?
Student B: It's here. (Student B points to the map.)

Student B: Excuse me, where are the elevators?
Student A: They are here. (Student A points to the map.)

Evaluation 1   7–10 mins. ■■■

Ask volunteers to perform their conversations in front of the class.

Presentation 2   10–15 mins. ■■■

D. INTERPRET Write the letters next to the correct symbols.

Do this activity as a class. Look at the floor plan of the hospital emergency room and discuss any new vocabulary with students. Test their comprehension to find out which words are new for them. Then, ask where specific hospital areas or features are located. Ask students to point to the sites on the directory in their books as they say: *It's over here.*, *They're over here.*, etc. Review the plural and singular use of the *be* verb in the present tense.

Prepare students to do the practice activity and show them how they will substitute information.

Practice 2   7–10 mins. ■■

E. Practice the conversations. Ask questions about places in the directory.

Ask students to practice the exchanges in pairs. Make sure they understand to use *over there* when a particular site is far away and *over here* when it is close by.

To make the activity more challenging, ask students to use prepositions of location such as *next to*, *around the corner*, and *between*. You may want them to refer to page 121.

Evaluation 2   7–10 mins. ■■

Observe the pair activity. Ask volunteers who are using prepositions in their responses to perform the exchange in front of the class.

INSTRUCTOR'S NOTES

_____

_____

_____

_____

_____

_____

_____

_____

_____

_____

_____

_____

_____

_____

_____

_____

_____

Presentation 3
10–15 mins. ■■■

Briefly review the prepositions of location. Write a few new phrases on the board including *center*, *in the front*, *in the back*, and *down the hall*. Go over the floor plan on the previous page using these new words. Then, ask students where the sofas are. This will prepare them for the listening.

F. Listen to the conversations. Complete the sentences.

> **LISTENING SCRIPT** 🎧 CD 2 TR 22–25
>
> 1. **Visitor:** *Excuse me. Where are the elevators? I can't seem to find them.*
>   **Staff:** *They are down the hall.*
>   **Visitor:** *Where?*
>   **Staff:** *They are close to the restrooms.*
>   **Visitor:** *Thanks.*
>
> 2. **Staff:** *Can I help you?*
>   **Visitor:** *Yes. I am looking for the wheelchair entrance. Is it close by?*
>   **Staff:** *Yes, it is. It is through the lobby and to your left.*
>   **Visitor:** *Where? I don't understand.*
>   **Staff:** *It is in the emergency room.*
>   **Visitor:** *Oh, thanks.*
>
> 3. **Visitor:** *I need to make a call. Where are the phones?*
>   **Staff:** *The pay phones are close to the entrance.*
>   **Visitor:** *Oh, I see them now. Thanks.*
>
> 4. **Visitor:** *Can you help me?*
>   **Staff:** *What can I do for you?*
>   **Visitor:** *I am looking for Information.*
>   **Staff:** *This is Information.*
>   **Visitor:** *Right here in the lobby?*
>   **Staff:** *Yes. Information is in the lobby.*

Prepare students for the practice in Exercise G.

Practice 3
7–10 mins. ■

G. Ask a partner for information. Ask about the elevators, the wheelchair entrance, the pay phones, and Information.

Evaluation 3
5–7 mins. ■

Observe the activity and ask volunteers to demonstrate in front of the class.

Application
20–30 mins. ■■■

H. CREATE In groups of four, prepare a role-play.

I. Find a hospital directory on the Internet. Share the information you find with the class.

Refer students to *Stand Out 1 Workbook*, Unit 6, Lesson 4 for more practice with *who*, *what*, and *where*.

Go to the *Activity Bank* online for suggestions on promoting digital literacy and using the Internet to enhance this lesson.

MULTILEVEL WORKSHEETS

Unit 6, Lesson 4, Worksheet 1: Emergencies

Unit 6, Lesson 4, Worksheet 2: Hospital Vocabulary

INSTRUCTOR'S NOTES

_____

_____

_____

_____

_____

_____

_____

_____

_____

_____

_____

_____

_____

_____

F. Listen to the conversations. Complete the sentences.

CD 2
TR 22-25

1. The elevators are close to the _____ restrooms _____.

2. The wheelchair entrance is in the _____ emergency room _____.

3. The pay phones are close to the _____ entrance _____.

4. Information is in the _____ lobby _____.

G. Ask a partner for information. Ask about the elevators, the wheelchair entrance, the pay phones, and Information.

Student A: Where are the restrooms?
Student B: They are close to the elevators.

H. CREATE In groups of four, prepare a role-play.

Student 1: You work at the Information desk.
Student 2: You are very sick.
Student 3: You are a family member.
Student 4: You are a nurse.

I. Find a hospital directory on the Internet. Share the information you find with the class.

LESSON **5** Staying healthy

A. Look at the picture. Why is exercise important? Then, read about exercise.

We need to exercise. It is good for our heart, muscles, flexibility, and weight. Everyone should exercise. People can run, swim, clean the house, or work in the yard. Doctors say we should exercise every day.

B. Write the letters of the pictures next to the words.

_____d_____ 1. muscles   _____c_____ 2. weight   _____b_____ 3. flexibility   _____a_____ 4. heart

a.

b.
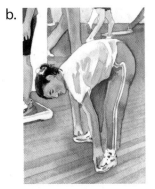

c.

d.

Goal: Develop an exercise plan

Grammar: Infinitives

Academic Strategies: Graphs, focused listening

Vocabulary: Exercise and health vocabulary

Agenda

- Write questions with *who, what, where.*
- Describe healthy practices.
- Talk about exercise.
- Read and make a bar graph.
- Make goals with *want to.*

Resources

Multilevel Worksheet: Unit 6, Lesson 5, Worksheet 1

Workbook: Unit 6, Lesson 5

Audio: CD 2, Tracks 26–29

Heinle Picture Dictionary: Daily Activities, pages 34–35

Stand Out 1 Assessment CD-ROM with ExamView®

Pacing

- 1.5 hour classes
- 2.5 hour classes
- 3+ hour classes

STANDARDS CORRELATIONS

CCRS: RI1, RI7, SL4, L1

CASAS: 1.1.3, 3.5.9, 7.1.1

SCANS: **Resources** Allocate human resources

Information Acquire and evaluate information

Basic Skills Reading, writing, listening, speaking

Thinking Skills See things in the mind's eye

Personal Qualities Self-management

EFF: **Communication** Read with understanding, convey ideas in writing, speak so others can understand, listen actively

Decision Making Plan

Lifelong Learning Take responsibility for learning, reflect and evaluate

Warm-up and Review   20–30 mins.

Write *who, what,* and *where* on the board. Ask students to write questions about an imaginary accident using the three question words. Tell them to imagine that they are 911 operators. Ask them to try to do it without their books at first. After they struggle for a few minutes, let them open their books and improve their sentences. Then, ask volunteers to share their sentences with the class and write them on the board.

Introduction   7–10 mins.

Write the words *healthy* and *unhealthy* on the board and see if students understand what they mean. Ask students about healthy and unhealthy foods. Make a list on the board. You may want to refer to Unit 3. State the goal: *Today, we will talk about making an exercise plan.*

Presentation 1   20–30 mins.

A. Look at the picture. Why is exercise important? Then, read about exercise.

Ask students to look at the picture at the top of the page. Then, ask them why they think exercise is important.

Next, ask students to read the paragraph silently and underline any words they don't know. Have them try to figure out the meanings by using the context. Then, read the paragraph together with the class and discuss the new vocabulary.

B. Write the letters of the pictures next to the words.

These are difficult words, but work with students to help them understand. First, ask them to look carefully at each picture. Second, read each word out loud while students listen. Then, ask students to write the letters of the pictures next to the words.

Have students compare their answer to a partner's after they have finished. Then, ask volunteers to share their answers with the class. Review and discuss as necessary.

INSTRUCTOR'S NOTES

_____

_____

_____

_____

_____

_____

_____

C. ANALYZE Study the bar graph and answer the questions about Alta, Wisconsin.

Study the bar graph with students. Help them understand how to read it. Ask questions to confirm that students understand.

Go over students' answers and make sure they understand how to read the bar graph in preparation for the upcoming practice.

Practice 1   5–7 mins. ■■■

Ask students to make a bar graph. Write the information you would like them to include on the graph. For example:

running: 10%

swimming: 5%

working in the yard: 5%

going to the gym: 15%

walking: 25%

no exercise: 40%

There is a bar graph template available in the template folder on the Multilevel Worksheets Activity Bank if you prefer to give students some structure.

Evaluation 1   20–30 mins. ■■■

Ask students to compare their graphs.

Presentation 2   7–10 mins. ■■■

Ask students what kind of activities around the house might be considered exercise. Ask them to look at the pictures in Exercise D. Talk about each picture and ask students if they do the activities.

Practice 2   7–10 mins. ■■

D. Listen to the conversations about exercise. Write the number under the correct picture.

LISTENING SCRIPT   CD 2
                                          TR 26–29

1. **A:** *I am so tired.*
   B: *Why?*
   A: *I think I need to exercise more. I don't feel very healthy.*
   B: *I swim every day at the gym. It is great exercise.*
   A: *Maybe I'll try that.*

2. **A:** *I don't get any exercise.*
   B: *Yes, you do.*
   A: *What do you mean? I never even leave the house.*
   B: *You vacuum every day. That is exercise.*
   A: *Oh, I never thought of that.*

3. **A:** *What do you do for exercise?*
   B: *I jog.*
   A: *What is jogging?*
   B: *I run slowly and enjoy nature with my dog.*
   A: *That sounds great.*

4. **A:** *I exercise every day.*
   B: *Me, too.*
   A: *What do you do?*
   B: *I get most of my exercise outside in the yard. Gardening can be good exercise, too.*
   A: *Really?*
   B: *Sure, why not?*

Evaluation 2   3–5 mins. ■■

Go over the answers with students.

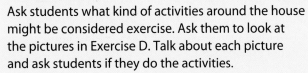

C. ANALYZE Study the bar graph and answer the questions about Alta, Wisconsin.

Alta, Wisconsin (Exercise Per Week)

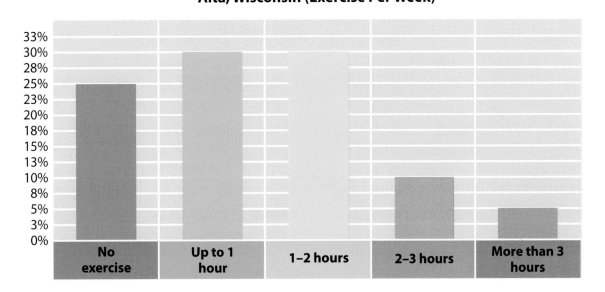

1. What percentage of people don't exercise?

   a. 0%   b. 30%   c. 10%   (d. 25%)

2. What percentage of people exercise more than three hours a week?

   (a. 5%)   b. 30%   c. 10%   d. 25%

3. What percentage of people exercise more than one hour a week?

   a. 0%   b. 30%   (c. 45%)   d. 50%

D. Listen to the conversations about exercise. Write the number under the correct picture.

CD 2
TR 26-29

a.

3

b.

1

c.

2

d.

4

E.   Study the chart with your classmates and teacher.

Infinitives			
Subject	**Verb**	**Infinitive (*to* + base)**	**Example sentence**
I, You, We, They	want	to run	I want **to run.**
		to exercise	We want **to exercise.**
		to walk	They want **to walk.**
He, She, It	wants	to ride	He wants **to ride** a bicycle.
		to do	She wants **to do** yard work.
		to go	She wants **to go** to the gym.

F.   APPLY Write three exercise goals. Use the ideas in Exercise D.   Answers will vary.

1. I want to _____.

2. _____.

3. _____.

G.   Ask three classmates about their exercise goals. Write their goals.   Answers will vary.

1. She/He wants to _____.

2. _____.

3. _____.

H.   SURVEY Talk to four classmates. Complete the chart.   Answers will vary.

Student A: How much do you exercise every week?
Student B: I exercise about one hour every week.

Amount of Exercise per Week					
Name	**0 minutes**	**0–1 hour**	**1–2 hours**	**2–3 hours**	**more than 3 hours**

Before You Watch

A. Look at the picture. Complete each sentence.

1. Mr. Sanchez has a

   back _ache_____.

2. He has a ___*thermometer*_____ in his mouth.

3. Hector is going to

   ____Answers will vary.____.

While You Watch

B. 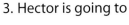 **Watch the video. Check Mr. Sanchez's symptoms.**

Symptom	True	False	Symptom	True	False
headache	X		sore throat	✓	
dizziness	✓		backache	✓	
fever	✓		shoulder ache	✓	
stomachache	✓		runny nose	✓	

Check Your Understanding

C. Match the statements and responses.

Patient

1. My back aches.
2. I have a sore throat.
3. I'm tired all the time.
4. I have a bad headache.
5. I cut my finger.

Doctor

a. Have some aspirin.
b. Take a pain reliever.
c. You need to get more rest.
d. I will clean it with alcohol.
e. You should take some cough syrup.

Review

A. Look at the picture. Write the words.

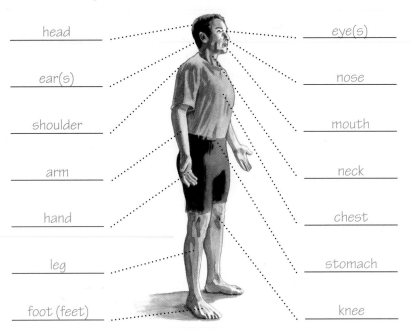

head

ear(s)

shoulder

arm

hand

leg

foot (feet)

eye(s)

nose

mouth

neck

chest

stomach

knee

B. Look at the pictures and complete the sentences.

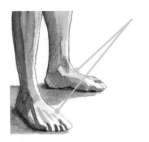

1. My ___feet___ hurt.

2. I have a _stomachache_.

3. I have a _headache_.

4. I have an _earache_.

5. My _hand_ hurts.

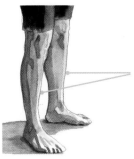

6. My _legs_ hurt.

Goal: All unit goals

Grammar: All unit grammar

Academic Strategies: Reviewing, evaluating, developing study skills

Vocabulary: All unit vocabulary

Agenda

- ☐ Discuss unit goals.
- ☐ Complete the review.
- ☐ Evaluate and reflect on progress.

Pacing

- ■ 1.5 hour classes
- ■ 2.5 hour classes
- ■ 3⁺ hour classes

STANDARDS CORRELATIONS

CCRS: RI1, RI7, L1, RF3

CASAS: 2.5.1, 3.1.1, 3.3.1, 3.3.2, 3.3.3, 3.5.9

SCANS: **Information** Acquire and evaluate information, organize and maintain information

Basic Skills Reading, writing, speaking

Personal Qualities Responsibility, self-management

EFF: **Communication** Speak so others can understand

Lifelong Learning Take responsibility for learning, reflect and evaluate

Warm-up and Review   7–10 mins. ■■■

With their books closed, ask students to help you make a list on the board of all the vocabulary they can come up with from the unit. Then, have a competition where students in groups will write page numbers for each item on the list. The first group to have the correct page number for each item wins.

Introduction   5 mins. ■■■

Write all the goals on the board from Unit 6. Show students the first page of every lesson so they understand that today will be review. Complete the agenda.

Presentation   10–15 mins. ■■■

This Presentation and Practice will cover the first three pages of the review. Quickly go to the first page of each lesson. Discuss the goal of each. Ask simple questions to remind students of what they have learned.

Practice   15–20 mins. ■■■

A. Look at the picture. Write the words. (Lesson 1)

B. Look at the pictures and complete the sentences. (Lesson 1)

BEST PRACTICE

Recycling/Review

The review and the project that follows are part of the recycling/review process. Students at this level often need to be reintroduced to concepts to solidify what they have learned. Many concepts are learned and forgotten while learning other new concepts. This is because students learn but are not necessarily ready to acquire language concepts.

Therefore, it becomes very important to review and to show students how to review on their own. It is also important to recycle the new concepts in different contexts.

INSTRUCTOR'S NOTES

_____

_____

_____

_____

_____

_____

_____

_____

_____

_____

_____

_____

_____

_____

_____

Practice *(continued)*

C. Match the symptom and the remedy. (Lesson 3)

D. Practice the conversation with a partner. Make similar conversations. (Lessons 2 and 3)

E. Read the medicine bottles and complete the chart. (Lesson 3)

INSTRUCTOR'S NOTES

C. Match the symptom and the remedy.

_d_ 1. fever   a. lozenges

_c_ 2. feel tired   b. syrup

_a_ 3. sore throat   c. rest

_b_ 4. cough   d. pain reliever

D. Practice the conversation with a partner. Make similar conversations.

Student A: What's the matter?
Student B: I have a headache.
Student A: You should take a pain reliever.
Student B: Thanks. That's a good idea.

E. Read the medicine bottles and complete the chart.

1.

Directions:
For minor sore throat pain.
Directions:
Take two tablespoons every four hours.
Warning:
Not for children under 12 years of age.

2.

INDICATIONS:
For temporary relief of minor aches and pains.
DIRECTIONS:
Take two tablets every three hours.
WARNING:
DO NOT DRIVE WHEN TAKING THIS MEDICINE.

3.

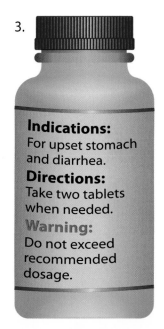

Indications:
For upset stomach and diarrhea.
Directions:
Take two tablets when needed.
Warning:
Do not exceed recommended dosage.

	How many?	How often?
1.	two tablespoons	every four hours
2.	two tablets	every three hours
3.	two tablets	when needed

F. Complete the sentences with *should* or *shouldn't*.

should

1. He _____should_____ take medicine.

2. We _____should_____ rest.

3. They _____should_____ go to the doctor.

4. We _____should_____ exercise every day.

shouldn't

1. I _____shouldn't_____ drink and drive.

2. He _____shouldn't_____ take four tablets.

3. We _____shouldn't_____ go out.

4. They _____shouldn't_____ drive and take this medicine.

G. Read the conversation and put the sentences in the correct order.

___2___ **Victor:** There's a car accident.

___1___ **Operator:** 911, what is the emergency?

___4___ **Victor:** Yes.

___6___ **Victor:** It's on Fourth and Bush.

___3___ **Operator:** Is anyone hurt?

___7___ **Operator:** OK. The police and ambulance are on the way.

___5___ **Operator:** Where is the accident?

H. Write six items you can find in a hospital. Answers will vary.

_____   _____   _____

_____   _____   _____

I. Ask three classmates about their exercise goals. Complete the chart. Answers will vary.

Name	What exercise do you want to do?	When do you want to do this exercise?	How long do you want to do this exercise?
Nadia	swim	8 a.m. on Saturdays	40 minutes

Practice (continued)

F. Complete the sentences with *should* **or** *shouldn't* **(Lesson 3).**

G. Read the conversation and put the sentences in the correct order. (Lesson 4)

H. Write six items you can find in a hospital. (Lesson 4)

I. Ask three classmates about their exercise goals. Complete the chart. (Lesson 5)

Evaluation   15 mins. ■■■

Go around the room and check on students' progress. Help individuals when needed. If you see consistent errors among several students, interrupt the class and give a mini lesson or review to help students feel comfortable with the concept.

Presentation   5 mins. ■■■

Learner Log

Review the concepts of the Learner Log. Make sure students understand the concepts and how to complete the log including circling the answers, finding page numbers where the concept is taught, and ranking favorite activities.

BEST PRACTICE

Learner Logs

Learner Logs function to help students in many different ways.

1. They serve as part of the review process.
2. They help students to gain confidence and to document what they have learned. Consequently, students see that they are progressing in their learning.
3. They provide students with a tool that they can use over and over to check and recheck their understanding of the target language. In this way, students become independent learners.

Practice   10–15 mins. ■

Ask students to complete the Learner Log.

Evaluation   2 mins. ■

Go over the Learner Log with students.

Application   5–7 mins. ■■■

Ask students to record their favorite lesson or page in the unit.

Assessment   ■■■

Use the Stand Out 1 Assessment Activity Bank with ExamView® to create a post-test for Unit 6.

Refer students to *Stand Out 1 Workbook*, **Unit 6, Lesson 1 for more practice with** *yes/no* **questions with** *should* **and Lesson 4 for more practice with** *wh-* **questions.**

Go to the *Activity Bank* **online for suggestions on promoting digital literacy and using the Internet to enhance this lesson.**

MULTILEVEL WORKSHEETS

Unit 6, Computer Worksheets

Unit 6, Internet Worksheets

INSTRUCTOR'S NOTES

STANDARDS CORRELATIONS

CCRS: SL1, SL2

CASAS: 2.5.1, 3.1.1, 3.3.1, 3.3.2, 3.3.3, 3.5.9, 4.8.1

SCANS: **Resources** Allocate time, allocate materials and facility resources, allocate human resources

Information Acquire and evaluate information, organize and maintain information, interpret and communicate information

Interpersonal Participate as a member of a team, teach others, exercise leadership, negotiate to arrive at a decision, work with cultural diversity

Systems Understand systems, monitor and correct performance

Basic Skills Reading, writing, listening, speaking

Thinking Skills Think creatively, make decisions, solve problems, see things in the mind's eye

Personal Qualities Responsibility, sociability, self-management

EFF: **Communication** Read with understanding, convey ideas in writing, speak so others can understand, listen actively, observe critically

Decision Making Solve problems and make decisions, plan

Interpersonal Cooperate with others, advocate and influence, resolve conflict and negotiate, guide others

Lifelong Learning Take responsibility for learning, reflect and evaluate

Introduction   5 mins.

TEAM PROJECT

Create a role-play about an emergency

In this project, students will create a role-play about an emergency. Each group will perform for the class. Each member of the group will have a role to play. There is a template that teams may use for this project on the Multilevel Worksheet Activity Bank (Unit 6, Project, Worksheet 1).

Stage 1   15–20 mins.

COLLABORATE Form a team with four or five students.

Help students form groups and assign positions in their groups. On the spot, students will have to choose who will be the leader of their group. Review the responsibility of a leader and ask students to write the name of their leader in their books. Do the same with the remaining positions.

Help students understand that they will all be part of the conversations. They should write their role assignments in the book.

Stage 2   10–15 mins.

Choose an accident or illness. Write down the injured or sick person's symptoms. Who is the patient in your group? What is his or her name in the role-play?

Ask students to choose an accident. You might want to list some ideas on the board. Include things like a car accident, a fire, a medical emergency, etc. Students may prefer to choose an illness. It is very important for students to make these decisions before they start writing the skit. Some students will want to start without proper preparation. Have them decide the names of the characters in the role-play.

Stage 3   20–30 mins.

Write a conversation with a 911 operator.

Offer help to the groups as necessary.

Stage 4   10–30 mins.

Write a conversation with a doctor. Write a medicine label with directions. In the conversation, the doctor gives a prescription.

The patient should read a label in the conversation and the doctor should give advice.

Stage 5   30 mins.

Write a conversation with a family member of the patient.

Offer help as needed.

Stage 6   30 mins.

Put the conversations together.

Tell students to combine their three conversations to make one skit that they can act out for the class.

Stage 7   10–30 mins.

Present the role-play to the class.

Have groups present their conversations and medicine labels to the class. Videotaping the presentations can greatly enhance the learning experience.

MULTILEVEL WORKSHEETS

Unit 6, Project, Worksheet 1: Emergency

Unit 6, Extension, Worksheet 1: Home Remedies

Unit 6, Extension, Worksheet 2: Reading Medicine Labels

TEAM PROJECT ✓ Create a role-play about an emergency

In this project, you will create a role-play. Members of your group will be a patient, a family member, a 911 operator, a doctor, and a hospital worker.

1. **COLLABORATE** Form a team with four or five students. In your team, you need:

Position	Job description	Student name
Student 1: **Team Leader**	Check that everyone speaks English. Check that everyone participates.	
Student 2: **Secretary**	Write out the role-play with help from the team. Make sure there is a part for everyone.	
Student 3: **Director**	Direct the role-play.	
Students 4/5: **Spokespeople**	Introduce the role-play.	

2. Choose an accident or illness. Write down the injured or sick person's symptoms. Who is the patient in your group? What is his or her name in the role-play?

3. Write a conversation with a 911 operator.

4. Write a conversation with a doctor. Write a medicine label with directions. In the conversation, the doctor gives a prescription.

5. Write a conversation with a family member of the patient.

6. Put the conversations together.

7. Present the role-play to the class.

About the Explorer

Grace Gobbo is an ethnobotanist from Tanzania. Grace uses the lush nature of her home continent to help find holistic remedies for people who cannot afford to buy expensive medication. Medication used to help people with a wide range of ailments including chest infections and ulcers is sometimes unaffordable in some countries like Tanzania, so Grace interviewed traditional healers to find out what they used to treat illnesses in their communities. She is working to catalog this information so that it's not lost. She is also teaching people about the environment in which they live and how they can use it to help themselves.

About the Photo

This photo shows Grace researching holistic remedies. Grace works with the Jane Goodall Institute's Greater Gombe Ecosystem program. This program helps preserve the chimpanzee habitat in western Tanzania. As Grace becomes more successful in showing people the health benefits of their environment, the institute is able to protect the natural habitat of the primates who depend on the area for survival.

- Introduce the explorer. Tell students to look at the photo and say, "This is Grace Gobbo."
- Read the title out loud. Then, ask students what they think medicinal plants are. Discuss as a class.
- Ask a volunteer to read the quote out loud. Define vocabulary that students may not be familiar with.
- Ask students what they think the link is between the title and the quote. Discuss as a class.

Searching for Medicinal Plants

"It's so rewarding to help people understand the value of conservation, sustainable agriculture, and holistic remedies."
—Grace Gobbo

A. A remedy is something we use when we are sick. Match the remedy to the illness.

1. Drink water very fast.	a. cough
2. Take honey.	b. stomachache
3. Drink homemade ginger tea.	c. hiccups
4. Put heat on the belly.	d. headaches

B. **PREDICT** Read the title of the paragraph. What do you think it is about? Tell a group.

Answers will vary.

a. I think the story is about plants that make you sick.

b. I think the story is about plants used to help sick people.

c. I think the story is about drug companies who make medicine from plants.

d. I think the story is about expensive medicine.

158 Unit 6

CCRS FOR READING

RI1, RI2, RI7, L3

A. A remedy is something we use when we are sick. Match the remedy to the illness.

- Explain to students that a home or natural remedy is something we use when we are sick.
- Go over each remedy in the left-hand column. Then, ask students to match the remedy to the illness.
- Have volunteers write their answers on the board and review.

C. Read about Grace Gobbo.

Plants and Medicine

Grace Gobbo wants to help sick people. She lives in Tanzania. Medicine is very expensive there. Traditional healers help people who are ill. Traditional healers find less expensive medicines for chest problems, stomachaches, coughs, and many other illnesses and symptoms. These medicines come from plants in the rainforest. Grace wants to share these medicines with her people. She believes people in her country should be healthy, and they shouldn't pay a lot of money for medicine.

D. **ANALYZE** Study the paragraph and discover new words. Answer the questions.

1. A healer is someone who helps people when they are sick, but they are not always doctors or nurses. What do *traditional healers* do?
   - (a.) They use plants to help sick people.
   - b. They talk to people about the government.
   - c. They buy medicine at a pharmacy to help people.

2. A forest is a group of trees. What do you think a *rain*forest is? Which picture is probably a rainforest and why do you think so?

3. Grace wants to *share* the medicine with her people. What do you think *share* means and what does she want to do? Read the next sentences in the paragraph to help you.
   - a. She wants to buy medicines for her people.
   - b. She wants to sell medicines to make money.
   - (c.) She wants to teach people about the medicines.

E. In a group, make a list of medicines you buy for stomachaches, colds, or coughs. Estimate the cost of each item on the list. Then, share your list with the class.

F. **CREATE** In a group, describe a home remedy.

READING STRATEGIES

Checking Comprehension

Students should become accustomed to monitoring their own comprehension. They should also know how to identify what they do not understand. Asking students to underline or circle unfamiliar vocabulary is an effective strategy towards building better comprehension. Once new words have been defined and explained, students can re-read a text to check if their understanding improves.

B. **PREDICT** Read the title of the paragraph. What do you think it is about? Tell a group.

Have students form small groups. Then, read the title out loud and ask them what they think the title is about. Have students discuss in groups and choose their answer.

C. Read about Grace Gobbo.

Ask students to read about Grace Gobbo.

D. **ANALYZE** Study the paragraph and discover new words. Answer the questions.

- Tell students to carefully re-read the paragraph and underline or circle any words they do not understand.
- Ask students to read the questions and choose the correct answer.
- Have students check their answers with a partner. Then, review as a class.

E. In a group, make a list of medicines you buy for stomachaches, colds, or coughs. Estimate the cost of each item on the list. Then, share your list with the class.

- Have students work in small groups. Then, ask them to make a list of medicines they buy for stomachaches, colds, or coughs. Ask them to think of the cost of each item on their list and write the price next to it.
- Have students compare their lists with one or two other groups and discuss.
- Discuss as a class.

F. **CREATE** In a group, describe a home remedy.

Ask students to describe a home remedy in groups.

Working On It

About the Photo

National Geographic photographer Joel Sartore took this photo. It shows three mine repair workers standing inside a "dipper" at the Bingham Canyon copper mine in Salt Lake City, Utah. The men are posing and looking very serious; however, there is a fourth worker in the photo. He is operating the machine and is looking through the top of the giant shovel. The Bingham Canyon Mine has been in operation since 1906, and the pit is a National Historic Landmark.

- Introduce the unit. Read the title out loud. Ask students what they think the title means.

- Have students look at the photo. Then, ask the questions. Discuss as a class.

- Ask a volunteer to read the caption out loud. Then ask students what they think of this kind of job. Discuss as a class.

- Go over the unit outcomes.

UNIT **7**
Working On It

Three mine repair workers stand for a portrait inside a huge dipper in Utah.

UNIT OUTCOMES	GRAMMAR	VOCABULARY	EL CIVICS
• Identify common occupations • Interpret job information • Write your job history • Perform a job interview • Interpret performance reviews	• Simple present • Negative simple present • Modal: *can* • Simple past • Simple past: regular verbs, *be* • Questions with *can* • Simple present: *be* • Adverbs of frequency	• Occupations • Job ads • Benefits, vacation, salary • Simple verbs • Application, resume, appointment • Punctuality, improvement, superior, appearance, grooming	The skills students learn in this unit can be applied to the following El Civics competency area: • Employment Resources

Life Skills Link

In this unit, students will learn about common occupations. They will also learn what the occupations entail and the steps involved in acquiring them as well as keeping them.

Workplace Link

All lessons and units in *Stand Out* include basic communication skills and interpersonal skills important for the workplace. They are not individually identified. Other workplace skills are indicated. They include collecting and organizing information, making decisions and solving problems, and combining ideas and information.

UNIT OUTCOMES

- ☐ Identify common occupations
- ☐ Interpret job information
- ☐ Write your job history
- ☐ Perform a job interview
- ☐ Interpret performance reviews

Look at the photo and answer the questions.

1. What do you see in the picture?
2. What are they wearing?
3. What kind of job do the workers have?

CASAS	SCANS	CCRS
Lesson 1: 4.1.8 Lesson 2: 4.1.3, 4.1.6, 4.1.8 Lesson 3: 4.1.2, 4.1.8 Lesson 4: 0.1.1, 0.1.6, 4.1.5, 4.6.1 Lesson 5: 4.4.1, 4.4.4 Review: 4.1.2, 4.1.3, 4.1.6, 4.1.8, 4.1.5, 4.4.1, 4.4.4, 4.6.1 Team Project: 4.1.2, 4.1.3, 4.1.6, 4.1.8, 4.1.5, 4.4.1, 4.4.4, 4.6.1, 4.8.1	Most SCANS are incorporated into this unit, with an emphasis on: • Organizing and maintaining information • Understanding systems • Creative thinking • Decision making (Technology is optional.)	RI1, RI2, RI5, RI7, RI9, W2, SL1, SL2, SL4, L1, L2, L5, RF2, RF3

LESSON ① What's your job?

GOAL ■ Identify common occupations

A. IDENTIFY Write the jobs from the box under the pictures.

teller	nurse	office worker	server	mechanic

Alan
1. _____server_____

Michelle
2. _____office worker_____

Tony
3. _____mechanic_____

Huong
4. _____nurse_____

Isabel
5. _____teller_____

B. Practice the conversations. Then, ask questions about the people above.

Student A: What is Tony's job?   **Student B:** What does Tony do?

Student B: He is a mechanic.   **Student A:** He's a mechanic.

Goal: Identify common occupations

Grammar: Simple present and negative simple present

Pronunciation: Emphasis

Academic Strategies: Classifying, focused listening

Vocabulary: Job titles

Agenda

☐ Describe your job.

☐ Identify occupations.

☐ Listen to conversations about different occupations.

☐ Discuss occupations.

Resources

Multilevel Worksheet: Unit 7, Lesson 1, Worksheet 1

Workbook: Unit 7, Lesson 1

Audio: CD 2, Tracks 30–33

Heinle Picture Dictionary: Jobs 1, pages 146–147, Jobs 2, pages 148–149

Stand Out 1 Assessment CD-ROM with ExamView®

Pacing

■ 1.5 hour classes   ■ 2.5 hour classes
■ 3+ hour classes

CCRS: SL1, SL2, SL4, L1, L2, L5, RF2, RF3

CASAS: 4.1.8

SCANS: **Information** Acquire and evaluate information

Basic Skills Listening, speaking

Thinking Skills See things in the mind's eye

EFF: **Communication** Speak so others can understand, listen actively, observe critically

Preassessment (*optional*) ■■■

Use the Stand Out 1 Assessment CD-ROM with ExamView® to create a pretest for Unit 7.

Warm-up and Review   7–10 mins. ■■■

Write on the board: *What do you do?* Ask various students this question. At first, students may describe what they are doing at the moment.

Then, ask a few other students to name their jobs or occupations. Explain that the question *What do you do?* usually means *What is your job?*

Make a list on the board of students' jobs. Make sure they know that being a student or a homemaker is also a job. Help with pronunciation as needed.

Introduction   3–7 mins. ■■■

Look at the list you have created with students' input on the board. Ask students if they can think of any other jobs to add to the list. State the goal: *Today, we will identify common occupations.*

Presentation 1   20–30 mins. ■■■

Before students open their books, act out the five jobs pictured in Exercise A and ask students to identify the jobs. For job titles that are difficult to act out, give students additional verbal hints. For example, for *mechanic*, tell them that this person works with cars. Write their responses on the board even if they are not exactly accurate. Go over the words you have written on the board several times, correcting inaccuracies as you go.

Ask students to open their books and look at the five occupations.

A. IDENTIFY Write the jobs from the box under the pictures.

Do this exercise as a class. Then, quiz students to test their comprehension.

Prepare students for the practice by going over the exchanges in Exercise B.

Practice 1   7–10 mins. ■■■

B. Practice the conversations. Then, ask questions about the people above.

Tell students that they may try to expand upon the examples given in the book to form longer conversations.

Evaluation 1   3–5 mins. ■■■

Observe the activity and ask volunteers to demonstrate their questions and answers in front of the class.

Presentation 2

10–15 mins. ■■■

Follow the same pattern you did for Presentation 1.

1. With books closed, pantomime the occupations depicted on the page.
2. Write students' responses on the board. This time, if they don't know an answer, don't give it to them yet.
3. Go over the pictures in the book.
4. Quiz students with a student response technique described in the Best Practice below.

BEST PRACTICE

Monitoring student responses

An easy way to monitor responses is to have students respond verbally with a word.

With the above method, however, stronger students sometimes overwhelm students who need more time to think when asked for a verbal response. You may choose other ways for students to respond where students are less likely to "go along with the crowd." One such method could be to use 3-by-5 index cards where students choose the card with the correct answer and hold it up. If you choose to do this method, have students create the actual cards themselves so they also get writing practice.

There is another effective technique that doesn't require preparation. Students respond by showing the number of fingers that correspond to each picture. Start this method by first only saying the target word. Next, embed the word in a sentence, and then embed all the words in a paragraph.

C. Study the pictures with your classmates and teacher.

D. CLASSIFY Write the job titles from Exercise C in the correct column.

Do this classifying activity as a class. You might want to do a Venn diagram on the board. One circle would represent restaurants and the other would represent schools. Both might have *custodian* in common.

Practice 2

7–10 mins. ■■

E. Listen to each conversation. Circle the correct job title.

Play the recording several times if necessary.

LISTENING SCRIPT

CD 2
TR 30–33

1. **Supervisor:** *Hello, Maria. I have some important work for you today.*
   Maria: *Great. I am ready to work.*
   Supervisor: *One of your secretary responsibilities is to file, so please file all the papers.*
   Maria: *Yes, sir. I will have it finished by lunch.*

2. **A:** *What do you do?*
   B: *I am a cook at Market Street Grill.*
   A: *Wow, that's great. I hear the food is very good there.*

3. **A:** *My job is so great! I love working with people.*
   B: *Me, too. What do you do?*
   A: *I have the perfect job.*
   B: *Well, what is it?*
   A: *I am a teacher at an adult school in Fairmont.*

4. **Woman:** *I'm looking for a job.*
   Manager: *Do you have experience?*
   Manager: *Yes, I do. I worked at the theater down the street for three years.*
   Manager: *What was your job?*
   Woman: *I was a cashier.*
   Manager: *So, you are good with money and making change.*
   Woman: *Yes, I think I do a good job.*
   Manager: *OK, let's get you an application.*

Pause between listenings and allow students to discuss their answers.

Evaluation 2

7–10 mins. ■■

Go over the recording again, stopping the audio when a key word is spoken.

C. **Study the pictures with your classmates and teacher.**

1. cook/chef

2. server

3. custodian

4. cashier

5. secretary

6. teacher

D. **CLASSIFY** **Write the job titles from Exercise C in the correct column.**

Restaurant	School
cook/chef	secretary
server	custodian
cashier	teacher

E. **Listen to each conversation. Circle the correct job title.**

CD 2
TR 30-33

1. secretary	teacher	custodian
2. cashier	server	cook
3. secretary	teacher	custodian
4. cashier	server	cook

F.   Study the charts with your classmates and teacher.

Simple Present		
Subject	**Verb**	**Example sentence**
I, You, We, They	work	I **work** in an office.
He, She, It	works	He **works** in a restaurant.

Negative Simple Present			
Subject	**Negative**	**Verb**	**Example sentence**
I, You, We, They	do not (don't)	work	I **don't work** in an office. You don't work in a restaurant.
He, She, It	does not (doesn't)		He **doesn't work** in a school. She **doesn't work** in a hospital.

G.   Look at the jobs in Exercise C. Ask and answer questions about each job.

Student A: What does he do? (Point to the cook.)

Student B: He is a <u>cook</u>.

Student A: He works <u>in a school</u>, right?

Student B: No, he doesn't work <u>in a school</u>. He works <u>in a restaurant</u>.

INTONATION

Put emphasis on requested information and on corrected information.

He works IN A SCHOOL, right?

No, he doesn't work IN A SCHOOL. He works IN A RESTAURANT.

H.   SURVEY   Talk to three classmates. Complete the chart. Then, report to a group.

Huong is a nurse. She works in a hospital.

Answers will vary.

Name	What do you do?	Where do you work?
Huong	nurse	hospital

Presentation 3   30–40 mins. ■■■

Ask students again: *What do you do?* Also ask: *Where do you work?* Make sure you involve students who don't work out of the home, such as students and homemakers. Write down what students do in sentences on the board. For example: *Huong is a nurse. She works in a hospital.* After you have written several sentences on the board, show students that you have used the third-person singular *s*. Also, remind them again to use *a* or *an* before the name of the occupation.

Then, ask students to open their books and study the charts.

F. Study the charts with your classmates and teacher.

Continue writing examples on the board. Write negative sentences as well.

BEST PRACTICE

Recycling grammar

It is important that students learn to transfer the structures they have previously been exposed to to different contexts. The simple present has been introduced many times in this book. Make sure students see the connection of this explanation of the simple present with previous ones. Refer them to the following pages: 24 (*like*), 40 (*shop*), 87 (*live*), 127 (*write, eat, read*), and 140 (*hurt*). Show students that adding an *s* to the third-person singular verb is a consistent rule, with only a few exceptions. Ask students to help you choose other verbs and show how they are all formed in the same way.

Go over the conversation in Exercise G and help students prepare for the activity. Make sure you help them with intonation. This is also a clarifying skill. The emphasis always goes where a correction is made. Exaggerate this point so students will understand.

PRONUNCIATION

Emphasis

Students can hear rising intonation with ease. The amount of emphasis given in discourse is different in different languages. English gives more emphasis to corrections than many other languages, so students may need to be encouraged to really emphasize words. One way to do this is to have them stand and sit when they say the emphasized word or words. In this conversation, have students stand when they say *restaurant*.

Practice 3   7–10 mins. ■

G. Look at the jobs in Exercise C. Ask and answer questions about each job.

Evaluation 3   2–7 mins. ■

Ask volunteers to demonstrate in front of the class.

Application   10–15 mins. ■■■

H. SURVEY Talk to three classmates. Complete the chart. Then, report to a group.

Monitor students as they report to make sure they understand the task.

Refer students to *Stand Out 1 Workbook*, Unit 7, Lesson 1 for more practice with the simple present.

Go to the *Activity Bank* online for suggestions on promoting digital literacy and using the Internet to enhance this lesson.

MULTILEVEL WORKSHEET

Unit 7, Lesson 1, Worksheet 1: Job Titles

Goal: Interpret job information

Grammar: Modal: *can*

Academic Strategies: Focused listening

Vocabulary: Abbreviations used in classified ads

Agenda

- Interview a partner.
- Read classified ads.
- Listen for benefits.
- Choose jobs to match people's skills and schedules.
- Write a classified ad.

Resources

Multilevel Worksheets: Lesson 2, Worksheets 1–2

Workbook: Unit 7, Lesson 2

Audio: CD 2, Tracks 34–37

Heinle Picture Dictionary: Jobs 1, pages 146–147; Jobs 2, pages 148–149

Stand Out 1 Assessment CD-ROM with ExamView®

Pacing

- ■ 1.5 hour classes   ■ 2.5 hour classes
- ■ 3+ hour classes

STANDARDS CORRELATIONS

CCRS: RI1, RI7, RI9, SL1, SL2, L1, L2

CASAS: 4.1.3, 4.1.6, 4.1.8

SCANS: **Information** Acquire and evaluate information, organize and maintain information, interpret and communicate information

Interpersonal Participate as a member of a team

Basic Skills Reading, writing, listening, speaking

Thinking Skills Think creatively

EFF: **Communication** Read with understanding, convey ideas in writing, speak so others can understand, listen actively, observe critically

Interpersonal Cooperate with others

Warm-up and Review   10–15 mins. ■■■

Have students ask the questions in the application from the previous lesson in pairs. Make sure they practice with someone different. They should ask: *What do you do?* and *Where do you work?* Then, ask students to introduce the student to the class. For example: *Oscar is a cook. He works in a restaurant.*

Introduction   5–7 mins. ■■■

Ask the class where they can find out about jobs. List their responses on the board. Ask them if they know about help-wanted ads in the newspaper. Ask how many students read the help-wanted ads and if they have any trouble understanding them. State the goal: *Today, we will interpret classified ads from the newspaper.*

Presentation 1   15–20 mins. ■■■

Write the word *benefits* on the board and ask students what they think it means. Ask for examples. Also write *vacation, sick leave,* and *health insurance* on the board and make sure students understand the meaning of each term.

A. INTERPRET   Read the classified ads and discuss them with your teacher.

Have students open their books and look at the classified ads. Ask them to find the job titles, the pay, and the addresses.

B. COMPARE   Write the information in the chart.

Review the vocabulary with students to make sure they understand each word. Then, do this activity as a class.

Prepare students for the focused-listening activity in Exercise C.

Practice 1   7–10 mins. ■■■

C. Listen to the conversations. Check (✓) the correct benefits.

Note: The listening script for Exercise C appears on page 166a.

Evaluation 1   3–5 mins. ■■■

Go over the answers and listen to the recording again for confirmation.

BEST PRACTICE

Using audio scripts

Many textbooks include audio scripts. It is a good idea to ask students to follow the audio script from time to time while listening. Students can benefit from seeing what they hear. This approach also helps them with pronunciation of new vocabulary as well as pronunciation in general.

First, have students listen while reading. Then, ask them to listen without the audio script. You can repeat this process as many times as you think necessary.

LESSON **2** Job hunting

GOAL ■ Interpret job information

WORKPLACE CONNECTION
Exercise B: Collect and organize information.

A. INTERPRET Read the classified ads and discuss them with your teacher.

Cook Needed

Regal Diner

2 yrs exp, f/t or p/t,
gd bnfts, appl avail.
$10/hr. Call 555-7454 or
apply in person at 232
W. Broadway M-F, 8-6

BBQ Madness

Position : Cook
Location : 8258 River Road
Hourly Rate : $12
Type : full-time

Summary:
Responsible for preparing foods and performing all other responsibilities as directed by management. 1 year experience.

Essential Functions:
• Read and follows recipes
• Clean equipment
• Operate kitchen equipment

Benefits
• 1 week vacation annually
• medical insurance

Apply

B. COMPARE Write the information in the chart.

	Regal Diner	**BBQ Madness**
Position / Job Title	cook	cook
Location	W. Broadway	8258 River Road
Pay / Wages / Salary	$10/hr	$12/hr
Full- or Part-time?	Full-time or part-time	Full-time
Benefits	Yes	1 week vacation, medical insurance
Experience	2 years	1 year

C. Listen to the conversations. Check (✓) the correct benefits.

CD 2
TR 34-36

1. Listen to Roberto and his boss. Check (✓) the benefit.

   ☑ vacation   ☐ sick leave   ☐ insurance

2. Listen to Anya and her supervisor. Check (✓) the benefit.

   ☐ vacation   ☐ sick leave   ☑ insurance

3. Listen to Steve and his manager. Check (✓) the benefit.

   ☐ vacation   ☑ sick leave   ☐ insurance

D. EVALUATE Study the information in the chart about jobs.

Position	Experience	Full-time / Part-time	Benefits (Yes/No)	Pay
1. Nurse	2 years	F/T	Yes	$22/hr
2. Server	No	P/T	No	$10/hr + tips
3. Driver	No	F/T or P/T	Yes	$18/hr
4. Cashier	No	P/T	No	$8/hr
5. Mechanic	No	F/T	Yes	$12/hr

E. Practice the conversation and then create new conversations with information from the chart.

Applicant: I am interested in the <u>nurse</u> position.

Manager: Great. Do you have any questions?

Applicant: Yes. Is the position full-time or part-time?

Manager: It's <u>full-time</u>. The pay is <u>$22 an hour</u>.

Applicant: And benefits?

Manager: <u>Yes, there are benefits.</u>

Applicant: Thank you for the information. I will apply online.

> **YES / NO**
> Yes, there are benefits.
> No, there are no benefits.

F. Listen and write the missing words.

CD 2
TR 37

We need a _____ cook _____ for our restaurant in San Francisco. The salary is _____ $12 _____ an hour. You need _____ 2 _____ years experience for this job. This is a full-time position with benefits. We offer _____ sick leave _____ and a two-week _____ vacation _____ every year. Apply in person at 3500 West Arbor Place, San Francisco, California.

1. **Manager:** *Roberto, you need to take a vacation right away.*
   Roberto: *Well, I'm not sure I have time.*
   Manager: *If you don't take vacation now, then you will lose it. You have five days.*
   Roberto: *OK, I'll talk to my wife and see what she says.*

2. **Anya:** *I have a problem.*
   Manager: *What can I do for you?*
   Anya: *My husband had an accident.*
   Manager: *An accident? What happened?*
   Anya: *He was in a car accident and broke his leg.*
   Manager: *What can I do?*
   Anya: *Is he covered by my insurance?*
   Manager: *Of course. Your whole family is covered by your insurance.*

3. **Steve:** *I'm sorry. I have to call in sick.*
   Manager: *I'm sorry to hear that.*
   Steve: *Yes, I have a fever. Maybe I have the flu.*
   Manager: *How long will you be out?*
   Steve: *Do you know how much sick leave I have left?*
   Manager: *I'll check on it for you.*

Presentation 2

10–15 mins.

D. EVALUATE Study the information in the chart about jobs.

Ask students to go over the chart. Point out that there are five positions. Ask students what other information is given and discuss as a class. Ask specific questions about the information shown in the charts. Have volunteers look for and report their answers.

Practice 2

7–10 mins.

E. Practice the conversation and then create new conversations with information from the chart.

Students can do this activity in pairs or in small groups. Allow them plenty of time to work. Ask students to read the conversation before they make new ones. Have volunteers demonstrate the conversation in front of the class.

Evaluation 2

3–5 mins.

F. Listen and write the missing words.

Review the completed charts with students. Then, give them the cloze listening activity. After the listening, see if students can put the new information in the appropriate places in Exercise D.

We need a cook for our restaurant in San Francisco. The salary is $12 an hour. You need two years experience for this job. This is a full-time position with benefits. We offer sick leave and a two-week vacation every year. Apply in person at 3500 West Arbor Place, San Francisco, California.

INSTRUCTOR'S NOTES

_____
_____
_____
_____
_____
_____
_____
_____
_____
_____
_____
_____
_____
_____
_____
_____
_____
_____
_____
_____

Presentation 3 — 10–15 mins. ■■■

G. Read about Silvia, Anh, and Amal.

Go over the modal *can* with students. You may want to review the modal *should* from the previous unit to show that the two modals operate in the same way. *Can* is a verb in many languages, but it functions as a modal in English—it doesn't change form in the simple present. Have students repeat all the sentences with *can* and *can't* under the pictures.

BEST PRACTICE

Group work

At this level, it is important to model group activities with a few students. In group work, it is good to limit groups to five, with four being ideal for maximum participation. Whenever possible, be aware of the mix of students.

A variety of grouping strategies are suggested depending on the task. Some considerations might include the following:

- Allow students to self-select groups. Students sometimes perform well with friends or people they feel comfortable with.
- Arrange groups according to similar abilities. Sometimes proficient students in groups with other proficient students can be allowed to excel, while less proficient students don't feel intimidated by more proficient students.
- Arrange groups in diverse-ability groups. More proficient students often enjoy helping the less proficient, and you'll have several mentors in the class instead of just one teacher.
- Avoid putting students in homogeneous language groups when possible to encourage the use of English.

BEST PRACTICE

Random selection

Random selection of groups may be a consideration. To randomly select groups try the following techniques:

1. Count heads.
2. Use playing cards. Count out the number of cards. All students who have 3s, for example, would be in the same group.
3. Do a corners activity to form groups. Ask students to go to a corner based on criteria that you set. You might have homemakers in one corner, students in another, people who work part-time in another, and full-time workers in the final corner. Then, take one student from each corner and form a group, repeating the process until every student has been placed in a group.

Practice 3 — 10–15 mins. ■

H. ANALYZE Work in a group. Look at the information in Exercise D. Write the jobs that are good for Silvia, Anh, and Amal.

Evaluation 3 — 5–7 mins. ■

Ask groups to report to the class.

Application — 10–15 mins. ■■■

I. CREATE In a group, make a classified ad for the Internet. Use another sheet of paper. Include the information below. See Exercise A for an example.

Ask students to choose an imaginary job or a job that one of the members of the group has.

J. Look in a newspaper or on the Internet to find a job you want. Tell the class about the job.

Refer students to *Stand Out 1 Workbook*, Unit 7, Lesson 2 for more practice with can.

Go to the *Activity Bank* online for suggestions on promoting digital literacy and using the Internet to enhance this lesson.

MULTILEVEL WORKSHEETS

Unit 7, Lesson 2, Worksheet 1: Job Vocabulary
Unit 7, Lesson 2, Worksheet 2: Daily News Classifieds

WORKPLACE CONNECTIONS
Exercise H: Interpret and communicate information; Interact appropriately with team members.
Exercise I: Combine ideas and information.
Exercise J: Apply technology.

G. **Read about Silvia, Anh, and Amal.**

Silvia	Anh	Amal

Silvia

Skills:

She can drive.

She can speak English.

She can speak Spanish.

She can work at night.

Needs:

She needs a part-time job.

Anh

Skills:

She can't drive.

She can speak English.

She can't work at night.

She can't speak Spanish.

Needs:

She needs a part-time job.

Amal

Skills:

He can drive.

He can speak English.

He can't speak Spanish.

He can work at night.

Needs:

He needs a full-time job.

H. **ANALYZE** **Work in a group. Look at the information in Exercise D. Write the jobs that are good for Silvia, Anh, and Amal.**

Silvia	Anh	Amal
driver	server	nurse
server	cashier	mechanic
cashier		driver

I. **CREATE** **In a group, make a classified ad for the Internet. Use another sheet of paper. Include the information below. See Exercise A for an example.** Answers will vary.

business name	job title	location	hourly rate
full- or part-time	experience needed	benefit information	

J. **Look in the newspaper or on the Internet to find a job you want. Tell the class about the job.**

LESSON **3** What was your job before?

GOAL ■ Write your job history

A. PREDICT Look at the picture. What is Francisco's job? Does he work inside or outside? Then, read about Francisco.

My name is Francisco. I'm from Guatemala. Now, I work in the United States. I'm a mail carrier. I deliver mail to about two hundred houses every day. I started my job in July of 2010. Before I moved to the United States, I was a cook from March 2005 to July 2010. I cooked hamburgers and french fries in a fast-food restaurant.

B. SUMMARIZE Answer the questions in complete sentences and then tell a summary to a partner.

1. Where is Francisco from? _____ Francisco is from Guatemala. _____

2. What is his job now? _____ He is a mail carrier. _____

3. What does he do in his job? _____ He delivers mail. _____

4. When did he start his job? _____ He started his job in July of 2010. _____

5. What was his job in Guatemala? _____ He was a cook. _____

6. Where did he work in Guatemala? _____ He worked in a fast-food restaurant. _____

C. Complete the job history for Francisco.

Job History				
POSITION	**COMPANY**	**FROM**	**TO**	**DUTIES (Responsibilities)**
Mail carrier	US Government	July 2010	Present	delivers mail
Cook	Mr. Burger	March 2005	July 2010	cooked hamburgers and french fries
Server	La Cantina	March 2002	March 2005	served customers

Goal: Write your job history
Grammar: Simple past: regular verbs, *be*
Academic Strategy: Focused listening
Vocabulary: Job history vocabulary

Agenda

- Do a corners activity about employment status.
- Read about Francisco.
- Complete a job history for Francisco.
- Use the past tense.
- Complete a job history form about yourself.

Resources

Multilevel Worksheets: Unit 7, Lesson 3, Worksheets 1–2
Workbook: Unit 7, Lesson 3
Audio: CD 2, Track 38
Heinle Picture Dictionary: Jobs 1, pages 146–147; Jobs 2, pages 148–149
Stand Out 1 Assessment CD-ROM with ExamView®

Pacing

- 1.5 hour classes
- 2.5 hour classes
- 3+ hour classes

STANDARDS CORRELATIONS

CCRS: RI1, SL1, SL2, SL4, L1
CASAS: 4.1.2, 4.1.8
SCANS: **Information** Interpret and communicate information
Basic Skills Reading, writing, listening, speaking
Personal Qualities Self-management
EFF: **Communication** Read with understanding, convey ideas in writing, speak so others can understand, listen actively
Lifelong Learning Reflect and evaluate

Warm-up and Review   7–10 mins. ■■■

Do a corners activity. Send students to corners of the room based on these categories: *employed, unemployed but looking, unemployed and not looking,* and *retired.* If necessary, you can adjust these categories to better suit your class. **Note:** If your school uses the demographic forms for CASAS, you can say *unemployed* and *not employed* for the categories above.

Ask students to interview each other in their corners. Give them these questions:

Employed: Where do you work? When do you start work?
Unemployed but looking: What job do you want? Where do you want to work?
Unemployed and not looking: What do you do? Where do you live?
Retired: What do you do? Where do you live?

Introduction   3–5 mins. ■■■

Write your current and previous jobs on the board. Tell students a little about your job history. State the goal: *Today, you will write your job history.*

Presentation 1   15–20 mins. ■■■

Ask students to look at the picture. Ask the questions. Make sure that students have the paragraph beside the picture covered up so they don't refer to it to answer the questions. With the rest of the page covered, ask students the questions in Exercise B. At this point, they will be guessing so accept any answer. This method will help students prepare to read. They are predicting what they will read based on the picture.

A. PREDICT Look at the picture. What is Francisco's job? Does he work inside or outside? Then, read about Francisco.

Ask students to read the paragraph about Francisco by themselves and complete Exercise B.

B. SUMMARIZE Answer the questions in complete sentences and then tell a summary to a partner.

These comprehension questions are the same questions asked when the section was covered up. Go over the questions and compare the ideas students came up with to what they actually read. Go over any new words in the reading. Use your job history on the board to show how the most recent job always goes first.

Practice 1   12–15 mins. ■■■

C. Complete the job history for Francisco.

Allow students to do this activity on their own.

Evaluation 1   3–7 mins. ■■■

Ask students to peer-edit each other's work.

Presentation 2 15–20 min. ■■

Draw a timeline on the board. Label the center as the present. Put an arrow going to the left and an arrow going to the right. Write *past* and *future* in the appropriate places.

D. Study the charts with your classmates and teacher.

Go over the charts thoroughly with the class. Have students repeat the sentences. Show students examples of the simple past in the paragraph in Exercise A.

BEST PRACTICE

Past-tense endings

At this level, students may not be ready for a discussion of the three pronunciations of regular past-tense verbs. They will have trouble applying the pronunciation concept if you present it at this point.

However, it is appropriate to have them repeat the correct pronunciation after you without explanation.

Practice 2 10–15 mins. ■■

E. Complete each sentence with the correct form of the word in parentheses.

Ask students to work individually to complete this activity.

Evaluation 2 7–10 mins.

Ask volunteers to write their completed sentences on the board and go over them as a class.

BEST PRACTICE

Fill-in-the-blank activities

Teachers can easily expand fill-in-the-blank activities to give students more practice (particularly when the correct verb form is required). Teachers can write both the correct and incorrect verb forms on the board and ask students which one fits into the sentences. Teachers can ask students to create new sentences using the same verb form. Teachers can also ask students to add more sentences to the example to provide more detail.

INSTRUCTOR'S NOTES

D. **Study the charts with your classmates and teacher.**

Simple Past: Regular Verbs			
Subject	**Base verb + *ed***		**Example sentence**
I, You, He, She, It, We, They	cleaned	tables	I **cleaned** tables.
	cooked	hamburgers	You **cooked** hamburgers.
	prepared	breakfast	He **prepared** breakfast.
	delivered	packages	She **delivered** packages.
	counted	the money	I **counted** the money.
	helped	other workers	We **helped** other workers.
	moved	to the United States	They **moved** to the United States.

Simple Past: *Be*			
Subject	***Be***		**Example sentence**
I, He, She, It	was	a mail carrier	I **was** a mail carrier.
We, You, They	were	happy	You **were** happy.

E. **Complete each sentence with the correct form of the word in parentheses.**

1. Anya was an office worker.
   She _____typed_____ (type) letters.

2. Ernesto was a delivery person.
   He _____delivered_____ (deliver) packages.

3. David was a cashier.
   He _____counted_____ (count) money.

4. Anita was a nurse.
   She _____helped_____ (help) the doctors.

5. Eva and Anya were teachers.
   They _____worked_____ (work) in a school.

6. Derek was a salesperson.
   He _____talked_____ (talk) to customers.

7. So was a mechanic.
   He _____fixed_____ (fix) cars.

8. Mary was a cook.
   She _____prepared_____ (prepare) lunch.

9. Agatha was a manager.
   She _____supervised_____ (supervise) the other workers.

10. I was a ___Answers will vary.___.
    I ___Answers will vary.___.

WORKPLACE CONNECTIONS
Exercise F: Interpret and communicate information.
Exercises G, H: Complete tasks as assigned.

F. **Practice the conversation with your partner. Then, make new conversations using the information below.**

Miyuki: What was your last job?

Anya: I was <u>an office worker</u>.

Miyuki: What did you do as <u>an office worker</u>?

Anya: I <u>typed letters</u>.

Miyuki: What do you do now?

Anya: I am <u>a student</u>. I <u>study English</u>.

Before	**Now**
1. office worker / type letters	student / study English
2. teacher / help students	writer / write books
3. mechanic / fix cars	driver / drive a taxi
4. mail carrier / deliver letters	salesperson / sell computers
5. cook / cook hamburgers	server / serve food
6. busboy / clean tables	cashier / count money

G. **Listen and complete the job history. Then, practice the conversation in Exercise F again with the new information.**

CD 2 TR 38

POSITION	COMPANY	FROM	TO	DUTIES (Responsibilities)
Nurse	Arch Memorial Hospital	February 2012	Present	help doctors and people
Office worker	Arch Memorial Hospital	May 2009	February 2012	typed letters
Receptionist	Arch Memorial Hospital	January 2006	May 2009	talked on the phone

H. **APPLY** **Complete the job history for yourself.** Answers will vary.

POSITION	COMPANY	FROM	TO	DUTIES (Responsibilities)

I. **Get a job application from a business or find one on the Internet. How much can you complete? Can you complete the job history section?**

Presentation 3
7–10 mins. ■■□

Ask students what their last job was. Ask what they did at that job. Help them express themselves and write new verbs on the board. Make a job history section from a job application on the board, similar to the one in Exercise H. Ask a few students for their job history information and complete the chart on the board for them.

Go over the conversation with students. Work on their intonation and pronunciation of key words. Show them how to do the practice substituting the information.

Also, go over the past tense of each of the verbs in the *Before* column.

Practice 3
10–15 mins. ■

F. Practice the conversation with your partner. Then, make new conversations using the information below.

Evaluation 3
5–7 mins. ■

Go over the past tense of the verbs again before doing the listening.

G. Listen and complete the job history. Then, practice the conversation in Exercise F again with the new information.

LISTENING SCRIPT
🎧 CD 2 TR 38

My name is Nadia. My first job I ever had was as a receptionist. I worked very hard. I did that job for over three years and learned a lot. I talked to people every day on the phone. I started my second position in 2009. I was an office worker. I typed letters all day, every day. Now I am a nurse. I help doctors and people. It is a great job.

Have students check their work in pairs before they practice the conversation again. Play the recording again if necessary as they check their work.

Application
15–20 mins. ■■■

H. APPLY Complete the job history for yourself.

I. Get a job application from a business or find one on the Internet. How much can you complete? Can you complete the job history section?

Refer students to *Stand Out 1 Workbook,* Unit 7, Lesson 3 for more practice with the past tense.

Go to the *Activity Bank* online for suggestions on promoting digital literacy and using the Internet to enhance this lesson.

MULTILEVEL WORKSHEETS

Unit 7, Lesson 3, Worksheet 1: Job History

Unit 7, Lesson 3, Worksheet 2: Past Tense

INSTRUCTOR'S NOTES

_____

_____

_____

_____

_____

_____

_____

_____

_____

_____

_____

_____

_____

_____

_____

_____

_____

_____

Goal: Perform a job interview

Grammar: Questions with *can*

Pronunciation: Intonation with clarification questions

Academic Strategies: Clarification strategies, brainstorming

Vocabulary: Job interviews

Agenda

- Review job histories.
- Evaluate job interview behavior.
- Make an appointment.
- Discuss what to say in an interview.
- Discuss interview questions.
- Practice an interview.

Resources

Multilevel Worksheets: Unit 7, Lesson 4, Worksheets 1–2

Workbook: Unit 7, Lesson 4

Audio: CD 2, Tracks 39–41

Heinle Picture Dictionary: Jobs 1, pages 146–147; Jobs 2, pages 148–149

Stand Out 1 Assessment CD-ROM with ExamView®

Pacing

- 1.5 hour classes
- 2.5 hour classes
- 3+ hour classes

STANDARDS CORRELATIONS

CCRS: RI1, RI9, W2, SI2, SL3, L1, L5, RF2

CASAS: 0.1.1, 0.1.6, 4.1.5, 4.6.1

SCANS: **Information** Interpret and communicate information

Interpersonal Participate as a member of a team

Basic Skills Listening, speaking

Personal Qualities Self-management

EFF: **Communication** Speak so others can understand, listen actively, observe critically

Interpersonal Cooperate with others

Lifelong Learning Reflect and evaluate

Warm-up and Review   10–15 mins. ■■■

Ask students to work with a partner. One student should report their job history orally, while the other student takes notes. Then, have them reverse roles. Tell them to use Exercise H from the previous lesson to help them.

Introduction   15–20 mins. ■■■

Turn to a student and shake his or her hand. Remind the class of how to shake hands the American way by curling the fingers around the other person's hand firmly. Write on the board: *I'm looking for a job. Do you have any openings?* Shake hands with a few more students and say the statement and ask the question. Call on volunteers to do the same. Then, have all students walk around the room and practice the exchange. You can also add to the board typical responses such as: *Yes, here is an application.* State the goal: *Today, we will perform job interviews.*

Presentation 1   15–20 mins. ■■■

Role-play a bad interview with a volunteer. The volunteer will be the person who represents the hiring company. You might include in your presentation sloppy attire, uncombed hair, gum chewing, and an imaginary smoking habit.

Ask students what they found wrong with the interview. Make a list on the board. Then, ask students to open their books.

A. Look at the pictures. What is good at a job interview? What is not good?

Go over each picture carefully with students. Help them understand the new vocabulary.

Work on focused listening by talking about each item. Ask students to identify what you are talking about. For example, you might say: *I'm going in for an interview today, and I really need some help. I'm so hungry. Maybe I'll chew some gum so my stomach won't growl.*

Practice 1   10–15 mins. ■■■

B. CLASSIFY Use the words above to complete the chart. Then, add your own ideas.

After students have added to their lists, ask them to form groups to compare lists. Send representatives to other groups to add to their lists.

Evaluation 1   10–12 mins. ■■■

Draw the chart on the board and ask group representatives to enter the information. If students disagree, for example, about whether or not bright clothing is good for an interview, discuss how different cultures might view these things differently.

GOAL ■ Perform a job interview

A. Look at the pictures. What is good at a job interview? What is not good?

chewing gum

checking texts

firm handshake

eye contact

good posture

bright clothing

B. **CLASSIFY** Use the words above to complete the chart. Then, add your own ideas.

Good at a job interview	Not good at a job interview
firm handshake	chewing gum
eye contact	checking texts
good posture	bright clothing
Answers will vary.	Answers will vary.

C. Read the chart.

Questions with *Can*				
Can	**Subject**	**Base verb**	**Example questions**	**Example answers**
Can	I	ask answer	Can I ask you a question? Can you answer a few questions?	Yes, of course. Absolutely.
	you	work follow speak	Can you work on weekends? Can you follow directions? Can you speak English well?	No, I'm sorry. I can't. Yes, I can. I believe so. I am studying in school.

CD 2
TR 39-41

D. PREDICT Complete with a question from the chart. Then, listen for the correct answer.

1. **Applicant:** _Can I ask you a question_ _____?

   Interviewer: Yes, please do.

   Applicant: What are the benefits?

2. **Interviewer:** _Can you work on weekends_ _____?

   Applicant: Yes, on Saturday, but not on Sunday.

   Interviewer: OK, that's good to know.

3. **Interviewer:** _Can you speak English well_ _____?

   Applicant: I think I do. I am studying in school.

   Interviewer: Yes, I think you do, too. I just want to make sure.

E. CLARIFY Match each question with a clarification question. Draw lines.

1. What is your name?   a. Experience for this job?

2. What do you do?   b. My name?

3. Do you have experience?   c. Full-time?

4. Can you work eight hours?   d. On the weekends?

5. Can you work on Saturdays? e. What is my job now?

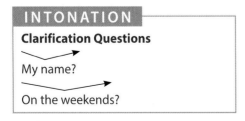

INTONATION

Clarification Questions

My name?

On the weekends?

Presentation 2   15–20 mins. ■■■

C. Read the chart.

Ask students to look at the chart. Then, review the information on questions with *can*. Go over the subjects, base verbs, and the example questions and answers.

D. PREDICT Complete with a question from the chart. Then, listen for the correct answer.

Ask students to look at the conversations in Exercise D. Go over the responses. Make sure students understand all the responses. Ask them to predict which phrase goes with which conversation.

LISTENING SCRIPT
CD 2
TR 39–41

1. **Interviewer:** *Thank you for answering all our questions. We will contact you soon to let you know about the position.*
   Applicant: *Thank you. I am very interested. Can I ask you a question?*
   Interviewer: *Yes, please do.*
   Applicant: *What are the benefits?*
   Interviewer: *We offer medical and dental insurance. We also have sick leave and six days of vacation every year.*
   Applicant: *Thanks.*

2. **Interviewer:** *Well, I think you look very good for the position. We must speak to many other applicants. We are open every day of the week including Saturday and Sundays. Can you work on weekends?*
   Applicant: *Well… yes, on Saturday and not on Sunday.*
   Interviewer: *OK, that's good to know.*
   Applicant: *Is that something that is required?*
   Interviewer: *No, not really. We have many opportunities here.*
   Applicant: *OK, thank you.*

   CD 2
   TR 40

3. **Interviewer:** *In this job, you have to talk to customers all the time. I hear that you speak English a little. Do you speak English well?*
   Applicant: *I think I do. I am studying in school.*
   Interviewer: *Yes, I think you do, too. I just want to make sure. Where do you study?*
   Applicant: *At the adult school around the corner.*
   Interviewer: *Perfect!*

   CD 2
   TR 41

Now, ask students to listen again for intonation. Point out that the intonation used here involves clarification. Have them study the pronunciation box at the bottom of the page. Practice with students by asking them questions similar to the ones in Exercise D.

Practice 2   7–10 mins. ■■

E. CLARIFY Match each question with a clarification question. Draw lines.

Have students do this activity in pairs.

Evaluation 2   5–10 mins. ■■

Write the phrases on the board as students are working. When they have completed the practice, ask volunteers to draw the lines on the board.

INSTRUCTOR'S NOTES

_____

_____

_____

_____

_____

_____

_____

_____

_____

_____

_____

_____

_____

_____

_____

_____

_____

_____

_____

_____

_____

_____

Presentation 3   10–15 mins. ■■■

F. Look at the picture. Who is Miyuki talking to? What is she doing? Then, study the phrases with your teacher. What are your strengths?

Ask students to look at the picture and ask the questions. Then, go over each phrase in the box. Explain any vocabulary that students do not understand. Then, ask them what their own strengths are.

G. CONTRAST Write the phrases from Exercise F in the chart next to the weakness.

Point out that one column shows strengths and the other shows weaknesses. Have students read the statements in the column under "Weaknesses." Then ask them to write a phrase from Exercise F that matches each weakness. Tell students that these phrases are strengths.

Practice 3   7–10 mins. ■

H. INTERPRET Read the paragraphs about Mary and Neda.

Allow students to read on their own or take turns reading in pairs.

Evaluation 3   5–7 mins. ■

Ask students to summarize the paragraphs in pairs. Then, have pairs present their summaries to another pair in the class.

Application   20–30 mins. ■■■

I. APPLY Write your own Work or School Inventory on another sheet of paper. Use Exercise H as an example.

J. Write and practice a job interview. Use the information from this lesson to help you with the questions.

Refer students to *Stand Out 1 Workbook*, Unit 7, Lesson 4 for more practice with questions using *can*.

Go to the *Activity Bank* online for suggestions on promoting digital literacy and using the Internet to enhance this lesson.

MULTILEVEL WORKSHEETS

Unit 7, Lesson 4, Worksheet 1: *Can*
Unit 7, Lesson 4, Worksheet 2: Job Interviews

INSTRUCTOR'S NOTES

F. Look at the picture. Who is Miyuki talking to? What is she doing? Then, study the phrases with your teacher. What are your strengths?

I communicate well.	I am a hard worker.
I am punctual.	I listen and follow directions well.

G. **CONTRAST** Write the phrases from Exercise F in the chart next to the weakness.

Strengths	Weaknesses
I am punctual.	Sometimes, I'm late.
I am a hard worker.	I like to take a lot of breaks.
I listen and follow directions well.	I don't always listen.
I communicate well.	Sometimes people don't understand me.

H. **INTERPRET** Read the paragraphs about Mary and Neda.

SYNONYMS

employee = worker

Mary's Work Inventory

I am a good employee.* I work hard. Sometimes I'm late. I always listen and follow directions well. I am learning English. Sometimes people don't understand me. I want to be a great employee. I need to communicate well and to come to work on time.

Neda's School Inventory

I don't work. I go to school. I am punctual. I don't always listen well. I am learning English. Sometimes people don't understand me. Sometimes I don't do my homework. I want to be a great student. I need to communicate well and do my homework every day.

I. **APPLY** Write your own Work or School Inventory on another sheet of paper. Use Exercise H as an example. Answers will vary.

J. Write and practice a job interview. Use the information from this lesson to help you with the questions. Answers will vary.

LESSON ⑤ He's a good worker

GOAL ■ Interpret performance reviews

WORKPLACE CONNECTIONS
Exercises A, B Collect and organize information;
Combine ideas and information.

A. Look at Fernando's evaluation. What is good? What is a problem?

EVALUATION FORM

DATE: May 4, 2016
COMPANY: Paul's Radio and CD
NAME: Fernando Gaspar
POSITION: Sales Clerk
SUPERVISOR: Leticia Garcia

Punctuality:

Superior   Good   (Needs improvement)

Appearance (professional dress and grooming):

(Superior)   Good   Needs improvement

Communication Skills:

Superior   (Good)   Needs improvement

Product Knowledge:

Superior   (Good)   Needs improvement

Fernando is a good employee. I worked with him for eight hours on
April 28 to evaluate his performance. He talked with the customers
well. He was ten minutes late to work. This is a problem. He said he
had a problem with his car. Fernando is a good salesperson and he
has very good knowledge of the product.

SIGNED: *Leticia Garcia*

B. EVALUATE Look at the evaluation and answer the questions.

1. Where does Fernando work? _____ Paul's Radio and CD _____

2. What is his supervisor's name? _____ Leticia Garcia _____

3. What does Fernando do well? _____ communicates, knows products _____

4. What does he do very well? _____ appearance _____

5. What does he need to improve? _____ punctuality _____

Goal: Interpret performance reviews

Grammar: Simple past: *be*, adverbs of frequency

Academic Strategies: Scanning, focused listening, ranking

Vocabulary: *Punctuality, improvement, superior, appearance, grooming*

Agenda

- Review and practice interviews.
- Read an evaluation form.
- Use the *be* verb in the simple past.
- Listen to an evaluation.
- Rank job skills.

Resources

Multilevel Worksheet: Unit 7, Lesson 5, Worksheet 1

Workbook: Unit 7, Lesson 5

Audio: CD 2, Track 42

Heinle Picture Dictionary: Working, pages 150–151

Stand Out 1 Assessment CD-ROM with ExamView®

Pacing

- ■ 1.5 hour classes
- ■ 2.5 hour classes
- ■ 3+ hour classes

STANDARDS CORRELATIONS

CCRS: RI1, RI7, SL1, SL2, SL4, L1, L2

CASAS: 4.4.1, 4.4.4

SCANS: **Resources** Allocate human resources

Information Acquire and evaluate information, organize and maintain information, interpret and communicate information

Interpersonal Participate as a member of a team

Basic Skills Reading, writing, listening, speaking

Thinking Skills Make decisions

Personal Qualities Self-management

EFF: **Communication** Read with understanding, convey ideas in writing, speak so others can understand, listen actively, observe critically

Decision Making Solve problems and make decisions

Interpersonal Cooperate with others

Lifelong Learning Reflect and evaluate

Warm-up and Review   10–15 mins. ■■■

Ask students to practice their new interviews from the application activity in the previous lesson and present them to the class. Teach students appropriate etiquette when students are performing in front of the class. Other students should be paying attention and not doing other work or talking.

Introduction   7–10 mins. ■■■

Write *punctuality* on the board. Give a brief definition. Take a class vote to determine which student is the most consistently punctual in the class. State the goal: *Today, we will interpret performance reviews.*

Presentation 1   15–20 mins. ■■■

Ask students what makes a good worker. Write their ideas on the board. Help them with challenging words. Write new vocabulary next to the ideas students suggest. For example, write *punctuality* next to *comes to work on time.*

A. Look at Fernando's evaluation. What is good? What is a problem?

As a class, go over each area of the evaluation form.

BEST PRACTICE

Presenting material

Asking questions is one of the best ways to introduce and present material. Allow students to answer. Ask all the questions in Exercise B and several other questions of your own. Make sure students are not completing Exercise B at this time. You may even ask them to cover it up so they are not tempted.

Ask the easier questions to the group and the more challenging questions to individuals whom you believe can answer. Keep everyone's attention by asking students to find items and to point to them in their book at times.

Make it a point to ask students who have more trouble communicating easy questions and then be ready to guide them if you need to. Another way to include these students is to ask a question to the class and give students time to think before you call on an individual.

Practice 1   10–15 mins. ■■■

B. EVALUATE Look at the evaluation and answer the questions.

Evaluation 1   3–5 mins. ■■■

Go over the answers with students.

Presentation 2 20–30 mins. ■■■

C. Study the charts with your classmates and teacher.

Look back to the evaluation form on the previous page to make additional example sentences. Write the examples on the board and allow students to copy them down. Go over the past tense and remind students about the regular past tense that they studied in this unit. Explain that the *be* verb is an irregular verb.

Remind students of the adverbs of frequency. These were last introduced in Unit 5 on page 127.

Practice 2 10–15 mins. ■■

D. Complete the sentences with the correct form of *be*.

This activity is more difficult than it looks. Have students work in pairs and then ask the pairs to check and compare with another pair, forming a group of four.

Evaluation 2 7–10 mins. ■■

Go over the answers with students and then do the next activity.

E. ANALYZE Read about Alberto. Underline the *be* verbs.

Read the paragraph with the class and make sure that students understand the *be* verb. See if they can also identify the present and the past in every sentence.

BEST PRACTICE

Forming groups

Teachers often ask students to form groups by simply calling out the number of group members needed. Although quick and easy, this approach is not really the best for the grouping process. Groups should be mixed with students at different performance levels and should be varied as much as possible. Students themselves may tend to group with friends, people from their own countries, the same age, or the same sex. Try using one of the following techniques to form mixed groups:

1. Ask each student to pick a partner. Then, combine pairs to make groups.
2. Write students' names on small cards. Then, randomly pick cards to make groups.
3. Give students specific categories for making their own groups. For example, have them choose classmates wearing jeans, a blue shirt, black shoes, etc.
4. Have students get into small groups of four. Then, ask one student from each group to raise his or her hand. Choose those with raised hands to form a new group. Repeat the process with the remaining students.

INSTRUCTOR'S NOTES

_____

_____

_____

_____

_____

_____

_____

_____

_____

_____

_____

_____

_____

_____

_____

_____

_____

C. **Study the charts with your classmates and teacher.**

Simple Present: *Be*			
Subject	**Be**		**Example sentence**
I	am		I **am** always early.
He, She, It	is	early late	He **is** sometimes late. She **is** a good worker.
We, You, They	are	on time punctual	We **are** often early. You **are** never on time. They **are** always punctual.

Adverbs of Frequency

0%	50%	100%

never   rarely   sometimes   usually   always

Simple Past: *Be*			
Subject	**Be**		**Example sentence**
I, He, She, It	was	early late	I **was** early yesterday. He **was** often late. She **was** always a good worker.
We, You, They	were	on time punctual	We **were** early on Saturday. You **were** on time today. They **were** never punctual.

D. **Complete the sentences with the correct form of *be*.**

1. Mario and Alberto _____*were*_____ early to work yesterday.

2. I _____*was*_____ never on time last year, but now I _____*am*_____ always on time.

3. She _____*was*_____ punctual every day last year.

4. We come to work on time every day. We _____*are*_____ rarely late.

5. You _____*are*_____ a good worker. You always work well with customers.

E. **ANALYZE** **Read about Alberto. Underline the *be* verbs.**

Alberto <u>is</u> a good worker. He works at night. He <u>is</u> punctual. The customers love him. Last night, Alberto <u>was</u> late for work. He had a problem with his car. His car <u>is</u> old. He called a tow truck with his cell phone and the tow truck <u>was</u> late.

F. **Listen to John's evaluation. Circle the correct rating** *(Needs Improvement,* *Good,* **or** *Superior).*

CD 2
TR 42

EVALUATION FORM

DATE: May 4, 2016
COMPANY: Paul's Electronics
NAME: John Perkins
POSITION: Sales Clerk
SUPERVISOR: Leticia Garcia

Punctuality:
Superior   (Good)   Needs improvement

Appearance (professional dress and grooming):
Superior   Good   (Needs improvement)

Communication Skills:
(Superior)   Good   Needs improvement

Product Knowledge:
Superior   Good   (Needs improvement)

Comments:

I worked with John for four hours. He is new. He needs to learn more

about the product. He doesn't dress well and he needs to comb

his hair. He said he was tired today. I think he has three jobs.

This is a problem. John communicates well with the customers.

Signed: *Leticia Garcia*

G. **RANK** **In a group, rank the areas 1–4. Number 1 is the most important.**

Answers will vary.

_____ Punctuality

_____ Appearance

_____ Communication

_____ Product Knowledge

Presentation 3

7–10 mins. ■■■

Look at the evaluation form with students. Ask questions to make sure students understand the new vocabulary. Read the comments together. This reading will help students predict what information the listening will give them. Ask students to predict what ratings John will get for the three areas. Then, play the recording.

Practice 3

10–15 mins. ■

F. Listen to John's evaluation. Circle the correct rating (*Needs Improvement, Good,* or *Superior*).

Play the listening several times and allow students to discuss their answers between listenings.

LISTENING SCRIPT

CD 2
TR 42

Supervisor: *John, I think in time you will become a good worker. You certainly speak well and you are great with the customers. I gave you a superior for communication skills. This is why I am sure you can be a great employee in time. I did notice that overall you come on time. You were late once, but only by a few minutes. For punctuality, I have given you a good.*

I know that you are trying to work hard and make extra money through commissions. You will do better if you dress better and keep your hair neat. Do this and you will see your sales soar. For now, I had to give you a needs improvement on appearance. You are new so don't worry too much about this last one. You will learn quickly if you apply yourself. I gave you a needs improvement for product knowledge. I am sure that will change in no time.

Evaluation 3

3 mins. ■

Go over students' answers. Play the recording and pause it when appropriate to confirm the correct answers.

Application

10–15 mins. ■■■

G. RANK In a group, rank the areas 1–4. Number 1 is the most important.

Refer students to *Stand Out 1 Workbook,* Unit 7, Lesson 5 for more practice with the present and past tense of *be* and adjectives.

Go to the *Activity Bank* online for suggestions on promoting digital literacy and using the Internet to enhance this lesson.

MULTILEVEL WORKSHEET

Unit 7, Lesson 5, Worksheet 1: Adjectives and Adverbs

INSTRUCTOR'S NOTES

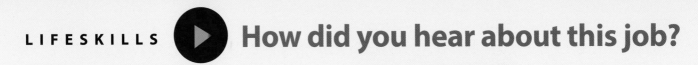

Before You Watch

- Ask students if they have a job. Ask volunteers what jobs they have.
- Ask students how people find jobs. Discuss different ways as a class.

A. Look at the picture. Complete each sentence.

- Have students look at the picture. Then, ask them to complete each sentence.
- Ask volunteers to write their answers on the board. Then, review as a class.

While You Watch

B. Watch the video. Read the statements. Write T for *True* and F for *False*.

- Tell students they will watch the video. Then, tell them to read each statement and decide if it is true or false.
- Play the video and ask students to watch and listen.
- Ask students to read the statements. Then, play the video again.
- Play the video once more so that students can check their answers. Then, review answers as a class.

Check Your Understanding

C. Complete the dialog. Use the words in the box.

- Ask students to look at the words in the box. Review the words as a class.
- Explain to students that they will complete the dialog between Mr. Patel and Hector with the words from the box.
- Ask students to work individually. Then, have students check their answers in pairs.
- Ask students to practice the dialog with their partners. Then, ask them to take turns acting out the dialog with another pair.

INSTRUCTOR'S NOTES

LIFESKILLS ▶ How did you hear about this job?

Before You Watch

A. Look at the picture. Complete each sentence.

1. Hector is at a
   _____*a job interview*_____.

2. Mr. Patel is reading Hector's
   _____*application*_____.

3. He is going to ask about Hector's
   _____*experience*_____.

While You Watch

B. ▶ Watch the video. Read the statements. Write T for *True* or F for *False*.

1. Hector does not have an appointment for an interview.   _**F**_

2. Mr. Patel is the store manager.   _T_

3. Hector saw an ad for the job.   _T_

4. Hector can work in the mornings and evenings.   _F_

5. Mr. Patel hires Hector.   _T_

Check Your Understanding

C. Complete the dialog. Use the words in the box.

answered	~~application~~	assistant	did	experience	history

Mr. Patel: Let's take it one step at a time . . . Did you bring an (1) _____*application*_____?

Hector: Yes, here it is. I know I don't have very much (2) _____*experience*_____.

Mr. Patel: Never mind that. Tell me about your work (3) _____*history*_____. What was your last job?

Hector: I was an . . . (4) _____*assistant*_____.

Mr. Patel: And what was it that you (5) _____*did*_____ as an "assistant"?

Hector: I (6) _____*answered*_____ the phones and took messages.

Review

WORKPLACE CONNECTIONS
Exercises B, C: Collect and organize information.

A. **Write the name of the job below each picture.**

1. _____custodian_____ 2. _____mail carrier_____ 3. _____mechanic_____

B. **Read the ads and complete the chart below.**

1.
Office Assistant
f/t, gd bnfts,
4 yrs exp nec,
$17/hr,
Call 555-2298.

2.
Restaurant Manager
p/t, restaurant exp nec,
$14/hr, no bnfts,
Apply in person
at 2222 E. Fourth St.
8am to 12pm, M-F.

3.
Delivery Person
p/t, work 7 days, no bnfts,
$8/hr, no exp, will train,
current driver's license,
speak Eng. and Span.
Call 555-5477.

4.
CARPENTER
f/t, good bnfts, no exp,
$22 an hour,
must be 18 yrs. old.
Apply in person at
3333 W. Broadway
during office hours.

5.
Mechanic
Mike's Garage
f/t, night shift,
$12/hour, no exp nec,
will train, bnfts,
Call 555-7469.

Position	Experience	F/T or P/T	Benefits	Pay
1. Office Assistant	yes (4 years)	full-time	yes	$17/hr.
2. Restaurant Manager	yes	part-time	no	$14/hr.
3. Delivery Person	no	part-time	no	$8/hr.
4. Carpenter	no	full-time	yes	$22/hr.
5. Mechanic	no	full-time	yes	$12/hr.

Goal: All unit goals

Grammar: All unit grammar

Academic Strategies: Focused listening, reviewing, evaluating, developing study skills

Vocabulary: All unit vocabulary

Agenda

☐ Discuss unit goals.

☐ Complete the review.

☐ Evaluate and reflect on progress.

Stand Out 1 Assessment CD-ROM with ExamView®

Pacing

■ 1.5 hour classes   ■ 2.5 hour classes

■ 3+ hour classes

STANDARDS CORRELATIONS

CCRS: RI1, W2, L1, L4, RF3

CASAS: 4.1.2, 4.1.3, 4.1.5, 4.1.6, 4.1.8, 4.4.1, 4.4.4, 4.6.1

SCANS: **Information** Acquire and evaluate information, organize and maintain information

Basic Skills Reading, writing, speaking

Personal Qualities Responsibility, self-management

EFF: **Communicate** Speak so others can understand

Lifelong Learning Take responsibility for learning, reflect and evaluate

Warm-up and Review   10–15 mins. ■■■

With their books closed, ask students to help you make a list on the board of all the vocabulary they can come up with from the unit. Then, have a competition where students in groups will write page numbers for each item on the list. The first group to have the correct page number for each item wins.

Introduction   5 mins. ■■■

Write all the goals on the board from Unit 7. Show students the first page of every lesson so they understand that today will be review. Complete the agenda.

Presentation   10–15 mins. ■■■

This Presentation and Practice will cover the first three pages of the review. Quickly go to the first page of each lesson. Discuss the goal of each. Ask simple questions to remind students of what they have learned.

Practice   15–20 mins. ■■■

A. **Write the name of the job below each picture. (Lesson 1)**

B. **Read the ads and complete the chart below. (Lesson 2)**

BEST PRACTICE

Recycling/Review

The review and the project that follows are part of the recycling/review process. Students at this level often need to be reintroduced to concepts to solidify what they have learned. Many concepts are learned and forgotten while learning other new concepts. This is because students learn but are not necessarily ready to acquire language concepts.

Therefore, it becomes very important to review and to show students how to review on their own. It is also important to recycle the new concepts in different contexts.

INSTRUCTOR'S NOTES

_____

_____

_____

_____

_____

_____

_____

_____

_____

Practice *(continued)*

C. **Write a classified ad for a receptionist. (Lesson 2)**

D. **Complete the paragraph with the past tense form of the verbs in parentheses. (Lesson 3)**

E. **Complete the job history for Jarek. (Lesson 3)**

Learner Log

I can write my job history.   I can ask good questions at a job interview.
☐ Yes ☐ No ☐ Maybe   ☐ Yes ☐ No ☐ Maybe

C. Write a classified ad for a receptionist. *Answers will vary.*

Company: _____

Position: _____

Location: _____

Hourly Rate: _____

Type: _____

Benefits: _____

D. Complete the paragraph with the past tense form of the verbs in parentheses.

In 2005, Jarek was a carpenter. He _____*constructed*_____ (construct) homes for Builders Plus Company. In 2007, Jarek was a custodian. He _____*cleaned*_____ (clean) the offices for Clean Sweep Maintenance Company. In 2010, Jarek was a server. He _____*talked*_____ (talk) to customers at the Polish Café. Now Jarek is a teacher. He helps students at Jefferson Adult School.

E. Complete the job history for Jarek.

POSITION	COMPANY	FROM	TO	DUTIES (Responsibilities)
server	The Polish Café	2010		talked to customers
custodian	Clean Sweep Maintenance Company	2007	2010	cleaned offices
carpenter	Builders Plus Company	2005	2007	constructed homes

F. Label the pictures and circle *good* or *bad* for a job interview.

1. **ch**ewing _____ gum _____   good / (bad)

2. **g**ood _____ posture _____   (good) / bad

3. **f**irm _____ handshake _____   (good) / bad

4. **ch**ecking _____ text message _____   good / (bad)

5. **br**ight _____ clothing _____   good / (bad)

6. **e**ye _____ contact _____   (good) / bad

G. Complete the paragraph with the correct form of the verbs from the box. Choose the present or past tense. You will use one of the verbs two times.

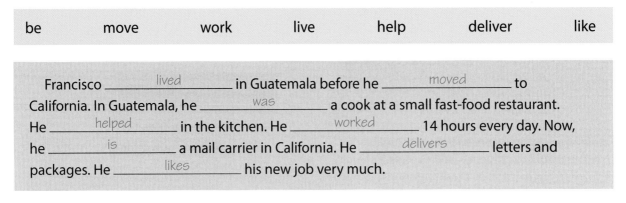

| be | move | work | live | help | deliver | like |

Francisco ___lived___ in Guatemala before he ___moved___ to California. In Guatemala, he ___was___ a cook at a small fast-food restaurant. He ___helped___ in the kitchen. He ___worked___ 14 hours every day. Now, he ___is___ a mail carrier in California. He ___delivers___ letters and packages. He ___likes___ his new job very much.

H. Match the words and definitions. Draw lines.

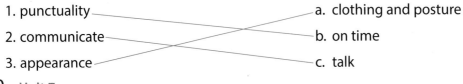

1. punctuality   a. clothing and posture
2. communicate   b. on time
3. appearance   c. talk

Practice (continued)

F. Label the pictures and circle *good* or *bad* for a job interview. (Lesson 4)

G. Complete the paragraph with the correct form of the verbs from the box. Choose the present or past tense. You will use one of the verbs two times. (Lessons 3 and 5)

H. Match the words and definitions. Draw lines. (Lesson 5)

Evaluation   15 mins. ■■■

Go around the room and check on students' progress. Help individuals when needed. If you see consistent errors among several students, interrupt the class and give a mini lesson or review to help students feel comfortable with the concept.

Presentation   5 mins. ■■■

Learner Log

Review the concepts of the Learner Log. Make sure students understand the concepts and how to complete the log including circling the answers, finding page numbers where the concept is taught, and ranking favorite activities.

BEST PRACTICE

Learner Logs

Learner logs function to help students in many different ways.

1. They serve as part of the review process.
2. They help students to gain confidence and to document what they have learned. Consequently, students see that they are progressing in their learning.
3. They provide students with a tool that they can use repeatedly to check and recheck their understanding of the target language. In this way, students become independent learners.

Practice   10–15 mins. ■

Ask students to complete the Learner Log.

Evaluation   2 mins. ■

Go over the Learner Log with students.

Application   5–7 mins. ■■■

Ask students to record their favorite lesson or page in the unit.

Assessment   ■■■

Use the Stand Out 1 Assessment CD-ROM with ExamView® to create a post-test for Unit 7.

Refer students to *Stand Out 1 Workbook,* Unit 7, Lesson 1 for more practice with the past tense of *be* and Stand Out 1 Workbook, Unit 7, Lesson 2 for more practice with the future with *will*.

Go to the *Activity Bank* online for suggestions on promoting digital literacy and using the Internet to enhance this lesson.

MULTILEVEL WORKSHEETS

Unit 7, Computer Worksheets

Unit 7, Internet Worksheets

INSTRUCTOR'S NOTES

_____

_____

_____

_____

_____

_____

_____

_____

_____

_____

_____

_____

_____

WORKPLACE CONNECTION

Make decisions and solve problems; Collect and organize information; Combine ideas and information; Make decisions; Exercise leadership roles; Manage time; Complete tasks as assigned; Interact appropriately with team members; Interpret and communicate information.

Introduction   5 mins.

TEAM PROJECT

Get a new job

In this project, one student will prepare to complete the process for getting a job. Discuss the art on the student book page before beginning.

Stage 1   15–20 mins.

COLLABORATE Form a team with four or five students. In your team, you need:

Help students form groups and assign positions. Review responsibilities of the positions.

Stage 2   3–5 mins.

Choose one member of your team to look for a new job. Decide on a position he or she is interested in.

Ask students to choose one person whom they will prepare for a job interview.

Stage 3   15–20 mins.

Write a classified ad describing the position.

Ask groups to design a classified ad for the new job that the team member wants. There is a classified ad template available on the Multilevel Worksheets (Unit 7, Project, Worksheet 1).

Stage 4   10–15 mins.

Write a real or imaginary job history for the person looking for a job.

Have students write a real or imaginary job history for the student they have selected. There is a job application template available on the Multilevel Worksheets (Unit 7, Project, Worksheet 2).

Stage 5   10–15 mins.

Write an imaginary job evaluation from an old job.

Ask students to make an imaginary evaluation form for one of the jobs from the student's job history. There is an evaluation template available on the Multilevel Worksheets (Unit 7, Project, Worksheet 3).

Stage 6   10–30 mins.

Write a conversation of a job interview and practice the conversation.

Ask students to write a job interview and practice it with others from the team.

Stage 7   20–30 mins.

As a team, make a presentation of all the previous steps and perform the conversation.

Ask teams to practice their presentations before presenting to the class.

Students often prepare better for formal presentations if they are videotaped.

MULTILEVEL WORKSHEETS

Unit 7, Project, Worksheet 1: Daily News Classifieds

Unit 7, Project, Worksheet 2: Job Application

Unit 7, Project, Worksheet 3: Evaluation

Unit 7, Extension, Worksheet 1: Warning Signs

Unit 7, Extension, Worksheet 2: Signs and Must

TEAM PROJECT ✓ Get a new job

In this project, you will prepare one member of your team to complete the process for getting a job.

1. **COLLABORATE** Form a team with four or five students. In your team, you need:

Position	Job description	Student name
Student 1: **Team Leader**	Check that everyone speaks English. Check that everyone participates.	
Student 2: **Writer**	With help from the team, write a classified ad, a job history, and a job evaluation.	
Student 3: **Director**	With help from the team, write and direct an interview.	
Students 4/5: **Spokespeople**	With help from the team, organize a presentation to give to the class.	

2. Choose one member of your team to look for a new job. Decide on a position he or she is interested in.

3. Write a classified ad describing the position.

4. Write a real or imaginary job history for the person looking for a job.

5. Write an imaginary job evaluation from an old job.

6. Write a conversation of a job interview and practice the conversation.

7. As a team, make a presentation of all the previous steps and perform the conversation.

READING CHALLENGE

About the Explorer

Thomas Taha Rassam (TH) Culhane is an urban planner. He is the co-founder of Solar C.3.I.T.I.E.S, a non-governmental organization that benefits low-income families in Cairo, Egypt who have no hot running water. Thomas' organization installs rooftop solar water heaters on the families' roofs. Thomas' job history has varied over the years. He has worked as a researcher for Harvard University; he has also worked as a teacher. His first job is probably the most interesting though: He worked as a clown for the Ringling Brothers Circus.

About the Photo

This photo shows Thomas helping to install a rooftop solar water heater on the roof of a low-income family in Cairo, Egypt. The system generates 200 liters of hot water and 200 liters of cold water each day. Thomas and his team do not just turn up with everything they need to install; each installation is unique. This is because the team tries to utilize as many of the available resources on the roofs as possible. This may look like garbage to the untrained eye, but these are the resources helping people of Cairo to get what they need.

- Introduce the explorer, Thomas Culhane, and read the title out loud. Then, ask students to look at the photo and describe what Thomas is doing.

- Explain to students that Thomas runs an organization. Ask them if they can guess what kind of organization Thomas runs.

A. Look at the picture. Read about Thomas Culhane's organization.

- Read the quote out loud. Ask students what the problem in

READING CHALLENGE

EXPLORER THOMAS CULHANE

Solar Power Provider

"This is not a new or exotic technology. I believe Egypt could solve at least half its energy needs by immediately going solar."
—Thomas Taha Rassam Culhane

A. **Look at the picture. Read about Thomas Culhane's organization.**

> Thomas Culhane also teaches people to build passive solar heated food-waste-to-fuel-and-fertilizer biodigesters.

a. Solar C3ITIES is an organization co-founded by Thomas Culhane.

b. It makes power from the sun.

c. It helps people heat water.

d. It works with poor people all over the world.

B. **PREDICT** The words below are in the reading about Thomas Culhane. Match the letter of the definition to the word.

_d_ solar	a. to make something
_a_ build	b. a machine to make water hot
_e_ co-founder	c. what you do when something is funny
_b_ water heater	d. from the sun
_c_ laugh	e. someone who started something with another person

182 Unit 7

CCRS FOR READING

RI1, RI2, RI5, RI10, SL1, SL2, L3

C. On another sheet of paper, combine the sentences in Exercise A into a paragraph.

D. Read about Thomas Culhane and his organization.

> **Solar for the Poor**
>
> Thomas Culhane is a National Geographic Explorer and the co-founder of Solar C3ITIES. He helps poor people all over the world. They need hot and cold water in their homes. Thomas says that poor people have skills. They are carpenters, plumbers, glassworkers, etc. Thomas helps them build water heaters that are powered by the sun. Before working in countries like Egypt, Thomas was a teacher. He was also a researcher at Harvard University. In 1976, Thomas made people laugh as a job. He was a clown for the Ringling Brothers Circus.

E. INTERACT Find answers in the paragraph.

1. Do you think Thomas builds the water heaters by himself? Find one or two words that help you answer the question.

No, helps them

2. Is Thomas a clown now in the Ringling Brothers Circus? Find one or two words that help you answer the question.

No, was

3. What are examples of the *skills* Thomas is talking about.

carpentry, plumbing, glassworking

F. APPLY Why do people need hot and cold water? In a group, make a list.

Answers will vary.

to wash clothes

READING STRATEGIES

Question-Answer Relationship

Question-Answer Relationship is a reading strategy that requires students to analyze types of questions asked and where to find answers in a reading. The strategy is used after students have read. Question types are usually those that

- require student to use background knowledge to answer.
- have answers coming from different parts of the reading.
- are literal and have answers using the same words.
- ask students to relate the question to their own personal experience.

Egypt is. Then, ask them what the solution is.

- Ask students if they know a place or someone that uses solar energy. Discuss as a class.

B. PREDICT **The words below are in the reading about Thomas Culhane. Match the letter of the definition to the word.**

Ask students to match the words to the definitions.

C. **On another sheet of paper, combine the sentences in Exercise A into a paragraph.**

Have students use the sentences in Exercise A to write a complete paragraph.

D. **Read about Thomas Culhane and his organization.**

- Have students read about Thomas Culhane and his organization.
- Ask students to re-read the paragraph and underline or circle the name of the organization and find who the solar energy is for in the paragraph.

E. INTERACT **Find answers in the paragraph.**

- Ask students to re-read and find answers in the paragraph.
- Read each question out loud. Then, ask students to work individually or in pairs to find their answers. Discuss as a class.

F. APPLY **Why do people need hot and cold water? In a group, make a list.**

Ask students why people need hot and cold water. Ask them to make a list of possible answers in small groups.

Lifelong Learning and Review

About the Photo

Idaho-based photographer Glenn Oakley took this photo. It shows musician Johnny Thomsen sitting outside his self-built home with a banjo. Johnny plays a wide variety of instruments: guitar, recorder, dobro, harmonica, mandolin, flute, autoharp, accordion, and, of course, banjo. Johnny performs in many different places, including schools and folk festivals. Johnny has held a number of different jobs over the years. He was once a Forest Service fire lookout.

- Introduce the unit by reading the title. Then, go over the unit outcomes.

- Ask students to look at the photo and answer the questions. Discuss as a class.

- Have a volunteer read the caption out loud. Ask students to discuss what types of events would be considered to be a community gathering.

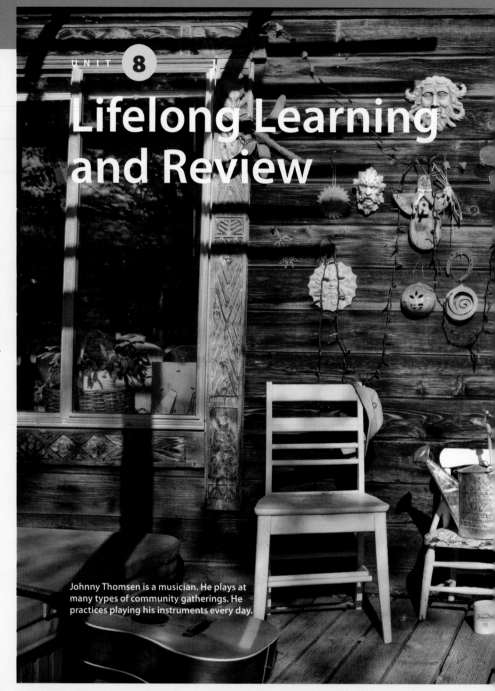

UNIT 8

Lifelong Learning and Review

Johnny Thomsen is a musician. He plays at many types of community gatherings. He practices playing his instruments every day.

UNIT OUTCOMES	GRAMMAR	VOCABULARY	EL CIVICS
• Evaluate study habits • Organize study • Identify learning opportunities • Identify vocational preferences • Develop goals	• Past tense: regular and irregular verbs • Modal: *can* • Modal: *should* • Verb + infinitive • Verb + noun • Future: *going to* and *will*	• Study words • Skills • Life skills • Educational agencies • Goals	The skills students learn in this unit can be applied to the following El Civics competency areas: • Employment Resources • Employment Soft Skills

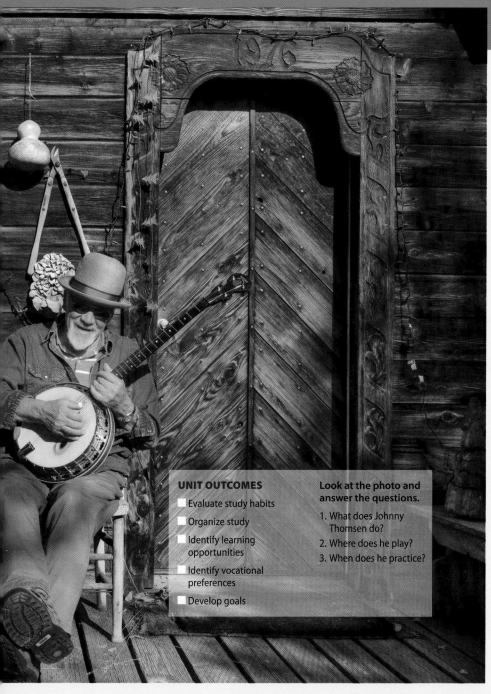

UNIT OUTCOMES

- [ ] Evaluate study habits
- [ ] Organize study
- [ ] Identify learning opportunities
- [ ] Identify vocational preferences
- [ ] Develop goals

Look at the photo and answer the questions.

1. What does Johnny Thomsen do?
2. Where does he play?
3. When does he practice?

- Ask students what type of musical instrument they see in the photo. Point out that a *banjo* is an instrument used in traditional music. Ask students what other musical instruments might be used in traditional music. Discuss as a class.

Life Skills Link

In this unit, students will review what they have learned throughout *Stand Out 1*. They will also learn how to develop future goals pertaining to academia and the workplace.

Workplace Link

All lessons and units in *Stand Out* include basic communication skills and interpersonal skills important for the workplace. They are not individually identified. Other workplace skills are indicated. They include collecting and organizing information, making decisions and solving problems, and combining ideas and information.

CASAS	SCANS	CCRS
Lesson 1: 7.4.1 Lesson 2: 7.1.4, 7.4.1, 7.4.9 Lesson 3: 2.5.5, 7.1.1 Lesson 4: 7.1.1, 7.5.1 Lesson 5: 7.1.1, 7.1.2 Review: 7.1.1, 7.1.4, 7.4.1, 7.4.9, 7.5.1 Team Project: 4.8.1, 7.1.1, 7.1.4, 7.4.1, 7.4.9, 7.5.1	Most SCANS are incorporated into this unit, with an emphasis on: • Understanding systems • Monitoring and correcting performance • Knowing how to learn • Self-management (Technology is optional.)	RI1, RI2, RI5, RI7, SL1, SL2, L1, L2, L4, L5, RF3

LESSON 1 How are your study habits?

GOAL ▮ Evaluate study habits

WORKPLACE CONNECTION
Exercise B: Collect and organize information.

A. PREDICT Look at the picture. What is Nubar doing? Why? Then, read about Nubar.

Nubar is a good ESL student at Franklin Adult School. He comes to school every day. He also studies at home. Some students practice English at work. Others practice English with their families. Nubar learns two or three new words a day at home. Sometimes Nubar watches TV or listens to the radio.

B. CLASSIFY In a group, write different ways to study or practice English.

Answers will vary.

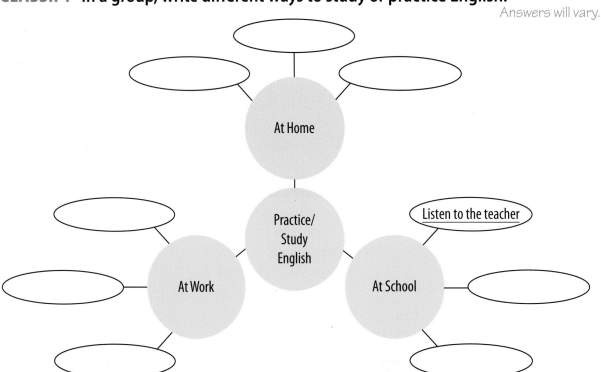

AT-A-GLANCE PREP

Goal: Evaluate study habits
Grammar: Past tense: regular and irregular verbs
Academic Strategies: Self-assessment, focused listening
Vocabulary: Study skills

Agenda

▢ List activities you do outside of school.

▢ Evaluate study habits.

▢ Use past tense verbs.

▢ Listen for good habits.

▢ Evaluate your study habits.

Resources

Multilevel Worksheet: Unit 8, Lesson 1, Worksheet 1
Workbook: Unit 8, Lesson 1
Audio: CD 2, Track 43
Heinle Picture Dictionary: Classroom, pages 18–19
Stand Out 1 Assessment CD-ROM with ExamView®

Pacing

■ 1.5 hour classes   ■ 2.5 hour classes
■ 3+ hour classes

STANDARDS CORRELATIONS

CCRS: RI1, SL1, SL2, L1, L2, RF3

CASAS: 7.4.1

SCANS: **Resources** Allocate time, allocate materials and facility resources, allocate human resources

Interpersonal Participate as a member of a team

Basic Skills Reading, writing, listening, speaking

Personal Qualities Responsibility, self-management

EFF: Communication Read with understanding, convey ideas in writing, speak so others can understand, listen actively, observe critically

Decision Making Plan

Interpersonal Cooperate with others

Lifelong Learning Take responsibility for learning, reflect and evaluate

Preassessment *(optional)*   ■■■

Use the Stand Out 1 Assessment CD-ROM with ExamView® to create a pretest for Unit 8.

Warm-up and Review   7–10 mins. ■■■

Ask students what they do when they are not in school. Make a list on the board. The list may or may not include *study*. Ask students if they study at home.

Introduction   3 mins. ■■■

Write *habit* on the board. Ask students if they know what the word means. Tell them that it is when they do things over and over again. Explain that there are good and bad habits. Ask for examples of both. State the goal: *Today, we will learn to evaluate study habits.*

Presentation 1   10–15 mins. ■■■

Ask students to look at the picture of Nubar. Tell them to cover up the reading and the activity that follows. Ask the questions in the box and any others that you consider appropriate.

Prepare students for the reading by asking them for ideas on how to study English at home. List their ideas on the board. Tell students that they will have a limited time to read about Nubar. Then, they will be told to close their books.

Practice 1   10–15 mins. ■■■

A. PREDICT Look at the picture. What is Nubar doing? Why? Then, read about Nubar.

Ask students to read the paragraph silently. Only give them one minute. Then, ask them to close their books, whether they have finished or not. Students will be given more time to read in the next activity if they didn't finish.

Ask comprehension questions to see how much students retained from the paragraph and then ask them to get into groups to do the next activity.

B. CLASSIFY In a group, write different ways to study or practice English.

Groups can use ideas from the paragraph and add any other ideas they may have.

Evaluation 1   3–5 mins. ■■■

Ask groups to report to the class.

Reading

As mentioned earlier, some students read slowly because they think it is better than reading fast. Some students will read and vocalize what they are reading. Teach students that this is not a productive way to read. Some students will want to stop and check words in the dictionary. Ask them instead to underline words they don't know and not stop reading. Teach students that reading is like focused listening in that they may not understand every word, but they can still understand the important information.

Presentation 2   10–15 mins. ■■■

C. Study the charts with your classmates and teacher.

Reintroduce the simple past tense. Explain to students that there are many irregular forms that they will need to memorize. This is merely an introduction, however, so don't expect students to memorize the verbs at this point.

Practice 2   20–30 mins. ■■■

D. Rewrite the sentences in the past tense. Then, use the sentences to write a paragraph in your notebook.

After students do the exercise, ask them to string the sentences together in paragraph form. You may need to teach the form. Ask them to use the model on page 186.

Evaluation 2   7–10 mins. ■■■

Check students' answers. Ask volunteers to write their sentences on the board.

Presentation 3   3–5 mins. ■■■

Prepare students for listening by going over all the choices in Exercise E.

Practice 3   5–7 mins. ■

E. Listen to Angela talk about her study skills. Check (✓) the things she did to study.

Play the recording several times and allow students to discuss the recording between listenings.

LISTENING SCRIPT   CD 2 TR 43

My name is Angela Sheldon. I am in college now. I studied English in school so I could go to college here in the United States. I took advantage of every opportunity so I could learn quickly. For example, I came to class on time every day. I wrote down new words in my notebook. I learned new words every day. At home, I watched TV. It was really good for me. I watched the news and other programs. I think the best thing I did was I helped and taught other students. Now I am in college. I am happy to be here.

Evaluation 3   3–5 mins. ■

Play the recording one more time to confirm that students heard all of the information. Stop the recording when necessary.

_____

_____

_____

_____

_____

_____

_____

_____

_____

_____

_____

_____

_____

_____

_____

_____

C. Study the charts with your classmates and teacher.

Regular Past Tense Verbs	
Base	**Simple past**
study	studied
participate	participated
help	helped
listen	listened
watch	watched
practice	practiced
learn	learned

Irregular Past Tense Verbs	
Base	**Simple past**
come	came
see	saw
write	wrote
speak	spoke
read	read
teach	taught

D. Rewrite the sentences in the past tense. Then, use the sentences to write a paragraph in your notebook.

1. Nubar comes to class every day.

    Nubar came to class every day.

2. Nubar studies at home.

    Nubar studied at home.

3. Some students practice at work.

    Some students practiced at work.

4. Some students watch TV or listen to the radio.

    Some students watched TV or listened to the radio.

5. Nubar reads for one or two hours a day at home.

    Nubar read for one or two hours a day at home.

E. Listen to Angela talk about her study skills. Check (✓) the things she did to study.

CD 2
TR 43

☑ came to class every day

☑ came to class on time

☑ helped other students

☑ learned new words every day

☐ listened to the radio

☐ participated in class

☐ practiced at work

☐ studied at home

☑ taught other students

☑ watched TV

F. EVALUATE Answer the questions about this course. Check (✓) the correct answer.

Answers will vary.

Study Habits Questionnaire

1. How often did you come to class?

☐ a. most of the time   ☐ b. more than 50%   ☐ c. less than 50%

2. Did you come to class on time?

☐ a. most of the time   ☐ b. more than 50%   ☐ c. less than 50%

3. How much did you study at home each week?

☐ a. more than 10 hours   ☐ b. 5–10 hours   ☐ c. less than 5 hours

4. Did you speak English in class and participate?

☐ a. most of the time   ☐ b. more than 50%   ☐ c. less than 50%

5. Did you teach and help other students in class?

☐ a. a lot   ☐ b. a little   ☐ c. never

6. Did you listen to the radio in English?

☐ a. a lot   ☐ b. a little   ☐ c. never

7. Did you watch TV in English?

☐ a. a lot   ☐ b. a little   ☐ c. never

8. Did you ask the teacher or other students questions when you didn't understand?

☐ a. a lot   ☐ b. a little   ☐ c. never

How many *a* answers, *b* answers, and *c* answers do you have?

# of *a* answers _____	# of *b* answers _____	# of *c* answers _____

Do the math below.

\# of *a* answers x 3 = _____
\# of *b* answers x 2 = _____
\# of *c* answers x 1 = _____
            Total = _____

Score: **20–24** Super – You have great study habits!

Score: **16–19** Good – You have great study habits.

Score: **Under 16** – You need to change your study habits.

Application

10–15 mins. ■■□

F. EVALUATE Answer the questions about this course. Check (✓) the correct answer.

Ask students to calculate their rating. You may decide that it would be interesting if students interviewed one another instead of evaluating themselves.

Refer student to *Stand Out 1 Workbook,* Unit 8, Lesson 1 for more practice with the past tense of irregular verbs.

Go to the *Activity Bank* online for suggestions on promoting digital literacy and using the Internet to enhance this lesson.

MULTILEVEL WORKSHEET

Unit 8, Lesson 1, Worksheet 1: Studying Outside of Class

BEST PRACTICE

Student-to-student interviews

Having students conduct their own interviews is an excellent way for them to practice their English and the lesson goals. Treating the interview as a real-life experience will also be a fun and engaging activity for students. With this goal in mind, teachers should provide students with a few effective tips on conducting interviews.

1. Ask students to review the interview questions beforehand. This allows them to sound less stilted when asking their questions and makes the interview go along more smoothly. Tell them that it is very important that the interviewer know the information that he or she is looking for.
2. Help students pick a pre-determined location to conduct their interviews. It can be in different locations around the classroom, for example. This gives students as much privacy as possible with a minimum chance of interference from other classmates.

3. Ask students to open their interview with small talk (*How are you doing today? What country are you from? Where do you live?*). Small talk is a good warm-up and helps students feel more comfortable with each other before they participate in the interview process.
4. Discourage students from interrupting each other. Instruct them to ask the question and let the interviewee respond with his or her own answers, whatever they may be. Explain that this provides them with more reliable data and it also give each student the chance to speak his or her own mind without interruption.

INSTRUCTOR'S NOTES

Goal: Organize study

Grammar: Modal: *can*

Academic Strategies: Focused listening, organizational strategies, self-assessment

Vocabulary: Life skills

Agenda

☐ Talk about study skills.

☐ Organize study time.

☐ Identify life skills.

☐ Organize a notebook.

☐ Write in a journal.

Resources

Multilevel Worksheets: Unit 8, Lesson 2, Worksheets 1–2

Workbook: Unit 8, Lesson 2

Audio: CD 2, Track 44

Heinle Picture Dictionary: Classroom, pages 18–19

Stand Out 1 Assessment CD-ROM with ExamView®

Pacing

■ 1.5 hour classes   ■ 2.5 hour classes

■ 3+ hour classes

STANDARDS CORRELATIONS

CCRS: RI1, SL2, L1, L2

CASAS: 7.1.4, 7.4.1, 7.4.9

SCANS: **Resources** Allocate materials and facility resources, allocate human resources

Information Acquire and evaluate information

Interpersonal Participate as a member of a team

Systems Understand systems, monitor and correct performance, improve and design systems

Basic Skills Reading, writing, listening, speaking

Personal Qualities Responsibility, self-management

EFF: Communication Read with understanding, convey ideas in writing, speak so others can understand, listen actively, observe critically

Interpersonal Cooperate with others

Lifelong Learning Take responsibility for learning, reflect and evaluate

Warm-up and Review   15–20 mins. ■■■

Write the word *study* on the board. Ask students what they should study if they want to learn English. Help them get started by writing *vocabulary* on the board. They may need additional help, so lead them through aspects of classroom study, such as *grammar*, *vocabulary*, and *life skills*.

Introduction   5–7 mins. ■■■

Ask students which of the items they mentioned in the warm-up are most important to them. Take a class poll. State the goal: *Today, we will learn how to organize study*.

Presentation 1   15–20 mins. ■■■

A. Talk about the pictures with your classmates and teacher.

Ask students to cover up Exercise B and see how many photos they can identify without the word box. Talk about each picture and then, as a class, do Exercise B.

B. What do you learn in English class? Write a word from the box for each picture above.

C. COLLABORATE In a group, think of other things you learn in English class.

Have students work in small groups of three or four to complete this exercise.

Practice 1   10–15 mins. ■■■

D. APPLY Complete the chart about yourself. Use the words from Exercise B.

Write the chart headings on the board. Make sure students understand them. Share with the class something that you personally do well. As another example, point out a student who speaks very well in the class.

After students have had five or ten minutes to complete the chart, do a corners activity. Designate the corners of the room as *reading*, *writing*, *listening*, and *speaking*. Then, ask students to go to the corner that represents which skill they do best. While in their corners, have students ask one another which skill they do second best.

Evaluation 1   5–7 mins. ■■■

Observe the activity. Discuss what students discovered from the activity. For example, discuss if there is a consensus on what students do well or if students have different strengths.

GOAL ■ Organize study

WORKPLACE CONNECTION
Exercise C: Interact appropriately with team members.

A. Talk about the pictures with your classmates and teacher.

1. ___listening___

2. ___writing___

SIMPLE PRESENT

I like . . .

He / She likes . . .

3. ___grammar___

4. ___teamwork___

5. ___speaking___

FOR RENT

2 bed, 3 bath apt.
a/c, elect. pd.
Call Margaret for
more information–
555-2672.

6. ___life skills___

7. ___reading___

8. ___vocabulary___

B. What do you learn in English class? Write a word from the box for each picture above.

grammar	~~listening~~	speaking	writing
life skills	reading	teamwork	vocabulary

C. COLLABORATE In a group, think of other things you learn in English class.

Answers will vary.

_____   _____

_____   _____

D. APPLY Complete the chart about yourself. Use the words from Exercise B.

Answers will vary.

Things I do well	Things I need help with

E. **Make a study guide. Make one page for each skill from Exercise B and add a page for a journal.** Answers will vary.

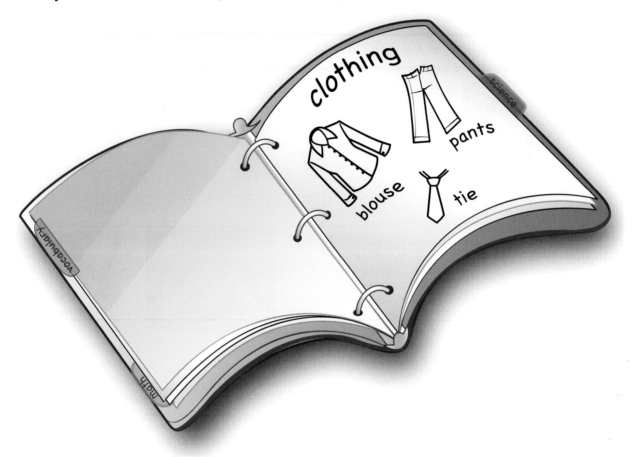

F. **Write new words in the Vocabulary page. List one or two new words you learned from each unit in this book. Add the words to the Vocabulary page.** Answers will vary.

G. **In a group, write on the Listening page ways you can practice listening outside of class.** Answers will vary.

H. **REFLECT** **On the Grammar page, write the name of the grammar tenses you have learned in this book. Use pages 214–219 to help you with this.**

CAN
I **can** listen to the radio.
You **can** listen to …
He/She **can** listen to …
We **can** listen to …
They **can** listen to …

Answers will vary. Sample answers are given.

We can listen to friends.

We can listen to the TV.

We can listen in the language lab.

We can listen on the computer.

We can listen to people talking.

Presentation 2 15–20 mins. ■■■

Show students a notebook and dividers before they see this page. Tell them that notebooks and journals are good ways to organize their work.

E. Make a study guide. Make one page for each skill from Exercise B and add a page for a journal.

Encourage students to make their own notebooks or journals. If they can't buy dividers, suggest they make dividers out of file folders. Discuss notebook sections with students by referring to ideas on the previous page.

Encourage students to choose *vocabulary* and *listening* as important sections in their notebooks. Go through Unit 1 in the book with students. Ask them which words they think are most important. Tell students to do Exercise F for homework.

F. Write new words in the Vocabulary page. List one or two new words you learned from each unit in this book. Add the words to the Vocabulary page.

Go over the small grammar review box and remind students how to use *can*.

Practice 2 10–15 mins. ■■

G. In a group, write on the Listening page ways you can practice listening outside of class.

H. REFLECT On the Grammar page, write the name of the grammar tenses you have learned in this book. Use pages 214–219 to help you with this.

Evaluation 2 3–5 mins. ■■

Ask groups to report their ideas to the class.

INSTRUCTOR'S NOTES

Presentation 3

10–15 mins. ■■■

With books closed, ask students what *life skills* are. Tell students that they will read a paragraph that will describe what a life skill is.

I. What are life skills? Read the definition.

Ask students to first read the definition by themselves. Then, read the definition as a class and answer any questions about meaning. Encourage students to go through the book and look for other life skills. Ask volunteers to share their examples and discuss as a class.

Prepare students for focused listening.

Practice 3

30–40 mins. ■

J. Listen and write the life skills you hear in the conversation. Then, write them on your study guide page for Life Skills.

Play the recording several times.

LISTENING SCRIPT

CD 2
TR 44

Nadia: *English is very important to me. I need to learn it well so I can go to college.*
Phuong: *You need to study a lot.*
Nadia: *I know, but school will be out for two months. What can I do?*
Phuong: *Life is practice.*
Nadia: *What do you mean?*
Phuong: *When you read a bus schedule, that is a life skill and you practice English.*
Nadia: *I see. So, reading the newspaper is a life skill, too, right?*
Phuong: *That's right.*
Nadia: *How about calling the doctor for an appointment? Is that a life skill?*
Phuong: *Yes, it is. So is making a notebook.*
Nadia: *I guess you're right. I can practice English every day. Making this notebook will really help.*

Evaluation 3

5 mins. ■

Go over students' answers as a class. You may need to introduce gerunds if students are confused, but this isn't the goal of the activity, so any explanation should be short and simple.

Application

10–15 mins. ■■■

K. Read the journal notes.

Go over the journal notes with students. Show them how a simple journal can be maintained to help them keep track of their learning. Help students understand that journal entries don't need to be lengthy and that often just a few words will help speed their learning.

L. CREATE What did you do today to help you practice English? Write the information here and in your study guide.

Ask students to write their own journal entry.

M. Now that you have made a study guide, make a notebook. Put each page of the study guide in a section of your notebook.

Refer students to *Stand Out 1 Workbook*, Unit 8, Lesson 2 for more practice with *can*.

Go to the *Activity Bank* online for suggestions on promoting digital literacy and using the Internet to enhance this lesson.

MULTILEVEL WORKSHEETS

Unit 8, Lesson 2, Worksheet 1: My Journal
Unit 8, Lesson 2, Worksheet 2: Identify Study Skills

INSTRUCTOR'S NOTES

_____

_____

_____

_____

_____

_____

_____

_____

_____

I.   What are life skills? Read the definition.

> Every lesson in this book teaches a life skill. Life skills are what we do often every day, like reading a bus schedule or making a doctor's appointment.

J.   Listen and write the life skills you hear in the conversation. Then, write them on your study guide page for Life Skills.

CD 2
TR 44

reading a bus schedule

reading the newspaper

calling for a doctor's appointment

K.   Read the journal notes.

New Words: checkout, counter, cough
Skill: I practiced in the supermarket. "Where is the medicine?"
Book: I reviewed pages 10–15 in the textbook from last semester.
Listening: TV—I watched Channel 20 for ten minutes at 7a.m.
Writing: I wrote in my journal.

L.   CREATE What did you do today to help you practice English? Write the information here and in your study guide.   Answers will vary.

M.   Now that you have made a study guide, make a notebook. Put each page of the study guide in a section of your notebook.

LESSON ❸ Schools in the United States

GOAL ▪ Identify learning opportunities

WORKPLACE CONNECTION
Exercise B: Collect and organize information.

A. **ANALYZE** Read the diagram with your classmates and teacher.

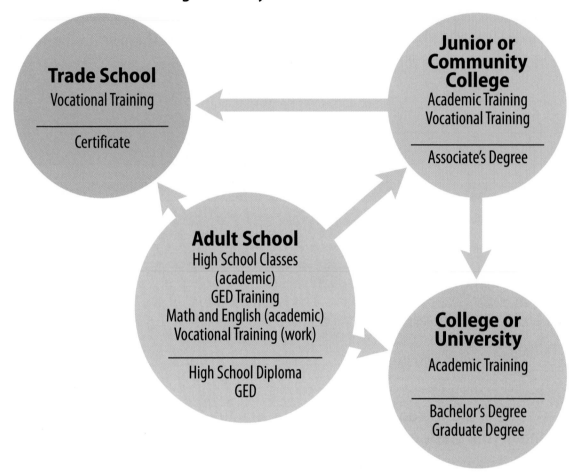

B. **INTERPRET** Complete the chart about learning opportunities.

School	Degree or diploma
Adult School	High School Diploma or GED
Trade School	Certificate
Junior or Community College	Associate's Degree
College or University	Bachelor's or Graduate Degree

Goal: Identify learning opportunities

Grammar: Modal: *should*

Academic Strategy: Focused listening

Vocabulary: Educational choices, learning opportunities

Agenda

- Review new words from Units 1–7.
- Identify learning opportunities.
- Listen to advice from counselors.
- Think about your future plans.

Resources

Multilevel Worksheet: Unit 8, Lesson 3, Worksheet 1

Workbook: Unit 8, Lesson 3

Audio: CD 2, Tracks 45–50

Heinle Picture Dictionary: Life Events, pages 30–31

Stand Out 1 Assessment CD-ROM with ExamView®

Pacing

- 1.5 hour classes
- 2.5 hour classes
- 3+ hour classes

STANDARDS CORRELATIONS

CCRS: RI1, RI7, SL1, SL2, L1

CASAS: 2.5.5, 7.1.1

SCANS: **Resources** Allocate materials and facility resources, allocate human resources

Information Acquire and evaluate information, organize and maintain information, interpret and communicate information

Basic Skills Reading, writing, listening, speaking

Personal Qualities Responsibility, self-management

EFF: **Communication** Read with understanding, convey ideas in writing, speak so others can understand, listen actively, observe critically

Lifelong Learning Take responsibility for learning, reflect and evaluate

Warm-up and Review   10–15 mins. ■■■

Ask students to share the words they came up with from each unit. (This was the homework assignment in the previous lesson from Exercise F.) Write the vocabulary on the board.

Introduction   5–7 mins. ■■■

Ask students if they have any future plans for their education. Have a short discussion about possible educational paths. State the goal: *Today, we will learn about educational opportunities.*

Presentation 1   30–40 mins. ■■■

A. ANALYZE Read the diagram with your classmates and teacher.

Discuss the different possible paths students can take. Briefly explain each one and the number of years a full-time student might go to school. Ask students if this system is similar to or different from the system they are familiar with in their native countries.

You might consider discussing your own educational path as an example.

BEST PRACTICE

Lecture and student-centered instruction

When there is a lot of information for students to learn, it is tempting to teach with little interaction with students. It is important to make a connection with students and work on making it a discussion even though students have minimal English language skills at this point.

Try asking questions such as: *Do you have a high school diploma from your country? Who wants to go to college? Who likes math? Do you have trade schools in your country? Does anyone have vocational training? What kind of vocational training do you have?*

B. INTERPRET Complete the chart about learning opportunities.

Evaluation 1   5 mins. ■■■

Check students' answers in their books as they are working.

Presentation 2

15–20 mins. ■■■■

C. PREDICT Read the information about the students. What kind of education do you think they need?

Do this activity as a class. Write the word *counselor* on the board. Explain what a counselor does. Ask students to predict what a counselor would say to the people depicted in Exercise C. Prepare students for focused listening.

D. Listen to the conversations and check the correct information in Exercise C.

Do the first item of the listening as a class so that students understand how to complete the rest of the activity.

LISTENING SCRIPT

CD 2
TR 45–50

1. **Ahmed:** *I want to be a computer technician, but first I need to learn more English.*
   Counselor: *That's very important. Do you have a high school diploma?*
   Ahmed: *No, I don't.*
   Counselor: *Well, that is always a good place to start. Maybe you can get work without it, but it's very important.*
   Ahmed: *Yes, I know. That's one of my plans.*
   Counselor: *You can learn to be a computer technician in a trade school, or you can go to a two-year college.*
   Ahmed: *Which one is better?*
   Counselor: *They are both good, but a trade school will help you find a job later.*

2. **Akiko:** *I want to understand computers in the United States so I can get a good job in web design.*
   Counselor: *First, you have to speak English very well.*
   Akiko: *If I study at home and come to adult school, I think that will be enough.*
   Counselor: *You should plan to go to college and take technology courses, too. It's hard, but you need the experience.*

3. **Counselor:** *That's great that you want to be a teacher.*
   Minh: *Yes, but I do need to learn English.*
   Counselor: *That's right. You have your high school diploma, so you can start at a two-year college or go right to the university.*
   Minh: *Which is better for me?*
   Counselor: *They are both good. The college is cheaper and you can take English classes while you take other classes.*

---

4. **Counselor:** *Alan, you want to be a cook, right?*
   Alan: *That's right.*
   Counselor: *Do you want to be a chef in an expensive restaurant where you can make special food?*
   Alan: *I don't know. I like to cook. Is it hard to be a chef?*
   Counselor: *You need to go to school—maybe a trade school.*
   Alan: *That sounds like a lot of work, but I'll think about it.*

5. **Mario:** *I just need a little English and I can go to work. I am already a good mechanic.*
   Counselor: *Do you have a GED or high school diploma?*
   Mario: *No. Do I really need one?*
   Counselor: *A GED can really help. A good mechanic needs to read instructions and manuals. Please think about it.*
   Mario: *Thanks, I'm going to think about it.*

6. **Counselor:** *Nursing is a good job. You can take special classes at a university.*
   Marie: *I already have plans to go to community college here in town. Do I need to be a citizen?*
   Counselor: *No, but you do need to be a state resident or it will cost you a lot of money.*
   Marie: *Good. I am a state resident.*

Practice 2

7–10 mins. ■■■

E. Practice the conversation with a partner. Ask about the students in Exercise C.

Go over the grammar box as a class before students practice the exchange in pairs.

Evaluation 2

5 mins. ■■

Observe students as they practice the exchange. Make sure they use *should* correctly.

C. **PREDICT** Read the information about the students. What kind of education do you think they need?

1.

Ahmed wants to be a computer technician.

☑ High School Diploma
☑ Community College
☐ University
☑ Trade School

3.

Minh wants to be a teacher.

☐ High School Diploma
☑ Community College
☑ University
☐ Trade School

5.

Mario wants to be a mechanic.

☑ High School Diploma
☐ Community College
☐ University
☐ Trade School

2.

Akiko wants to be a Web designer.

☐ High School Diploma
☑ Community College
☐ University
☐ Trade School

4.

Alan wants to be a cook.

☐ High School Diploma
☐ Community College
☐ University
☑ Trade School

6.

Marie wants to be a nurse's assistant.

☐ High School Diploma
☑ Community College
☑ University
☐ Trade School

D. Listen to the conversations and check the correct information in Exercise C.

CD 2
TR 45–50

E. Practice the conversation with a partner. Ask about the students in Exercise C.

SHOULD
I **should** go to college.
You **should** go …
He/She **should** go …
We **should** go …
They **should** go …

Student A: Where should Ahmed go to school after the adult school?
Student B: He should go to a trade school.

F. Look at the pictures. What are the people doing? Then, in a group, make a list of three or four places you can go to for advice about learning opportunities.

Answers will vary.

_____

_____

_____

_____

_____

G. **APPLY** What do you want to do after adult school? Fill in the boxes and talk to a partner. Answers will vary.

| Adult School | → | _____ | → | _____ |

H. What books or Internet sites can help you with your educational choices? Tell the class.

Presentation 3 7–10 mins. ■■■

Look at the photos with the class. Ask questions about what the people might be doing, where they might be, and other questions that seem relevant.

Practice 3 10–15 mins. ■

F. Look at the pictures. What are the people doing? Then, in a group, make a list of three or four places you can go to for advice about learning opportunities.

Evaluation 3 5 mins. ■

Ask groups to report to the class.

Application 10–15 mins. ■■■

G. APPLY What do you want to do after adult school? Fill in the boxes and talk to a partner.

H. What books or Internet sites can help you with your educational choices? Tell the class.

Refer students to *Stand Out 1 Workbook,* Unit 8, Lesson 3 for more practice with *should*.

Go to the *Activity Bank* online for suggestions on promoting digital literacy and using the Internet to enhance this lesson.

MULTILEVEL WORKSHEET

Unit 8, Lesson 3, Worksheet 1: Choices for the Future

BEST PRACTICE

Asking students to conduct research

Often exercises call for students to conduct research on their own. This may be via the Internet or finding information in books or other print resources. This is nothing new to most students. However, they may be at a lost about where to begin, particularly when the language is not their native tongue.

Teachers should always help students start their research on the Internet by providing them with a list of useful websites. It is beneficial if the list contains the website names, brief one-line descriptions of content, and the URL (web addresses). Teachers may print these lists and distribute them to the class or simply e-mail them to students. If choosing the latter, they may consider authoring the list with active *hyperlinks*. This means that students will only have to point and click on the link to reach the target Internet source.

The same advice applies to having students use books and other print resources. Teachers should provide students with directions as to where to look. They should always be clear about what to look for (i.e., a bibliography) Students may not be familiar with the local library or even how it works. If students take along a suggested bibliography, it will be easier for them to start looking on their own or ask for assistance from library personnel.

Exhaustive or long bibliographies are not necessary, but teachers should give students enough to get them off to a good start. Research activities should be enjoyable and a beneficial addition to the lesson. If planned and well-conducted, students will learn more and start to look forward to conducting research. Teachers will also gain valuable insight into students' grasp of lesson goals.

INSTRUCTOR'S NOTES

_____

_____

_____

_____

_____

_____

_____

_____

_____

_____

_____

AT-A-GLANCE PREP

Goal: Identify vocational preferences
Grammar: Verb + infinitive, verb + noun
Academic Strategies: Focused listening, self-evaluation
Vocabulary: Goals

Agenda

☐ Identify work preferences.
☐ Predict jobs.
☐ Discuss your preferences.
☐ Take a personal inventory survey.

Resources

Multilevel Worksheet: Unit 8, Lesson 4, Worksheet 1
Workbook: Unit 8, Lesson 4
Audio: CD 2, Tracks 51–53
Heinle Picture Dictionary: Jobs, pages 146–149
Stand Out 1 Assessment CD-ROM with ExamView®

Pacing

■ 1.5 hour classes ■ 2.5 hour classes
■ 3+ hour classes

STANDARDS CORRELATIONS

CCRS: RI1, SL1, SL2, L1
CASAS: 7.1.1, 7.5.1
SCANS: **Basic Skills** Reading, writing, listening, speaking
Thinking Skills Make decisions, solve problems
Personal Qualities Responsibility, sociability, self-management
EFF: Communication Read with understanding, convey ideas in writing, speak so others can understand, listen actively, observe critically
Decision Making Solve problems and make decisions, plan
Lifelong Learning Take responsibility for learning, reflect and evaluate

Warm-up and Review
10–15 mins. ■■■

Write the word *counselor* on the board. Ask students if they have spoken to either a school counselor or a job counselor before. Ask students if they have any job goals for the future. Talk to students with goals and ask them what kind of education they would need for the jobs.

Introduction
5–7 mins. ■■■

State the goal: *Today, we will identify work preferences.*

195a Unit 8

Presentation 1
15–20 mins. ■■■

A. PREDICT Read the information about the students. Circle the job that you think is the best for each one.

Look at the pictures and the information. Ask students to predict what would be the best job for each of the people depicted in Exercise A.

B. Listen to the conversations. Check your predictions in Exercise A.

Play the recording several times so students have an opportunity to hear the information. Check to see if the class predictions were good predictions.

LISTENING SCRIPT

CD 2
TR 51–53

1. Roberto

My name is Roberto. I am a student at Pine Adult School. I like to study and go to school. I think I would like to be a student for my whole life, but I know I will have to get a job someday. I love history so maybe I should look into being a teacher. I think that would be a great profession for me.

2. Eva

I love people. Every chance I get, I talk to people. They are so interesting. I like to help people. For that reason, I am going to choose a career that will enable me to be around people who I can help. I think being a nurse would be very rewarding. My mother is a nurse, too. It might be fun.

3. Duong

My name is Duong. I have a lot of experience working with my hands. I like to fix things, too. I love to make things work. That's why I think being a mechanic might be a good job for me. I like cars, too, so I think that this is a good choice.

Practice 1
10–15 mins. ■■■

C. Talk to a partner. List three things your partner likes to do.

Encourage students to use the information from Exercise A to come up with ideas of their own.

Evaluation 1
3–5 mins. ■■■

Ask students to report to the class about their partners.

LESSON ④ Choosing the right job

GOAL ▪ Identify vocational preferences

A. PREDICT Read the information about the students. Circle the job that you think is the best for each one.

Position	Job
1. Roberto likes to study. He likes school. He likes history.	(teacher) mechanic doctor
2. Eva likes to help people. She likes to talk to people. She likes to study.	gardener (nurse) receptionist
3. Duong likes to work with his hands. He likes to fix things. He likes cars.	(mechanic) manager salesperson

B. Listen to the conversations. Check your predictions in Exercise A.

CD 2
TR 51-53

C. Talk to a partner. List three things your partner likes to do. Answers will vary.

_____   _____   _____

D. Study the charts with your classmates and teacher.

Verb + Infinitive			
Subject	**Verb**	**Infinitive**	**Example sentence**
I, You, We, They	like want need	to read to travel to work to talk to handle to study	I like **to read**. You want **to travel**. We need **to work** alone. They like **to talk** on the phone.
He, She, It	likes wants needs		He likes **to handle** money. She wants **to study**.

Verb + Noun			
Subject	**Verb**	**Noun**	**Example sentence**
I, You, We, They	like want need	cars computer books school food	I like **cars**. You want a **computer**. We need **books**. They like **school**.
He, She, It	likes wants needs		He likes **computers**. She wants **food**.

E. Complete each sentence with the correct form of the verb in parentheses.

1. They like _____to work_____ (work) outside.

2. He wants _____to study_____ (study) at school every day.

3. She needs _____to make_____ (make) money right now.

4. They want _____to handle_____ (handle) money.

5. I want _____to learn_____ (learn) English.

6. We like _____to read_____ (read) books.

7. I like _____to talk_____ (talk) on the telephone.

8. You want _____to work_____ (work) at the university.

F. Talk to a different partner than in Exercise C. List three things your partner likes to do. Report to a group. Answers will vary.

_____   _____   _____

Presentation 2

15–20 mins. ■■■

D. Study the charts with your classmates and teacher.

Go over the charts carefully. Help students to see that the purpose of this activity is to help them write their goals and what they like to do more clearly.

Practice 2

7–10 mins. ■■

E. Complete each sentence with the correct form of the verb in parentheses.

After students complete this activity, ask them if any of the sentences are true for them.

Evaluation 2

7–10 mins. ■■

F. Talk to a different partner than in Exercise C. List three things your partner likes to do. Report to a group.

BEST PRACTICE

The importance of example sentences in grammar charts

Studying grammar is an integral part of language learning. There is no escape; it has to be learned. Although most students understand this, they are rarely motivated to complete grammar exercises and rarely interested in reviewing grammar charts.

Teachers should point out that a grammar chart in itself is a straightforward and valuable tool, much like a dictionary. They should also mention that it is useful for grasping often complex grammar rules and that the example sentences in the chart are of equal importance.

Because most students prefer to learn grammar in a social context, teachers can take advantage of this inclination by calling attention to these example sentences. Teachers should let students know that the examples usually mimic lifelike social interactions. Teachers can further exemplify this by asking students to create a short and natural conversation in pairs using the featured grammar item. Students will see that some statements and responses in their conversations will match in form with the example sentences already provided.

INSTRUCTOR'S NOTES

Presentation 3
10–15 mins. ■■□

Review how to form questions with students. Write on the board: *Do you like to work outside?* Go around the room and ask students about each of the items in Exercise E. Ask students to make questions of each of the sentences in Exercise E using *Do you . . . ?*

Practice 3
7–10 mins. ■

Ask students to walk around the room and interview three of their classmates. They should ask questions using the eight sentences that they completed in Exercise E.

Evaluation 3
5–7 mins. ■

Ask volunteers to write their questions on the board.

Application
10–15 mins. ■■■

G. PLAN A counselor is going to ask you questions to help you with your future plans. Answer the questions about yourself. Check (✓) *Yes* or *No*.

H. Discuss your answers in a group.

Refer students to *Stand Out 1 Workbook,* Unit 8, Lesson 4 for more practice with *like, want,* and *need*.

Go to the *Activity Bank* online for suggestions on promoting digital literacy and using the Internet to enhance this lesson.

MULTILEVEL WORKSHEET

Unit 8, Lesson 4, Worksheet 1: Questions

BEST PRACTICE
Practice asking questions

Students have plenty of opportunities to answer questions, but seldom have as many chances to ask them. When presenting lessons that teach the correct forms for asking questions, it is important that teachers give students as much practice as possible. This can go beyond exercises in the book. Teachers should consider having students play games or participate in other fun activities after the model forms have been presented. Game or activity ideas like the following may be employed:

Guess the question

Divide the class into an equal number of groups. Ask students to make a list of a select number of answers to commonly asked questions they might hear (e.g., in school, at home, etc.). Next, have each group face an opposing group. Then, ask each group member to take a turn giving an answer and waiting for the opposing group member to come up with the correct question. Tell students that they only have one turn per answer. Have students play the game until all the answers have been used. The team with the highest number of correct questions wins the game.

INSTRUCTOR'S NOTES

_____

_____

_____

_____

_____

_____

_____

_____

_____

_____

_____

_____

_____

_____

_____

G. PLAN A counselor is going to ask you questions to help you with your future plans. Answer the questions about yourself. Check (✓) *Yes* or *No*. Answers will vary.

Personal Inventory

	Yes	No
1. Do you have a high school diploma?	☐	☐
2. Do you have good study skills?	☐	☐
3. Do you have experience?	☐	☐
4. Do you like technology (computers, machines)?	☐	☐
5. Do you like to do the same thing every day?	☐	☐
6. Do you like to handle money?	☐	☐
7. Do you like to read?	☐	☐
8. Do you like to study and to learn new things?	☐	☐
9. Do you like to listen to people?	☐	☐
10. Do you like to talk on the phone?	☐	☐
11. Do you like to travel?	☐	☐
12. Do you like to work with other people?	☐	☐
13. Do you like to work alone?	☐	☐
14. Do you like to work at night?	☐	☐
15. Do you like to work in the daytime?	☐	☐
16. Do you like to work with your hands?	☐	☐
17. Do you like your job?	☐	☐
18. Do you work now?	☐	☐
19. Do you have goals for the future?	☐	☐

H. Discuss your answers in a group.

LESSON **5** Making goals

GOAL ■ Develop goals

WORKPLACE CONNECTIONS
Exercises A, B: Collect and organize information.

A. Read Nubar's journal entry. Answer the questions about his study goals.

September 5
  I have many study goals for the next month. I am going to read the newspaper, listen to the radio, and talk to people in English every day. I am also going to study four pages from my textbook every night for 30 minutes in my bedroom.

1. When is Nubar going to study? _____ Nubar is going to study at night.

2. Where is Nubar going to study? _____ Nubar is going to study in his bedroom.

3. What is he going to study? _____ Nubar is going to study his English textbook.

4. How long is he going to study? _____ Nubar is going to study for 30 minutes.

B. Look at the clocks. Then, listen to Nubar talk about his plans. Write what he is going to do next to the clocks. Use the phrases from the box.

CD 2
TR 54

listen to the radio	read the newspaper	write in a journal
review vocabulary	study the textbook	

From (clock) to (clock) _____ read the newspaper

From (clock) to (clock) _____ study the textbook

From (clock) to (clock) _____ listen to the radio, review vocabulary

From (clock) to (clock) _____ write in a journal

Goal: Develop goals

Grammar: Future with *going to* and *will*

Academic Strategies: Focused listening, note taking

Vocabulary: Study plans, goals

Agenda

- Review what makes a good worker.
- Read and listen to Nubar's goals.
- Use the future with *going to* and *will*.
- Make personal goals.

Resources

Multilevel Worksheets: Unit 8, Lesson 5, Worksheets 1–2

Workbook: Unit 8, Lesson 5

Audio: CD 2, Track 54

Heinle Picture Dictionary: Life Events, pages 30–31

Stand Out 1 Assessment CD-ROM with ExamView®

Pacing

- 1.5 hour classes
- 2.5 hour classes
- 3+ hour classes

STANDARDS CORRELATIONS

CCRS: RI1, W2, SL1, L1

CASAS: 7.1.1, 7.1.2

SCANS: **Resources** Allocate time, allocate materials and facility resources, allocate human resources

Interpersonal Participate as a member of a team

Basic Skills Reading, writing, listening, speaking

Thinking Skills Make decisions, solve problems

Personal Qualities Responsibility, self-management

EFF: **Communication** Read with understanding, convey ideas in writing, speak so others can understand, listen actively, observe critically

Decision Making Solve problems and make decisions, plan

Interpersonal Cooperate with others

Lifelong Learning Take responsibility for learning, reflect and evaluate

Warm-up and Review
10–15 mins.

Ask students what makes a good worker. Make a list of the qualities they brainstorm on the board.

Introduction
10–15 mins.

Write *goal* on the board. Ask students for work, education, and family goals. State the goal: *Today, we will develop goals.*

Presentation 1
7–10 mins.

Ask students if they have any goals. Write on the board *long-term goals* and *short-term goals*. Explain that a short-term goal is one that helps you reach long-term goals. Ask students if they have made any study goals for the next month.

A. Read Nubar's journal entry. Answer the questions about his study goals.

Give students a time limit to read the entry. Then, ask them to answer the questions on their own.

Practice 1
10–15 mins.

B. Look at the clocks. Then, listen to Nubar talk about his plans. Write what he is going to do next to the clocks. Use the phrases from the box.

Evaluation 1
3–5 mins.

Go over the answers and play the recording for a final check.

LISTENING SCRIPT
CD 2
TR 54

I think that if I plan, I will be able to learn English well even when there is no school. I am going to read the newspaper, listen to the radio, and talk to people in English every day. Well, let's see. If I am going to do all this, I need to schedule these things. I will get home at 6:00 and then from 6:30 to 6:45 I will read the newspaper. I need to find time to study the textbook. I know—I will do that from 7:00 to 7:30. I will listen to the radio from 8:00 to 8:45. This should be good practice. During this time, I will review vocabulary, too. Then, from 9:00 to 9:15, I will write in my journal. I am going to do this for a full month. Then, I will make new goals.

BEST PRACTICE

Taking notes

This is an opportunity to teach students how to take notes. Some will want to write the entire phrase next to the clock and by so doing will miss all the other clues. Tell students that you will not stop the recording after every clue. Tell them that they will hear the recording only three times.

Show students how to write a word or two as a reminder to go back and add details later. They might write the first letter of the phrase or, even faster, number the clocks and write the number next to the phrase when they hear it.

Presentation 2

15–20 mins. ■■■

C. Study the chart with your classmates and teacher.

Practice the new sentence structure with students. Go back to the previous page so students can see how it is used in context. Prepare some example sentences and ask students to complete sentences on the board in the context of this lesson. The sentences might be the following:

I _____ (study) 30 minutes every day.

We _____ (listen) to the radio from 7:00 to 7:30.

They _____ (write) sentences every day.

She _____ (speak) at work in English.

You _____ (learn) three new words a day.

Practice 2

10–15 mins. ■■

D. Write sentences about Nubar's plans. Use the information from Exercise B.

Evaluation 2

10 mins. ■■

E. PLAN What are your study plans? Write sentences and share them with a group.

Go over what students have written.

BEST PRACTICE

Sharing work

Students may be initially reluctant to share their written work with classmates. They may be sensitive about possible errors and not want to feel inferior to others. Teachers should point out that mistakes are part of the learning process and that classmates can give valuable feedback from a student's perspective. Teachers should explain that checking someone else's work is also a good way to test their own understanding of the lesson. Encourage students to be respectful when giving feedback and/or criticism. Have students share work as much as possible. They will eventually become more comfortable with the practice.

INSTRUCTOR'S NOTES

C. **Study the chart with your classmates and teacher.**

Future with *Going to*			
Subject	*Going to*	**Base verb**	**Example sentence**
I	am going to (I'm going to)	learn	I **am going to** learn English.
You, We, They	are going to (you're/we're/they're going to)	listen practice	We **are going to** practice English.
He, She, It	is going to (he's/she's going to)	read speak study write	She **is going to** speak English.
Use *going to* for future plans that can change.			

D. **Write sentences about Nubar's plans. Use the information from Exercise B.**

Answers will vary.

1. He is going to read the newspaper from 6:30 to 6:45. _____

2. _____

3. _____

4. _____

E. **PLAN** **What are your study plans? Write sentences and share them with a group.**

Answers will vary.

1. I _____

2. _____

3. _____

4. _____

F. Study another way to talk about future plans.

Future with *Will*			
Subject	***Will***	**Base**	**Example sentence**
I, You, He, She, It We, They	will	study work get married	I **will** study every day. She **will** work hard. They **will** get married.
Use *will* for future plans you are very sure about.			

G. Read about Nubar's long-term goals.

> June 12
>
>   I have many goals for the future. Some of my goals will take a long time. I will study every day and get a high school diploma. After that, I will start college. I want to start in about three years. I also want to get married and have children sometime in the future. I will be a computer technician one day.

H. CLASSIFY Nubar wants to do many things. Write his goals in the chart.

Family goals	Educational goals	Work goals
He wants to get married.	He wants to get a high school diploma.	He wants to be a computer technician.
He wants to have children.	He wants to start college.	

I. APPLY What are your family, educational, and work goals? Write them in the chart.

Answers will vary.

Family goals	Educational goals	Work goals

Presentation 3

10–15 mins. ■■■

F. Study another way to talk about future plans.

Go over this structure as well. Play the listening from Exercise B and ask students to listen for this structure.

Write *Family Goals, Educational Goals,* and *Work Goals* on the board.

Practice 3

10–15 mins. ■

G. Read about Nubar's long-term goals.

H. CLASSIFY Nubar wants to do many things. Write his goals in the chart.

Allow students to do this activity in pairs or in groups.

Evaluation 3

5–7 mins. ■

Have groups or pairs report to the class.

Application

20–30 mins. ■■■

I. APPLY What are your family, educational, and work goals? Write them in the chart.

Refer students to *Stand Out 1 Workbook*, Unit 8, Lesson 5 for more practice with the future with *going to*.

Go to the *Activity Bank* online for suggestions on promoting digital literacy and using the Internet to enhance this lesson.

MULTILEVEL WORKSHEETS

Unit 8, Lesson 5, Worksheet 1: *Going to*
Unit 8, Lesson 5, Worksheet 2: Future Plans

INSTRUCTOR'S NOTES

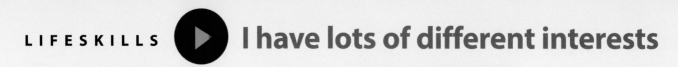

Before You Watch

- Draw a chart on the board and label it *My Interests*.
- Read the title out loud. Write a list with some of your own interests. Then, go over the list with the class.
- Ask students if they have lots of different interests.
- Ask students to work in small groups and complete a chart listing their interests.
- Have groups compare their lists with other groups.

A. Look at the picture. Complete each sentence.

- Ask students to look at the picture. Then, have them complete the sentences.
- Ask students to compare their answers to a partner's.
- Have volunteers read the sentences and their answers to the class.

While You Watch

B. Watch the video. Complete the dialog. Use the words in the box.

- Review the words in the box.
- Tell students they will watch the video and then complete the dialog with the words from the box.
- Read the example sentence out loud. Then, play the video once for understanding.
- Play the video again. Ask students to complete the dialog.
- Have students review their answers in pairs.
- Play the video once more. Then, ask students to act out the dialog with their partners.
- Have volunteers act out the dialog in front of the class.

Check Your Understanding

C. Read the statements. Write T for *True* or F for *False*.

- Ask students to read each statement and write T for *True* or F for *False*.
- Have volunteers read the statements and share their answers.

INSTRUCTOR'S NOTES

_____

_____

_____

_____

_____

_____

_____

_____

_____

_____

_____

_____

_____

_____

_____

_____

_____

_____

_____

_____

_____

Before You Watch

A. Look at the picture. Complete each sentence.

Answers will vary. Sample answers are given.

1. Hector is one of Mrs. Smith's

   _____ students _____.

2. Hector needs some

   _____ help _____.

3. Mrs. Smith is going to help him

   identify his _____ goals _____.

While You Watch

B. ▶ Watch the video. Complete the dialog. Use the words in the box.

gave	like	take	taking	took	~~wanted~~

Hector: That's hard. I'm interested in lots of things. First, I (1) _____ *wanted* _____ to be an actor. Then, I wanted to be a teacher. Now, I'm not sure. I'm taking lots of different classes.

Mrs. Smith: Tell me, which classes did you (2) _____ *take* _____ last semester?

Hector: I (3) _____ *took* _____ a class in public speaking. That was fun.

Mrs. Smith: Oh, really? You (4) _____ *like* _____ to speak in public?

Hector: Let's just say I'm not shy. I (5) _____ *gave* _____ a speech at least twice a week. And I took a class in world events, too.

Mrs. Smith: World events—very interesting. And what classes are you (6) _____ *taking* _____ now?

Check Your Understanding

C. Read the statements. Write T for *True* or F for *False*.

1. Hector needs to choose his classes for the new semester. _____ T _____

2. He's not sure what classes he's going to take. _____ T _____

3. Last semester he took a class in journalism. _____ F _____

4. Hector likes to watch and listen to news programs. _____ T _____

Review

A. What are six things you did in this course to help you study English? Use the verbs from the box. Write sentences in the simple past tense. *Answers will vary.*

participate	help	speak	ask	read	listen	~~come~~

1. I came to class on time.

2. _____

3. _____

4. _____

5. _____

6. _____

7. _____

B. Check (✓) the study skills.

☐ learn English   ☐ get a high school diploma   ☑ read

☐ go to college   ☑ listen carefully   ☑ write vocabulary words

☐ go to the supermarket   ☑ ask questions   ☐ eat a good breakfast

C. Write the things you can do well in class. *Answers will vary.*

1. I can _____.

2. _____

3. _____

D. Ask a partner: *What can you do well in class?* *Answers will vary.*

1. He can listen well. OR She can ask questions well.

2. _____

3. _____

4. _____

AT-A-GLANCE **PREP**

Goal: All unit goals

Grammar: All unit grammar

Academic Strategies: Focused listening, reviewing, evaluating, developing study skills

Vocabulary: All unit vocabulary

Agenda

▢ Discuss unit goals.

▢ Complete the review.

▢ Evaluate and reflect on progress.

Stand Out 1 Assessment CD-ROM with ExamView®

Pacing

■ 1.5 hour classes ■ 2.5 hour classes
■ 3+ hour classes

STANDARDS CORRELATIONS

CCRS: RI7, W2, SL2, L1, RF3

CASAS: 7.1.1, 7.1.4, 7.4.1, 7.4.9, 7.5.1

SCANS: **Information** Acquire and evaluate information, organize and maintain information

Basic Skills Reading, writing, speaking

Personal Qualities Responsibility, self-management

EFF: **Communication** Speak so others can understand

Lifelong Learning Take responsibility for learning, reflect and evaluate

Warm-up and Review   7–10 mins. ■■■

With their books closed, ask students to help you make a list on the board of all the vocabulary they can come up with from the unit. Then, have a competition where students in groups write page numbers where they can find each item on the list. The first group to have the correct page number for each item wins. Explain that this review will also include going through the entire book for information.

Introduction   5 mins. ■■■

Write all the goals on the board from Unit 8. Show students the first page of every lesson so they understand that today will be review. Complete the agenda.

Presentation   10–15 mins. ■■■

This Presentation and Practice will cover the first three pages of the review. Quickly go to the first page of each lesson. Discuss the goal of each. Ask simple questions to remind students of what they have learned.

Practice   15–20 mins. ■■■

A. **What are six things you did in this course to help you study English? Use the verbs from the box. Write sentences in the simple past tense. (Lesson 1)**

B. **Check (✓) the study skills. (Lesson 2)**

C. **Write the things you can do well in class. (Lessons 1 and 2)**

D. **Ask a partner:** *What can you do well in class?* **(Lessons 1 and 2)**

BEST PRACTICE

Recycling/Review

The review and the project that follows are part of the recycling/review process. Students at this level often need to be reintroduced to concepts to solidify what they have learned. Many concepts are learned and forgotten while learning other new concepts. This is because students learn but are not necessarily ready to acquire language concepts.

Therefore, it becomes very important to review and to show students how to review on their own. It is also important to recycle the new concepts in different contexts.

Practice *(continued)*

E. Complete the paragraph with the words from the box. (Lesson 3)

F. Complete the sentences with the correct form of the verb in parentheses. (Lesson 4)

E. **Complete the paragraph with the words from the box.**

| degree | college | trade | diploma | GED | adult | certificate |

In the United States, adults can go to school in many different places. They can go to an _____adult_____ school to learn English or to get a high school _____diploma_____ or _____GED_____. After adult school, students can study at a _____college_____ or a _____trade_____ school. Students who go to a trade school get a _____certificate_____ when they complete the courses. Some students get a _____degree_____ from a university after adult school.

F. **Complete the sentences with the correct form of the verb in parentheses.**

1. Javier likes _____to study_____ (study) in the afternoon.

2. The students _____want_____ (want) to learn English.

3. I _____like_____ (like) books.

4. She _____likes_____ (like) to read books.

5. We want _____to go_____ (go) to college.

6. You need _____to speak_____ (speak) to a teacher.

7. Eva _____wants_____ (want) to see the homework.

8. He likes _____to work_____ (work) at night.

G. Write sentences about Nam's future goals. Use *be going to*.

Nam

Now: Alton Adult School

Educational Goals: learn English, go to junior college

Work Goal: become a chef

Family Goal: buy a house

1. Nam is going to learn English.

2. Nam is going to go to junior college.

3. He is going to become a chef.

4. He is going to buy a house.

H. Write sentences about Gabriela's future goals. Use *will*.

Gabriela

Now: Alton Adult School

Educational Goals: get a high school diploma, go to a trade school

Work Goal: become a nurse

Family Goal: get married

1. Gabriela will get a high school diploma.

2. She will go to a trade school.

3. She will become a nurse.

4. She will get married.

Practice (continued)

G. Write sentences about Nam's future goals. Use *be going to*. (Lesson 5)

H. Write sentences about Gabriela's future goals. Use *will*. (Lesson 5)

Evaluation   10–15 mins. ■■■

Go around the room and check on students' progress. Help individuals when needed. If you see consistent errors among several students, interrupt the class and give a mini lesson or review to help students feel comfortable with the concept.

Presentation   5 mins. ■■■

Learner Log

Review the concepts of the Learner Log. Make sure students understand the concepts and how to complete the log including circling the answers, finding page numbers where the concept is taught, and ranking favorite activities.

BEST PRACTICE

Learner Logs

Learner Logs function to help students in many different ways.

1. They serve as part of the review process. They help students to gain confidence and to document what they have learned.
2. Consequently, students see that they are progressing in their learning.
3. They provide students with a tool that they can use over and over to check and recheck their understanding of the target language. In this way, students become independent learners.

Practice   10–15 mins. ■

Ask students to complete the Learner Log.

Evaluation   2 mins. ■

Go over the Learner Log with students.

Application   5–7 mins. ■■■

Ask students to record their favorite lesson or page in the unit.

Assessment   ■■■

Use the Stand Out 1 Assessment CD-ROM with ExamView® to create a post-test for Unit 8.

Refer students to *Stand Out 1 Workbook*, Unit 8, Lesson 1 for more practice with future *will* and *Stand Out 1 Workbook*, Unit 8, Lesson 2 for more practice with future *will* and contractions.

Go to the *Activity Bank* online for suggestions on promoting digital literacy and using the Internet to enhance this lesson.

MULTILEVEL WORKSHEETS

Unit 8, Computer Worksheets

Unit 8, Internet Worksheets

INSTRUCTOR'S NOTES

_____

_____

_____

_____

_____

_____

_____

_____

_____

_____

_____

_____

_____

_____

_____

_____

STANDARDS CORRELATIONS

CCRS: RI7, W2, SL1, SL2

CASAS: 4.8.1, 7.1.1, 7.1.4, 7.4.1, 7.4.9, 7.5.1

SCANS: Resources Allocate time, allocate materials and facility resources, allocate human resources

Information Acquire and evaluate information, organize and maintain information, interpret and communicate information

Interpersonal Participate as a member of a team, teach others, exercise leadership, negotiate to arrive at a decision, work with cultural diversity

Systems Understand systems, monitor and correct performance

Basic Skills Reading, writing, listening, speaking

Thinking Skills Think creatively, make decisions, solve problems, see things in the mind's eye

Personal Qualities Responsibility, sociability, self-management

EFF: Communication Read with understanding, convey ideas in writing, speak so others can understand, listen actively, observe critically

Decision Making Solve problems and make decisions, plan

Interpersonal Cooperate with others, advocate and influence, resolve conflict and negotiate, guide others

Lifelong Learning Take responsibility for learning, reflect and evaluate

Introduction   5 mins.

TEAM PROJECT

Meet your goals

In this project, students will plan a personal study schedule and write two paragraphs pertaining to their study goals.

In a positive atmosphere, students can rely on each other for assistance and peer-review. Students may use templates and checklist in Multilevel Worksheets CD-ROM (Unit 8, Worksheets 1–4) as guides.

Stage 1   10 mins.

Complete a calender for this month and next month. Write what days and what times you are going to do the following activities.

Ask students to develop their calendars individually.

Stage 2   10 mins.

COLLABORATE Discuss your plans with your team.

Have students compare their calendars.

Stage 3   40–50 mins.

Write a paragraph about your goals on another piece of paper. Start your paragraph like this.

Ask students to write a paragraph about their goals.

Stage 4   40–50 mins.

Write another paragraph about your plans for developing good study habits. Are you going to come to school every day? Are you going to arrive on time? What are other things you are going to do?

Ask students to write another paragraph detailing their specific study habit goals.

Stages 5 and 6   20–30 mins.

Ask members of your team to edit your paragraphs. Then, rewrite them. Then, read your paragraphs to your team.

Ask students to peer-edit each other's work within their teams.

Stage 7   15–20 mins.

As a team, design a goal chart that you can each put in your home to remind you of your goals.

Have students organize their goals into a chart.

Stage 8   15–20 mins.

Present your calendar, paragraphs, and goal chart to the class.

Encourage students to bring the goal chart home and put their calendars in a place they'll check regularly.

MULTILEVEL WORKSHEETS

Unit 8, Project, Worksheet 1: Calendar
Unit 8, Project, Worksheet 2: Goals
Unit 8, Project, Worksheet 3: Study Plans
Unit 8, Project, Worksheet 4: Editing Checklist
Unit 8, Extension, Worksheet 1: Personal Inventory

✔ Meet your goals

In this project, you will plan your study time on a calendar. You will also write out your goals and plans in two paragraphs. You will work with a team, and your team will help you polish your paragraphs and calendar. Then, you will present your paragraphs and calendar to the class.

1. Complete a calender for this month and next month. Write what days and what times you are going to do the following activities:

   - study your textbook

   - listen to the radio

   - read the newspaper

   - watch TV

   - review flash cards

   - write in your journal

2. **COLLABORATE** Discuss your plans with your team.

3. Write a paragraph about your goals on another piece of paper. Start your paragraph like this:

   > I have many goals. I'm going to be able to speak to Americans, understand TV programs in English, and find a job that requires English. First, …

4. Write another paragraph about your plans for developing good study habits. Are you going to come to school every day? Are you going to arrive on time? What are other things you are going to do?

5. Ask members of your team to edit your paragraphs. Then, rewrite them.

6. Read your paragraphs to your team.

7. As a team, design a goal chart that you can each put in your home to remind you of your goals.

8. Present your calendar, paragraphs, and goal chart to the class.

About the Explorer

Jack Andraka is a researcher, scientist, and inventor from Maryland. Born in Ohio in 1997, Jack is a rising talent in the science world. When he was only 15 years old, Jack developed an inexpensive early detection method for pancreatic, lung, and ovarian cancer. He developed the test after a close family friend died from pancreatic cancer, and it won him the grand prize at a 2012 science and engineering fair, among other awards.

About the Photo

The photo shows Jack holding a model pancreas. The pancreas is an essential part of the digestive system and helps control blood sugar levels in the body. Cancer of the pancreas is fatal in the majority of cases. Jack's test not only detects the onset of pancreatic cancer early, but it is also extremely cheap—three cents! It is also 90 percent accurate. Jack hopes that one day his test will be available for everyone to use.

- Introduce the explorer and tell students that the young man in the photo is Jack Andraka. Ask them how old they think Jack is.

A. PREDICT Look at the picture and answer the questions.

- Read the title out loud and ask students what they think Jack discovered. Ask them what his job is. Have them look carefully at the photo and discuss.
- Ask a volunteer to read the quote to the class. Then, ask the class what they think Jack means. Discuss.

READING CHALLENGE

EXPLORER JACK ANDRAKA

Making Discoveries

"I think innovation often stems from a willingness to take risks that can lead to discoveries."
—Jack Andraka

A. PREDICT Look at the picture and answer the questions.

1. How old is Jack in the picture?
   a. 17   b. 30   c. 50

2. What is his job?
   a. a mechanic   b. a cook   c. a researcher

B. Match the word with the definition.

1. researcher   a. a serious illness
2. discover   b. a person who looks for answers to questions or problems
3. cancer   c. life with friends and family
4. social life   d. to find something

206 Unit 8

CCRS FOR READING

RI1, RI2, RI10, L4

C. Read about Jack Andraka and his discovery.

In 2015, Jack Andraka was 17 years old and a high school student. At the same time, he worked in a lab on important experiments, traveled, and shared his story with people all over the world. He is famous because, at 15 years old, he discovered a way to identify some forms of cancer. He is a researcher now. He continues to work and receive awards. In the future, he will study and learn more. He is learning to balance school, work on his experiments, and to have a social life with speaking about his discovery with other researchers.

D. CLASSIFY Complete the timeline about Jack's life.

Past		Present	Future
2013	2015		
Discovered _____ a way to identify some forms of cancer.	went to high school worked in a lab traveled shared his story	works receives awards	will study learn more learn to balance school, work, social life, and speaking

E. CREATE Complete a timeline for you. Answers will vary.

Past	Present	Future

B. Match the word with the definition.

Ask students to match each word with the correct definition.

C. Read about Jack Andraka and his discovery.

Have students read about Jack Andraka and his discovery.

D. CLASSIFY Complete the timeline about Jack's life.

- Ask students to look at the chart. Tell them it is a timeline about Jack's life.
- Direct students' attention to the columns for the past and the present. Point out that 2013 and 2015 are in the past.
- Ask students to complete the timeline. Tell them to refer back to the reading to check their answers.
- Ask students to compare their timelines with another student. Then, review as a class.

E. CREATE Complete a timeline for you.

Ask students to complete a timeline for themselves and then share in small groups.

READING STRATEGIES

Sequencing

Being able to sequence demonstrates that students fully comprehend a reading. Sequencing is identifying the beginning, middle, and end of a story and/or putting key events or details in the correct order. If students can understand information in the order that it is presented, they can better recall and retell a complete story without just focusing on the parts that interest them.

About the Photo

This photo was taken at the Ceiba Pentandra Park. It shows Maritza and a group of children. Each section of the park focuses on a different environmental issue. As Maritza believes in shaping future leaders, she empowers some of the children as teachers at the park. Maritza has been trying to raise awareness from a very young age. When she was ten years old, she founded HUNAB (Humanity United to Nature in Harmony for Beauty, Welfare, and Goodness). Her project grew and now, at the Ceiba Pentandra Park, children learn how to care for the environment.

▶ VIDEO CHALLENGE

The Engaging Environmentalist

Before You Watch

A. **Read the words and their definition. Check (✓) the ones you already know.** Answers will va

☐ **natural resource** thing we use that comes from nature	☐ **environment** the land, water, and air where people, animals, and plants live	☐ **movement** a group of people who work together because they believe the same thing	☐ **solution** the answer to a problem	☐ **school curriculum** courses that every student studies in school
☐ **advocacy** showing you believe in someone or something	☐ **mentorship** helping someone with less experience	☐ **pollution** damage to air, land, and water where people, animals, and plants live	☐ **extinction** when a type of animal or plant no longer lives	☐ **invest** to put time into something because you believe it is important

208   The Engaging Environmentalist

B. Complete the sentences. Use the words from Exercise A.

1. Teachers _____*invest*_____ a lot of time in their students' education.
2. Water is a ___*natural resource*___ for every person, plant, and animal.
3. Our ___*school curriculum*___ needs more classes about the environment.
4. What is the best _____*solution*_____ for stopping air pollution?
5. Before its _____*extinction*_____, there were more than 5 billion passenger pigeons on Earth.

C. Look at the map of Yucatan, Mexico. Circle the things you can find in the environment.

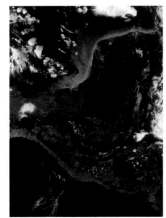

birds
cold temperatures
jungle
snow
fish
monkeys
trees
the ocean
mountains
hot temperatures
elephants
desert

While You Watch

D. Watch the video. Then read each question. Choose the correct answer.

1. Does *Ceiba Pentandra* have boats?
   a. Yes, it does.   b. No, it doesn't.

2. Does Maritza Morales Casanova have a dog?
   a. Yes, she does.   b. No, she doesn't.

3. Does *Ceiba Pentandra* have classrooms?
   a. Yes, it does.   b. No, it doesn't.

4. Do the children have video games at the park?
   a. Yes, they do.   b. No, they don't.

5. Does *Ceiba Pentandra* have a shopping mall?
   a. Yes, it does.   b. No, it doesn't.

6. Do the children have plants to take care of?
   a. Yes, they does.   b. No, they don't.

Before You Watch

A. Read the words and their definition. Check (✓) the ones you already know.

Ask students to read each word and its definition. Then, have them check the ones they already know.

B. Complete the sentences. Use the words from Exercise A.

- Ask students to complete the sentences using the words from Exercise A.
- Have students check their answers with partners.
- Ask volunteers to read their sentences out loud.

C. Look at the map of Yucatan, Mexico. Circle the things you can find in the environment.

- Ask students to look at both maps of the Yucatan.
- Go over the list of words as a class.
- Have students circle the thing they think they can find in the Yucatan environment. Discuss as a class.

While You Watch

D. Watch the video. Then read each question. Choose the correct answer.

- Have students watch the video.
- Ask students to read each question and then choose the correct answer.
- Play the video once more and check answers as a class.

E. Watch the video again. What activities do you see the children doing? Check the correct answers.

- Have students watch the video again. Then, ask them what activities they see the children doing.
- Ask students to check the correct answer.
- Review as a class.

F. Watch the video again. Read each sentence. Circle T for *True* or F for *False*.

Ask students to watch the video again. Then, have them read the sentences and circle T for *True* or F for *False*.

E. Watch the video again. What activities do you see the children doing? Check the correct answers.

_____ riding in a bus	_____ fishing for food	✓ painting pictures
✓ watering plants	_____ watching TV	_____ swimming in a pool
_____ riding bicycles	✓ playing games	_____ talking on a cell phone

F. Watch the video again. Read each sentence. Circle T for *True* or F for *False*.

1. Maritza Morales Casanova studies the environment. (T) F
2. *Ceiba Pentandra* is a theme park in the United States. T (F)
3. The environment is a main subject in Mexico's schools. T (F)
4. The word for explorer in Spanish is *explorador*. (T) F
5. Maritza believes that the worst problem for the environment is pollution. T (F)

After You Watch

G. Write the correct type of environmental pollution under each picture.

light pollution	land pollution
noise pollution	water pollution
air pollution	

1. _____ air pollution _____

2. _____ land pollution _____

3. _____ noise pollution _____

4. _____ water pollution _____

5. _____ light pollution _____

210   The Engaging Environmentalist

H. Read each sentence. Circle the environmental problem.

1. Marisa can't sleep at night because of the traffic on the street.

   a. water pollution   (b. noise pollution)   c. land pollution

2. The city's parks are too dirty for families to have picnics.

   (a. land pollution)   b. air pollution   c. light pollution

3. Hundreds of birds are hurt when they fly into the buildings.

   (a. light pollution)   b. air pollution   c. noise pollution

4. The smoke from the cars and buses hurt our eyes.

   a. water pollution   (b. air pollution)   c. land pollution

5. Most of the fish in the lake are dead.

   (a. water pollution)   b. noise pollution   c. air pollution

I. List some subjects students can study to learn about protecting the environment. Discuss in small groups. Answers will vary.

School Curriculum: Environment
_____   _____
_____   _____

J. What new information did you learn from watching the video? Compare your answers in small groups. Answers will vary.

Video Challenge **211**

APPLICABLE STRATEGIES

True/False statements. Explain to students that there are strategies for correctly answering *true/false* statements.

1. Look for extreme modifiers that might make the question or statement false, such as *all, always, never, only, none,* and *nobody*.

2. Look for qualifying word that might make the question or statement true, such as *usually, probably, often, most,* and *sometimes*.

3. Look for negative words and prefixes, such as *not* and *un-*.

After You Watch

G. Write the correct type of environmental pollution under each picture.

- Review the types of environmental pollution as a class.

- Have students look at each picture. Ask them to write the correct environmental pollution under each picture.

H. Read each sentence. Circle the environmental problem.

Ask students to read each sentence then circle the environmental problem.

I. List some subjects students can study to learn about protecting the environment. Discuss in small groups.

- Have students form small groups.

- Ask students how they can learn about protecting the environment at school.

- Have groups complete the chart by listing different subjects they can take.

- Ask volunteers to share their answers with the class. Discuss.

J. What new information did you learn from watching the video? Compare your answers in small groups.

Ask students what information they learned from watching the video. Then, ask them to compare and discuss their answers in small groups.

STAND OUT VOCABULARY LIST

PRE-UNIT
Greetings 3
Numbers 7
Instructions
listen 9
read 9
speak 9
write 9

UNIT 1
Personal information
age 14
divorced 16
height 17
marital status 14
married 16
single 16
weight 17
Hairstyle
curly 19
long 19
short 19
straight 19
wavy 19
Family
aunt 21
brother 20
children 21
daughter 21
father 21
granddaughter 21
grandfather 21
grandmother 21
grandson 21
husband 21
mother 21
nephew 21
niece 21
parents 20
sister 20
son 20
uncle 21
wife 21
Hobbies
books 23
computers 23
games 23
movies 23
music 23
parks 23

restaurants 23
sports 23
TV 23

UNIT 2
Stores
bookstore 39
clothing store 39
convenience store 39
department store 39
shoe store 39
supermarket 39
Money
bill 42
check 43
dime 42
nickel 42
penny 42
quarter 42
Clothing
baseball cap 44
belt 47
blouse 44
coat 44
dress 44
hat 44
pants 47
sandals 47
shorts 47
skirt 44
sneakers 44
socks 44
suit 44
sweater 44
tie 44
T-shirt 44
Colors
black 47
blue 47
brown 47
green 47
orange 47
red 47
white 47
yellow 47
Adjectives
big 51
large 50
medium 50
new 50

old 50
plaid 50
small 50
striped 50
used 50

UNIT 3
Food and meals
apples 66
avocados 65
bread 66
breakfast 62
carrots 65
cereal 63
cheeseburger 75
cookies 66
cucumbers 66
dinner 62
eggs 63
french fries 63
fried chicken 63
ground beef 65
hamburger 63
hot dog 76
lunch 62
milk 65
mustard 66
oranges 66
peanut butter 65
potato chips 66
roast beef 63
salad 74
sandwich 63
side order 74
soda 65
spaghetti 63
toast 63
tomatoes 65
yogurt 66
Containers/
Measurements
bag 66
bottle 66
box 66
can 66
gallon 66
jar 66
loaf 66
package 66
pound 66

UNIT 4
Housing
air-conditioning 93
apartment 86
backyard 91
balcony 91
bathroom 89
bedroom 89
car 98
carport 102
condominium 86
deck 91
dining room 90
door 100
driveway 91
electricity 93
family room 91
front porch 91
front yard 91
garage 91
gas 93
hall 91
kitchen 90
living room 90
mobile home 86
stairs 91
swimming pool 91
utilities 93
window 100
yard 91
Furniture
bathtub 98
bed 98
chair 98
coffee table 100
end table 100
lamp 100
painting 100
refrigerator 98
sofa 98
trash can 99

UNIT 5
**Place in the
community**
bank 116
bus station 117
city hall 114
dentist's office 115
doctor's office 115

For an extended Vocabulary List, refer to pages 212–213 of *Stand Out 1* student book.

STAND OUT GRAMMAR REFERENCE

Simple Present: *Be*

Subject	*Be*	Information	Example sentence
I	am	43 years old	I **am** 43 years old.
He, She	is	single	He **is** single. (Roberto **is** single.)
We, You, They	are	from Argentina single married from Russia	She **is** from Argentina. (Gabriela **is** from Argentina.) We **are** single. You **are** married. They **are** from Russia.

Simple Present

Subject	Verb	Example sentence
I, You, We, They	eat like need want make	I **eat** tacos for lunch. You **like** eggs for breakfast. We **need** three cans of corn. They **want** three boxes of cookies. I **make** sandwiches for lunch.
He, She, It	eats likes needs wants makes	He **eats** pizza for dinner. She **likes** tomato soup. He **needs** three pounds of tomatoes. She **wants** two bottles of water. She **makes** sandwiches for Duong.

Simple Present

Subject	Verb	Example sentence
It my leg my arm my foot my head	hurts	My leg **hurts.** My arm **hurts.** My head **hurts.**
they my legs my arms my feet my ears	hurt	My legs **hurt.** My feet **hurt.** My ears **hurt.**

Simple Present

Subject	Verb	Example sentence
I, You, We, They	work	I **work** in an office.
He, She, It	works	He **works** in a restaurant.

Negative Simple Present

Subject	Negative	Verb	Example sentence
I, You, We, They	do not (don't)	work	I **don't work** in an office. You **don't work** in a restaurant.
He, She, It	does not (doesn't)		He **doesn't work** in a school. She **doesn't work** in a hospital.

For an extended Grammar Reference, refer to pages 214–219 of *Stand Out 1* student book.

PHOTO CREDITS

Cover: Portra Images/Getty Images, **Bottom Images** (Left to Right) Jay B Sauceda/Getty Images, Tripod/Getty Images, Portra Images/Getty Images, James Porter/Getty Images, Mark Edward Atkinson/

Tracey Lee/Getty Images, Hero Images/Getty Images, Jade/Getty Images, Seth Joel/Getty Images, LWA/Larry Williams/Getty Images, Dimitri Otis/Getty Images, **02** (tl) (tc) Portra Images/Getty Images, (tr) Mark Edward Atkinson/Tracey Lee/Getty Images, (cl) Hero Images/Getty Images, (c) Jade/Getty Images, (cr) Seth Joel/Getty Images, **03** (tl) Andresr/Shutterstock.com, (tr) StockLite/Shutterstock.com, (bl) Mel Yates/Digital Vision/Getty Images, (br) Dmitry Kalinovsky/Shutterstock.com, **04** (l) Blend Images/Shutterstock.com, (r) Mel Yates/Digital Vision/Getty Images, **05** (tl) Mel Yates/Digital Vision/Getty Images, (tr) Dmitry Kalinovsky/Shutterstock.com, **07** Mel Yates/Digital Vision/Getty Images, **08** (tl) Mel Yates/Digital Vision/Getty Images, (tr) StockLite/Shutterstock.com, **09** (tl) antoniodiaz/Shutterstock.com, (tr) Asia Images Group/Getty Images, (cl) Nick Daly/The Image Bank/Getty Images, (cr) Minerva Studio/Shutterstock.com, **10** (tla) Walter B. McKenzie/Stone/Getty Images, (trb) maturos1812/Shutterstock.com, (tlc) Nick Daly/The Image Bank/Getty Images, (trd) Syda Productions/Shutterstock.com, (cl) Lucky Business/Shutterstock.com, (cr) Lighthousebay/Getty Images, (bl) Image Source/Getty Images, (br) Blend Images/Shutterstock.com, **11** Chris Bernard/Getty Images, **12–13** DESIGN PICS INC/National Geographic Creative, **15** (tl) Andresr/Shutterstock.com, (tr) Dasha Petrenko/Shutterstock.com, (cl) LuckyImages/Shutterstock.com, (bl) StockLite/Shutterstock.com, (bc) Mel Yates/Digital Vision/Getty Images, (br) Andresr/Shutterstock.com, **17** (tl) Andresr/Shutterstock.com, (bl) Dmitry Kalinovsky/Shutterstock.com, (br) StockLite/Shutterstock.com, **18** Portra Images/Getty Images, **23** (tl) Rorem/Shutterstock.com, (tc) Graja/Shutterstock.com, (tr) Ferenc Cegledi/Shutterstock.com, (c) Dien/Shutterstock.com, (c) Johnnie Davis/Getty Images, (cr) Leren Lu/Taxi Japan/Getty Images, (bl) Donatas1205/Shutterstock.com, (bc) Tutti Frutti/Shutterstock.com, (br) MongPro/Shutterstock.com, **29** © Cengage Learning, **32** (tla) KPG Payless2/Shutterstock.com, (trb) Andre Babiak/Alamy, (tlc) Dmitry Naumov/Shutterstock.com, (trd) (cl) Angela Hampton Picture Library /Alamy, (cr) Image Source/Getty Images, (bl) Ahmet Misirligul/Shutterstock.com, (br) Gavran333/Shutterstock.com, **33** David Sacks/Getty Images, **34** Gordon Wiltsie/National Geographic Creative, **36–37** Dave Yoder/National Geographic Creative, **42** (t1) (t2) (t3) (t4) (c5) (c6) (c7) (c8) United States Government/Public Domain, (bl) Ilizia/Shutterstock.com, (bc) Fotoslaz/Shutterstock.com, (br) Mega Pixel/Shutterstock.com, **45** (tl) Angelika Smile/Shutterstock.com, (tr) Aleksandr Lobanov/Getty Images, (cl) Michael Kraus/Shutterstock.com, (cr) Africa Studio/Shutterstock.com, (bl) Numforest/Shutterstock.com, (br)

PhotoNAN/Shutterstock.com, **50** (t1) ollyy/Shutterstock.com, (t2) Valeriy Lebedev /Shutterstock, (t3) Jessicakirsh/Shutterstock.com, (t4) Marvin Dembinsky Photo Associates/Alamy, (c1) Maksim Toome/Shutterstock.com, (c2) Neale Cousland/Shutterstock.com, (c3) Buturlimov Paul/Shutterstock.com, (c4) Ruslan Kudrin/Shutterstock.com, (b1) Focal point/Shutterstock.com, (b2) Gulei Ivan/Shutterstock.com, (b3) Surrphoto/Shutterstock.com, (b4) Paci77/Shutterstock.com, **52** (c1) Monkey Business Images/Shutterstock.com, (c2) Bikeriderlondon/Shutterstock.com, (c3) Monkey Business Images/Getty Images, (c4) racorn/Shutterstock.com, **53** © Cengage Learning, **54** (tl1) Ollyy/Shutterstock.com, (tl2) Luciana Pampalone/AGE Fotostock, (tl3) Mega Pixel/Shutterstock.com, (cl1) KWL/Shutterstock.com, (cl2) Ronstik/Shutterstock.com, (bl1) Karkas/Shutterstock.com, (bl2) Nito/Shutterstock, (bl3) Buturlimov Paul/Shutterstock.com, **55** (bl) Elenovsky/Shutterstock.com, (bc) Shyamalamuralinath/Shutterstock.com, (br) Karkas/Shutterstock.com, **58** Brent Humphreys/Redux, **60–61** Henry Sudarman/500px.com, **64** (tl) Valerio Pardi/Shutterstock.com, (tr) AI1962/Shutterstock.com, (cl) Anna Shepulova/Shutterstock.com, (cr) AS Food studio/Shutterstock.com, **69** (tl) Christopher Gardiner/Shutterstock.com, (tc) Tatiana Popova/Shutterstock.com, (tr) Jaimie Duplass/Shutterstock.com, (cl) Danilaleo/Shutterstock.com, (c) Donatas1205/Shutterstock.com, (cr) Christian Draghici/Shutterstock.com, **70** Ayatgali Tuleubek/Alamy, **72** Sheila Fitzgerald/Shutterstock.com, **75** Elxeneize/Shutterstock.com, **77** © Cengage Learning, **81** CandyBox Images/Shutterstock.com, **83** Sarah Dixon/Corbis News/Corbis, **84–85** Francesco Riccardo Iacomino/Core/500px prime, **101** © Cengage Learning, **105** Photobank.ch/Shutterstock.com, **106** Ben Horton/National Geographic Creative, **108** J. Norman Reid/Shutterstock.com, **109** BaLL LunLa/Shutterstock.com, **110** Janis Smits/Shutterstock.com, **112–113** Annie Griffiths/ National Geographic Creative, **114** EDHAR/Shutterstock.com, **115** (cl) ROBYN BECK/Getty Images, (c) Ken Wolter/Shutterstock.com, (cr) dpa picture alliance/Alamy, (bl) Tupungato/Shutterstock.com, (bc) Bruce Leighty/Getty Images, (br) SeanPavonePhoto/Shutterstock.com, **129** © Cengage Learning, **131** scyther5/Shutterstock.com, **132** (tl) ROBYN BECK/Getty Images, (tr) dpa picture alliance/Alamy, (cl) Ken Wolter/Shutterstock.com, (cr) Tupungato/Shutterstock.com, **133** WorldPictures/Shutterstock.com, **134** © Rolex Awards/François, **136–137** BENJAMIN NORMAN/The New York Times/Redux, **143** (cl) Fuse/Getty Images, (c) BSIP SA/Alamy, (cr) BJI / Lane Oatey/Getty Images, **147** Blend Images - Stewart Cohen/Brand X Pictures/Getty Images, **149** Paul Bradbury/Getty Images, **151** (cl) Gorillaimages/Shutterstock.com, (cr) efenzi/Getty Images, (bl) Dana Menussi/Getty Images, (br) Ryan McVay/Getty Images, **153** © Cengage Learning,

157 Image Point Fr/Shutterstock.com, **158** The Jane Goodall Institute, **159** (cl) Sascha Burkard/Shutterstock.com, (c) Christopher Meder/Shutterstock.com, (cr) xuanhuongho/Shutterstock.com, **160–161** Joel Sartore/ National Geographic Creative, **162** (tl) Comstock/Getty Images, (tc) Allison Michael Orenstein/The Image Bank/Getty Images, (tr) IT Stock Free/Polka Dot/Jupiter Images, (cl) Nicole Waring/Getty Images, (cr) STR/Getty Images, **163** (tl) Kayte Deioma/PhotoEdit, (tc) Golden Pixels LLC/Shutterstock.com, (tr) Echo/Getty Images, (cl) Marjorie Kamys Cotera/Bob Daemmrich Photography/Alamy, (c) Syda Productions/Shutterstock.com, (cr) Don Nichols/Getty Images, **167** (tl) ColorBlind Images/Iconica/Getty Images, (tc) Yellow Dog Productions Inc./Getty Images, (tr) Juanmonino/Getty Images, **168** Dann Tardif/LWA/Flirt/Corbis, **171** (tl) Africa Studio/Shutterstock.com (tc) Keith Bell/Getty Images, (tr) PhotoObjects/RF/Photos.com, (cl) Medioimages/Photodisc/Getty Images, (c) luminaimages/Shutterstock.com, (cr) Stewart Bremner/Getty Images, (c) CZQS2000/STS/Getty Images, **177** © Cengage Learning, **178** (tl) Andrey_Popov/Shutterstock.com, (tc) Tetra Images/Getty Images, (tr) Minerva Studio/Shutterstock.com, **180** (tl) Africa Studio/Shutterstock.com (tr) luminaimages/Shutterstock.com, (cl) PhotoObjects/RF/Photos.com, (cr) Keith Bell/Getty Images, (bl) Stewart Bremner/Getty Images, (br) Medioimages/Photodisc/Getty Images, **181** imtmphoto/iStock/Getty Images Plus/Getty Images, **182** TH Culhane/National Geographic, **184–185** Glenn Oakley, **189** (t1) leungchopan/Shutterstock.com, (t2) Jeremy Frechette/The Image Bank/Getty Images, (t4) Goodluz/Shutterstock.com, (c5) lightwavemedia/Shutterstock.com, (c7) Wavebreakmedia ltd/Shutterstock.com, (c8) Dragon Images/Shutterstock.com, **193** (tl) Phase4Photography/Shutterstock.com, (tc) PT Images/Shutterstock.com, (tr) Roxana Gonzalez/Shutterstock.com, (cl) Takayuki/Shutterstock.com, (c) Felix Mizioznikov/Shutterstock.com, (cr) Nadino/Shutterstock.com, **194** (tl) vlad.georgescu/Shutterstock.com, (tr) Ammentorp Photography/Shutterstock.com, (c) Hill Street Studios/Blend (RM)/Corbis, **195** (t) Blend Images/Shutterstock.com, (c) StockLite/Shutterstock.com, (cr) Dmitry Kalinovsky/Shutterstock.com, **201** © Cengage Learning, **203** g-stockstudio/Shutterstock.com, **204** (t) Amos Morgan/Photodisc/Getty Images, (b) Mel Yates/Digital Vision/Getty Images, **206** Ethan Hill/Redux, **208** © Rolex Awards/François Schaer, **209** (tr) B Christopher/Alamy, (cl) © Cengage Learning (c) UniversalImagesGroup/Getty Images, **210** (cl) WANG ZHAO/Getty Images, (c) joreks/Shutterstock.com, (cr) altrendo images/Altrendo/Getty Images, (bl) Signature Message/Shutterstock.com, (bc) mdmworks/Shutterstock.com, **211** Brian Overcast/Alamy.

STAND OUT SKILLS INDEX

ACADEMIC SKILLS

Check
Descriptions, 20, 47, 50, 89
Instructions, 9
Study habits, 186, 197
Study skills, 187
Work, 174

Charts, graphs, and maps, 6, 8, 14, 16, 18, 24, 25, 27, 28, 30, 40, 44, 48, 49, 50, 52, 54, 58, 59, 62, 63, 64, 65, 66, 67, 69, 70, 71, 72, 73, 74, 75, 76, 78, 79, 82, 86, 87, 88, 89, 90, 92, 94, 96, 97, 98, 102, 103, 104, 107, 116, 117, 118, 119, 120, 121, 122, 124, 125, 127, 130, 131, 135, 140, 142, 144, 146, 147, 148, 151, 152, 153, 155, 156, 163, 164, 165, 166, 167, 169, 171, 172, 173, 178, 186, 187, 189, 192, 194, 196, 199, 200

Critical thinking
Apply, 19, 35, 59, 64, 73, 83, 91, 100, 116, 125, 128, 140, 146, 152, 170, 173, 183, 189, 194, 200
Analyze, 59, 66, 82, 118, 142, 175, 192
Calculate, 42
Classify, 14, 18, 25, 38, 44, 47, 50, 64, 74, 98, 107, 115, 163, 171, 186, 200, 207
Collaborate, 33, 57, 81, 105, 133, 157, 181, 189, 205
Compare, 24, 25, 49, 73, 142, 165
Create, 22, 83, 88, 94, 95, 149, 159, 167, 191, 207
Design, 67
Evaluate, 71, 123, 124, 144, 166, 174, 188
Identify, 90, 162
Infer, 46, 114, 138
Interpret, 14, 17, 26, 41, 43, 44, 65, 66, 68, 73, 86, 88, 92, 94, 114, 120, 123, 126, 147, 148, 165, 173, 192
Investigate, 43, 46
List, 59, 98, 104, 114, 131, 138, 140, 159, 183, 194, 195, 196

Plan, 197, 199
Predict, 21, 34, 35, 39, 59, 63, 83, 89, 92, 95, 116, 138, 145, 168, 186, 193, 195, 206
Rank, 97, 135, 176
Report, 28, 40, 164, 196
Research, 95
Survey, 6, 16, 40, 62, 88, 116, 152, 164

Grammar
Adverbs, 127
Charts, 112
Future tense, 199, 200
Imperatives, 9, 117
Infinitives, 152, 196
in/on, 118
is/are, 4, 5, 16, 22, 42, 67, 148
Negative simple present, 143, 164
Past tense, 169, 175, 187
Plurals, 69, 74
Possessive adjectives, 48
Prepositions, 99, 121
Present continuous, 97, 127
Questions, 45, 76, 94, 125, 172
should, 146, 193
Simple past, 169, 175, 187
Simple present, 16, 18, 24, 40, 52, 70, 87, 127, 140, 143, 164, 175
Verbs
be, 16, 22, 42, 45, 67, 97
have, 18, 143
infinitives, 152, 196
live, 87
will, 200
want, 52
Yes/No questions, 5, 76, 94, 166

Group activities, 16, 19, 33, 39, 44, 46, 49, 57, 64, 67, 73, 83, 90, 91, 95, 97, 98, 115, 122, 123, 124, 131, 135, 140, 146, 149, 157, 158, 159, 164, 167, 176, 183, 186, 189, 190, 194, 196, 197, 199

Listening
Conversations, 20, 51, 68, 116
Descriptions, 18
Directions, 119
Emergencies, 147
Exercise, 151
Food, 75

Greetings, 4
Housing, 86, 89
Illnesses, 141
Instructions, 10
Job hunting, 163, 165, 166, 170
Job interviews, 172, 176
Numbers, 9, 89
Occupations, 163, 165
Performance evaluations, 176
Personal information, 15
Phone messages, 123
Preferences, 23
Prices, 41, 44, 54, 73, 75
Work preferences, 195

Matching
Illnesses, 153, 155, 158, 206
Job interviews, 172
Questions and answers, 15, 31, 101, 106, 125, 172
Words and definitions, 180, 206
Words and pictures, 10, 90

Partner activities, 4, 8, 11, 22, 25, 28, 39, 42, 45, 49–52, 56, 59, 69, 70, 76, 78–80, 88, 90, 91, 94, 98–100, 102, 120, 128, 130, 135, 147, 149, 155, 168, 170, 193–196, 202

Pronunciation
Intonation, 39, 94, 141, 172
/m/ sound, 5
Plurals, 69
Questions, 5, 94, 141, 172
Stress, 39
/v/ sound, 87
Yes/No questions, 5, 94

Reading
Advertisements, 65, 79
Body parts, 138
Charts, 67, 124, 172
Classified ads, 92–94, 102, 165
Conversations, 11, 139, 156
Directions, 118
Exercise, 150
Food orders, 74–76
Goals, 198
Housing, 86, 92
Illnesses, 145
Job hunting, 165
Learning opportunities, 192
Maps, 117, 118, 130
Medicine bottles, 155
Menus, 74, 80

For an extended Skills Index, refer to pages 221–223 of *Stand Out 1* student book.

STAND OUT VIDEO SCRIPTS

UNIT 1: Video 1: Where are you from?

Hector: I'll get it!

Naomi: I hope you're not busy.

Hector: Not at all. I was framing pictures. Let me introduce you to my family. This is the Sanchez family. That's my dad's side of the family.

Naomi: Which one is your dad?

Hector: Here he is. Dad, meet my friend Naomi. Naomi, meet my dad.

Naomi: Your father is very young.

Hector: I'm sure he would love you for saying that. Actually, this photo was taken a long time ago. My dad's 45 years old.

Naomi: Where is your father from?

Hector: He's from Sinaloa. It's in Mexico.

Naomi: When did your father come to the U.S.?

Hector: When he was about 20. First he moved to San Diego, then he moved to L.A. He met my mom, and the rest is history.

Naomi: What is your mother's maiden name?

Hector: Yilmaz.

Naomi: That sounds like a Middle Eastern name.

Hector: You're right. It's Turkish. She was born in Istanbul. She moved to New York, and then to L.A.

Naomi How interesting. Is this your mom?

Hector: How did you guess?

Naomi: You look just like her.

Hector: You think so? I think I look like my father. I have his eyes.

Naomi: Yes, but you have your mother's smile.

Mrs. Sanchez: Oh, how sweet.

Hector: Mom, this is my friend Naomi.

Mrs. Sanchez: How nice to meet you, Naomi.

Naomi: Nice to meet you too, Mrs. Sanchez. Hector was showing me some of the family photos.

Mrs. Sanchez: Oh, was he? Well, this is my sister. She's married and she has two kids.

Naomi: So these are your cousins?

Hector: Yes, Aidan and Marta.

Mrs. Sanchez: Aidan is 10 and Marta is 8. Aren't they cute? Oh, and this is my brother, and these are my parents. They all live in New York. Oh, and over here we have my parents at their...

Hector: Ma, take it easy! Naomi doesn't need to know our whole family history.

Mrs. Sanchez: I was only saying... Oh, honey. Come meet Hector's friend. Her name is Naomi.

Mr. Sanchez: Hello, Naomi. Nice to meet you.

Naomi: Nice to meet you too, Mr. Sanchez.

Mrs. Sanchez: Naomi is from...Where are you from, dear?

Naomi: I'm from Pasadena, I was born in Washington. My father's from Japan, and my mother's from L.A.

Mrs. Sanchez: Do you have any brothers or sisters?

Naomi: No, I'm an only child, like Hector.

Mrs. Sanchez: Honey, where are the rest of the pictures?

Mr. Sanchez: There are a lot more in the photo album. I think it's right here. Here it is. Ahh. Here's a photo of Hector when he was 2.

Mrs. Sanchez: Wasn't he cute? Here's another picture of Hector. He's 10 years old in that picture. Oh, look at him!

Hector: Here we go!

Video 2: My Story: Family

Nick: I'm twenty-three years old and I'm single.

Agnes: I am thirty-one years old and I'm married. My husband's name is Gibrael. We have a son. His name is Kareem and he is two years old.

Denise: I have a son. His name is Ricardo and he's ten years old.

Alejandra: I am a single woman and I have no children.

Natalie: I am a single mother. My daughter is two years old. Her name is Leilanni and her birthday is April sixteenth.

Yelena: I am married. I have a husband. No kids yet . . .

Kumiko: This is my husband. His name is Paul Lieber.

Kevin: I am not married. . .which means I am currently single.

Catherine: My fiancé's name is Paul Ham. I like him a lot because he is very, very smart, and he's pretty cute.

UNIT 2: Video 1: Can I help you?

Mr. Patel: Good morning Mateo.

Mateo: Good morning.

Mr. Patel: Did you put that sign in the window?

Mateo: The one that says "Help Wanted"? Yes, I did. I put it in the window yesterday.

Mr. Patel: Good. Now I have something else for you. Here is a dress, a blouse, and a sweater. Can you put them away for me, please?

Mateo: Yeah. OK, sure.

Mr. Patel: Thank you. I'll be in my office.

Hector: Hey, Mateo!

Mateo: Hey Hector. What are you doing here?

Hector: I saw the sign in the window. It says "Help Wanted." Are you looking for sales clerks?

Mateo: Yeah, we are. But do you think you have what it takes to be a sales clerk?

Hector: Well you never know unless you try, right?

Customer: Excuse me.

Mateo: Yes? Can I help you?

Customer: I'm looking for a sweater. Do you have any blue sweaters?

Mateo: Well, is the sweater for you or for someone else?

Customer: It's for me.

Hector: Well, what about this sweater right here? I think this would look great on you.

Customer: I like it. It might be a bit big. What size is it?

Mateo: That is a large. Here is a small.

Customer: Yes, I think this is the right size. How much is it?

Mateo: It's $48.

Customer: Oh, no. I only have $40.

Hector: What about this green sweater? It's only $34.

Customer: I love it! And I really love the price. I'll take it.

Mateo: Are you sure? Because this red sweater is even less expensive. It's only $27.

Customer: It's perfect. And I'll still have extra money. Thank you so much.

Hector: Well, is there anything else we can help you with?

Customer: Well, my little brother wants a pair of blue jeans. Can you show me the way to the boy's section?

Hector: I would be happy to show you the way. Please follow me.

Mr. Patel: Who was that?

Mateo: That is my friend, Hector. He's a bit of a show-off.

Mr. Patel: He might make a good sales clerk. Why don't you ask him to come in for an interview?

Video 2: My Story: Clothing and Fashion

Dave: I really admire my sister's style because she's very independent.

Calum: One person whose fashion I admire is my friend Alex. He wears really nice clothes.

Dayanne: I have a friend that always wears cowboy boots to go to work. I think that she should wear something more stylish.

Dennis: The person I most admire is Robert Redford. I like the way he moves, the way he stands the way he carries his clothes…his hair...

Woo Sung: I've had this hair for a while and I think it's definitely time for a change. I need a haircut.

Dayanne: To improve my appearance, I should have a haircut and lose weight.

Calum: I think I could improve my appearance by wearing contact lenses instead of glasses.

UNIT 3: Video 1: Nobody has pizza for breakfast

Mrs. Sanchez: What was that?

Mr. Sanchez: Was that the refrigerator?

Hector: Probably.

Mrs. Sanchez: Hector! That was your stomach!

Hector: Sorry, Ma. I didn't eat breakfast.

Mrs. Sanchez: Why not? Breakfast is the most important meal of the day, you know.

Hector: It's OK. I can wait until lunch.

Mr. Sanchez: Hector, please eat something.

Hector: Like what?

Mr. Sanchez: We have fruit. Why don't you have an apple?

Mrs. Sanchez: Or I can make you some bacon and eggs with toast. Would you like that?

Hector: It's OK, Ma. Don't bother. There's some cold pizza. That's good enough.

Mrs. Sanchez: Pizza for breakfast? That is not a good way to start the day.

Mr. Sanchez: I agree with your mother. Nobody ever has pizza for breakfast.

Hector: Well, why not? People have toast for breakfast, and toast is bread, right? Well so is pizza, basically. Now all I need is some potato chips.

Mr. Sanchez: Really, now. This is too much.

Hector: OK, OK.

Mrs. Sanchez: You should have real food for breakfast: eggs, milk, fruit. Please, let me make something for you.

Hector: How about some cake? Cake has eggs and milk and fruit!

Mrs. Sanchez: It also has sugar in it. Lots and lots of sugar. Isn't there anything else in the refrigerator besides pizza and cake?

Hector: Let's see. Well, there's vegetables, cheese, and eggs.

Mr. Sanchez: Why don't you make an omelet?

Mrs. Sanchez: That's a wonderful idea. Give me a hand, will you, dear? It will only take about 15 minutes.

Hector: What should I do?

Mrs. Sanchez: First, you take a few eggs and you beat them in a bowl. Then you pour some milk into the bowl. Then you can add some grated cheese if you like . . .

Mrs. Sanchez: Now isn't this better than having pizza and cake for breakfast?

Hector: It sure is. Thanks, Ma.

Mr. Sanchez: Can you pass the pepper?

Hector: Sure, here you go, Dad. Can you pass me that sugar?

Mr. Sanchez: Sugar? What do you want sugar for?

Hector: I like to put sugar on my omelet.

Mr. Sanchez: What?

Hector: I was only kidding!

Video 2: My Story: Food and Nutrition

Alyssa: When I go shopping I buy lots of fruits and vegetables. I'm vegetarian so I never buy meat.

Miyuki: I buy a lot of meat, a lot of cheese and grab some eggs. I usually buy some rice and I try to buy some vegetables as well.

Kevin: I normally buy fruits, vegetables, some deli meats like turkey and ham, orange juice, milk, bread, and maybe a few magazines and some potato chips

Dayanne: In my refrigerator I have a bottle of orange juice, a bottle of milk, some bread and some apples.

Jennifer: I hate grocery shopping. My refrigerator is empty. Not even ice cubes.

UNIT 4: Video 1: Are utilities included?

Apartment Manager: Hello?

Naomi: Uh, hello. I'm calling about the apartments for rent.

Apartment Manager: Hello. Yes, we have several apartments available. What kind of apartment are you looking for?

Naomi: I'm looking for a one-bedroom apartment with a pool and near a bus stop. Do you have any one-bedroom apartments?

Apartment Manager: Uh, no, but we do have a studio apartment available. It's small, but it does have a kitchen area with a microwave, a refrigerator, and a very nice view of the city.

Naomi: Oh. Well, does it have a swimming pool?

Apartment Manager: No. It doesn't have a swimming pool, but it does have a parking area for your car.

Naomi: Oh. Well, I don't have a car. I'm looking for something near a bus stop. Is there a bus stop near the apartment building?

Apartment Manager: Uh, the building is about six blocks from a bus stop, but the highway is very near.

Naomi: The highway is very near?

Apartment Manager: It goes right by the back of the building! It's very useful.

Naomi: But I don't have a car.

Apartment Manager: Do you have any pets?

Naomi: No.

Apartment Manager: Good, because we don't accept pets. Do you smoke?

Naomi: No.

Apartment Manager: Good. This is a non-smoking apartment building.

Naomi: That's good. What about electricity and water? Are the utilities included in the rent?

Apartment Manager: Yes, some utilities are included. Water and garbage are included, but you have to pay for the electricity. Do you want to make an appointment to come look at the apartment? It has a very nice view. I'm sure you'll like it.

Naomi: Well, how much is the rent?

Apartment Manager: It's only $900 a month, plus electricity. But the parking is free!

Naomi: Um, I don't have a car. Well, let's see: $900 a month, plus electricity—

Apartment Manager: Don't forget, it's close to the highway. It has a nice view!

Naomi: Okay...near the highway, has a nice view. But it's six blocks to the nearest bus stop, and it doesn't have a swimming pool—Wait . . . Oh, I'm sorry. Can I think about it? Thank you—bye!

Apartment Manager: Good-bye?

Video 2: My Story: Living Situations

Hana: I live in a dorm in my school.

Dave I live in a dorm with a roommate. There's not much in it besides myself, my roommate, and two beds. That's all there's room for.

Vanessa: In my room, I have one roommate and there are two beds, two dressers and two desks.

Calum: My dorm is very big and very old. There are a lot of people in my dorm so it's very noisy, especially at night. My dorm room is very small and in the dorm room there is a desk, shelves, an alarm clock, a few books, and a rug.

Video Challenge 1
How Your T-Shirt Can Make a Difference

Cotton is everywhere—in your furniture, in your food, in your wallet, in your closet.

Cotton has a major impact on the planet. Take your favorite cotton t-shirt.

It takes 2,700 liters of water to make one t-shirt. Enough for one person to drink for 900 days.

It also takes a lot of energy to grow, manufacture, transport Mostly, it needs energy to care for it.

One load of drying uses five times more energy than washing. One load of washing uses 40 gallons of water. Now think how often you wash and dry your t-shirt.

Don't we have plenty of resources? Plenty of water? Yes, but 97% is salty. Nearly 2% is locked in snow or ice. That leaves less than 1% that we can access. And 70% of that grows our crops.

Cotton is a very thirsty crop.

Now, think how many t-shirts are in your closet.

Now, think how many t-shirts are in your city.

Now, think how many t-shirts are in your country.

Now, think how many t-shirts are on the planet.

How many t-shirts do you need? How often do you need to wash and dry them?

There is a solution.

We can use less water and less energy. Skip the drying and ironing and save one third of your t-shirt's carbon footprint.

Choices make a difference. Make each choice count.

World Wildlife Fund logo

National Geographic logo

worldwildlife.org/choicescount

UNIT 5: Video 1: How do I get there?

Naomi: Wow. Mateo is really late. Where is he?

Hector: You know Mateo. He's probably lost again. He has a terrible sense of direction. That's probably him now. Hello?

Mateo: Yo, Hector. This is Mateo.

Hector: I know who you are. The question is where you are.

Mateo: I'm not sure. I'm in front of the bookstore. The bookstore is next to a coffee shop.

Naomi: Ask him what street he's on.

Hector: What street are you on? Do you see any street signs?

Mateo: Yeah, I'm on the corner of Atlantic and Broadway.

Hector: He's on the corner of Atlantic and Broadway.

Naomi: Tell him to walk straight for two blocks.

Hector: Walk straight for two blocks.

Mateo: On Atlantic or Broadway?

Hector: On Atlantic or Broadway?

Naomi: On Atlantic. Go towards City Hall.

Hector: Walk down Atlantic towards City Hall.

Mateo: OK. Then what?

Hector: Then what? Here, you talk to him.

Naomi: Did you hear that? Walk down Atlantic two blocks.

Mateo: Then what?

Naomi: Then turn right and walk one block. The diner is on the left.

Mateo: Turn right, walk down one block, the diner's on your left, right?

Naomi: Right, I mean correct.

Mateo: OK, see you in a few minutes.

Hector: See, I told you Mateo isn't good with directions.

Naomi: I wouldn't be surprised if he calls us again.

Hector: Hello.

Mateo: Hector, I'm here at the diner, but I still can't find you guys. Where are you?

Hector: It's complicated. I'll try to explain this to you. Take two steps back.

Mateo: Two steps back? Well, OK then.

Hector: Now, turn around.

Mateo: Very funny!

Naomi: Come sit down and have some coffee. I think you need it!

Video 2: My Story: Around Town

Dennis: There's a big mall in my neighborhood and in that mall you can find several stores like there's a CD shop, there are clothes stores, a restaurant and a supermarket where you can get groceries.

Jennifer: In the mall near my neighborhood there are department stores, there are clothing stores, shoe stores, there is a stationery store and a bookstore.

Agnes: In Senegal we don't have big shopping malls. We have a lot of little markets and nice little shops and that's where I go shopping.

UNIT 6: Video 1: You'd better call the doctor

Mrs. Sanchez: Victor? Are you feeling alright?

Mr. Sanchez: Not really. My head hurts . . . I feel dizzy . . . I'm too warm.

Mrs. Sanchez: Here, sit down on the couch. You don't look well. And you have a fever. You are not going to work. You need to see the doctor.

Mr. Sanchez: No, no, I'm fine. I need to go to work . . .

Mrs. Sanchez: I don't think so. Sit!

Mr. Sanchez: Really, I'm okay.

Hector: Morning Mom. Morning, Dad. What's the matter with Dad?

Mrs. Sanchez: He's sick. Can you get the thermometer?

Mr. Sanchez: And some water? With ice?

Mrs. Sanchez: Hello? Dr. Badaoui? This is Miriam Sanchez. My husband, Victor Sanchez, seems to be very sick.

Dr. Badaoui: What are his symptoms?

Mrs. Sanchez: He has a headache. He's dizzy. And he feels warm.

Dr. Badaoui: Any aches and pains?

Mrs. Sanchez: Do you have any aches and pains?

Mr. Sanchez: My knees ache...

Hector: His back aches. His shoulders ache too. His elbow aches?

Mrs. Sanchez: Yes, he has aches and pains.

Dr. Badaoui: Does he have a fever?

Mrs. Sanchez: Does he have a fever?

Hector: Yes, he does have a fever. One-oh-one-point-two.

Mrs. Sanchez: He does have a fever. One hundred and one point two. And now he has a cough.

Dr. Badaoui: He needs to rest. Give him lots of water, and keep him warm. Give him lots of Vitamin C. And give him some ibuprofen or acetaminophen for the fever and aches.

Mrs. Sanchez: Vitamin C, ibuprofen, and acetaminophen. Okay, Dr. Badaoui. Thank you very much.

Dr. Badaoui: No problem.

Mr. Sanchez: I need to get to work.

Mrs. Sanchez: Your only job today is to rest and get well. Nurse?

Hector: Yes, doctor.

Mrs. Sanchez: Get ready. Acetaminophen?

Hector: Check.

Mrs. Sanchez: Ibuprofen?

Hector: Check.

Mrs. Sanchez: Don't worry, Mr. Sanchez. You're in good hands.

Video 2: My Story: Staying Healthy

Kumiko: I'm a very healthy person. I have asthma, but I hardly ever get sick. To stay healthy— don't smoke. You should exercise every day, I don't do exercise, but you really should exercise everyday.

Jennifer: I go to the gym, I exercise and I try to eat good foods.

Dave: To stay healthy you must drink a lot of orange juice, wash your hands and eat right.

Danny: Drink a lot of fluids, get a good night's rest and exercise regularly.

Dayanne: Don't smoke, eat well and exercise.

UNIT 7: Video 1: How did you hear about this job?

Hector: Excuse me . . . I have an appointment for 3 o'clock.

Mr. Patel: Oh, yes--Mr. Sanchez is it?

Hector: Yes, Hector Sanchez. But you can just call me Hector.

Mr. Patel: Nice to meet you, Hector. You can call me Mr. Patel. I'm the store owner and manager. I supervise all the employees and make sure everything is going smoothly. What brings you here?

Hector: Well, I'd like to apply for the sales position.

Mr. Patel: Please have a seat. Tell me, how did you find out about this job?

Hector: I saw your ad, and I have a friend who works here.

Mr. Patel: Who is that?

Hector: Mateo Trujillo.

Mr. Patel: Oh yes, Mateo . . .

Hector: He said that you are looking for a part-time sales clerk, which is perfect for me, because I'm a student.

Mr. Patel: Let's take it one step at a time. . . Did you bring an application?

Hector: Yes. Here it is. I know I don't have very much experience.

Mr. Patel: Never mind that. Tell me about your work history. What was your last job?

Hector: I was an . . . assistant.

Mr. Patel: And what was it that you did as an "assistant"?

Hector: I answered the phones and took messages.

Mr. Patel: I see. And what do you do now?

Hector: I'm a student at Glendale Community College. I'm majoring in business, and taking classes in accounting, and some day I would like to be a store manager like yourself, Mr. Patel.

Mr. Patel: Can you work the cash register?

Hector: Not exactly, but I learn very quickly.

Mr. Patel: Well, Hector, let's be honest. You really don't have much work experience. But I like your attitude and I'd like to give you a chance. What hours can you work?

Hector: I can work the afternoons, and the evenings and on the weekends. But I can't work in the mornings because I have class.

Mr. Patel: That sounds fine. Now we have a few rules around here, Hector. Rule number one: Never be late. **Rule** number two: Have the right attitude. Rule number three: Always be on time.

Hector: Wait a second. Isn't rule number three the same as rule number one?

Mr. Patel: I was only testing you, Hector. I can tell you'll make a very good employee. Welcome to the staff.

Video 2: My Story: What do you do?

Natalie: I work for a television station that was launched ten years ago and I have been working there for about a year.

Dan: I work with computers at a hospital and I have been doing that for three years.

Gian: I am a marketing manager. I make brochures, I send out e-mails and I work on the web.

UNIT 8: Video 1: I Have lots of different interests

Mrs. Smith: Hello, Hector. How nice to see you. What can I do for you today?

Hector: Well, we're starting a new semester in a few weeks.

Mrs. Smith: I know!

Hector: And we need to choose our classes.

Mrs. Smith: The sooner the better. Which classes are you going to take?

Hector: I'm not sure yet. That's why I came to see you. Do you have any suggestions?

Mrs. Smith: That depends. Have a seat. What's your goal? What do you want to study?

Hector: That's hard. I'm interested in lots of things. First I wanted to be an actor. Then I wanted to be a teacher. Now I'm not sure. I'm taking lots of different classes.

Mrs. Smith: Tell me, which classes did you take last semester?

Hector: I took a class in public speaking. That was fun.

Mrs. Smith: Oh, really? You like to speak in public?

Hector: Let's just say I'm not shy. I gave a speech at least twice a week. And I took a class in world events, too.

Mrs. Smith: World events. Very interesting. And what classes are you taking now?

Hector: This semester? I'm taking English, Social Studies, and Business.

Mrs. Smith: And which class do you like the most?

Hector: English. I like to read, and I really like to write reports. Last month I wrote an investigative report.

Mrs. Smith: What was it about?

Hector: Local politics, the upcoming election.

Mrs. Smith: I see. What else do you like to do?

Hector: After class, I usually go to the gym. Sometimes I play soccer. When I get home, I like to watch TV or listen to the radio.

Mrs. Smith: What kinds of programs do you like?

Hector: Oh, definitely the news. I watch the local news report every night. After dinner I watch another news program, and I listen to the BBC on the radio at least three times a week.

Mrs. Smith: I think I see a pattern. You like taking English, and you like watching the news. Last semester you took a class in public speaking. You liked that, too. You seem to be interested in the media and communications. Did you ever think about studying journalism?

Hector: Journalism? I never thought about it. But I should think about it. I like to watch the news, I like to listen to the radio. Plus I like English. It makes perfect sense. "This is Hector Sanchez, reporting from Los Angeles." Yeah, I can imagine that.

Mrs. Smith: Mr. Hopkins is going to teach a class in journalism next semester. Why don't you take it?

Hector: I think I will take Mr. Hopkins' class. I think I'm going to take another English class, too.

Mrs. Smith: That's an excellent idea. Sign up for the Journalism class soon, though. I think it's going to fill up.

Hector: OK, I'll sign up today. Thanks for talking to me, Mrs. Smith. I really appreciate it.

Mrs. Smith: It was my pleasure, Hector. I'm glad I could help you. Let me know if you have any other questions.

Hector: I will. See you soon.

Mrs. Smith: Take care. See you in class.